Shadworth Hollway Hodgson

The theory of practice

an ethical enquiry in two books

Shadworth Hollway Hodgson

The theory of practice
an ethical enquiry in two books

ISBN/EAN: 9783741156397

Manufactured in Europe, USA, Canada, Australia, Japa

Cover: Foto ©Thomas Meinert / pixelio.de

Manufactured and distributed by brebook publishing software (www.brebook.com)

Shadworth Hollway Hodgson

The theory of practice

THE
THEORY OF PRACTICE.

LONDON:
ROBSON AND SONS, PRINTERS, PANCRAS ROAD, N.W.

THE

THEORY OF PRACTICE

AN

Ethical Enquiry

IN TWO BOOKS

BY

SHADWORTH H. HODGSON.

IN TWO VOLUMES.
VOL. II.

LONDON:
LONGMANS, GREEN, READER, AND DYER.
1870.

[Reserve of Rights.]

THE THEORY OF PRACTICE.

BOOK II.—SYSTEMATIC.

THE LOGIC OF PRACTICE.

VIE PIÙ CHE' 'NDARNO DA RIVA SI PARTE,
PERCHÈ NON TORNA TAL, QUAL EI SI MUOVE,
CHI PESCA PER LO VERO, E NON HA L'ARTE.

CONTENTS OF BOOK II.

CHAPTER I.

THE LOGIC OF PRACTICE.

§		PAGE
76. The method of volition	.	3
77. Instances of this method	.	16

CHAPTER II.

THE LOGIC OF ETHIC.

78. The Summum Bonum in Ethic	. .	20
79. The Motive in Ethic		31
80. The Criterion in Ethic . . .		35
81. Comparison of this with other systems .		44
82. On the application of this logic . .		62
83. Relation of the criterion to happiness .		67

CHAPTER III.

THE LOGIC OF POLITIC.

84. The relation of Ethic and Law .		70
85. The ends of Law		86
86. The criteria and motives of Law .		92

CONTENTS OF BOOK II.

§		PAGE
87.	The motives of society	95
88.	The spontaneous organisation of society	100
89.	The voluntary organisation of society	130
90.	Analysis and classification of Law	162
	Public Law	171
	Civil Law	180
	Procedure and Evidence	210
	Table of the General Classes of Law	213
91.	Policy	213

CHAPTER IV.

LOGIC OF THE PRACTICAL SCIENCES.

92.	Practical sciences and Arts of Action	234
	Cultus and Theology	241
	Criticism and Fine Art	242
	Art of War	243
	Diplomacy	244
	Medicine	244
	Education	245
93.	Philology	249
	Parts of speech	255
	Inflection and Syntax	263
	Style	270
94.	Political Economy	274
95.	Statical Logic of Exchange	286
96.	Statical logic of money	367
97.	History	453
98.	Historical Science	464
99.	Arrangement of the Sciences	475
100.	Relativity of Existence	491

THE
THEORY OF PRACTICE.

BOOK II.

CHAPTER I.

THE LOGIC OF PRACTICE.

"There is, or rather there ought to be, a *logic* of the *will*, as well as of the *understanding*."

Bentham.

§ 76. 1. PURE Logic is that system of forms which voluntary redintegration necessarily and universally assumes, or that abstract method which it follows, in its process. Necessity, as has been shown continually in "Time and Space," is but the subjective correlate or subjective aspect of universality. Whatever forms or whatever method voluntary redintegration takes universally, without exception in any instance, these are its necessary forms or method. Hence the laws of pure logic are discovered solely by metaphysic, that is, by metaphysical analysis of the process of voluntary redintegration, and discovered in or as belonging inseparably to that process. This discovery is what was attempted in Chapter vii. of "Time and Space," where the concept-form or the postulates of logic were shown to arise from the operation of volition in the forms of time and space, which are the formal element in all consciousness and in all its perceptions. Pure logic, which makes abstraction of all particular aim or content of volition, and is applicable solely to voluntary redintegration as such, no matter what the redintegrated representations may be, contains only such abstract and general forms of thought as are founded on the postulates or on the concept-form alone. But the moment any particular object or content of the volition is assumed, that moment the logic ceases to be pure, and takes up into its own abstract and general forms other forms and distinctions belonging to the objects represented in the redintegration. The logic then becomes a mixed or applied logic; mixed because its abstract forms are exhibited in shapes derived from the particular object, and applied because its abstract method is directed to the investigation of an object-matter distinguishable from itself. But still the more concrete forms of mixed logic are inherent and discoverable in the objects represented in the logical redintegrations, just as the abstract forms of pure logic are in voluntary redintegration taken in the abstract.

2. Every particular object of voluntary redintegration has in this way a mixed logic of its own; the particular way of dealing with it, of directing the redintegrations which contain it, must be learnt from the object itself; but every particular way of dealing with it, whether right or wrong, must as a matter of fact be a mode of pure logic, a movement of thought in the method of the concept-form or the postulates, differentiated by the forms of the object itself. Every object so treated is moulded, as it were, into shapes developing and differentiating the first or most obvious shapes which the logical treatment observes in it; and the most complete investigation of it possible,

the most complete coordination and subordination of its parts, is but the continuation of the same process of redintegration which observed its first or most obvious distinctions. In other words, the science of any object or set of objects, the objects themselves in their scientific arrangement, is the complete establishment and development of the logic of that object or set of objects; or, a science is the completion of a logic, a logic the foundation of a science. The logic and the science of any object-matter are not two things but one thing; the same thing considered as to its growth in knowledge is logic, and considered as to its fulness and arrangement when grown is science. There are no distinctions of logic which are not distinctions between facts of science, there are no facts of science which are not members of a distinction of logic. The organon of discovery consists in the facts and distinctions already discovered.

3. Throughout the whole history, therefore, of any branch of knowledge, its science and its logic are two inseparable, correlated, aspects of each other. Nevertheless there comes a point in the history of every science, at which we are accustomed to say, here the logic ends and the science begins. This point is where we are in possession of such a fund of distinctions and of facts, that we can use them as a whole for the deduction of other new facts and new distinctions; where we possess in the already acquired fund of knowledge an organon for the deduction of new truths in the science. This fund is then called the Logic of the Science in a special sense; as being that firmly established body of facts and distinctions which are regarded as being beyond the power of future discoveries to disprove, or as the

conditions of the truth of facts and distinctions still to be discovered. The science is then said to have entered on its deductive stage.

4. It is a Logic in this second sense of the term which is at present in question with respect to the object-matter of practice, whether there is such a logic discoverable, and in what it consists. What then are the characteristics of this object-matter? Two are plainly discoverable at first sight; the redintegrations in question are processes, 1st, of consciousness, 2nd, of volition. Now all processes which take place in unconscious things, such as physical, mechanical, chemical, vegetable, processes, seem to be completely exhausted logically by being considered under two aspects, the statical and the dynamical; when any state of them is abstracted from states antecedent and subsequent to it and thus examined statically, and then its connection with those states and the movement or series of which it forms a part are added to the former examination, the logic thus applied seems sufficiently searching to leave no corner of the phenomena unexplored. These phenomena are thus examined objectively. But when the phenomena in question are states, and sequences of states, of consciousness, then they assume a double aspect, subjective as well as objective, and the connection between every former and latter state is both a fact in the object perceived or represented and a fact in the perception or representation of that object; depends, in the former character, upon the features of the object represented, in the latter character, upon the nerve movements supporting the perception or representation. There is a threefold character imprinted on the process, for in the statical analysis

the subjective and objective aspects coincide, are inseparably the same, while in the dynamical analysis the track followed by thought differs from that followed by nature and discovered by thought in the objects redintegrated. We thus get the distinction, established in "Time and Space" § 40, into the three orders, Essendi, Existendi, and Cognoscendi. These three orders seem equally to exhaust processes of consciousness as those of statical and dynamical analysis exhaust processes of unconscious objects.

5. But the application of these distinctions directly to the object-matter in hand would be to consider that object-matter from the outside, as it were, or objectively, as if it were an unconscious object-matter. Since it is a process of consciousness, the important question is, not what distinctions we may perceive in it, but what distinctions it perceives in itself while in action; in other words, what shape these same distinctions, now perceived by us in its process, assume to the Subject who has the redintegrations. Only the distinctions so perceived can be the logic of the process, the method followed by the redintegration itself. The redintegrations of practice have two branches, as shown in § 56, that in which we choose the best, and that in which we judge of the best; that in which we aim to be or do the best, and that in which we aim to know what is the best. In both alike we exercise volition, in choosing either between images or between feelings. In both therefore we start from a known and felt representation, and aim at one which is only known or felt in outline. By calling this "the best" it is meant to include in it all ends, aims, or purposes, whatever; "the best" is the widest term possible

for the ultimate end of volitions, be they what they may. And in all of them we start from some state of feeling and thought which is actual, and proceed by aiming at some dimly or partially seen state, some ideal, which we try to realise, or make actual in experience. We proceed from the one towards the other by media or middle steps, which in the branch of judgment are evidences of the desired truth, in the branch of choice are means to the desired pleasure. Both kinds of media may be called by the common name criteria, since both branches of the process are processes of consciousness, and even the means to a desired pleasure must be judged to be such means, or they would not be chosen to lead to it. The criteria of the branch of judgment have predominantly the character of imagery or framework, those of the branch of choice predominantly the character of feeling or emotion.

6. Now the terminus a quo in both branches corresponds to the order essendi in the objective logic of the process. It is a state of consciousness known for what it is, and it is what it is known as. The same may be said of the terminus ad quem in both branches; it is an ideal at first, and when reached is a state realised, just as was the terminus a quo; its nature is defined only by the knowledge of it, or its nature means its known nature. The same may be said of any of the intermediate states of consciousness between the two termini, when considered statically or each by itself. The two termini differ not from each other in belonging to a different order, for they both belong to the order essendi, but in being the one actual, the other ideal. Within the movement from one to the other lies the distinction cor-

responding to that between the orders existendi and cognoscendi, just as this latter distinction arose within the dynamical analysis of unconscious objects. In each of the two branches, of judgment and of choice, and in the criteria which are the steps of their movement, two different elements or strains are apparent, first, the kind of knowledge or feeling which constitutes these states what they are in point of nature, secondly, the strength or degree of pleasure which makes one arise in preference to another, or which guides the train of representations. The former of these corresponds to the order of knowledge, the latter to the order of existence. Yet both are phenomena of consciousness, phenomena seen subjectively, or as they appear to the redintegrating Subject.

7. We have, therefore, for our first distinctions in the logic of practice the three following, corresponding to the orders of logic, of history, and of knowledge, namely, the distinctions between the nature of states of consciousness, whether these are actual or ideal; the efficient cause of their production or reproduction in consciousness, the energy of which is measured by their degree of pleasure; and the cause of our knowing what the redintegration tends towards, which is the analysis or knowledge of each intermediate step. Let us now see how each branch of practice fits itself into these distinctions in actual working, and how in doing so it works also in the forms or method of pure logic, the concept-form and the postulates. Here we must attend to the second characteristic of the object-matter, namely, that it is a process of volition. The concrete shape of every process of conscious volition must assume both the sets of forms, causæ existendi and causæ cognoscendi,

now pointed out; and the question is, how these as well as the concept-form and the postulates, are involved in that concrete shape, or what that concrete shape is which involves them.

8. In the judgment branch of practice the redintegration starts from some present state of the Ego, a state which is defined only by the desire to judge between two or more mediate ends, two or more representations, at present imperfectly known, and to decide which of them is the best. Here the ultimate end of the voluntary redintegration, by which the present state of the Ego is defined, is the general idea of the good or best, a general idea requiring to be specialised and known in relation to the two or more mediate ends or representations, which spontaneous redintegration offers, and between which the volition is to judge. But the ultimate end, or idea of the best, general as it is, is yet to some extent known or imagined; and so far as it is known or imagined it becomes the middle term, or criterion, of a syllogism, of the syllogism of practical judgment, the conclusion of which is one or other of the mediate ends or representations between which the volition had to judge. These formed the quæstio of the syllogism, and one of them now forms the conclusion, the others being excluded from the known or imagined part of the idea of the best, which is the middle term. For instance, suppose the quæstio to be whether this particular act of strict honesty, A, or that particular act of loosely conceived honesty, B, or another of honesty apparently strict, but really dishonest, C, is the best; and suppose the idea of the best, as now known to us, to include only justice, veracity, and zeal for truth; the first step in

the syllogistic process is to unite the middle term with the general idea of the best, or, what is the same thing, with the present state of the Ego, the second and third to exclude from that middle term loose honesty and apparent honesty, as refusing to coalesce with its characteristics, zeal for truth and veracity. The conclusion binds together the Ego with the third term of the quæstio, strict honesty, as the only one which coalesces with all the characteristics of the middle term. The syllogism then stands thus:

> The particular act of strict honesty, A, is (contained in) justice, veracity, and zeal for truth;
> Justice, veracity, and zeal for truth, are (coincident with) the present state of the Ego, or general idea of the best;
> ∴ The particular act of strict honesty is (contained in) the present state of the Ego, or general idea of the best.

Or as a negative syllogism, thus:

> The particular acts, B and C, are excluded from justice, veracity, and zeal for truth;
> Justice, veracity, and zeal for truth, are (coincident with) the present state of the Ego, or general idea of the best;
> ∴ The particular acts, B and C, are excluded from the present state of the Ego, or general idea of the best.

Both syllogisms belong to the 2nd figure given in "Time and Space" § 56.

9. It is now to be noted that the conclusion of

this syllogistic process, the particular act of strict honesty, is an interpretation both of what the Ego is, and of what the Ego understands the ideal best to be. The imperfect knowledge of the ideal best has been differentiated, and thereby perfected; it now includes consciously that act which is strictly honest, as well as those emotions, justice, veracity, and zeal for truth, which were assumed as its known meaning. This differentiation is of course due to the previous habits of redintegration, by which such and such representations have been put together in times past. The Ego also is differentiated and made more perfect by one more judgment that such and such characteristics belong to its idea of good. The concluding term in short becomes a new criterion in the process above described, where the Ego passes from a present state towards the realisation of an ideal state; for this criterion, inasmuch as it is an actual judgment or act of the Ego, is an actual step in its history, or order of existence; and, inasmuch as it is a differentiation of the general or imperfectly known ideal, is a test or evidence of the nature of that ideal, added to the evidence by which alone it was previously known. The middle term, whatever it may be, is itself supplied by spontaneous redintegration like the rest; it is the most certain part of the knowledge at the time, having been the fruit of previous redintegrations and syllogisms; while those parts of the idea which are still unknown, or doubtful, the known part of it being the middle term, are viewed by the Subject as an unknown ideal to which he is tending, or the knowledge of which he is seeking, by means of the voluntary redintegration. The criterion which his reasoning produces, the conclusion of his syllogism, becomes in turn a new criterion of the nature, still unknown otherwise, of the ideal which he seeks to know.

10. Turning now to the branch of choice in practice, it will be well to refer to the dictum of Aristotle, Eud. Eth. v. 2. already quoted in § 20. 3, that pursuit and avoidance are in desire what affirmation and denial are in understanding. 'Desire' it was there said 'is affirmation that an object makes part of our trains of association, asserts that it belongs to our consciousness; dislike or repulsion of an object is negation of it, or denying that it is part of our train.' But for this distinction the method of the two branches of practice is the same. Suppose any one has an actual choice proposed to him between doing or having two or more objects, A, B, C. These are representations offered successively by spontaneous redintegration; his general habit of choosing whatever is most agreeable or best is, in choice, what his general idea of best is in judgment; that is, instead of proposing to himself, or identifying himself with, the idea of the best or greatest pleasure, he acts on the habit without converting it into an image or proposition. The conflicting pleasures, A, B, C, are then compared with each other, not by comparison of judgment, but by actual weight, intensity, or power of fixing the redintegration; that which is the most intense is the determining motive of the choice, and corresponds to the middle term in judgment; this is also the one which finally remains in possession of consciousness, which in other words is the one chosen; and thus becomes for other persons a criterion or evidence, not indeed of what the Ego knows, but of what he feels at the time to be most pleasureable,

the criterion of what he feels to be best. It is in choice the criterion and the conclusion of judgment both in one; and in the character of conclusion, or practical decision arrived at, is the differentiation of the Ego by a new act tending towards an ideal good, and evidencing, when its nature is analysed, not indeed the state of the agent's knowledge, but that of his feelings, not the clearness of his judgment but the relative strength of his motives. If this process is represented in syllogistic form, as it may readily be, the syllogism will be in the 4th figure given in "Time and Space" § 56, as those representing practical judgment were in the 2nd figure; the reason being that the train of redintegration as a whole is pictured by the syllogism, and that the train or movement of choice, being not consciously analytic like that of judgment, excludes not by mentioning and denying, but by simply omitting, what it rejects. The syllogism, then, to take the former instance, will stand thus:

> The present state of the Ego coincides with justice, veracity, and zeal for truth;
> Justice, veracity, and zeal for truth, coincide with this act of strict honesty;
> ∴ The present state of the Ego coincides with this act of strict honesty.

The Ego itself is represented as passing through three states in succession; identifying itself first with the middle term, then with its specialisation; the pleasure which is the determining motive being the same throughout, first as criterion, secondly as conclusion.

11. The processes in the two branches of judgment and of choice are precisely the same in point

of kind, but differ in the proportion in which the
criterion or middle term of each contains the two
elements of emotion and imagery. Action, it has
been shown, depends upon the strength of pleasurable emotion, judgment upon clearness of its framework. But just as all action is judgment and all
judgment action, so all motives of action are evidences in knowledge, and all criteria of judgment are
motives in action. It was necessary for the sake
of clearness to discriminate and describe separately
the two branches of practice; to begin by treating
the two cases as different, in order to demonstrate
their fundamental sameness. But this having been
done, we may now reduce both to one and the same
logical form. Voluntary redintegration, we may now
say, as a concrete process, moves in a method distinguished by three fundamental characteristics. It
has a general aim, end, or ideal; it has an evidence
or test applicable at present, of what that ideal will
consist in; and it has a motive power, known or
felt as the greatest immediate pleasure, which is the
efficient cause, operative at present, of the attainment
of that ideal. These three things are actually felt
by the Subject in voluntary redintegration; they are
the forms in which the abstract forms of pure logic,
the concept-form and the postulates, are clothed in
any concrete case of voluntary action or reasoning.
We all distinguish our knowledge of what is right,
or prudent, or ultimately most for our happiness,
from our feeling of what is most intensely pleasureable at the moment; we often find these two things
leading to different results; the clashing between the
two, and the frequent victory of the latter, when for
instance we do what we know clearly to be not only

wrong but highly imprudent, have been the theme of moralists and satirists times without end. The analysis of the foregoing Book enables us now to reduce them under the present logic of practice, with its three moments, the End, the Criterion, the Motive. The End is the ideal greatest good, or Summum Bonum, in whatever it may be discovered to consist. It is considered statically not dynamically, as part of the order of logic, not of knowledge or of history. It is what it will be ultimately known as. The Criterion is the cause of our knowing more perfectly than before this ideal end; it belongs to the order of knowledge. The Motive, which is the greatest immediate pleasure, the evidence of the nerve movement which is strongest at the time, a pleasure which can only be known to be the greatest at the time by its actually prevailing or remaining in consciousness, is, with nerve movement on which it depends, the efficient or dynamical cause, tending to the production or modification of the ultimate ideal end, and belongs to the order of history. For this End has also both characteristics in itself, that of being a state of consciousness and that of being a real fact, requiring, in the latter character, an actual train of efficient causes before it can itself become actual.

§ 77. 1. Many writers on ethic endeavour to crowd all its phenomena together under two heads of logic, usually called the questions as to the nature of right or good, and the causes or motives which lead us to pursue or enable us to attain it. The evidence of what is good, my second point, is then treated either under the question of nature or under that of motive. But it is often clear, from the very manner in which these heads of enquiry are laid down, that two alone are an insufficient logical apparatus for the discussion. Thus, for instance, in Adam Smith's Theory of Moral Sentiments, Part vii. Section i: entitled "Of the questions which ought to be examined in a theory of moral sentiments," we read as follows : " In treating of the principles of morals there are two questions to be considered. First, wherein does virtue consist—or what is the tone of temper, and tenor of conduct, which constitutes the excellent and praiseworthy character, the character which is the natural object of esteem, honour, and approbation ? And, secondly, by what power or faculty in the mind is it that this character, whatever it be, is recommended to us ? or, in other words, how and by what means does it come to pass, that the mind prefers one tenor of conduct to another ; denominates the one right and the other wrong ; considers the one as the object of approbation, honour, and reward, and the other of blame, censure, and punishment?" Here we might almost doubt whether the illustrious author intended to include the efficient motives of action in the enquiry ; and when he comes, in the third Section, to treat of the second class of questions, he sums them up as an enquiry " concerning the principle of approbation." It is true that approbation itself is a strong motive of action ; but is it the only motive, or a condition sine qua non of any other feeling becoming one ? Do not these questions by themselves show the necessity of treating the question of motive, or dynamic power in conscious action, separately from the question of judgment or approbation ?

2. The distinction between motive and criterion is very clearly drawn and strongly insisted on by

Bentham. For instance, in his Principles of Morals and Legislation, Chap. ii. xix. he says: "There are two things which are very apt to be confounded, but which it imports us carefully to distinguish:—the motive or cause, which, by operating on the mind of an individual, is productive of any act, and the ground or reason which warrants a legislator, or other bystander, in regarding that act with an eye of approbation. When the act happens, in the particular instance in question, to be productive of effects which we approve of, much more if we happen to observe that the same motive may frequently be productive, in other instances, of the like effects, we are apt to transfer our approbation to the motive itself, and to assume, as the just ground for the approbation we bestow on the act, the circumstance of its originating from that motive. It is in this way that the sentiment of antipathy has often been considered as a just ground of action. Antipathy, for instance, in such or such a case, is the cause of an action which is attended with good effects: but this does not make it a right ground of action in that case, any more than in any other. Still farther. Not only the effects are good, but the agent sees beforehand that they will be so. This may make the action indeed a perfectly right action: but it does not make antipathy a right ground of action. For the same sentiment of antipathy, if implicitly deferred to, may be and very frequently is, productive of the very worst effects. * * * * * The only right ground of action, that can possibly subsist, is, after all, the consideration of utility, which, if it is a right principle of action and of approbation, in any one case, is so in every other. Other principles in abundance, that is, other motives, may be the reasons why such and such an act *has* been done: that is, the reasons or causes of its being done: but it is this alone that can be the reason why it might or ought to have been done."

3. Here it is to be noticed that Bentham distinguishes really three things, the actual motive of an action, the intention or knowledge of the effects of the action, and these effects themselves as seen by a bystander; in other words, he distinguishes the actual motives which may be good or bad indifferently, the right motive which is the consideration of utility, and the right effects which are utility itself. Only when the consideration of utility is the actual as well as the right motive, would he say that both agent and act were perfectly right. He makes three heads of logic, so to speak, and in two of them places Utility, in case the act and agent are good. The consideration of utility is the right motive, utility itself is the end realised or aimed at. What I call criterion he calls consideration of the effects of the action, or right intention; the logic, had Bentham drawn it out, is the same, though the filling up or application of it may be different. Whereas Adam Smith allows the important point of motive or dynamic power to be almost dropped out of view, in his care to distinguish the nature of right from the criterion of right, all that is wanting in the passage quoted from Bentham is the explicit distinction of the end from the criterion, and the explicit statement of the three logical moments, end, criterion, and motive, which nevertheless are clearly discernible therein.

CHAPTER II.

THE LOGIC OF ETHIC.

Βίος γὰρ ἐφ' αὑτοῦ ἑκάστῳ, καὶ ἐν τῇ ἐνεργείᾳ τὸ εὖ.

Plotinus.

§ 78. 1. THE logical forms established in the preceding Chapter exhaust the whole process of practice or voluntary redintegration. It remains to apply them to the object-matter analysed in Book i., that is, to discover the best and simplest forms which practice can assume when its multifarious processes are combined with these which are the necessary or universal forms of all its processes alike; by which it is intended to convey that the task before us is no longer a discovery merely of the actual, but of a distinction to guide choice, a construction as much as a discovery of logic. We take up at this point a position ab extra, and endeavour to deduce, from the analysis of the object-matter and from its necessary and most general logic, that sort of continuation of the logic which is properly called science (§ 76, 3). It is clear that from this point onward there both may be and is the greatest divergence of practical systems. The task before us, then, is to criticise these, and, so far as they are found faulty or deficient, to supply their place with one more accurate. With this view I undertake, in this Chapter, that branch of the logic of practice which considers man as an individual person, reserving for the following one the consideration of the action and reaction of men on each other in society; the former branch being properly called the logic of ethic, the latter that of politic.

2. The method to be followed in this enquiry must flow from the logical distinctions established in the preceding Chapter. I will accordingly apply separately and successively the three heads of logic, the end, the motive, the criterion. And first the end, since to determine this is nothing else than to determine the nature of what is best, the nature of what is right and good. In the first place it is evident, that this is not immediately known to any one. All we know about it, in the first instance, is that it bears the general character of right and goodness, using 'goodness' as the most general expression for pleasure of feeling and emotion, and that it carries these qualities to their highest pitch, or possesses them in their greatest degree. This preliminary determination of the object sought is obviously most general, nothing more than is required for the expression of the question we ask about it; since without knowing *something* of what we want we could not ask or seek at all. When we put the question What this Summum Bonum is, we clearly want a further determination of it. The answer must therefore be given, if at all, by reason, or reasoning reflection. It must consist in something not obvious at first sight; and it must be an analysis of the na-

ture of the Summum Bonum, an answer to the question τί ἐστι, and not to the questions, how it comes to exist, how we reach it, or what consequences it produces. And since the answer is given by reason, it must be an answer giving the true nature or truth of the ideal which is sought, that is, an analysis of it which will stand the test of the most continued and the most searching enquiry.

3. In the next place, the Summum Bonum exhibited by the analysis which is here to be given must be capable of serving as the ideal end of all men and all characters alike, no matter what the special bent of their character, the special emotion predominant in them, may be; otherwise it would not be the Summum Bonum or End of a general, universally applicable, science of ethic. It must be neither too special or small to embrace all men, nor too indefinite or large to serve as an aim of conduct. It must be capable of interpretation by criteria which all men, however different in character, can perceive and apply. This character of the End points out at once its most important feature; for there is no other emotion but that of Justice, perfectly fulfilled by Love, in other words, the sense of Moral Right (§ 37), which combines these features of universality and definiteness. Love is the perfect fulfilment of the law, that is, of the moral law, the law of justice. The end is therefore definite and of universal validity. But no further or special developments of this principle can be included in the summum bonum of ethic, as an universally applicable science. All such further developments belong in different measures to different types of character, and there is not one among them which can be imposed

as an universally valid rule on all. The conduct,
and emotions, and objects, whatever they may be,
which this or that man finds, at any time or from
time to time, inseparable from his own sense of moral
right, and therefore commanded by his conscience;
for instance, the religious creed, the religious practices, which he cannot imagine not to be imperative,
are not to be imposed on others, not to be included
in the general End of ethic, either by himself or by
the ethical enquirer. Future agreements of characters, future harmonies of moral ends, must be left to
the future. The point of actual universal agreement
is the point to be insisted on in all cases; the diverg-
ences from this point onwards, the different modes
of realising what is still left indefinite in its ideal,
must be left undetermined; only the ideal itself, defined by the traits universally recognised, is the Summum Bonum of ethical science. These traits are the
common starting-point; the ideal of these traits, unknown except that it contains them, is the common
goal. Here is the rock on which most systems of
ethic have made shipwreck, some from adopting an
End too small and special, others from adopting one
too large and indefinite, as will be shown presently.

4. Another thing which we know about the End
of ethic, and which is a condition fulfilled by that
now exhibited, is that it consists in energy or in action. It is not a thing to be possessed or enjoyed,
but a life; something for a man to do, something for
him to be. He is to be a Subject so and so defined,
that is, defined as feeling, thinking, and doing, justice
and love,— οὐ γνῶσις ἀλλὰ πρᾶξις. Accordingly the
End embraces not only single emotions, acts, thoughts,
but habits and characters springing from and formed

out of these. It is a Character; as yet ideal, it is true, except that it contains the universally recognised traits; but still a character containing those tendencies, not merely a single state of consciousness containing them; a character not merely a moment of character; or rather, to apply Aristotle's words, a moment of character,—ἔτι δὲ ἐν βίῳ τελείῳ, a character and a life as well.

5. Finally, since there are two universally recognised traits in the End of ethic, and these are to be predominant not only over other emotions, thoughts, and actions, but also over these exhibited in characters; are to be themselves dominant in a character, bringing other types of character into agreement with that ideal type, as yet only distinguished by these traits; therefore we know something more of this End of ethic than merely these traits, and that they are to have ideal perfection; we know that they are to be, in their ideal state, a harmony of emotions, thoughts, and actions, and a harmony of characters formed from them. We do not, it is true, know in what this harmony will consist, we do not know it in its first intention; for to know this would be to know the ideal End itself in its first intention. We only know a second intention of it, its character of being a harmony of emotions, thoughts, actions, and characters. This general or characterising determination of the End lies in the two traits themselves, which are its known part or definition, justice and love. They cannot be operative without tending to such a harmony. Farther, we may characterise this harmony, and the ideal state which it pervades, as happiness, Aristotle's εὐδαιμονία. It is certainly a kind of εὐδαιμονία, a kind of happiness; though whether it

be the *greatest* happiness I cannot say, for I know of
no means of measuring happiness, the amount of one
kind against the amount of another kind, one man's
happiness with another man's. Had εὐδαιμονία been
capable of definition by analysis, Aristotle would
no doubt have so defined it. Happiness, then, characterises the ideal Summum Bonum, but does not
enter into its analysis. The kind of happiness which
it contains is definable only by the traits of love and
justice, and of the harmony which springs from them.
Everything in the Summum Bonum is referable to
these two traits, and explicable by them only.

6. Some of the Ends which have been proposed
by ethical writers as the account of the nature of
good and right seem to be too small and special for
the purpose, and so to require a justification themselves rather than to be the source of justification for
other principles. Benevolence, for instance, or sympathy; for thus stated alone, as the End of ethic, it
is of course opposed to self-love or care for one's own
interest. Clearly, when benevolence is put forward,
we always ask the further question Why is it right?
So also of self-love, even supported by enlightened
prudence, and shown to be not incompatible with the
interests of others. We again always ask Why is it
right? So too of both together, "the greatest happiness of the greatest number;" it is too small in one
respect, namely, that it requires a justification. Happiness is happiness, true; but is happiness right? I
mean by putting the question not to dispute that
happiness is compatible with right, but to show that
the two things are distinct, that the question can be
asked. That is to say, happiness may exist de facto
without its being known to exist de jure. Happiness

offers no handle to the judgment; it is a general name for pleasureable feeling, the material element, the emotional element only apart from the formal. At most it can contain only the motive of conduct. This it does contain, as will be seen.

7. In another respect, happiness, even the apparently more definite "greatest happiness of the greatest number," is too large and indefinite to serve as the End of ethic. All kinds of emotions have their pleasures, or are capable of pleasure; pleasure can only be defined by the emotion to which it belongs or in which it arises; to say that the greatest pleasure is the End of ethic is to tell us nothing about the End at all; the question always recurs, What sort of pleasure is the greatest? Again, to say that the End consists not only in pleasure, but in the greatest pleasure or in the greatest pleasure or happiness of the greatest number, is to add two still more obscure explanations to the already obscure explanation of happiness or pleasure by itself. The greatest pleasure,—true, but what sort of pleasure is the greatest; of the greatest number,—true, but may not your pleasures diminish in dignity as they increase in area? May not the smallest amount of pleasure be shared among the largest number of people? Bentham, I am aware, has met these questions by showing that there is a pretty general agreement about the relative amount or greatness of pleasures. But he has not shown that pleasure can be weighed against pleasure except by the actual choice of one and neglect of another. It is the habit, the character, formed by repeated acts of choice, which enables this opinion to be formed, and produces the general agreement of opinions. But we are seeking not only a more definite

conception of the End than we have at present, but we are seeking one which is to be the justification of habit, not one of which habit is the justification. If the opinion of such and such pleasures being greater than others, of such and such pleasures enjoyed by one number of men being greater than such and such pleasures enjoyed by another number of men, an opinion founded on habit and on agreement among men of different habits, is the ultimate End of ethic, then habit and agreement, irrespective of *what* is habitual and agreed upon, irrespective of the End itself, is the only source of what is good and right. De facto habit and agreement alone, that which above everything needs to be judged and criticised, is made in this theory the ultimate and only source of judgment and criticism; a rule of thumb becomes accepted as the moral law.

8. Wherever there is such an agreement on the relative greatness of pleasures, the pleasures are always defined by the emotion or its framework, in which they arise; they have no other definition. These emotions and frameworks are really that which is meant by the term pleasures. (See Bentham's Principles of Morals and Legislation, Chap. iv.) When we say that we prefer, or have found by experience that we prefer, such and such pleasures to others, or think them greater than others, what we mean is, that such and such emotions or frameworks have been found to predominate in actual frequent acts of choice over others, or to exclude others. It is the emotions and their frameworks that are compared, and furnish the means of comparing the pleasures. If, therefore, we wish to have an End of ethic not merely given by de facto habit, but founded on a

knowledge and comparison of the nature of the feelings selected and selected from, it is to the analysis of the emotions and their frameworks that we must go, and not to the general characteristic or description of these by the greatest pleasure. I am very far from depreciating the immense services rendered by Bentham to practical morals and legislation; very far from forgetting how needful it was to break through the trammels of narrow special systems of ethic, as well as of barbarous laws. But I must still think that the great principle which he placed as the ultimate ground of moral approbation, the greatest happiness principle, or the principle of utility,—admirable as a lever, admirable as an appeal ad populum,—is entirely untenable in the position he assigned to it in ethic, as the ultimate End of action. It may characterise that End, be a description, a "second intention" of it, if I may again use this technicality; but it gives us no knowledge of the End itself, and affords no ground of justification for actions tending towards it. Such a determination of the End supplies us with a tribunal for judging actions, a tribunal which consists of all those who happen to take the same general view of happiness; but it offers no means of finding criteria more special than itself, or of effecting any further agreement among men by proof founded on such criteria and their relation to the End. We ask, as it were, for a principle of jurisprudence, and it gives us the custom of a court.

9. I venture to insist still farther on this objection drawn from my distinction between first and second intentions. It is the cardinal distinction in all metaphysical method, and was so stated in "Time and Space" § 10. I had occasion to apply it, in

that work, to the examination of Hegel's Logic; it
is equally applicable to Bentham's Ethic. The distinction briefly stated is this. An object in its first
intention is an object abstracted from all other objects, and considered, analysed, in relation to consciousness alone, that is, considered as *what* it is;
and it makes no difference whether the object is
large or small, simple or complex. An object in its
second intention is one considered in relation to
some other object or objects in consciousness, and
the terms describing it as so related are terms describing it in some one or more of its second intentions, which are as numerous as the objects with
which it is related; its causes and effects, its relative
size, intensity, and number, are among such second
intentions. It is clear that, before we can know any
second intention of an object, we must know something of the object in its first intention, for we must
know what the object is which we then are to consider in relation to other objects. Second intentions
then in all cases are founded upon first intentions,
and are relations between them; and no second intention can be the ultimate ground of a system.
For either the first intentions, between which it is
the relation, are known, in which case the whole object, the relation and its parts together, forming an
object in its first intention, is the ground of the system; or the first intentions are not known, and then
there is no relation sufficiently definite to serve as
such a ground.

10. Now Bentham's "greatest happiness" is a
relation between pleasures; but pleasures are only
known in their first intention by the emotion and
framework in which they arise; this gives the kind

of pleasure; and their relative quantity, intensity, or amount, is only known by observing which emotions and frameworks usually supplant others, as described in § 54 (and see also § 57, 7-10). The "greatest happiness principle" therefore picks out two relations between emotions, relations known and definable only by knowledge of the emotions themselves, and makes these relations, expressed by the term "greatest happiness," the ultimate ground and basis of a system of ethic; all its power of serving as such ground being due, not to the relations, but to the emotions between which they subsist. The definite meanings of the terms 'ought,' 'right,' 'wrong,' are thus suspended upon the indefinite meaning of 'utility.' "When thus interpreted," says Bentham, Chap. i. x. of work cited, "the words *ought*, and *right* and *wrong*, and others of that stamp, have a meaning: when otherwise, they have none."

11. The very vagueness of the terms, utility, greatest happiness, and so on, serves to win them credit, since no moralist denies that what is morally best and right is the highest utility, the greatest happiness; that is, that these, being known, are what will turn out to be beneficial in the highest degree we can conceive. But the question in ethic is, which of these two characters is the known one, which known only through the other. It is the most known one which must be the basis of an ethical system. Is pleasure the source of right? No, it is not even coextensive with it, for some bad things are pleasant. But is the greatest pleasure? May be; but what is the greatest pleasure? We are thrown back upon analysis.

12. This cannot be called, to use a phrase of

Bentham's, a "trifling verbal difficulty;" it is an objection both just and important. Just, for the reasons already given; and important, because from the substitution of a perfectly indefinite τέλος, or Summum Bonum, happiness in place of some definite emotion or emotions, flows directly the consequence that habit and opinion are made supreme in ethical questions, and that the question, What is de jure right, is transformed into the question, What is commonly and de facto supposed to be so. It is true that we are in no worse position than was Aristotle, with his appeal to ὡς ὁ ἀγαθὸς ὁρίσει. So much I admit; but have we not grounds for claiming a better position?

§ 79. 1. If a conjecture is permissible, it may be conjectured that the circumstance of the greatest pleasure being attached to the determining motive, in all particular cases of choice and conduct, was that which led to this characteristic being adopted as the definition of the Summum Bonum. Of a good thing we all choose to have much rather than little, of a bad thing little rather than much. This being the general character of all our actions in particular, it seemed only necessary to express it in the most general terms, to sum the cases, in order to find the general character of the whole. But it was forgotten that this process could only give the general character of what all action is, not of what all action ought to be. Again, the relative degrees or intensities of pleasure in particular cases, apart from the emotions and frameworks to which they belong, are just as indefinite and uncommensurable as in the general sum of the whole.

2. Therefore, although we may say, and indeed

infer with great probability, that the actual determining force in any or all cases of action is characterised or accompanied by the greatest pleasure, we do not derive from this any law of the actual course of choice or action; we know that what is, has been, or will be done is accompanied by the greatest pleasure possible at the time, but not that what we think the greatest pleasure possible at the time is, has been, or will be done. Knowing what is done, we may say it is the most pleasureable course open; but, conversely, the most pleasureable course open is only known by knowing what is actually done. Only when by experience, observation and remembrance, we know what objects, what pleasures, have been preferred to others, we may infer, conversely, that, when the known objects and pleasures are in question, the most pleasureable will be actually done.

3. There is, therefore, very little to be said about the motive in the logic of ethic. The actual motives of choice and action are, on the other hand, the principal object of thought for those who aim at reforming actual customs, opinions, actions, and institutions, or at erecting new principles and standards of opinion. It is upon them that the chances of success depend; they must be appealed to and swayed. The study of the actual course of events, so as to distinguish first what is alterable from what is unalterable, and secondly, in the former, what is desirable from what is undesirable, in detail, and with a view to immediate practice, this is the field where the motives of choice and action require a lengthy treatment.

4. All kinds of emotion and passion have their pleasures as well as their pains; all may at different

times and in different circumstances become actually operative motives, and of course with different degrees of force, measured we may say generally by the intensity of the pleasure. Motives which have been or may be actual, or de facto causes of choice and action, de facto in point of kind, though not always operative, these are the material, as it were, of ethic, the matter to be moulded, by means of the two conceptions, the Summum Bonum and the Criterion. Among these de facto motives are always found some which are de jure. The practical problem of ethic and of action is to find which are de jure, and to make these the actual motives. The problem of the logic of ethic is to find what the leverage for this consists in, that is, what is the nature of the Summum Bonum, and what of the Criterion. The detailed application is the practical problem, which alone requires the detailed consideration of the material or field of action, the Motives of actual conduct.

5. Much has been said about persons acting from mixed motives, and much acuteness is sometimes displayed in pointing out an element of self-love or self-interest in the motives of actions which appear to flow from motives of benevolence or public feeling alone. It is sometimes thought also that to prove a mixture of self-interest in a motive is to condemn that motive as a low one. The truth is, that all motives which can be analysed at all are mixed; they contain an element of pleasure which is the evidence of their motive power, and they contain a certain kind of emotion and framework which furnishes the definition of what they are. Without the pleasure we should not know that they were motives,

without the emotion and framework we should not know what kind of motives they were. Two kinds of elements are discoverable in every motive, first the pleasure, which is the evidence of the causa existendi of the course actually followed by the redintegration; secondly, the emotion and its framework, which are the causa cognoscendi, or evidence of the kind of actions selected and selected from. From this latter element in motives is selected, by the logic of ethic, the criterion of the right and the good. The criterion may be itself pleasureable, and in this respect a de facto motive.

6. Had Bentham placed Utility under the head of motive, in his logic, and excluded it from the heads of end and criterion, instead of the reverse, he would, I think, have been nearer the truth. The de facto motive is that to which is attached the greatest attainable pleasure, the greatest pleasure of those in contemplation at the time of action. This truth, that pleasure is the universal motive power, spreads itself wrongly, in his theory, over the domains of the other two heads; wrongly because pleasure offers no cause of knowing the nature of emotions or states of consciousness, because the greatest of any two pleasures is distinguished, in the last resort, only by the fact of its supplanting the other. The immediately practical purpose of Bentham's writings it was which no doubt led him to fall into this confusion, and assume the end and the criterion of morals to be nothing more than the motive repeated, though on a larger scale. When he asked for the criterion, he really asked how we came to choose this rather than that, and received for answer the de facto motive; and again, when he asked for the ultimate end, he really

asked, not what it was, but how we came to have one, and here also the answer was given in the same terms in which it was put, namely, By the urging force of the actual motive, pleasure. It may be surmised also, that the very generality and vagueness of the End, in Utilitarianism, the greatest happiness of the greatest number, has chiefly contributed to win for the theory its great number of adherents among practical reformers, too busy for logic; whatever was the particular class of objects which each reformer might have most at heart, the existence of a professedly all-embracing theory afforded him a banner and watchword under which to fight, a justification in the eyes of the public at large for his efforts at reform, while at the same time its vagueness and generality bound him to no particular view or special aim, but left him free to interpret the "greatest happiness" in his own way. He enlisted in a service which was irreproachable, and required no sacrifices; the theory lent its name, (it was all it had to lend); he lent that name his adherence.

§ 80. 1. The Criterion is the point upon which hinges the greater part of the most practically important questions in ethic. Of the two elements in voluntary action, the historical or de facto element is exhausted by the Motive. The causa cognoscendi of what is right and good, the reason for immediate approbation of one act over another, remains; this is the Criterion. It makes no difference whether the approbation, the reason or criterion of which is now sought, is the approbation of one person for the acts of others, or for his own acts, nor whether, in either case, it is approbation after the fact, or before it, or so immediately before it as to combine with the motive of action. The criterion must be the same in all cases; and therefore I shall keep before me especially the last-mentioned case, as always speaking, where possible, from the point of view of the Subject engaged in action. The question then is, what is the criterion which the Subject adopts, or ought to adopt, as the reason for his approving one act and not another, in the moment of choice between them.

2. By a Criterion is meant not that feature which makes the act right, but that which makes us suppose it right; not that which will make us judge it right ultimately, but that which makes us judge it right now; the evidence which we have at our command, at the moment of action, that the act indicated by it will prove to be right and good when examined according to truth. We have no immediate knowledge of the true goodness or rightness of any act; this depends on its conformity, its quality of leading up to the true ideal, the true End or Summum Bonum. The End makes everything right that is right, even the Criterion itself. The determination of the End, therefore, logically precedes that of the Criterion. We, in logic of ethic, can only judge and establish a criterion by reference to the End; while, in actual choice and in the particular actions of every day, the criterion is our guide for conducting them towards the End. It stands between the two, being less general and abstract than the End, more general and abstract than the particular act. Two or rather perhaps three things are requisite in order to an act being ultimately or truly right, first the End must be truly conceived, secondly a true Criterion must be correctly applied. Or, as Abélard says in his Ethica, or Scito teipsum, Cap. xii. "Non est intentio

bona dicenda, quia bona videtur, sed insuper quia talis est, sicut existimatur." The truth of the criterion depends on that of the End, from which it is derived; yet the End is not less subjective than the criterion. Truth in ethic, no less than in speculation, means that view of the phenomena which will stand the test of the most rigorous and continued examination; and it is just as possible to adopt a false End as to adopt a false criterion of conduct. Truth in ethic, as well as in speculation, is suspended upon the result of future experience, that is, it is an ideal. ("Time and Space" § 62.) For the purpose of the present argument, however, I assume the End already given to be the true one.

3. The importance of distinguishing the criterion from the End is shown by the consequences of confusing them, namely, that acts flowing from the upright application of the criterion are thought to be eo ipso invested with the goodness of the End; whereas, not only may a wrong criterion be adopted, but also the application of a right one is subject to mistake, being dependent upon the degree of knowledge and state of feeling of the actor. Both errors however are reducible to one; a wrong criterion is never adopted except by mistake in the application of a right one, supposing the End to be the true one; for the general and abstract feature, which, being derived from the End, makes the criterion what it is, is derived immediately from the End, and only becomes a wrong criterion by being combined with other feelings, with emotions and frameworks, owing to experience of life, to habits and tendencies of character, which from that very combination are thought good and right, yet may turn out not conformable

to the End, when they are examined by the light of truth. This consequence of confusing the criterion and the End is the error to which religious systems are most exposed, just as an opposite error, arising from confusion of the motive with the End, the error of eliminating de jure considerations from ethic altogether, attaches most to utilitarian theories.

4. The upright application of a criterion honestly believed to be true, in any action, justifies the act and the actor, that is to say, secures him from remorse, secures to him a good conscience, as well as the approbation of others, so far as that act alone is concerned. But it does not secure their approbation or his own to other features of his character, to his other modes of reasoning or feeling, or to the series of acts as a whole, to which the single act in question belongs. If his whole conduct is governed by the same criterion, his whole conduct is justified by it; but it may happen that there is a discrepancy between his conduct as a whole and a single act which is part of it. The justification derived from the upright application of a criterion honestly believed to be true extends both to the act and to the agent; but it extends no farther, in either, than it has been actually determinant of conduct. Again, other persons may disbelieve in the agent's criterion, or he himself may come to disbelieve in it; that is, it may turn out a false criterion. This does not invalidate its justification of acts determined by it while it was believed true. The blame is then thrown not on the agent nor on his act, but on his erroneous belief in his criterion, and the question becomes, how far he is to blame for this. Third persons will say, 'Believing as he does, he is right

in his act, but his character and conduct as a whole
is wrong, as we believe.' A slovenly way of expressing this is to say, 'The agent is right, but his
act wrong;' as if the two could be separated. What
is an act? An agent in motion. The reason for
taking this false distinction between agent and act
lies, no doubt, in the facility with which the effects
of overt acts can be classed and judged of, compared
to the difficulty of judging immanent acts of choice
alone. But it is with immanent acts of choice that
we are chiefly concerned here, and with overt acts
only as judged in foro conscientiæ; and in these the
character of the act, as good or bad, is inseparable
from that of the agent in the act.

5. The first condition, then, which the criterion
to be selected by the logic of ethic must fulfil, is that
it must be such as to justify or secure our approbation of particular acts and the agents in them. The
second condition is, that the criterion must justify
or secure approbation not only of particular acts, but
also of particular kinds or tendencies of character.
In other words, we want something which shall guide
us towards the formation of a right and good character, as well as towards the choice of right and
good acts. Unless an act chosen conduces to the
formation of a good character in the actor, besides
being an addition to the number of good acts, the
good done, as it were, with one hand is undone with
the other, and a discrepancy is introduced into the
laws of conduct, which might be fatal to their success
in leading to the End. A criterion which did not
provide for both points would be, on that ground
alone, convicted of being a false criterion. Inatten-
tion to this condition of a true criterion of right has

led to many mistakes; for instance, to the famous apparent paradox of private vices being public benefits. The state is not served in the best way possible, when riches, for instance, increase but character deteriorates.

6. It will now be evident in what way I propose to fill up the third head of logic, what I propose as the criterion. It is the Moral Sense, the Conscience. This when obeyed honestly, and not merely professedly, and in the true and strict meaning of the term Moral Sense (§ 37), provides both for the approbation of the act and for the approbation of the character; obeying it both justifies the act and tends to produce the habit of acting rightly. The abstract and general features of justice and love are the features which are sought for in the act to be chosen; the pleasures inherent in them are the actual motive force in choosing; and the same features again are the reason of approving when the choice has been made. They are the de jure element, the justification of the act, and the justification of the character. The other features, the other emotions, which in different persons and at different times may be combined with these, forming a complex and more concrete state of feeling, are not to be confused with these, nor to be considered as contributing to justify the act. It is not these other features, nor yet the state of feeling as a whole, variable as they are indefinitely from time to time, from person to person, from place to place, but these two elements, justice and love, alone, which are the de jure, the justifying, element. And these it imports us to distinguish and apply in practice, no less than in the logical theory; to distinguish from their habitual, and often it may be

from their seemingly inseparable accompaniments; and to insist upon and endeavour their enforcement, and their enforcement alone, in our thoughts and actions.

7. Now it may seem, at first sight, as if two criteria and not one were here laid down, conscience in its concrete, accidental, shape being one, justice combined with love the other. To this point it is necessary to call particular attention, for we are at the very centre of the whole system of ethic, that central link upon which the whole fabric depends. Here too is the great difficulty peculiar to all systems of the Moral Law school of ethic, the objection which may be urged against them in claiming universal validity for conscience, drawn from the opposition between the dictates of conscience, in different persons, of different countries, different modes of education, different states of civilisation; so that that which claims to be universally valid is yet shown to command opposite duties, which would be also contradictory ones were they commanded at the same moment. This difficulty is that with which we have to cope in establishing a criterion. Now the criterion can only be single; which of the two then is to be selected? Conscience in its concrete, accidental, shape. Conscience is the test, or criterion of choice, in definite, particular, cases; of choice between this, that, and the other, of certain particular actions in the concrete, brought before us in representation at any moment of action. Its dicta therefore are particular and concrete,—do this, avoid that; and to such cases the perceptions of justice and love are not always immediately and directly applicable. What then is the function of these perceptions, and why have they

been introduced here? They are the analysis of conscience, the element of moral validity in its concrete dicta, or, as it were, the conscience of conscience itself. But to lay them down as the criterion or immediate guide of conduct would be to lay down what might indeed be both subjectively and objectively demonstrated, but would not be also subjectively obvious or immediately applicable. It is not every one that would accept them, since it requires an analytical process to discern them; while conscience, containing always these elements, but holding them in combination with other principles derived from particular circumstances and education, is known and admitted by all. Conscience then in its concrete, accidental, shape is to be obeyed; justice and love, the analysis of what is permanent and universal in it, used to correct conscience itself; just as, to take an illustration, the existing law of the land is to be enforced even where it works harshly, and afterwards repealed or reformed for future application. Nor do I fear to say with Abélard, taking an extreme case by way of illustration, of the persecutors of Christ and Christian martyrs "qui tamen gravius culpam peccassent, si contra conscientiam eis parcerent." Ethica, Cap. xiv.

8. If this analysis of what is permanent in conscience is the true one, obedience to conscience will bring, as its result, these elements to the light, and establish them in universal practice. That which has been the guiding principle in constituting and forming conscience will be the guide in its action afterwards, for this action itself is nothing but a continuance of the same process of formation. Again, if any of the utilitarian analyses of conscience, or criteria, were the true one, we could only expect that obedience to

conscience would produce its elements of analysis; if conscience had been really formed by habitual obedience to superior force, obedience to it would result in confirmed habits of such obedience; if by constant seeking of self-interest, such self-seeking would be the habit confirmed; if by constant self-sacrificing benevolence, the confirmed habit of self-sacrificing benevolence would arise; or if by any or all of these combined, then their combination would appear as the ultimate issue of obedience to conscience. But justice and love alone afford, as the analysis of conscience, a logically valid ground for assuming conscience to be always morally valid as a criterion of conduct. For the criterion can have no greater moral or de jure validity than is conferred by the elements of which it consists. If pleasure, in any of its kinds, high or low, is the element constituting conscience, then the moral validity of conscience is not greater than that of the pleasure or pleasures which are its source. Thus the analytical part of ethic contains the ground or reason of the systematical part, the doctrines of the logic of practice. The validity of the criterion of conduct reposes on its analysis. Why do I believe conscience in all its diversity to be the criterion of acts? Because I believe that the analysis of what is permanent in it, of that which makes it felt to be right, is justice and love. And the End, upon which the criterion depends, is itself grounded on a similar analysis, or justified by it, in the eye of philosophy, as the true End of action.

9. Every act done or chosen, considered as occupying a certain duration of time, is parted between two elements, parallel or intertwined throughout its dura-

tion, the motive and the criterion. Every act to be done or chosen the same; only that here the criterion is double, one part of it being affirmative, the other negative, one the principle of selection, the other of neglect or omission. All the past is irreversible; at any moment of choice, we, the volition, have to choose only between the next actions possible at the moment. Here again there is a part with which we have nothing to do, the motive. God or Nature provides for that; we have to do only with the criterion. The criterion contains under it, or applies to, all our knowledge about the acts to be chosen or avoided, including all that we know or suspect about the probable strength of motives, drawn from past experience. The strength of the motive in the present act is that which at the present moment is about to exhibit itself in actual trial.

§ 81. 1. Let us now institute a brief comparison between this system and others, and chiefly the Utilitarian theory. In the first place, the Utilitarian theory places its whole trust in acquired habits and acquired knowledge of what is preferable; I say its *whole* trust because both its End and its Criteria are placed by it in acquired knowledge, and not in emotions belonging to the nature of man itself, or the nature of his character. In the present system, on the contrary, both the End and the Criterion are found in that nature and character, and in features of them which are at once universally present and capable of extension to any circumstances and any degree of development. This expansibility of these principles renders them equally adaptable with the generality of the corresponding Utilitarian principles to the circumstances of life; and they have besides the advantage, in a systematic or scientific point of view, of being founded in the nature of man, not in his knowledge, which is wanting to the others. They are capable of embracing conceptions of what is de jure, as well as what is de facto.

2. It has sometimes been objected to the Utilitarian theory, that it requires what is impossible in requiring an anticipatory pursuit of the furthest consequences of acts, in order to judge whether they are according to, or likely to produce, the greatest happiness. This however is a mistake, as Mr. J. S. Mill has well shown, in his Utilitarianism, Ch. ii. p. 34. We have acquired habits and acquired knowledge as to what kinds of acts are most likely to produce happiness, and the media axiomata thus stored up are our criteria of particular acts, when the moment of choice comes. Between the kinds of pleasures again, and between the kinds of character most desirable and most conducive to happiness, we may have recourse to the opinions and experience of "the most competent judges" in such matters. This objection then falls to the ground, but I must still urge, as I have already done, that such habits and knowledge, whether our own or of "the most competent judges," are neither founded on an adequate criterion of right themselves, nor able to furnish one to us who have recourse to them. What is needed is an immediate criterion of right, as well as a probable judgment about advantage. This is supplied by the Conscience, analysable, in its permanent part, into the emotions of love and justice, a criterion immediately applicable to every case of action by ourselves, and among the rest to the judgments which we form as to who are "the most competent judges;"

for this too is a question which has to be decided; the tribunal itself must be tested as to its competence by some criterion. The question between the Utilitarian theory and the present theory is this, Whether the *ultimate* source of justification lies in the judgment of a tribunal, ὡς ὁ ἀγαθὸς ὁρίσειεν, or in the principle of that judgment, namely, in some particular emotion contained in it. Or, to put the question of a tribunal aside, does the ultimate source of justification of a judgment lie in the judgment itself as a whole, a judgment that pleasure A is better than pleasure B, or in an element of the judgment, the criterion which it assumes to form itself by. To rest in the judgment as a whole seems to me analogous, in ethic, to resting, in metaphysic, upon the fact that objects are objects of consciousness, as an ultimate datum, instead of resting on the analysis of such objects, (see "Time and Space" § 11); to rest in the judgment of a tribunal, or ὡς ὁ ἀγαθός, seems analogous to resting in the dicta of a book, or a priest, or a council, in theology, instead of in a further judgment of our own about the validity of those tribunals. It might indeed be the case, that we were compelled to do so; that we could push analysis no farther; but if analysis can be pushed farther it would be well; our effort must be to push it as far as it will go; the attempt to analyse farther is the counsel of hope, the ambition of philosophy.

3. To turn for a moment to another theory of ethic, the one most opposite to that of Bentham, the theory of Kant. The objection of impracticability in application of the criterion to practice, which does not lie against Bentham's theory, does seem to me to lie against Kant's. I have not entered into a criticism

of Kant's theory in this work, because it is founded on an Ontological basis, and the reasons urged against all Ontology in "Time and Space" seem to me to render it as inapt to be the foundation of an ethical as of a purely metaphysical superstructure. Kant's universal criterion in ethic is the following general law: "So act that the maxim of thy will may be valid at all times alike as the principle of an universal lawgiving;" Kritik der Praktischen Vernunft, Book i. Chap. i. § 7. In other words, Take as your criterion that state of mind which will be valid as a motive principle, not only for you now and here, but for all men everywhere and always. Now it is quite true, that the criterion of ethic must be capable of universal application, that all beings constituted as those are who would establish the criterion must be conceived as amenable to the law which it prescribes. But to assume this characteristic, this "second intention," of the criterion as the criterion itself, is to put a generality in the place of an analysis, to assume as an ultimate criterion a statement about criteria generally, to adopt as a criterion something which must derive its whole force, its whole applicability as a criterion of conduct, not from itself but from facts, or choices, or judgments, already known, or known from other sources, to be capable of subsumtion under it; in short it is to commit the very same error, in point of kind, which is committed by the Utilitarian theory according to the preceding paragraph, only in the name and interests of a supposed Absolute Moral Law from above, instead of a general search for Happiness from below. Kant's criterion would, in the first place, require for its application a series of media axiomata drawn from experience, just as much as Bentham's does, though this alone is no objection against either; and in the second place, and here is the true objection, is applicable only by those who have attained the conception of a law binding on all reasoning beings, as such. To adopt it as a criterion would be like adopting justice and love, by themselves, and not as involved in particular consciences, as if in that abstract shape they were universally recognised.

4. In what has been here said in criticism of the Utilitarian theory, nothing can be farther from my meaning than to deny that the greatest happiness of the greatest number is or ought to be the result of all conduct. It will no doubt characterise all results of conduct in greater measure according as the conduct is right. My objection lies against the theory as a theory of ethical logic or science. It substitutes, in its End and in its Criterion, an incident, a κατὰ συμβεβηκός, an "accident," though probably an "inseparable" one, for the thing itself which ought to be called End and Criterion. It is adopted chiefly, I believe, from the prevalence of the so-called practical point of view, and certainly it is founded on a popular not on a strict analysis. It is as if botanists should content themselves with the distinction between flowers and fruit, instead of distinguishing corolla, pistils, stamens, ovary, and seed. The analysis here proposed is intended to remedy this defect without involving, even theoretically, any loss of happiness in the ultimate result, though the happiness is denied to be that which is the proper aim and end of action. It is added, as lawyers say, "by the act of God."

5. Bentham himself was fully aware of the logical inconsistency involved in the popular language which

he adopted. He distinguishes, as has been seen, motives from intentions, motives being the various pleasures, which he calls springs of action, and intentions the conceptions of the particular acts aimed at in particular cases, and prompted by motives. "The causes of intention," he says, in Chap. viii., xiii. of the work already cited, "are called *motives*." But in thus adopting motives as one of his categories, he adopts a word and a thing full of ambiguity. See his Chapter x. Of Motives. In one sense it is true, as he asserts, Chap. x., x., "that *there is no such thing as any sort of motive that is in itself a bad one.*" This is true when motive is taken to mean solely motive power, without any distinction of kind imported into it. But in popular phrase a motive always means a pleasure of a particular kind, and motives in this use of the term are always good or bad, and have also some degree of goodness or badness. "To speak of motives," he says in sec. xiii., "as of anything else, one must call them by their names. But the misfortune is, that it is rare to meet with a motive of which the name expresses that and nothing more." He means that the name expresses not only the kind of motive, but some approbation or disapprobation as well. Bentham however, though aware of this difficulty in the language he had to use, apparently thought that the knot of the difficulty lay in the name combining the expression of approbation or disapprobation with the kind of the motive, and not in its combining the kind of motive with the circumstance of motive power. Three things being expressed by the name of any motive, namely, motive power, kind of it, and praise or blame, he endeavoured to sunder, he drew a distinction between, the second and third, and not between the first and second. Motives accordingly became with him pleasures of different kinds, all of them good, or not bad, in themselves, and bad or good, secondarily, only in respect of their consequences. "If they are good or bad, it is only on account of their effects: good, on account of their tendency to produce pleasure, or avert pain: bad, on account of their tendency to produce pain or avert pleasure." He thus deprives himself of all means of judging motives in or by themselves, notwithstanding that they are all pleasures of certain kinds; also of the means of judging of the character of agents as distinguished from their actions, if it is true that the kind of pleasures which are their favourites is what makes the characters of men good or bad. Perhaps it will be said, Not so, for, though he cannot judge of the motive, he can of the intention, and through this of the character. But here too he is precluded, for the intention also is suspended on the result; it is the known or supposed effect of an action, as good or bad, which makes the intention to do that action good or bad. The intention is good if the effect is thought to be good, and bad if it is thought to be bad. And similarly with omissions. The strength of will, again, in doing or neglecting an act whose effects are supposed to be known, or known to some extent, belongs to motives; it is a question of their comparative strength. A weak volition to do a good thing, a strong volition to do a bad one, are bad, and conversely; but the goodness or badness of the strength in volition depends on that of the acts done or omitted, and this falls under one or both of the heads, motive and intention; and both of these, according to Bentham, are dependent on their anticipated results. Bentham, therefore, can judge of nothing but the *resulting* pleasures or pains; the pleasures which, either as motives or as intentions, tend to produce these, and the characters of the men who act from these causes, are withdrawn from his scrutiny by his own logic; he can logically and consistently judge a *man* to be good or bad in no other way, and in no other sense, than he judges a hard winter or a genial spring to be so. And yet, if he can judge the pleasures or pains which *result* from motives, the characters *formed* by motives, as good or bad, why cannot he judge them while they are operating as motives and forming characters? He judges them in and by themselves in the one case; why not also in the other? There must be a radical error in the Utilitarian logic here.

6. It will be already clear in what I conceive this error to consist. It consists in drawing the line, where Bentham draws it, between the kind of motive and the approbation or disapprobation, and in not drawing it between the motive power in the abstract and the kind of all or any particular motives. This latter distinction is the one drawn and exhibited in the foregoing §§. We obtain as result the distinction between motive and criterion, in place of Bentham's distinction between motive and intention, a metaphysical in place of an empirical distinction. With Bentham motives are the causes of intentions, feelings causing and preceding thoughts, in full agreement with the psychological analysis of emotions, criticised in § 14. My Criterion on the other hand, like all mental states in representation, consists equally of emotion and framework; it is one of the emotions already analysed in Chap. ii. Book i.

Bentham too, like the psychological school generally, seems to take as much pains to keep emotion and framework apart, to make them stand in a causal relation to each other, as I do to bring them together, to form a theory in which they appear together, as they do in nature. But while in the psychological analysis of emotions it was the emotions which were caused by the frameworks, here, in Bentham's ethical theory, it is an element in emotion, the emotional pleasure, which appears as the cause of the framework. So far indeed rightly; since here we are engaged with voluntary, outward-going, there with involuntary, inward-going, action; there with causes as efficient, here with causes as final. This agreement however only serves to show the intimate coherence of the two schools, the psychological school in analysis, the Utilitarian in constructive ethic.

§ 82. 1. It is requisite, in the next place, to give some account of the character which the logic here offered assumes in application to particular circumstances and acts, to give some notion of the mode of its practical working, and of the colour which it imparts to life. Its application means the application of its criterion in cases of choice. Much depends, in the first place, on the nature of the criterion itself. The term Conscience, which characterises this criterion, is in itself as vague as the term Utility; it may be honestly used to cover almost any choice or any action, because the combinations of justice and love may be indefinitely various. But it is here maintained, that the peculiar sense of moral validity, which is the meaning of the term Conscience in its first intention, is, as a matter of fact, attached exclusively and permanently to one combination of feeling only, justice and love themselves; that, wherever this peculiar sense of validity is felt, it arises from the presence of, or from association with, those feelings. Let any one examine honestly for himself what he means by the term, and he will find that he means this by it and nothing else. We cannot then dispense with the distinction of Conscience, or with the term expressing it, for we want a term to express immediately felt moral validity, in whatever concrete shape it may be clothed; but we must analyse and define it, in order to rescue it from vagueness, and to secure ourselves against its abuse. Justice and love, which are the definition of what is valid in it, speak for themselves. If a man, for instance, says that his conscience bids him persecute opinion, ask him whether his sense of justice and love so bids him; if not, be sure it is not his conscience that does, but something which he falsely takes for conscience. This is the testing of conscience by its analysis, spoken of in § 80. 7, the distinction of what it appears now from what it in truth is. At the same time, whether so tested or not, it is conscience that must be obeyed; the sense of moral validity, the importance of duty, is that which is to be held fast and deepened; for in intensifying this feeling alone lies the chance of bringing out its elements of analysis into new distinctness, and into their true proportions.

2. In the second place, the law imposed by this criterion is a law, perhaps the only law, of Liberty. It is a necessary characteristic of liberty that the character, in the strict sense of the term, as defined in § 59, should be free from the domination of influences coming from nervous organs which are not

its own, as explained in § 57. 13; that it should act from principles springing from itself and from its own organ. The criterion, therefore, imposing a law of liberty must be at least a reflective emotion. Direct emotions are coloured too much by their representations, the representations of visible and tangible objects and events, to allow them to rule the character with freedom. This follows from § 64. 1, where it was shown that the character can only be determined by analysis of the reflective emotions. So far any reflective emotion might furnish a law of liberty; the preeminence of the emotion of moral sense depends on its universality and harmonising power, which no other emotion possesses. It is σύνδεσμος τῆς τελειότητος, the bond of perfectness. It imparts the gift of liberty, not only from external, but also from the conflict of internal laws. The proof of these propositions, as matters of fact, depends on the analysis in Book i.

3. Again, since the criterion is a reflective emotion, it is a criterion of the agent, or person acting, and of his character, as well as of the act done. If we had not a reflective emotion as criterion, we could have no criterion of characters or of persons. But this is what is required of ethic, that it should point out some direct means of judging persons and characters. Now the character of acts, apart from agents, is to be mere events; acts are events coloured by emotions. In knowing the emotions we have therefore necessarily some knowledge of the acts; but in knowing the acts, apart from the emotions, we have no knowledge of them but as events. To know the acts as events, together with their consequences, that is, with the feelings which they cause in others, or

in oneself, as distinguished from the feelings of which
they consist or by which they are caused in oneself,
is still to know them only as events, just as we might
know an earthquake, for instance, and the feelings
which it caused. It is the feelings in which the act
consists, not those which it causes, that are the analysis of the act; and to have a criterion for judging
these is to have a criterion both of the act and of
the agent. To examine and judge of acts solely by
their consequences, even if emotions are among such
consequences, is to examine and judge them apart
from character; is not strictly speaking an ethical
enquiry at all; unless we have also some criterion of
the emotions, as such, which are their consequences,
and apply the two criterions in the same enquiry.
But those who decline to apply a criterion of emotions and of characters, when they appear in or as
the acts themselves, will probably be led to decline
it also when they appear as the consequences of acts;
at least, if they had such a criterion to apply, why
should they not apply it at first as well as at last?
Probably therefore the recourse to consequences in
judging of acts, the finding the criteria of acts in
their consequences alone, is an indication that those
who so reason have no sufficient criteria of emotions
and characters to apply. We may therefore expect
to find them judging actions, not by the reflective,
but by the direct emotions which are their consequences, as being the kind of feelings most commonly
understood among men, and the relative values of
which are most widely agreed upon. The judging
by consequences will accordingly tend to make direct
emotions the principal criteria, and their pleasures
or satisfactions the principal ends of conduct. But

the problem of ethic is not solved without a criterion of the reflective emotions, of the character of the agent as well as of his transeunt or overt acts. If we are to have an ethic at all, this is the point which sooner or later must be settled, What is the criterion of character.

4. In all voluntary redintegrations, whether immanent or transeunt, the emotion of moral sense is that which justifies or condemns them, whether it is included in them at the time or not. It is by no means requisite that it should be included in the redintegrations which it is to justify; the attempt to have it so included would involve perpetual anxiety about the criterion, about conduct in minutiæ being conformable to it, which is not a course or habit of mind which the criterion itself would probably recommend to us. Some men may be too careless, others too anxious. A certain freedom and boldness in action, a certain confidence in the goodness of our principles, seems to be a necessary characteristic of principles that are really good, as well as being the charm and ornament of a noble life. This only is requisite, that, when actions or redintegrations are recalled for the purpose of judgment being passed upon them, they should coalesce with this emotion, which is the criterion. This combination is their justification. Now if the necessity, first of some criterion, then of some reflective emotion being the criterion, is admitted, it will also, I think, be allowed that the moral sense is one which certainly is the criterion of all emotions below it, that is, of all those analysed before it in Chapter ii. Book i.; but not so readily perhaps that it is the criterion of those above it, the imaginative emotions, or of any emotions car-

ried up into imagination. The moral sense, it will be said, is the mere rudiments of morality; it is inadequate to test the duties of religion, or, by others again it will be said, the ideally perfect life of a poet. But in the first place it must be considered, that two things are requisite for a criterion; it must be universally recognised, and it must embrace, as a principle, all the possible developments of other principles as well as its own. Both characters are wanting to religion and to poetical emotion. The first is wanting to religion, because religion is an imaginative development of the moral sense which fashions itself differently in different individuals and different sects, and in different times and places; no religion, except so far as it contains the moral sense and in this element of it alone, is recognised as a valid moral duty by men beyond the small pale of its votaries. To endeavour to enforce it upon others is not to enforce a law of liberty, but to tyrannise. For the same reason no religion embraces as a principle the developments of other principles as well as its own; it is only the moral sense, contained in the religion, that does so. The same reasons apply with greater force to the emotion or emotions of poetical imagination; with greater force, because they do not necessarily contain the moral sense at all. If then the moral sense were not the universal criterion, there would be no such criterion possible. But the objection above stated is, not that religion or poetry supply a criterion, but that the moral sense does not supply a criterion for religion and poetry. It cannot test, it is said, what is greater and better than itself. Again then I ask, What is meant by a criterion? Universality of recognition; universality of applicability. There is no emotion not imaginative which the moral sense does not dominate as better and wider than it; of all these it is a positive test; of these when carried over into imagination, that is, of poetical imagination, it is a negative test, a limiting condition of their imaginative development; a condition from which they cannot escape, not in their special character of imaginations, but in their general character of actions; it does not direct their imagination to certain further ends, but limits it to certain hither ends; it does not point to imaginative perfection, but restricts imagination to be perfect as well as imaginative. The same is true of its action upon the imagination founded on itself, that is, on the moral sense; it restricts and limits this imagination, religion, to the observance of its own principle, the moral sense, whatever else it may add to or combine with it, or in whatever dress it may clothe it. Commanding positively all below, the moral sense commands negatively all above itself, and makes itself the sine qua non of right action. It is the narrow neck of the hourglass, through which all the sands must pass, from whatever part of the heap above they come, and upon whatever part of the heap below they fall. Its universal recognition makes it valid for all men; its smallness of content, love and justice alone, makes it valid for all feelings; it is no restriction upon the liberty either of men or of their actions; it can found no tyranny over men, nor any over their tendencies of character. All its laws are recognised by the conscience of every individual.

5. The preceding paragraph leads naturally to the consideration of the Sanctions of the moral law; by what feelings and by whom it is enforced. It

has been said that the moral sense, being the criterion of right, is the basis or most general law of right. But all law is command, and all command, being possibly disobeyed, has two alternative results, the effect of obedience and the effect of disobedience. When the effects of disobedience are painful, they are called sanctions of the command; and sometimes the effects of obedience, when they are pleasureable, are called sanctions also; the latter sanction being Reward, the former Punishment. Without entering on the question whether, in the philosophy of law, the wider or the narrower sense of the term sanction is most correct, I will here, in the logic of ethic, take it in the wider sense, for the sake of leaving no corner of the ground untrodden.

6. It is necessary to a sanction that it should be known to be connected with the law, as the consequence of obedience or disobedience; otherwise it is not the sanction of that law, but merely a pleasureable or painful occurrence unconnected with it. The only sanction of the moral sense, or moral law, consists in the pleasure of a good conscience, as the reward of obedience, and in the pain of remorse, as the punishment of disobedience. But as many kinds and special combinations of acts falling under the general command of the moral law, as many complex feelings and acts which are instances of obedience or disobedience to it, so many kinds of feelings are there included under the general heads of its sanction. There is one kind or modification of remorse for envy, another for ingratitude; one modification of good conscience for benevolence, another for veracity. The sanctions are as various as the acts sanctioned. So also in regret; regret is sorrow

for things not being or having been so well as they might have been, so far as this result is not due to infringement of the moral law. There are as many kinds of regret as there are kinds of failings in well being. There is no painful or pleasureable feeling which is a sanction of the moral law, except it is a modification of good conscience or of remorse; for only as good conscience or as remorse can it be known to be connected, as a consequence, with the violation or fulfilment of the moral law. Without either of these two feelings, the supposed sanction might be the object of the most poignant sorrow or regret, but it could not be a sanction of the moral law.

7. There are two branches of the sanctions of the moral law so important, and at the same time attended with such ambiguities, as to require special notice. The sanctions are two, self-approval and self-disapproval. It is clear that we do not travel out of our own self-consciousness in submitting to or applying them. Yet the most powerful motives for obeying the moral law are drawn from the approval or disapproval of other persons, either of the public at large, in the shape of public opinion, or of those more immediately and constantly surrounding us. This opinion, even when attended with no material consequences, as they are called, that is, when confined to the most tacit expression of opinion possible, and to acts of omission, has a most powerful operation on character, and on the immanent as well as the transeunt acts which form it. We know or we divine what others think and feel about us; and this gives us the acutest pleasure or pain. Yet it is no less true that we are ourselves the agents who apply these sanctions. It is with these sanctions just

as it is with all reflective emotions; part of their object or framework is the representation of the feelings of other persons towards the Subject of the emotions. (See this exhibited in § 23.) So it is also with the emotions of remorse and good conscience, which are the sanctions of the moral law. There are then two main branches of these sanctions; the first when we simply feel them ourselves, the second when we both feel them ourselves and represent the approval or disapproval of others towards us, founded on the same perception of facts. To us this second element, the approval or disapproval felt towards us by others, is a circumstance which is a natural consequence of our actions, and so far independent of our remorse or good conscience; to make us feel it depends on other persons, and to us it is, on that account, like any other natural consequence of our actions, and no more; so far it is not a sanction of the moral law. But inasmuch as we represent this approval or disapproval as founded on the same knowledge, of our own obeying or disobeying the moral law, as we have ourselves, and only so far as we so represent it, it becomes a part of our own approval or disapproval of ourselves, and thus a part of the moral sanction.

8. This explains, I think, what is often noted as a curious circumstance, and often considered as a proof of the depravity or deceitfulness of the human heart, namely, that we think lightly of our own crimes provided they are undiscovered, but feel their enormity first when they are brought to light, or are in danger of being so. "Peccato celato è mezzo perdonato," says an old Italian proverb. The truth is, not, as often insinuated when the above remark

is made, that man thinks lightly of moral evil, dreading like a coward only the punishment of it, but that the discovery of guilt, by adding the representation of other persons' condemnation to his own remorse, intensifies the remorse itself, enforces it upon the mind at every turn, and permits no escape from its infliction. This analysis also, I think, explains the feeling, that when a morally guilty person has been long suffering from the general condemnation of public opinion, it is just and right at length to grant him an amnesty, as it were; while his own moral condemnation of himself must last as long as his own memory. The condemnation of third parties or of public opinion is a punishment which cannot be measured solely and directly by the guilt which it condemns, since it depends upon causes in third parties, quite distinct from that guilt; for instance, upon their caprice, their malevolence or benevolence, their degrees of knowledge and experience; hence it is just, for fear of over severity, that the expression of public condemnation should be withdrawn at certain lengths of time. Here also is the explanation of the different degrees of sensibility to public opinion in different characters. The self-isolating character feels it the least, the affectionate the most strongly. According as the tendency of our emotional disposition is towards alliance, sympathy, and union with others, we are more and more exposed to the influence of the feelings which we represent in others towards us; a fact noticed in that passionate questioning recorded in the Life of F. W. Robertson, Vol. i. p. 264, "I do not understand why the tenderer the heart is, the more it is exposed to being torn, and rent, and tortured;" a fact which extends, beyond the mere question of sanctions, to all cases of the represented feelings of others as frameworks of our own emotions.

9. When we look at this second branch of the sanctions of the moral law from the side of the public, of those who are its instruments or organs, whose acts either of omission or commission suggest the approval and disapproval which the Subject incorporates with his own, there arises a very important class of questions, relating first to the right which third parties, or the public, have of allowing to be suggested such approval or disapproval, and secondly to the just limits of such a right. First as to the right itself. I think it may be shown that the right itself cannot be disputed, with respect to any action or feeling whatever, as object-matter of approval or disapproval. The encroachments of the authority of third parties upon individual liberty, dangerous as they are, cannot find in this point any limitation to their influence. The thoughts and the feelings of third parties are as free and as uncontrollable as those of the persons whom they judge, approve, or condemn. It is difficult to see how any object whatever can be subtracted from their competence, if it is de facto a possible object of their knowledge; their right in this respect can have no limitation but their power. If however the public have a right and a power of entertaining feelings and thoughts concerning all objects, they can hardly be denied the right of expressing them, whether by acts of omission or commission. Efferent nerves are so closely dependent on afferent, and both with the organs of representation, that it is impracticable, at the very least, to draw the line between the right of entertaining and the right of expressing any class of opinions, taken

as a whole, though there may be occasions on which the right of expressing an opinion may be restricted; to debar from expression is to forbid the opinion. No class of acts can be withdrawn from the competence of public opinion by a distinction drawn between acts themselves; such as, for instance, would be that between acts solely self-regarding and acts which regard other persons as well, drawn by Mr. Mill, On Liberty, Ch. iv., if it could be made applicable to opinion itself as well as to overt acts which are its consequences.

10. The line must be drawn in quite a different way. True, there is no class of objects or acts excluded by its nature from the competence of third parties or public opinion, so that they should be debarred either from entertaining or from expressing opinion and feeling upon it. But their opinion and feeling, and its expression by act, fall, like those of the Subject, under the same universal criterion, the moral sense; and their conformity to this criterion is subjected to the criticism of others, who are to them third parties. The opinions and feelings of third parties about other persons than themselves are to be judged by themselves, and by other persons, by the criterion of love and justice. There is no other criterion which they will or need accept. And the following consideration is sufficient, I think, to show the efficacy which this criterion if honestly applied would have, or which, in other words, it ought from its nature to have. Men are always popularly judged by their motives, real or supposed. The immense ignorance in which third parties are and must always be, even in the very clearest cases, of the history, the experience, and the strength of different motives, in

another person, of the mechanism of his mind, so to speak, and of the forces at work within it and upon it, must, when properly pondered, and governed by the moral sense, hinder any one from hasty, severe, confident judgments, especially when unfavourable. If this is not taken into account, the person judging, or acting as if he had judged, is himself guilty of a clear injustice, and renders himself liable to the adverse judgment both of his victim and of the public. I cannot but think that this is the true way in theory, and therefore also in practice, though apparently it must be very slow in operation, to obviate the pressing danger of a tyranny of public opinion. The danger comes from want of thought in the public, that is, in the mass of men; it can only be obviated by increasing their habit of thoughtfulness.

11. Third parties, then, both may in right and must in practice entertain feelings and thoughts about the acts and characters of other persons, without limitation drawn from the kind of those characters and acts. The limitation to which these feelings and thoughts of third parties are subject is drawn from the criterion of ethic itself, and is applied not only by their own conscience, but also by the feelings and thoughts of others in judging their judgments. The same universal extent, and the same limitation, apply also to the expression of the feelings and thoughts of third parties, to their expression by acts of omission or commission. As it is inevitable that opinions should be formed and entertained, so also it is inevitable that, when entertained, they should be expressed by word, by look, by gesture, by deed, or by the abstaining from the like. Such acts are the evidence of the opinions. No such expression is, on account

of its nature alone, excluded from the competence of third parties; that is, there is no class of such acts which, as a class, is not within the right of third parties to do as the expression of their opinion. The limitation comes as before from the criterion. The question is, What is the limitation of this criterion?

12. In the first place, the limitation is clearly set by the criterion; the act must be conformable to the principle of the moral sense, in the person doing it. I shall enter into no further detail of this application than to point out the one most general distinction which arises in it, and attaches to all cases of its application. It is a distinction of the kinds of influence which the expression of opinion has upon the person whose character or conduct is criticised. It is a common and a true remark, that hardly any expression of opinion is without some "material" result or import, beyond the feelings which it excites as a mere expression of opinion. Thus, for instance, if you give a man to understand that you think him untrustworthy, he knows not only that he has incurred your disapproval, but that he will lose, if occasion should arise, the visible and tangible advantages of being trusted by you and by those whom you influence; if you express kindly feeling towards any one, he knows that he may reckon on your good offices when they may have a visible and tangible effect. So also on a larger scale, when the approval or disapproval of the public is expressed towards, or known by, any individual, as in the loss or gain of custom or appointments. There are then two kinds of influence which the expression of opinion exerts; the one is the consequence of the knowledge of the opinion itself, the other of the visible and tangible

results of that opinion. Both kinds however are influences on the representation; both are operative as representations in the mind of the person criticised, and as emotions in those representations. The loss or gain of visible and tangible advantages is represented by him, and felt as a kind of grief or of joy. This makes them motives influencing his conduct and character. The two kinds of influence are distinguished by the two kinds or classes of emotion, the direct and the reflective. Here is the source or root, in human nature, of the well-known difference between the two kinds of influence. Direct emotions, it was shown in § 23, are those which arise in representations of sensations alone; reflective those which add to these the representation of emotions felt by other persons. So far as an expression of opinion calls up the former kind of representations and emotions, it acts by the influence of visible and tangible, or as they are called material, advantages or disadvantages; so far as it calls up the latter kind, it acts by what are called purely moral influences. It is not here the place to determine how far the application of either kind of influence is justified or justifiable by the criterion of ethic. If at all, this question can be settled only when men are considered as forming societies, and their mutual action and reaction upon each other, of the whole on its parts, and of the parts on the whole, are brought into discussion. So much is clear, that we have in the distinction now drawn the ground of the distinction, in political logic, between the two kinds of influence known by the names of the spiritual and temporal powers.

§ 83. 1. One point remains to be remarked in the application of this system of logic; it is the connection between its criterion and the promotion of happiness, or the practical tendency which obedience to the criterion has to obtain that feature of the End which consists in Happiness, which we may assume to be its general characterisation. It is true that happiness cannot be balanced against happiness, any more than pleasure against pleasure; but, since pleasure is the motive of all actions without distinction, it is an irresistible conclusion that some great sum of happiness is the result of actions, supposing them to be rightly governed; for, if actions could be rightly governed and yet lead on the whole to misery, there would be a contradiction in practice between the motive power and the End of ethic; a contradiction which would not only discredit the logic proposed, which goes on the supposition of an harmonious structure and function in the world of life, but would exhibit this supposition itself as erroneous. Contradiction would be thus discovered in the very construction and course of nature. And although it is true, as maintained above, that we cannot determine the right course of action by knowing the nature of the greatest happiness, since this is a knowledge we have not; yet, knowing the nature of the right course of action, we may have grounds, more or less probable, for supposing that it tends towards the greatest possible happiness, grounds derived from observing the results of such a course of action in particular cases, where following it has led to happiness, or neglecting it to the reverse.

2. The following passage in Dr. Newman's Sermons bearing on Subjects of the Day, Serm. xvii. "Sanctity the token of the Christian Empire," page 276, 2nd edit., was pointed out to me by my friend,

Principal Shairp, as an admirable statement of one of the cardinal points in this question: "In truth, so has it been ordered by Divine Providence, that in the Gospel Kingdom is instanced a remarkable law of Ethics, which is well known to all who have given their minds to the subject. All virtue and goodness tend to make men powerful in this world; but they who aim at the power have not the virtue. Again: virtue is its own reward, and brings with it the truest and highest pleasures; but they who cultivate it for the pleasure-sake are selfish, not religious, and will never gain the pleasure, because they never can have the virtue." I do not know any passage where the law here spoken of is more clearly or precisely stated. It is certainly one which is very striking, and which yet, I think, must be acknowledged as true. It would be well perhaps to call it, for the purposes of citation, Dr. Newman's law, from the profound writer to whom we owe this statement of it. The causes upon which this law, or general phenomenon, depends seem to be already at hand, in the arrangement of facts proposed in the present logic. He who seeks happiness, eo nomine, misses it, because, not knowing what happiness is, he takes as his criterion what he thinks will be happiness, neglecting the criterion which, not being happiness, leads to it, or is characterised by it in result. He who aims at duty finds happiness, because he chooses the right criterion, neglecting that which may be a result but is not the criterion of conduct.

3. But these grounds of admitting and explaining Dr. Newman's law are capable of further generalisation; they may be applied to more cases than that which he had in view in the passage quoted. He

who seeks or applies anything but the right criterion misses the particular end which he seeks, and the particular satisfaction contained in that end. Supposing the moral sense, defined by justice and love, to be the true criterion, then he who makes the Will of God, as he supposes it, the criterion of his conduct, or, in other words, seeks to do the will of God and not simply to do justice and love, does not do the will of God as it truly is, but something else which he puts in its place. The will of God for him is that he should endeavour to act solely on the criterion, the moral sense. The result of that action is in the hand of God. Bentham, I think, it was who acutely remarked, that, if the will of God was the criterion of right and wrong, we should still need a criterion of the will of God. The same remark may be made on the greatest happiness principle, that, if the greatest happiness is the criterion of right and wrong, we shall still need a criterion of the greatest happiness. Both ways of proceeding are erroneous on the same ground; they both substitute a generality for a speciality, a second for a first intention, as the criterion of conduct; both are erroneous in the same way, namely, by interpreting that generality, specialising it for application, without a criterion; that is, by an immediate, or unreasoned, assumption that acts from time to time in question are in the one case a doing of the will of God, in the other a procuring of the greatest happiness. Call the End of ethic by what general name you like, Will of God, Greatest Happiness, or Harmony of Functions, in every case it requires interpreting by a criterion distinct from itself, before it can be rightly applied to conduct in a single instance.

4. Austin in his Province of Jurisprudence Determined, Chapter ii., strives to connect the two theories of the Will of God and Utility, by making the latter serve as the criterion of the former. The benevolence of God is the ground of this connection; the will of a benevolent creator and governor of the world must be, it is said, the greatest happiness of his sentient creatures. This no doubt may be true, but the union of the two theories does not supply the defect under which they both alike labour. This defect is the want of a sufficiently precise definition, and therefore of a sufficiently precise criterion. Putting together two indefinites does not supply the want of definiteness, unless they limit each other, each excluding what the other admits. But in the present case both indefinites cover the same ground. If two disorganised armies join their forces, we wait to see whether they have thereby secured a new organisation; if not they will only be weaker than before.

5. The two theories of Utility and the Will of God fail to lead to their own proposed ends in different ways, and therefore for different reasons. The particular actions or objects which are assumed to embody the Will of God, in the second theory, fail of being the Will of God from the necessary imperfection of the knowledge which particular persons anywhere and at any time have concerning that Will. Any such particular action or object is as little likely to be the Will of God there and then as, we are told by comparative philologists, a word in the language of one Indo-European people is to be the same with one precisely similar to it in the language of another people of the same family. An action precisely harmonising with a particular person's view of the Will

of God must differ from what the true Will of God would require, were it perfectly known to him. To act on this particular view is to assume a perfect acquaintance with the Will of God. Partially right such an action may be; partially right it must be, so far as the moral sense is included in its determination. It is this alone which gives it validity; and the greater part this has in its determination, the more nearly will it approach to being wholly right. When such an action is challenged by other persons, and conscience is pleaded by the doer, this plea is not to them a sufficient justification, and ought not to be so to the doer, since he should learn to distinguish his own particular persuasion of what the Will of God consists in from the criterion of right itself. The plea is of value for justifying or proving the honesty and good faith of the doer; and will have de facto just so much weight with others as their previous knowledge of the person pleading it determines them to attach to it.

6. But now the question arises, whether or not the theory of Utility adds to this cause of error, which springs from imperfect knowledge, a cause which consists in the deceptiveness of pleasure. This may be exhibited best by considering the two branches of its aims separately, namely, the greatest happiness of the Subject himself, and that of Mankind or of the greatest number. In aiming at the happiness of the greatest number, error in judgment must arise from the same source, and in the same way, as in the former theory. The particular act or object attained can seldom if ever be the precise act or object which a perfect knowledge of the greatest happiness of mankind would have dictated. The second branch,

relating to the happiness of the Subject himself, contains the most plainly the question before us. A man fixes his hopes and directs his efforts to some object or mode of action, which he thinks not only morally justifiable, but also a noble, refined, elevated pleasure; he attains the object, he is enabled to perform the actions embodying it; there is no failure in any part of his "intention," in Bentham's sense of the term. Yet it is a constant complaint of moralists that the pleasure enjoyed is a feeble reflex of the pleasure anticipated, that we seem to have attained one purpose only to discover its hollowness, and be again attracted and again deluded by another. The point to be considered is, whether and how far this is a true complaint; whether there is, in any considerable number of instances, a delusion in pleasure attained and enjoyed, a delusion not arising from mistaking the character of the "intention," or from its imperfect attainment, or from circumstances not foreseen which injure its operation, but attaching solely to the emotional character of the act done or object attained, and consisting in a deceived expectation of its pleasureable character, everything else remaining as it was anticipated.

7. This question is not to be hastily and roughly answered by appeals to the dicta of moralists, such as the "Surgit amari aliquid" of Lucretius, or Pope's "Man never is but always to be blest." Indeed there are dicta equally forcible on the other side of the question; and among the most weighty perhaps are those words of Horace,

> "Ille potens sui
> Lætusque deget, cui licet in diem
> Dixisse, Vixi:"

Book II.
Ch. II.
§ 88.
Relation of the criterion to happiness.

words which, with their immediate sequel, contain the expression of a calm satisfaction with pleasures enjoyed, a satisfaction enduring in the retrospect of them. And many other such dicta might be quoted. There seem then to be two classes of pleasures, or at least two classes of characters; pleasures which are satisfactory and pleasures which are deceptive; characters which tend to be satisfied and characters which tend to be dissatisfied with attained enjoyment. If this is so, the aim at the greatest happiness of the individual cannot be the universal rule of conduct for all men. We shall need a criterion to distinguish for what pleasures and for what persons it is available. But the recourse to testimony on this point is fruitless; we shall get no farther than to the fact of their discrepancy. If a decision is to be looked for at all, it must be from a recourse to analysis, to grounds which, in respect to this point, are a priori.

8. Two classes of pleasure were distinguished in § 53. 4, 5, 9, 10, the general and the specific; and pleasures of the former class were found to attend the exercise of the reactive powers, and to be their exponents, the pleasures of cheerfulness and energy; while the specific pleasures were attached to specific sensations and emotions, and were the exponents of the retentive powers. We may call specific pleasures pleasures of indulgence, and general pleasures pleasures of control and government. This distinction was observed in spontaneous redintegration, and found to be carried on into voluntary, through every domain of action. These two classes of pleasures were farther compared in § 62. 1, and instances of their operation in character given. From this ana-

lysis it is likely, that only those objects of pursuit can give a pleasure in attainment equal to their pleasure in anticipation, which contain the pleasures of control, or combine these as the governing element with pleasures of indulgence; that only such objects of pursuit can give a pleasure of long duration at the time, or one which will also give pleasure in the retrospect. We thus obtain a distinction both between the satisfactory and unsatisfactory pleasures and between the satisfied and unsatisfied characters. We narrow the class of pleasures to be aimed at, and make it more precise; they must be pleasures arising from self-directing activity. This distinction is by no means owing to the greatest happiness principle, but is one introduced into it. Yet even this does not give a class of pleasures sufficiently precise to serve as the criterion of ethic. We know only that this criterion must belong to the class now marked out; and that the criterion here affirmed does so more certainly and more universally than any other emotion will be clear also, I think, from the analysis of the preceding Book, particularly from §§ 38. 72. I am not however now concerned to prove that this is the criterion of ethic, but to show that this alone has the promise of producing the greatest happiness of the individual, which nothing else proposed as a criterion can claim.

9. Generally speaking, the happiness of life consists in the energy, and its dependent cheerfulness, being fully or more than equal to the tasks imposed on it, or objects proposed to it, in a far greater degree than to the specifically pleasureable character of the acts done or the objects enjoyed. The former is the essential, the latter the incidental, condition

of happiness. Only so long as we have the energy can we enjoy any specific pleasure; without it, these pleasures become burthens. It may be strongly suspected therefore that, whenever happiness is attained by acting on the principle of pursuing happiness, or on that of doing the will of God, as it is no doubt frequently attained in the highest degree by both modes, the attainment of it is due to the self-control exercised, to the energy of the reactive movements displayed, and the power thereby stored up for the future. To seek for happiness eo nomine, that is, for specific pleasures and enjoyments, is thus the surest way to miss its attainment, since it is to make us imagine ourselves dependent on circumstances, to exexpose us to frequent disappointment, as well as to lessen the fund of self-reliant energy, which is the true and actual source of perennial enjoyment. Who is not familiar with the fact, that conditions of life, poverty, hardship, even comparison of our own state with that of others, are things almost indifferent to happiness? "Pleasure," says Wordsworth, "is spread through the earth In stray gifts to be claimed by whoever shall find." The greater part of enjoyment is that which comes unlooked for, but never without finding already, or calling out afresh, within ourselves a burst of reactive energy. Were it not for this law, the emotions of comparison would probably press upon us with a far greater weight than they do. As, in ascending the ladder of ambition, each new step gained is soon forgotten, and the next end in view is sought for with the same eagerness as the old ones, so, in descending it, that is, in losing old possessions or former honours, we forget our losses and think ourselves fortunate in the gain of the ever decreasing objects of desire, the attainment of whatever purpose may be immediately in prospect. We accommodate ourselves to our circumstances, be they what they may; and the near horizon is always the boundary within which our happiness lies. This interest in the immediate action, which detracts from the pleasures of comparison in successful ambition, is also an alleviation of its pains in failure and distress. If we do not compare ourselves with those whom we have far outstripped in the race, so neither do we with those who have left us far behind. Were it not so, the wish to be "aut Cæsar aut nullus" would become a torment, and no one would be content with his position in life, since no one could in every respect be Cæsar.

10. We thus come back again to Dr. Newman's law, which was the point from which we started. Nothing but acting on a true criterion can lead to happiness; and the cause in nature which enables this to do so is its being an expression of the reactive energies. To have an indefinite criterion is probable failure, to have specific pleasures for a criterion is certain failure. The latter however is not an error into which moralists are likely to fall in theory. The great danger to theory is indefiniteness. Indefiniteness attaches to the Will of God, to the greatest happiness of the individual, to that of the greatest number, that is, of mankind at large, or of all sentient beings, certainly a magnificent conception. It is clear however that, if we make the greatest happiness of others our aim, we must at least take care to aim at the development of the energies of those we are caring for, to aim at this in the first place, at their material advantages in the second. Here too we

shall need another and more precise criterion, a criterion of the means to make others self-reliant, and secure to them the habit of self-control; otherwise we might destroy their happiness while we secured our own, and ruin the client to benefit the patron.

11. The efficacy, then, of obedience to conscience in producing happiness, like that of obedience to any other criterion which may be adopted, is due to its being the expression of the predominance of the reactive over the retentive powers. It is a case subsumed under a general law of the production of pleasure. The greatest pleasure results from the greatest vigour of the reactive mental powers; and that kind of conduct produces the most pleasure or greatest happiness, in the long run, which the most preserves and fosters this mental energy. This is a repetition, in another shape, of that phenomenon which was noticed in § 57. 7, namely, that health and strength of the physical organisation is accompanied with pleasure, weakness and disease with pain, an ultimate though general fact in physiology. And this law it is which supplies the connection between physiology and ethic, between the phenomena of the de facto constitution and working of the organism and the practical criterion of choice which becomes, in application, the Moral Law.

CHAPTER III.

THE LOGIC OF POLITIC.

Τί οὖν ὁ νόμος; τῶν παραβάσεων χάριν προσετέθη, * * * Ὥστε ὁ νόμος παιδαγωγὸς ἡμῶν γέγονε * * .

St. Paul.

§ 84. 1. THE Logic of Ethic embraces all actions whether immanent or transeunt, and all feelings whether sensations, direct, or reflective, emotions, in its scope, for there are none of these which are not modifiable by volition indirectly if not directly. Its scope is coextensive with consciousness itself. But its immediate domain or object-matter, in and with which it works, consists in voluntary redintegration only, embracing in this the guidance both of direct and of reflective emotions, both of immanent and of transeunt actions. Similarly and for the same reasons the scope of the Logic of Politic is the same with that of the logic of ethic. But its immediate domain or object-matter is more restricted, consisting in voluntary transeunt actions alone. Immanent actions fall back into the scope. They are part of the field of objects modified or to be modified by transeunt actions; transeunt actions are both objects to be modified and the means of effecting the modification. The logic of politic is coextensive with the science and art of Law. Both deal only with transeunt, or, as they are usually called, overt acts of will. A law is a command to do or omit an overt act, directed to a volition, and enforced by a sanction. Hence the sole method of politic or law, when it operates upon immanent acts, emotions, or characters, is to work by means of transeunt acts which it commands or forbids; its operation is from without inwards; while the principal, or at least the characteristic, method of ethic is to work from within outwards, to modify the habitual acts by first modifying the habitual emotions. Every law is therefore an infringement upon the liberty of action exercised by the organs of pure representation, which are the organs of the character. Without the law prescribing or forbidding an overt act, the immanent action of redintegration might have taken a different course with respect to it.

2. It is not here said that laws ought not to influence character and its immanent acts; they not only do but often ought to influence them. But it is said that laws do not, as a fact, prescribe or forbid them. Laws require by their definition, that the acts prescribed or forbidden should be overt or transeunt acts. Otherwise the laws belong not to politic but to ethic; they are moral laws only. The tenth command of the Decalogue, "thou shalt not covet," revealed to St. Paul, as we may gather from Rom. vii. 7, that the Law was spiritual; in other words, a moral and not only a political law. The term "moral law," which seems to add something to the definition of law, to make it more full and precise, so that a moral law must be a law at least and something else be-

sides, does not in reality do so. That is to say, it is not political law which is thus laid at the basis of moral law, but law generally, law as a rule of conduct indefinitely. The moral law is then a rule of conduct, felt to be valid by the agent, prescribing or forbidding feelings as well as acts. The political law is still narrower in extent and fuller in characteristics; it is a rule of conduct prescribing or forbidding overt acts only.

3. Conduct towards other persons as well as towards oneself is prescribed by moral as well as by political law; the domain of both kinds of law is in this respect the same; but only transeunt or overt acts are prescribed by political law; immanent acts as well as transeunt only by moral law. How far, or in what cases, political law is justified in commanding or forbidding transeunt acts towards oneself, or acts which are chiefly and primarily self-regarding, is a question for another place. Here it is only to be said, that no overt acts are excluded from the domain of political law by a mere consideration of its nature or scope, just as it was shown that no immanent acts or feelings were excluded from the cognisance of public opinion, in § 82. 9 et seqq.

4. All law, moral as well as political, has and enforces some sanction. The sanctions of the moral law consist in remorse and its modifications (§ 82. 6, &c.). The sanctions of political law are punishments, overt acts causing pain to the transgressor of a political law, in consequence of his transgression of it. Strictly speaking, rewards for obedience are as much sanctions of political law as punishments; but the immense preponderance of punishments in actual use, the principle of both being the same, will render it

unobjectionable to speak of punishments only under that term; especially since some of the best jurists hold this view to be the strictly correct one (Austin's Province of Jurisprudence, Lect. i. p. 8, 2nd ed.). The truth is that, restrict it as we may to punishments, the term sanction inevitably embraces rewards as well. The hope of reward may be a feebler motive to obedience, so feeble as to be properly called persuasion rather than enforcement; but the difference is only one of degree. And besides, wherever there is fear there is hope, and conversely; so that a promised reward urges by the fear of its being withheld, as well as by the hope of its being given; and a threatened punishment urges by the hope of escaping it as well as by the fear of incurring it. Still it remains true, that by far the greater part, both in number and weight, of the sanctions of law consists of punishments; so that we shall be in small danger of error by adopting this simplification of the term.

5. The difference between the sanctions of ethic and of law gives rise to a distinction between the duties imposed by them, the acts or feelings commanded or forbidden. The duties imposed by law are termed duties of perfect, those imposed in ethic by conscience of imperfect obligation. The sanction of moral duties flows directly from the conscience itself in remembering its act, that of legal duties flows from the lawgiver who punishes for the act. Here the act is separate from the command, and the command from the punishment; all three are overt acts; the obvious and overt nature of the punishment, which completes the efficacy of the command, seems to be the reason why the obligation is called perfect. The remorse of conscience is unseen in its

operation, and to the public therefore uncertain in its efficacy; hence the obligation is called imperfect. Yet the distinction of the whole series of acts into commanding power, command, and sanction, is just as clear in the one case as in the other. And since obligation is a term which has in ordinary use a distinctly moral sense, it would be better to substitute for it the term enforcement, and to speak of Duties of perfect and imperfect enforcement, instead of obligation. Some classes of commands imposing overt acts, which are usually called laws, have no legal sanction. Such are International laws and Constitutional laws. (Austin, Work cited, Vol. i. pp. 225-235, 2nd ed.) The sovereign which imposes them being divided, and the command thus consisting of an agreement either express or tacit between the parties concerned, the violation of the command by one or more of the parties prevents the sanction being applied by the same parties who imposed the command. In this case law is at an end, and the place of sanction is filled by war. Moral law remains in this case unassailed; but political law has vanished. The duties of international and constitutional law are therefore duties of imperfect enforcement, and in this character subject, as before, to moral law, and similar to moral duties, notwithstanding that they consist of overt acts commanded or forbidden, and notwithstanding that they are formed into elaborate systems, and administered by regular tribunals. Every political law has the moral law for its basis; a law which endures beyond the power of overt acts or events to overthrow; a law which judges at its tribunal and by its criterion every political law which can be imposed.

6. The following consideration again shows the universality of moral law, and its supremacy over political. The person or persons imposing the commands of political law are called the sovereign. In England, for instance, Parliament consisting of the King and the two Houses is the sovereign; that it is so depends on the Constitution; the Constitution is its de jure basis, and the actual recognition of its power is its de facto basis. The Constitution may be regarded as a de jure sovereign only; but this is not a sovereign in the strict sense of the term. The Parliament is de facto sovereign over the Constitution as well as over its subjects; but this is not perfect sovereignty, because it lacks the de jure element, which there is nothing to give it except the moral law in the hearts of the whole people. Only over its subjects is it full sovereign, de facto and de jure as well. It is essential to a political sovereign that it should have actual power of enforcing obedience to its commands by means of punishment. The laws are laws of perfect enforcement; hence the sovereign must at least have de facto supremacy. But the justification of the laws, of that supremacy itself, flows from a source above the sovereign, from the moral law.

7. In political law the sovereign who imposes the commands and the subjects on whom they are imposed are distinct persons. The acts commanded being overt acts, if the characters of sovereign and subject were united in the same person or persons, the sanction would be inefficacious; the sovereign would remit the punishment when it became disagreeable to him, that is, at the moment when its efficacy was required; and the only sanction remain-

ing would be that of the moral law. In political law, therefore, the sovereign and the subjects are distinct. But since every individual is subject necessarily to the moral law in all his acts, whether immanent or transeunt, the sovereign who imposes political laws is so; and in this way also the political laws, being acts of the sovereign, are subordinate to moral. The same is true of the obedience rendered by the subjects; obedience or disobedience is an act of the individual subject, and in this character dependent on his conscience for justification.

8. In the next place it is to be remarked, that in the case of political laws there is no single person able to judge them in their moral character without appeal. One person commands and another obeys, each responsible morally for his own act; but there is no single conscience judging the act, made up of command and obedience, as a whole. Yet at the same time every political law has effects upon immanent acts and feelings, and upon reflective emotions; and the lawgiver is therefore morally bound to aim at the results, of this nature, which are commanded by the moral law. The same is the case with laws international and constitutional, which reside in the breasts of men, and are bound by the considerations which conscience imposes. All law, which is not itself moral law, is therefore de jure subordinate to it, and flows from it so far as its de jure character is concerned. The separation which is possible between these two elements of right and fact in political laws is the ground of divided allegiance to a temporal and to a spiritual sovereign, a question which can only be settled, whenever it arises, by the conscience of the individual.

9. It is because law has ends beyond itself, in immanent acts and feelings, ends belonging solely to the jurisdiction of conscience and to the province of ethic, that attempts to judge ethic by law, or by a logic derived from law, are liable to failure. Between the ends proper to law itself and the ultimate ends of ethic there lies a gulf, a region of phenomena for which law supplies no guidance, where ethical analysis alone is of service. The ends proper to law itself require tracing across this region to their ultimate end; whereby the character of this ultimate end itself becomes more definitely perceived. Without this guidance by ethical analysis the ultimate end is caught up hastily and indicated vaguely, conceived as the greatest happiness for instance; and thus the application of law logic to ethic directly is one cause of utilitarianism. Another consequence of the same cause is the material or sensational nature of the sanctions attributed to the moral law. If the moral law has sanctions, it is said, they must be efficacious; hence the adoption by legal moralists of the conceptions of endless reward and punishment after death; the sanctions gain intensity at the cost of their purely moral character. Hence too comes the notion of the commands and judgments of God being definite words and phrases pronounced by men and written in books; for political laws must be clear and precise, it was said, or the punishments for transgressing them would be unjust; since, then, God's laws and sanctions are ex hypothesi just, the language in which they are conveyed must be definite and unmistakeable. Lastly the moral character of the moral law is lessened by the expectation that an actual, universal, and de facto, obedience is essential

to its nature. Political laws were not de jure binding, unless there was de facto power to enforce them; and accordingly, moral laws which are not de facto enforced are, by a false analogy, held not de jure binding either. It is then forgotten, or not perceived, that the moral law is a plant of feeble growth at first, having its roots in the reflective emotions; that its validity depends solely on what it is by its nature, not on the success with which it may be propagated, or on the extent of obedience which it may command; that its complete triumph may, or rather must, be in the far distant future, when the kingdoms of the world shall become kingdoms of righteousness and peace. But it is clear that, if only such laws are morally good as actually and visibly prevail in the world, the moral law must lose much of its morality, the conquered cause never be the right one; the gods of the moment always right, Cato always wrong.

10. The questions touched in the foregoing paragraph lead to one which has been much discussed, the question of primacy between ethic and law in historical development. History is the realisation of the moral law, which develops as every other element in man's nature develops in the changes of times. The moral law known to man ages ago is not the same in content as the moral law known to him now; nor the moral law known to him now as that which will be known to him ages hence. It is a mistake to imagine a moral law always the same, always equally perfect and complete. There is no evidence for such a thing. It would be absolute, transcendent, impossible. One element of the moral law only is unchanging. The moral law, as we know

it by experience, is gradually realised by history, is strengthened and increased in clearness and fullness with every step in the development of man's nature and knowledge. Its realisation includes its own growth as well as its increasing command over obedience. Now a change in law, now a change in morals; now a moral ideal becoming fixed and secured by a legal provision, now a legal provision cultivating the growth of a new moral ideal; as far back and as far forwards as we can see, each precedes the other, each is followed by the other. There is no question of precedence in order of time alone, for the process is in infinitum, in both directions. It is the nature of the two steps, the legal and the moral, which decides the question of the primacy between them. If the primacy means in point of de jure supremacy, it is clear that it belongs to the moral step, at every stage of the historical process.

§ 85. 1. Since law is subordinate to ethic, or, in other words, since both those who command and those who obey are bound morally to regard, in the last resort, the commands of the moral law, it follows that the ultimate ends of law are suspended upon that of ethic, deducible from it, and justifiable by it. The logic of law is a reproduction of that of ethic, but applied to overt acts only. Where immanent acts are judged, they are judged directly by the logic of ethic and not by that of law. Laws stand to moral duties in the same relative position as transeunt to immanent acts; they fix, embody, and give them permanence. Laws and systems of laws, which are institutions, codes, recognised customs whether written or unwritten, are fixed landmarks, known to all men, difficult to alter or remove, inasmuch as, obtaining all the force of habit, they offer in the venerable names of Law and Custom a battle cry and a rallying point to all those who are not prepared to give up habits of thought, action, and feeling, or are unable to perceive when the growth of a new morality demands the reformation of an old law. Hence arises the alternation spoken of in the preceding paragraph, the change effected in law by morality, the progress assured to morality by law. The alternation is in some sort a conflict between the two principles of law and morality. Yet throughout the alternation or the conflict, and at every step of it, the appeal always lies from law to the principles and logic of ethic. It is these that are invoked by both parties to resist or to justify a proposed change. The question is, what are the proper ends of law as determined by the logic of ethic.

2. Since the End of ethic is the ideal perfection of justice and love, but laws deal only with overt acts, the End of law must be to command such overt acts as lead toward the establishment of this ideal, to forbid such overt acts as lead away from or prevent it. But justice and love are emotions, immanent acts, which cannot be commanded by any law; nor can the immanent acts or emotions which lead toward their establishment be commanded, nor their opposites forbidden, by law. So far as the End can be furthered by overt acts, law has a positive duty to regulate such acts; so far as it can be furthered by immanent acts, law has a negative duty to abstain from regulation. Of these two branches, exhausting the whole duty of law, the first is to establish justice, the second to respect liberty.

3. Justice comprises the whole duty of law in the

first branch for this reason, that justice alone has a part which consists in overt acts; and it is only the overt acts which embody justice, the overt acts which embody injustice, which can be commanded or forbidden by law. The kind of acts which are here in contemplation will be evident from the instances of justice and injustice given in §§ 32, 33. They are such as fall under the heads of the law of status, of property, and of contract. It is not at this moment in place to enter upon an analysis or classification of law in these respects. All overt acts which are thought to embody justice and injustice are immediate objects of legal regulation. It is clear that the justice and injustice of one state of society consists in very different acts from the justice and injustice of another state. Justice between persons in the early days of Rome, for instance, consisted in very different acts from justice between persons in the Feudal Regime, and both from the justice of the present day. It is the duty of law to establish and enforce by its sanctions the justice proper to the state of society existing at the time, and from time to time. To maintain an antiquated justice is injustice. This would be a transgression of the second branch of the duty of law, the duty of respecting liberty.

4. The term Liberty is here employed in the sense which has been given to it throughout, the free self-determination of the mechanism of pure and reflective representation. This liberty is not the so-called freedom of the will; nor yet is it license, or freedom from the moral law; nor yet is it freedom from restraint generally. Of these uses of the term Liberty, the first is a chimera; the second an immorality; the third an impossibility. Yet this third

sense is the one which is currently adopted in this country. It involves the same conception as the first sense does, that of freedom of the will; the conception of something acting by itself, arbitrarily, without rule or order of nature, an ontological entity; for if not, liberty being freedom from restraint generally, perfect liberty would be perfect annihilation; the subject of the freedom must therefore be supposed, by these reasoners, to exist per se not subject to law of any kind. Of course I am well aware that this consequence would be rejected and denied by those who insist on the notion of liberty being freedom from restraint; but I do not see how it can be rejected logically and consistently. Legal moralists as well as psychologists are ontologists at bottom; some ontological "person" or "self" is the fundamental unanalysed unit with which they start. But the sense of the term liberty here intended is the liberty of self-determination in reflective redintegration, as explained in § 57. 12-16; the free play of the motive powers therein comprised, uninfluenced by feelings consisting solely of direct emotions, or of frameworks composed solely of sensations; uninfluenced therefore by the pain or pleasure inflicted by the overt acts which are sanctions of law.

5. Ethic, then, commands law to do two things, to leave the moral being of every individual free to be governed by motives arising within itself, including the security of this freedom from the encroachments of others, or of violence which is illegal law; and to enforce by sanctions the overt acts of justice as conceived by the political society of the time. The first duty is the provision for Progress, the second for Order; the first the provision for reformation of

the law, the second for its stability. Much has been said about the necessity for combining the two features of order and progress; in general terms nothing can be more true; but such generalities require always interpretation, analysis, reduction to their "first intention." So reduced their names are these, justice and liberty.

§ 86. 1. The ends of law having been pointed out, the next question concerns the criteria for knowing in the future what laws are adapted to secure them, and for judging past laws by their apparent tendency to these results. There can be no single criterion of law, as there was of ethic, because there is not one but two ends; and we should want a criterion not only for each separately, but also for their combination as ends of a single law. The establishment of legal criteria is therefore much more complicated and difficult than of the ethical one. Again, since the criteria are to be applied to laws commanding and forbidding overt acts, and not to the character of the lawgiver or sovereign, a knowledge of overt acts, in their different kinds and enormous variety, is requisite before we can discover in them features which may serve as criteria; we shall require to know what features have been found to lead to improved justice and more perfect liberty; in other words, we shall want a knowledge of history generally, and of the histories of particular states. Again, since the sanctions are motives of obedience, a knowledge of the operation of different kinds of sanctions is requisite; and since the operation of laws themselves when obeyed, of institutions when established, takes place by means of motives acting on individuals, it will be necessary to have, on this account too, some very considerable knowledge of the various kinds of human actions, and the means of their modification.

2. All this is clearly impossible in the present work. Such an historical and experimental enquiry is far beyond its purview. I must therefore renounce the attempt to establish any criteria for judging laws favourably or unfavourably, except so far as the Ends already pointed out are criteria, and their character plainly and directly discernible in the laws to be judged. Even this, however, affords no small guidance; a light on the horizon may direct the belated traveller, though it does not show him the immediate path. More than this could not be attempted without our becoming involved in the discussion of particular laws, and in the merits of particular controversies; without our transgressing the limits of a logic, as stated generally at the end of Book i. in § 75. For the truth is, that the further construction of a logic of politic, in this direction, depends upon a further analysis and classification of the phenomena of society than has hitherto been given, at least with admitted success.

3. When however we turn to the remaining logical head, that of Motives, we find ourselves in a different position. The analysis of the operation of social and political forces, as they are now actually at work, or have been actually operative in past times, apart from the judgments to be passed on them, as conducive or not conducive to the ends of law, has been pushed to a great degree of perfection, by works which would fall under the general description of Philosophy of History. All pleasures and pains, of whatever kind, are motives of action in individuals; all may be motives in masses of indi-

viduals. But the question is, How is the operation of motives affected when masses act upon masses, individuals upon each other and the whole, and the whole upon the individuals; What constitutes a mass of individuals, what binds it together; What particular kinds of motives, of pleasures and pains, are found de facto to have had most weight when witnessed in society? In the individual, the resulting choice proved the amount of one pleasure to be greater or less than that of another, and the greater pleasure became the will of the individual. A group of men often act as if they had a single will, a will to gratify a single desire; what then is the comparative force of the different groups, and of the different desires which seem to animate them? Of such kind are the questions which are the preliminary to any further question about criteria. The de facto forces at work in the social organism must be known, before a criterion can be discovered; just as, in the study of the individual, the analysis of the emotions and their redintegration was the condition of pointing out the criterion of ethic. That further analysis and classification of the phenomena of society, just spoken of as a pre-requisite to the discovery of the criteria, may be sketched in outline at least under the logical head of the de facto motive forces in society.

4. Thus in the logic of politic the question of motives, and the analysis of organs and functions belonging to that head of logic, occupy at present the most prominent position, the position which in the logic of ethic was occupied by the question of criterion, while the question of criterion is in politic a question of the future, reserved for a more com-

plete state of knowledge. The analysis corresponding to the present one in the study of the individual was that contained in Book i. Were the means at hand for offering one equally complete of society, it would not be attempted for the first time in the logical part of the investigation. In other words, the logic of the structure and functions of society is still only in its tentative stage, because the phenomena have not been yet sufficiently examined, or discovered in their true relations. Contrary to the usual opinion I cannot but think, that the knowledge which we have of the structure and functions of the individual consciousness is more complete and accurate than that which has been attained of the corresponding structure and functions of society.

5. Yet it is not a compendium or a sketch of the philosophy of history, so-called, that is here to be offered. It is an attempt to construct an applied logic, to give a metaphysical analysis, of the social organism, in respect of its de facto motive forces and of the organs which embody and apply them, of the mechanism of society both statical and dynamical; an attempt which could not have been made without the previous, more empirical, examination of the same phenomena by philosophic historians, especially by Auguste Comte, perhaps the greatest among the illustrious historians of that country the genius of which is pre-eminently historical.

§ 87. 1. Character is the last point in individual or ethical analysis, the first in political or analysis of the state. The ultimate units in character are emotional states of consciousness; the ultimate units of a mass or group of individuals are characters, or individuals defined by their character. The de facto empirical motives of individuals are the different degrees of pleasure contained in and defined by different emotions; the de facto empirical motives of a group of individuals are the actions of the individuals flowing from their character. This is not a conclusion from the analogy which a group or body politic bears to an individual person, but a simple fact of observation; no group is supposed by it to exist previously to the action, the overt action, of individuals. These actions, which display the tendencies of character, are the causes of the formation of groups in the first place, and in the next of the determination of their action when formed. In history, indeed, we can never reach a beginning; groups precede actions and actions groups, alternately, as far back as we can see, nor can we imagine men existing in isolation from each other, and not formed into groups. It is a parallel case to that of law and ethic, in § 84. 10; and here also it is not an historical but a logical first that is intended, in saying that actions are the causes of groups. That the reverse is not true in logic is shown by this, that, when groups are formed, it is not the group but the actions of the group which modify other groups, and are modified by their action in turn. The group may be entirely explained, when its nature is analysed, by the actions of individuals; but the actions of individuals can only be partially explained by their belonging to such and such a group.

2. The actions which form groups are actions displaying similar and compatible tendencies of character in the individuals who perform them. The pleasure which one individual takes in certain actions is increased or secured by similar and compatible ac-

tions in other individuals. These individuals are drawn together into a group by the perception of this mutual benefit. It makes no difference in the general nature of the case, whether the interests thus gratified, the benefits thus received, are received and gratified by the natural or birth position of the persons, or in consequence of a late discovery on their part; the persons in question may be mother and child, or they may be two hunters agreeing to meet for exchange of booty, or two students for interchange of ideas; the essential nature of the actions which bind these persons into groups remains the same, namely, actions satisfying similar and compatible tendencies of character. These groups, the smallest that can be formed, of whatever kind they may be, have individuals defined by character for their units; and they themselves are the units of larger, more complex, and more organised groups, which are nations or states. The organs of society are such units, that is to say, are groups by which a society performs its different functions, and operates on its own members or on other societies, groups incorporated into the society itself. All the organs of society are such groups, but it is not every group that is a separate organ of society. The organs must be defined by distinctness of function as well as by distinctness of group.

3. When Auguste Comte, insisting rightly on the necessity of regarding as unit of society an aggregate of individuals, interposed as it were between the individuals and the society as a whole, proceeds to lay it down that the family is the unit of the state, he seems to me to take too narrow a basis, and to erect upon it too artificial an edifice. Families, it is true,

are groups strongly coherent, bound together by natural not artificial interests; but they are not the only groups which are spontaneously formed by the action of individual interests. To analyse society sufficiently, and to classify its phenomena correctly, all the kinds of groups which the play of individual character produces, into which it throws individuals together, must be taken into account. Otherwise the society as a whole is judged of by too limited a standard, its freedom and variety is disregarded. It would perhaps be hopeless to expect the first successful movement towards such a complete analysis of the phenomena of society from a simple historical inspection of them. The first really available hypothesis may be expected to arise from an analysis of individual character, since it is in this that the motive causes are found which form and bind groups together, and which then determine their action on each other and on the whole. It is not said that all groups are important in the same way, or in equal degrees, but that all must be taken into account, as operative units and organs of society as a whole, whatever may be their character and importance.

4. The groups formed by unity of interest need not be locally distinct from each other, nor locally united in themselves. Sometimes a common local position forms a group, as in the case of islands, fortified towns, or towns with a particular trade. But it is by identity of interest that the peculiarity of local position operates to form the group. On the other hand, a family remains an united group, notwithstanding that one son may be in Australia, another in America. It is not always or necessarily so; but this depends upon the counteracting interests

of other groups; for instance, if an emigrant son or
brother marries and founds a family, this weakens
his connection with the family at home; if he finds
himself surrounded by enemies, or in distress and unable to form alliances in his new country, this binds
him more closely to his old family. Time again is
in a certain class of cases indifferent to groups; that
is, the members of them may be scattered over long
periods of time, as others are over large tracts of
space. The members of different trades are an instance of the latter kind of separation, the members
of different scientific pursuits of the former. It is
at this point that the enormous influence of improved
means of communication between men is exerted, of
the invention of printing, for instance, of the Post,
of railways, of telegraphs. Printing has no direct influence on intellectual power or knowledge; it brings
minds into communication with minds removed in
time and in space, modifying their knowledge and
feelings, forming groups and disforming them, a sol-
vent of old organisations, a constructor of new and
more complex ones; it makes common property of
knowledge and of feelings which before were confined to individuals, and spreads the knowledge that
it is common. The knowledge is increased only by
being combined and held in common; it is so much
the more food for logic.

5. Again, the same individual belongs to several
groups; it is hardly possible that he should belong
to one only. Each prominent trait in his character
brings him into unity of interest with other men
similarly formed; and as member of one group he
may be often at variance with himself as member of
another. The religious and the domestic interests or

duties are often in conflict. "He that loveth father or mother more than me is not worthy of me" is recorded as a saying of Christ. So patriotism with family affection, as in the story of Brutus. Here is not only a conflict of motives in the individual, but a conflict of laws, of allegiance to groups of men as members of a covenanted society. The logic now exhibited is sufficiently large to take in all stages of society; it applies equally to the earliest conceivable formation of groups and to the most complex stage of social and political development. The only difference, it will be remarked later on, is one which arises within this logic itself, the difference between less and greater degrees of self-consciousness, less and greater consciousness of purpose in volition. At the same time, the circumstance which is selected as the motive power of society is sufficiently precise; the unity of interest in groups, the interest of different kinds of actions in individuals. All the phenomena can be embraced in the scope, all can be referred to the central principle, of the logic of motives, which it now remains to apply definitively.

§ 88. 1. Since society operates in many ways, exerts influence, and displays character, and yet there is no single consciousness to which these actions and feelings can be referred, but only an aggregate of conscious persons, the first question in regard to society's action is, By what organs this action operates, or what mechanism it is which renders it possible. Thus approaching from the side of the whole, the same question is put as when we approached from the side of the individual members. There we found individuals forming themselves into groups by actions flowing from interests; here we find that society requires an analysis into groups, in order to the conception of its character and action. But these groups can be no other than those formed by the action of the individuals composing the aggregate society; for to assume any other mechanism would be to assume society already known to us, beyond the knowledge, barely more than denotative, that it is an aggregate of individuals.

2. It is impossible to enumerate or describe all the groups into which different tendencies of character cause individuals to fall; such an exhaustive treatment at least is not to be attempted here. The general kinds or classes of groups alone can be given by reference to the main distinctions in individual character; and these will serve as a logical framework for future arrangement of groups as they may be discovered. Society organises and distinguishes itself into the minutest sections; a group is no sooner established than it begins to unfold explicitly subordinate groups, bound together by subtiler interests, opposed to each other by finer distinctions. And not only does every man, as already remarked, belong to many of these groups at the same time, but also the groups themselves are incessantly changing in the men, and in the number of men, whom they contain, in obedience to the knowledge of changing circumstances, and to changes in the feelings, of the individual members themselves. As clouds in wind they limn and dislimn perpetually, and their torn-off fringes melt into other masses. No greater error can be committed than that of supposing the whole number of the members of any group, united for the time in any purpose or policy, to be individually and permanently supporters of that policy, or bound to effect

that purpose. It is the preponderating influence, within a group not yet dissolved, which determines its overt action at any moment on a given question. The distinctions therefore which are now to be exhibited are distinctions of logic, not of history; the classes of groups logical not historical classes. Their lines will run often through individuals, having the same individual on both sides, distinguishing one interest of his from another; often through groups formed by other lines of distinction. The empirical or historical groups of permanent value, formed by the coincidence or superposition of portions of several logical groups, are not the first object of logic, but fall within the province of history and of practical policy. But these remarks will perhaps be only understood by the actual analysis which follows.

3. The main distinction of classes of groups in society is derived from the distinction between the interests of direct and the interests of reflective emotions. Each of these two main classes of interests consists of, or contains within itself, particular interests, the foundation of special groups; and from the combination of particular classes of each kind there arise groups in which the motives of coherence and action are of a mixed character. The interests of direct emotions are the interests of bodily or material well-being, to use the term 'material' in its ordinary sense of sensational feeling presented or represented. Material commodities or material wealth are the object at which all direct emotions aim, which they have either for their framework or for their desired end. But some emotions, enumerated as direct, are carried up so immediately and so closely combined with reflective emotions, as to be undistinguishable

from these in their operation as motives. This is the case with the direct emotions arising from the form, which are carried up into imagination, and thence into poetry; and this is the case with the direct emotions of comparison, wonder and the logical instinct, which are the foundation of the intellectual tendencies of character, leaving only the sensational matter in which they arise to distinguish them as direct emotions. In other words, whenever the direct emotions of form and of comparison exist in sufficient strength to be noticeable as motives at all, they are motives of reflective action more than of direct, and must be counted as motives of groups formed by reflective interests. Only the purely direct emotions and passions are thus left to serve as the foundation of groups of direct emotional character, aiming at pleasures of sense and of enjoyment; these are the direct kinds of joy, grief, fondness, aversion, hope, and fear; and they have for their object or aim material enjoyments and material possessions. (See § 17 and § 20. 1.)

4. The binding power which the acquisition of material possessions and material enjoyments exerts, in grouping men together, is derived from a physical law of the visible and tangible objects in which those possessions consist, which are the means of the enjoyments; namely, the law of increase, that the objects acquired are the source of further acquisitions. Every acquisition may either be consumed, in which case it produces enjoyment, or it may be saved and employed, in which case it produces further acquisition and future enjoyment. Acquisition is an universal tendency; every man begins by acquiring some commodities, and these are the basis of the conception and recognition of property. In using acquisi-

tions for further acquisition, some man or men must be the agents; these have de facto property in the objects acquired. The recognition or allowance of such actual enjoyment and use of property flows directly from the perception that enjoyment and acquisition are increased by recognising it. The right of property may have other sources also, but, so far as this source goes, it is one founded on direct emotion. Acquisition of wealth and acquisition of property go hand in hand; and the physical law of increase of wealth, under these conditions, binds men together by satisfying their common desire of material possessions and enjoyments. This is one source, not the only one, but the first, most universal, and strongest, of society among large numbers of men.

5. The forms which wealth assumes, the distinctions which arise in it, at different periods of civilisation, are very different; and it is upon these forms and distinctions in possessions, different from time to time, that are built the most striking and important distinctions of classes of men in society. The distinction between acquired wealth, as a means to further production, and the powers of brain and muscle to apply these means is the distinction between capital and labour; and the possessors of each respectively have always fallen into two opposite classes in society. The further acquisition of wealth produces another distinction within capital itself, namely, that between capital employed for profit and capital lent at interest, or employed to procure for its possessors interest only and not profits. In highly civilised and wealthy communities, there will always be three classes in society which are distinguished from each other by the possession of these three

means of enjoyment, labour, capital and labour combined, capital alone,—the labourers, the profit-capitalists, the interest-capitalists. I have drawn this out at somewhat greater length in a little work, published in 1866, entitled Principles of Reform in the Suffrage; and, whatever the error of the practical suggestion, or rather illustration, contained in its concluding §, I still think it sound, so far as it goes, as a contribution to the Logic of Politic, which was its main purpose.

6. These three classes are the most general groups, exhaustive of the whole of any society, into which it tends to fall in consequence of the distinctions of wealth or property; class differences which are implicitly contained in every society, so far as it is bound together by the common pursuit of wealth or material well-being, and explicitly evolved in every such society so soon as the physical laws of acquisition and distribution of wealth come into fully developed action. But in this case again it must be remembered, that the forms which these classes, and these kinds of wealth, will assume in different countries, and at different times, will be very different, and that so will be also the relative social and political importance of the groups of men composing them. The first aim of logic is to give a general classification containing under it, but not necessarily specifying, the different shapes which its categories may assume according to different combinations of circumstances. Other circumstances not only may but must combine with those forming these groups, the limits of other groups must coincide with theirs, before these or any groups can take their place as recognised forces, or primary component members,

of a nation or state, before they can become objects of scientific history as well as of political logic.

7. It is next in order to examine the groups founded on the reflective emotions, emotions which are the constituents of character in the strict sense. Following the principle already adopted in the direct groups, we must take these emotions in their development and not in their germ, as the foundation of groups. Just as several direct emotions were excluded from forming groups, on the ground that they were only seen in action as contributories to reflective emotions, so here several reflective emotions will be excluded from forming groups on the ground that they have by themselves no career, and act only in modifying the groups formed by those that have. The reason of thus proceeding is clear; we are beginning here, in the logic, with society as a whole, endeavouring to break it up into its general logical constituents; we must therefore begin with those groups which are the largest, the most permanent, and the most important; but this can only be done by taking the most absorbing types of character, and by taking these in their full development or activity in their career. In this way are first excluded the groups formed by the ambitious type of character, founded on the emotions and passions of comparison; the objects of ambition are so numerous, that the groups formed are very small and very fluctuating; and ambition alone, apart from these its accidental objects, is not a bond of union but of separation, since all its emotions are so, being emotions of comparison. The same reasoning applies to the self-isolating type of character, and even to the kind of pride which is self-respect. It is only accidentally and temporarily

that alliances are formed from mutual satisfaction of these wishes. So again the irascible type is excluded; alliances may be formed to gratify common dislike or hatred, but they are fluctuating and temporary. Here is seen the importance, in the constitution of society, of the stress laid in Book i. Chap. iv. on the circumstance of a career. Emotions and passions which have no career do not enter into the de facto constitution of society as primary and permanent, but only as modifying elements. The "feeble folk" of amusement seekers are indeed in permanent alliance, but they are a group whose function has no defined purpose, and which serves only to clog the activity of the rest. They fall under the eye of history, but logic looks and passes on.

8. The remaining types of character, the affectionate, the duty-loving, and the erotic types, and the two intellectual tendencies, constructive and accumulative, form three groups in the following manner. The two first-mentioned types, together with the intellectual tendency, form in their development a group which may be called that of religious emotion; the third type, together with the intellectual tendency, with the desire of æsthetic beauty, and the various emotions with which this may be incorporated by imagination, forms the group of poetical emotion; and the two intellectual tendencies alone form the group of knowledge seekers for its own sake. These three groups, each bound together by permanent and strong interests, the interest of increasing and purifying the pleasures at which they aim, are the main groups founded on reflective emotions, of which other groups are the modification and differentiation. These three groups are or contain

the organs of the spiritual interests of society; their aims and their constitutive interests being the perfection of Religion, Art, and Knowledge, as ends in themselves, and apart from the influence they have on the aims of the direct groups, the increase of material possessions and enjoyments. The latter are a de facto condition of the former; the former a justifying condition of the latter.

9. The members of these three groups are scattered over every country and every time, they are not gathered up into locally united bodies commensurate with the groups; but the bonds of interest and of fellowship are not less powerful on that account, while they are far more secure from the interference of foreign interests. Organise a spiritual group as a civil or political corporation, and eo ipso its material interests begin to take the ascendancy over its spiritual ones. It begins to aim at material prosperity, and soon proceeds to motives of ambition and aggrandisement. But the subtil bonds of truly spiritual fellowship are perceived and acknowledged by the brotherhood all the world over, and across the barriers of time. The same traits of character, the same interest in promoting them, are recognised by their possessors, who hasten, wherever found,

" Di far al cittadin suo quivi festa."

Yet these groups are not without antagonism, chiefly between, but also within, themselves. Upon the antagonism of each group to the others there is no need to dwell; what has been said of the antagonism of the two types of character, the poetic and the religious, in § 73, may be applied to the groups which they form, and also to that formed by the intellectual tendency. Within itself, however, each group breaks up into subordinate groups, according to the influence of members of other groups which unite with it, or the predominance from time to time of particular reflective emotions, and to the different views which its members may take of the requirements of the time or of their particular circumstances. Thus, for instance, the man who belongs to the scientific group may belong also to some direct group, as a member of which his intellectual efforts are employed on some particular subject, engineering, mining, telegraphy, and so on; he of course is not uninfluenced by these circumstances in the view he takes of the relative importance of branches of knowledge. The general character of the purely scientific, reflective, group will be obviously modified from time to time by the prevalent pursuits and aims of different orders and kinds among its members. But, in following up farther the differentiation of groups, we should have to enter upon the domain of actual history, the analysis of character alone offering us no further ground for distinctions. It is enough in this paragraph to point out the mode in which the modification and differentiation of groups is effected.

10. The domain of actual history must however be entered, to some extent at least, by pointing out some of the most important groups which arise from the combination of motives direct and reflective. These groups are among the actual concrete groups which are within the cognisance of history, and their historical importance is the ground of selecting them for mention. And in the first place, intercommunication by means of speech or language, whether this consists in vocal or written utterances, or in picture

language, or in gesture only, is the most fundamental and elementary of all bonds of union. The whole human race is united by its means; and, within this limit, any particular language unites all those who understand and use it, and separates them from those who do not. This is carried down to the minutest shades of difference, to differences of phraseology current among separate cliques or sects, each clique having a slang system of its own. Now the interest of language is of two kinds, first reflective, the pleasure of communicating thoughts and feelings alone, to which must be added the pleasure of communicating particular thoughts and feelings for their own sake; secondly direct, the material advantages of concert, of which it is the condition. Unity of language often combines with unity of local habitation and with unity of race; these three interests in combination are those which mark out the actual historical groups known as nations or tribes; and it is evident that they combine with or contain the interest of common pursuit of wealth.

11. Unity of race again has a double origin, first the actual descent from a common stock, secondly the incorporation of new members into families and tribes as if they were actually so descended. The actual descent from a common stock rests ultimately on the family bond, which in its most rudimentary state is the bond between a mother and her offspring. Personal affection, first between mother and children, then between father and mother, and lastly between father and children, is the bond of the family at a later stage; but to reach this stage material interests must have come into play, as well as purely spiritual ones; and families in this stage may be regarded as

the most elementary molecules of a fully formed nation, molecules the atoms of which cohere too strongly to be sundered, notwithstanding that we can point out the motives which produce their cohesion. Of these motives some are reflective, others direct. The family, then, in some state or other, rudimentary or developed, is an ultimate empirical group in any mass of men which may be taken for historical examination.

12. But the origin of society is not yet completely accounted for; there remains the third element, unity of local habitation. We may break up a group into families, but it does not follow that the group has been formed out of those families; it may be that the group existed first, and was afterwards differentiated into the families. Physical circumstances may have thrown men together into a group, by giving them unity of habitation; and this may have been an indispensable condition for the family evolution. Here we should come upon the physical condition of society, which compared with the others is, so to speak, an irrational one, that is, not reducible to human motives, at least in the present state of our knowledge. The other conditions, language and the family bond, may be so reduced, because we can see from what kind of motives they derived their power. But these alone do not furnish a sufficient account of the origin of society; they suppose men to be already in some sort of communication with each other; they do not determine the numbers, or the outline, of a group as a whole. For this it seems recourse must be had to some physical conditions with which we are unacquainted, as well as with their mode of working on motives. A nation, then,

may be considered, at least provisionally, as consisting of the superposition and coincidence of groups of three kinds; first of those who speak the same language, secondly of those who belong, or are supposed to belong, to a common stock, and thirdly of those who are thrown together into a common local habitation.

13. Such is the outline, as I conceive it, of the groups into which men tend to arrange themselves, with the several sensations and emotions upon which they rest; let us now attempt to form some conception of the mental action by which this grouping is accomplished, and of the changes in mental imagery by which it is accompanied, at least in those directions which depend more immediately upon the character, and are most strictly entitled to the name of civilisation.

14. Besides the external circumstances affecting any tribe or nation, such as the physical features of its country and climate, and the tribes which come into contact or collision with it,—circumstances which may here be abstracted from,—its character is the source of its civilisation; the civilisation of a people being the result of the reaction of its character upon its circumstances. Those mental and moral features which constitute the character (§§ 59, 60) produce, in their operation upon the objects and events of life, those several imaginative structures which may be conveniently classified under the four heads, Law, Creed, Science, and Poetry; together with the associated systems of actions which are either necessary to their support or consequences of their existence, such as language, and legal, social, and religious observances. Along with the formation of these fea-

tures of civilisation, and springing from the same source, the primitive grouping of the people is modified by the superposition of groups whose special interest lies in any of these directions, such, for instance, as Kings or ruling families, priests, bards, physicians. Everything in the society has its root in the individual, everything in history has its root in nature.

15. It is a question not for this place but for special history, what has been the combination of character and circumstance which has produced the particular civilisation of this or that people, as well as to trace back the course of that civilisation, resolve it into its furthest elements and causes, and determine what and how much is due to the one cause, what and how much to the other. Only what is, or may properly be held, common to the civilisation of all people belongs here. I imagine to myself, then, the mental and moral activity of a community, in its earliest stage, as containing, implicitly and undistinguished, those trains and systems of thought and feeling which will afterwards one by one separate themselves from the parent stem, and organise themselves into the four above named systems of (1) Legal and Social institutions, (2) Religious beliefs, (3) Poetical imaginations, (4) Scientific or Philosophical conceptions. All these depend directly for their formation upon those emotions and tendencies which have been included in the term character, but upon these modified by the circumstances upon which they react, and themselves developed by the development of those systems which are their product. The predominance of different emotions in the character

of different nations is the ultimate source of their different systems of creed, law, or custom.

16. Let us endeavour to imagine the mode of origin of these systems, and their gradual distinction from each other. The first mode of conceiving phenomena is personification, that is, to conceive them as persons acting and feeling as the man who conceives them feels and acts. This 'judging others by oneself,' judging the unfamiliar by the familiar, the unknown by the known, is not only a fact to be assumed a priori from what we know of human nature, but is also established a posteriori by what we know of actual mythologies. And again, this tendency is not only the first step in human development, but its continuing method, upon which the unity of past, present, and future development depends. Personifying imagination is still the parent of poetry and of religion, though under widely different conditions of knowledge.

17. Man begins by personifying everything about him, all objects and all forces of nature. But those objects only which communicate with him by language are his allies; they alone respond to him, and express feelings like his own. The objects and forces of nature, though conceived by him as persons, are yet strange, uncommunicative, some indeed beneficent and friendly, but others hostile and destructive. Two kingdoms of persons are thus established in his imagination, his human compeers and his divine friends or foes. Hence human society on the one hand, divine or natural beings on the other. Gradually was made the discovery that the forces and objects of nature were not animated by consciousness, but were obedient to fixed laws, by obeying

which they were themselves conquerable. Then began the process of disintegration and reintegration of beliefs concerning them, which has never ceased, and in which we also are sharers. A similar process took place with the phenomena of the human kingdom, of which in like manner the social and political movement of the present day is the continuation. Let us begin with the latter; bearing in mind that both took place simultaneously, and in constant reaction on each other.

18. The state of association among men is one which has no antecedents; there never was a period of isolation. Not to speak of the bond which connects the mother with her offspring, there is a subtiler but hardly less powerful link between the individual and the group into which he happens to be born. The strange terrors of nature bind him to the society of his human compeers. He does not begin by feeling himself independent, and then form an association for mutual protection and advantage; he feels himself dependent from the first. To form an association for protection and advantage is, from its commencement, not a spontaneous but a voluntary act, an act done for a purpose lying beyond the act itself; were such an act the origin of society, we must begin with imagining men isolated and independent. But to herd together for the sake of companionship in presence of the uncommunicative powers of nature is a spontaneous act in its commencement, and from beginning to end aims at no satisfaction beyond what is contained in the act itself. Unless we go back to times not only prehistoric but prehuman, we shall never come to a period at which this motive of association is inoperative; and society is thus built upon

a spontaneous foundation in its origin, although it must soon have received accretions due to voluntary motives.

19. The society, of which the individual never felt himself independent, but of which he constantly felt himself a merged and incorporated member, was one half of his entire world, of which nature was the other; its image accompanied him, its power overshadowed him; and both society and nature he alike personified. He did not *know* himself and thus interpret nature and society; but he was *familiar* with himself and interpreted them thus. Society was one great personality, nature was another, but neither of the two originally distinguished into independent persons; these had first to be evolved out of the mass. The history of this evolution, with the analysis of its advancing states, is the history of religious and intellectual development on one side, of law on the other, and in both together of society itself and its members in relation to it. In other words, the personification of the society is the beginning of its actual historical evolution; and law, which is the relation between distinct members of society, the mode of coherence of its parts, some commanding, others obeying, begins with the first distinction drawn between its members, whether between the organ representing the whole society, the sovereign, and the rest, or between one member and another. The law of persons or status is thus the earliest law; the law of property followed, involving more complex distinctions. The personification of society is the origin of law, that of nature of theology.

20. I am disposed to see in this identification of self first with the society, and derivatively with the

several members of it, the root notion which rendered possible those various forms of substitution, vicarious suffering, and sacrifice, which meet us in the history of early times; for the gods, it was thought, would perceive the same identity between the persons. The difficulty to avoid transferring in thought one's own feelings and even conditions of existence to others, the inability to imagine separate in fact what has been associated in consciousness, a picture for instance from the person depicted, are well known features in uncultured nations. Add to this the tendency to consider one member of the society as equivalent to another, a tendency arising originally from the same transference of individual feeling, and we can at once see how such customs as the Couvade, such beliefs as that "the actions and food of survivors affect the spirits of the dead on their journey to their home in the after life," (see for both Mr. Tylor's Researches into the Early History of Mankind, Chap. x.), such precepts as the sanctification of the firstborn in Exodus xiii., such practices as the devotion of Decius in Livy viii. 9, and the sacrifices first of human beings, afterwards of animals in their stead, as shown, for instance, in the sealing of the ox for sacrifice, in Plut. De Iside et Osiride, xxxi., probably originated, and in what modes of thought they found their support. I do not say that the customs here mentioned arose exclusively from the transference of feeling with personification, but that this was one source from which they sprang. The Couvade, for instance, may also be connected, as Herr Bachofen suggests in his Das Mutterrecht, with the period of transition from kinship through females only to kinship through males also, the father thinking to prove his paternity by taking the place of the mother; "um die physische Wahrheit auf das Vaterthum zu übertragen, wird zuweile die Sitte angenommen, dass bei der Niederkunft des Weibes auch der Vater sich zu Bette legt und die Gebärende nachahmt." page 17. But to render this explanation conceivable, a basis of imaginative personification must be assumed.

21. The community of property in families, clans, and tribes, in the earliest times of history, is another circumstance which requires a corresponding community of personification to explain it. Had there not been from the first an overpowering sense of identification with the society, how could the common possession of property have continued to exist, in spite of the tendency to separate acquisition? "We hear nothing," says Mr. MacLennan, in his Primitive Marriage, p. 162, "in the most ancient times of individuals except as being members of groups. The history of property is the history of the development of proprietary rights *inside* groups, which were at first the only owners, and of all other personal rights—even including the right in offspring—it may be said that their history is that of the gradual assertion of the claims of individuals against the traditional rights of groups."

22. The researches of Herr Bachofen in his Das Mutterrecht,[*] and of Mr. MacLennan in his Primitive Marriage, and in his two papers on Kinship in Ancient Greece, in the Fortnightly Review, April, May, 1866, seem to me to have thrown an entirely

---

[*] Das Mutterrecht.—My thanks are here due to my friend Dr. C. Leitner for pointing out to me this and other works bearing on the subject in hand, as well as for his friendly and valuable criticism on my first sketch of these paragraphs.

new light on the prehistoric times of mankind. To adopt some expressions from the latter, 'the social unit was not the family but the tribe, and the first families, in which the conception of blood-relationship was involved, consisted of mothers and their offspring. This was the first step out of savagery.' The mental process was one of gradually disintegrating and organising an inorganic whole; and the moving powers in this process were the relation between mother and child on one side, and the necessity, springing from material needs, of seeking wives from without the tribe on the other. A series of changes in social relations was thus set on foot, which ended, at the beginning of the historical period, that from which contemporary records have come down to us, in the acknowledgement of the father as head of the family, and the system of relationship through males.

23. Every step in this progress was won by a hard struggle between the friends of the new and the friends of the old state of things; and the intensity of the contest was marked by the strictness and exclusiveness with which the victorious system was carried out. "Das römische Paternitäts-system weist durch die Strenge, mit welcher es auftritt, auf ein früheres, das bekämpft und zurückgedrängt werden soll, hin." Das Mutterrecht, Vorrede, p. viii. For, besides the personal interests which are always involved, every legalised system of society must repose upon some corresponding system of religious or at least theological convictions; without which correspondence the unity of human life would be impossible. Even the savage state of more or less promiscuous intercourse between the sexes was sanctioned

by religion, and marriage itself appeared at first as the transgression of a religious command. Only out of this state of things "erläutert sich der Gedanke, dass die Ehe eine Sühne jener Gottheit verlangt, deren Gesetz sie durch ihre Ausschliesslichkeit verletzt." And "daraus erklären sich nun alle jene Gebräuche, in welchen die Ehe selbst mit hetärischen Uebungen verbunden auftritt." Id. id. p. xix.

24. But let us now turn to the second branch of the development, religion. Three kinds of objects of religious personification may be pointed out; 1st, physical objects and events, 2nd, social objects and events of life, 3rd, mental powers and characteristics; but it is only the first of these which we can either suppose a priori, or find indicated a posteriori, to have been the object of religious personification in the earliest stage of all. . Later in the course of mental development, since, by the very fact of personification, the god created by it is created subject to the law of progress in the mind of which he is the creature, these divinities may either be themselves transformed into representations of the second and third class, which seems to have been the case, for instance, with the Greek Zeus, and with the Charites, the identity of whom with the Haritas, the horses of the sun, in the Vedas, is maintained by Prof. Max. Müller in his essay on Comparative Mythology; or they may receive as companions such divinities of independent though later origin, such as were apparently Hebe, Themis, Metis, the Muses, and many of the Heroes of Greek mythology. See K. O. Müller's Prolegomena zu einer wissenschaftlichen Mythologie, iv.

25. The physical objects and events which may be personified in the first instance are very numerous

and varied, and the choice of those which became the most prominent among different nations must, I think, have been determined at least as much by differences in the character as by differences in the circumstances of the people who were led to select them. Phenomena of the sky, storms, clouds, wind, light, and the changes of the day and year; terrestrial phenomena, rivers, mountains, sea, trees and forests, seedtime and harvest; the heavenly bodies themselves, the sun and moon, the planets, the stars; and especially, what must have appeared the most marvellous of all, the different animals, of earth, sea, and air, some wild and terrible, others capable of domestication, but all mysterious as bearing a half human character; such were the phenomena from which men must have selected the first objects of religious adoration. And the results of their choice may still be read incorporated in the later theology for which each nation was specially renowned, as, for instance, in the astrolatry and astrology of the Babylonians, and in the Egyptian worship of the heavenly bodies and of animals.

26. The next step in this development was the separation of the god from the phenomena which he once was and henceforth only ruled. The gods assumed a separate and independent existence. This opened the door to mythology on the one side, and on the other to the attribution of a new civil character and function to the gods whose origin was purely physical; and in this latter way law and religion again coalesce, by the presidency which is given to the gods over civil customs and institutions.

27. In the mythology, which arose from the separation of god from phenomenon, we may trace the

consequences of the separation. In Greece, for instance, there are two sets of Gods, the old and the new, the Titans and the Olympians, the gods of nature personified in their old form and the gods of nature transformed into new shapes, Phœbus Apollo side by side with Helios Hyperion. Although the public worship now became fixed in established forms, the mythology continued to undergo development at the hands of poets and antiquarians. The religion of the people in Greece must be looked for in the public sacrifices and ceremonies, and especially in the mysteries, which seem, from their character at once solemn and unexclusive, to have provided the chief means of satisfying the religious feeling.

28. But this is not the only direction of religious development. The distinction of sex is often found to play a prominent part in polytheistic creeds. The sexual relation, so important to men, is transferred to the Gods, and many natural processes, such as the fertilisation of the earth by rain and sunlight, are interpreted as the consequences of this relation between the personal beings into which the objects of nature were transformed. An abundant mythology may be traced back to this conception.

29. A far more subtil and probably a much later distinction is that between the principles of good and evil; and this too is one which may coalesce with the belief in older physical gods; which seems to have been the case in Magianism, the religion attributed to Zoroaster. Light, the original physical god, became identified with Ormuz the good spirit; and its opposite, darkness, with the evil spirit Ahriman. It is a case falling under the same general law as that of the conversion of Zeus, the upper air or sky,

into Zeus the administrator and upholder of justice among gods and men.

30. The most striking case in which the coalescence of religion and law, above mentioned, is observable is perhaps that of the Roman people; and this owing to their character, in which, while the love of home and family, of order and tradition, was strongly marked, there was a comparative absence of several traits which are prominent in other nations, —of poetical fancy such as distinguished the Greeks, of philosophical subtilty which seems to have dictated the two principles of Magianism, of profound religious feeling which, as will appear farther on, was the basis of the Mosaic creed. Here then the religious development assumes its most marked legal character; you might almost say that law, embodied in civil, family, and national tradition, and finding its home at the domestic and at the national hearth, was the religion of the Romans. The Lares and Penates, the Genii of the living, the Manes of the dead, the Vestal Virgins guarding the unextinguished fire in the national sanctuary, Janus the closer and opener of the gate which separates the future from the past, —these and such as these were the images which occupied the greater part of Roman religious thought. Such the people and such the religion from which sprang that system of law which has been the basis of all modern jurisprudence. Rome starved her mythology to feed her law; Greece starved her law to feed her mythology. The earliest remaining product of Greece is the Iliad, the earliest of Rome the Code of the Twelve Tables.

31. Judaism too begins with a Code, but with a Code how different from the Roman. Judaism too

had no poetical mythology, no mythology of fiction. In these points both nations alike are contrasted with the Greeks. Law is the common ground of similarity; it is within this that they are themselves contrasted. The love of home and family, of family and national tradition, is the feature upon which is built in each case the strong tendency to legal institutions. But the Hebrews were endowed with imagination, the Greeks with fancy, the Romans with neither. At the basis of the Hebrew character lay the same strong moral tendency as at the basis of the Roman, but combined with an equally strong tendency to poetical, that is, reflectively emotional, imagination. Two consequences may be traced to this fact, first, their rich mythology of ancestors assuming all the air of reality, secondly, their religious lyrics. Fiction was abhorrent to them, and therefore they believed in their fictions; a single system of thought was to them history, law, science, and religion in one.

32. With the Hebrews, then, law was not combined with, or placed under the sanction of, religion; but religion itself became law. It is from the Hebrews, or rather from that succession of prophetical minds, which never failed among them from Moses to Christ, that the world has learnt the true meaning of the term Religion. How much and what in the Mosaic legislation, and in its acceptance by the people, was due to the character, how much and what to the circumstances, of the nation, I will not attempt to decide. Much must have been due to the former. Nor perhaps may it ever be made out with certainty to what precise branch of Semitic religious development the previous Hebrew creed belonged, or how

much intellectual preparation had been received from Egyptian sources.

33. But the God who was revealed to Moses, and through him to the Hebrews, was of a very different nature from even the Good Spirit of Magianism, or from any Pervading Spirit of the Universe, if such an one should be thought to have been known in Egypt or elsewhere. The God who met Moses in his solitary journeys in the wilderness, whose abode was behind clouds on lonely mountain summits, was the God of conscience, "the father of the spirits of all flesh." The *I Am* is the second self of every man; that self to whom he goes, in imagination, for sympathy, comprehension, and support; that therefore 'unto whom all his heart is open, and from whom no secret is hid;' that who cannot approve what the man's conscience will disapprove; that to whom he must justify himself or forfeit his own self-respect; that, therefore, who is not only his second but his ideal self, so far as aims, longings, aspirations, are concerned; that to whom no second, no sharer in sovereignty is possible, being one as the self is one; that finally who cannot be torn from him, yet who is a friendly power, a shield, a rock, a secret source of strength, a Deliverer, as well as a justifier and sanctifier. Upon this God Moses and the people relied, and from this source they drew the law of their life. It was no intellectual monotheism which they held, no theory of the unity of the power sustaining and ruling all natural phenomena, such as might have commended itself to a philosophical intelligence, but an emotional choice; a religion not a creed. (See Dr. Ewald's powerful and philosophical delineation in his Geschichte des Volkes Israel, Vol. ii.

Book II.
Ch. III.
§ 68.
The spontaneous organisation of Society.

p. 138, 2nd edit. Das Wesen der Gesetzgebung, now fortunately accessible in an English translation.)

34. The common feature in all religions, that which justifies us in including them, however otherwise different, under a common name, is not the personification which they involve, for this underlies all directions of mental activity; it is that peculiar feeling of awe in presence of the immeasurable and mysterious powers of nature, which in early history are characterised as supernatural. It is a half truth to call this feeling fear; it was never fear simply, but fear of the immeasurable and mysterious; the feeling which led to those places being regarded as the special abodes of the Gods where the powers of nature made themselves most strongly felt, the solitudes of forests and mountains, the feeling which, accompanied in the earliest times by the sense of eeriness described in § 19. 4, has, in the latest development of it we are acquainted with, no other material object for its resting place than the infinite frame of nature as imaged not to the bodily but to the mental eye. All forms of divinity alike, whatever the mode of their production in belief, to whatever process of reasoning or of imagination they may have owed their origin, were held as exponents of these supreme powers of nature, and from this filiation, not from themselves, they derived whatever religious awe they were capable of inspiring. This awe the Mosaic religion had in common with all others; its God was conceived as the creator and sustainer of the world; that which distinguished it from other religions was that which it has been attempted to describe in the preceding paragraphs.

35. But it is time to turn to the two remaining

branches of the development, science and poetry. While the progress hitherto described has been taking place, while religions have succeeded to religions, and institutions have been supplanted by institutions, the changes in both cases alike have left behind a mass of recorded or unrecorded error, and have accumulated and organised a mass of more or less perfect truth. Men have won practical truth in winning individual liberty, and speculative in separating the laws of natural phenomena from the arbitrary action of imagined personalities. But in doing so their own individual powers have not been weakened but strengthened, not trammelled but set free. The separation of law from creed, and of both from ungrounded fancy, involves the separation and separate exercise of the mental activities which are principally engaged in each; involves the formation of distinct mental habits, or, as we are accustomed to say, of distinct faculties of mind. The reasoning powers are set free to examine the laws of phenomena, the imaginative to arrange those phenomena at pleasure, under the guidance of any emotion which may be selected. They now carry on, with full consciousness of its arbitrary nature, the same process which formerly issued in the production of mythologies once believed in as truths, but now perceived to have been without the warrant of reason. Poetry and science take their place by the side of religion and of law; four distinct branches from the parent stem in which they originally grew undistinguished.

36. The four branches divide the world between them, but the division is not empirical or exclusive. Each possesses the entire world, and impresses its own character upon it. No phenomenon which does

not or may not fall under the dominion of each in turn. All natural phenomena, being the objects of human energies, may be contemplated in the regulations of law; all are objects of scientific examination, all of imaginative metamorphosis; and all are parts of that great whole, the contemplation of which is the porch and antechamber of religion.

37. And here I must be allowed a word of homage to the illustrious founder of modern historical science, Giambattista Vico. The fundamental conceptions, which I am humbly endeavouring to apply, he was the first to proclaim. The conception of history in all its several branches, and among the several races of man, being the outcome of the human mind under various, but fundamentally similar, conditions, and explicable only by being referred to mental analysis, is the conception upon which the Scienza Nuova is based. "Ma in tal densa notte di tenebre, ond' è coverta la prima da noi lontanissima Antichità, apparisce questo lume eterno, che non tramonta, di questa Verità, la quale non si può a patto alcuno chiamar in dubbio; che *questo Mondo Civile egli certamente è stato fatto dagli uomini:* onde se ne possono, perchè se ne debbono, ritrovare *i Principj dentro le modificazioni della nostra medesima mente umana.*" The second Scienza Nuova, Vol. v. in Ferrari's edition of 1854. Lib. i. De' Principj, p. 136. Combined with this conception are others, among which the most important perhaps are, 1st, that which contains the distinction between spontaneous and voluntary action, "Gli *uomini* prima *sentono* senz' avvertire; da poi *avvertiscono* con animo perturbato e commosso; finalmente *riflettono* con mente pura." Lib. i. Degli Elementi, liii. p. 112; and 2nd, that in which the

origin of the various practical sciences is referred to the same moment as the perception of the object-matter with which they are concerned, "Le *dottrine debbono cominciare* da quando cominciano le *materie che trattano.*" Id. id. cvi. p. 131.

Book II. Ch. III.
§ 60.
The spontaneous organisation of Society.

37. The use which Vico made of principles like the foregoing, the kind of importance which they assumed in his eyes, may be gathered from his brief introduction to his historical construction of the earliest, or Poetico-theologic, stage of civilisation, Id. id. Lib. ii. p. 156. "PROPOSITIONE E PARTIZIONE DELLA SAPIENZA POETICA. Ma perchè la Metafisica è la Scienza sublime, che ripartisce i certi loro subbietti a tutte le scienze che si dicono subalterne; e la *Sapienza degli Antichi* fu quella *de' Poeti Teologi;* i quali senza contrasto furono i *primi Sapienti del Gentilesimo*—come si è nelle Degnità stabilito—e le *Origini* delle cose tutte debbono per natura esser *rozze;* dobbiamo per tutto ciò dar incominciamento alla SAPIENZA POETICA da una *rozza lor Metafisica;* dalla quale, come da un *tronco* si diramino *per un ramo* la *Logica,* la *Morale,* l' *Iconomica* e la *Politica* tutte *Poetiche;* e per *un altro ramo* tutte eziandio poetiche la *Fisica,* la qual sia stata madre della loro *Cosmographia,* e quindi dell' *Astronomia;* che ne dia accertate le due sue figliuole, che sono *Cronologia* e *Geographia.* E con ischiarite e distinte guise farem vedere, come i *Fondatori dell' Umanità Gentilesca* con la loro *Teologia Naturale* o sia *Metafisica* s' immaginarono gli Dei; con la loro *Logica* si trovarono le lingue; con la *Morale* si generarono gli Eroi; con l' *Iconomia* si fondarono le Famiglie; con la *Politica* le città; come con la loro *Fisica* si stabilirono i Principj delle cose tutte divini; con la *Fisica Particolare dell'*

Uomo in un certo modo generarono sè medesimi; con la loro *Cosmographia* si finsero un lor Universo tutto di Dei; con l'*Astronomia* portarono da Terra in Cielo i Pianeti e le costellazioni; con la *Cronologia* diedero principio ai tempi; e con la *Geographia* i Greci, per cagion d'esemplo, si descrissero il Mondo dentro la loro Grecia. Di tal maniera, che *questa Scienza* vien ad essere ad un fiato una *Storia dell' idee, costumi e fatti del gener umano*: e da tutti e tre si vedranno uscir i *Principj della Storia della Natura Umana*; e quest' esser i *Principj della Storia Universale*, la quale sembra ancor mancare ne' suoi Principj." The closeness of the parallel between these conceptions and those of modern scientific historians needs hardly to be pointed out. Modern knowledge may have escaped many of the errors as well as added much to the stock of truths contained in the Scienza Nuova, but its fontal principles are the principles of Vico.

§ 89. 1. Hitherto the organisation of society has been considered as entirely spontaneous; not that all the actions constituting it have not been voluntary acts so far as the individuals are concerned, but that there has been no action of the society as a whole, or of any of the groups, which has proceeded from a conscious purpose aimed at by the groups or by the society. It is true that we never find a group formed without finding it also acting voluntarily, as if it had a single consciousness and a single will; but from this action we have hitherto abstracted. The spontaneous and the voluntary action of a group, or of society, proceed in close connection with and interdependence on each other; the former being both the material modified and the means of its modification by the latter. It is with society in this respect precisely the same as with the individual; his volition arises in, and works with, the means and objects of movement provided by his spontaneous redintegrations, upon which it reacts and which it moulds to different purposes.

2. In the first place, and before proceeding to the distinction between the spontaneous and voluntary action of a group or groups, the very elements of the question must be cleared of an ambiguity which embarrasses them. The familiar use of the single term 'action of a group,' as if there was unity of person and of act in the group, leads us to imagine its action as a single thing, unanalysable, an ultimate entity. But this is not the case. Suppose that three persons A. B. C. form the group P. Any action said to be P's must be either three actions, precisely similar in every respect, done by A. B. C. separately; or it must be three different actions done by them separately but concurrent to one complex group of actions, as in building a house one mixes the mortar, another lays the bricks; or it must be one act done by one of the three, the others approving and consenting. The action of a group is always analysable into several actions of several members. The importance of insisting on this plain elementary truth is evident when we consider a further ambiguity which arises from neglecting it. It is often urged that examination of the actions of men in masses must precede examination of the actions of individuals, in order to lead to profitable results. There is a sense in which this both can and ought to be done; there is another sense in which it is impossible. The nature of the actions of a group, that is, of society, or of men in masses, can only be understood by prior

examination of the actions of individuals; this follows directly from what has just been said. But the history of particular actions, whether of individuals, or of groups, or of mankind collectively, must be entered on, laying first the enquiry into nature at the basis, by beginning with the actions of groups or masses; the reason for which is, that the collective actions of masses or groups are the most influential determinants of the particular actions of individuals. Hence in ethic, and in the logic of practice in all its branches, which deal with questions of nature and not of history, actions of individuals give the point of view from which the whole subject must be treated.

3. The distinction between the spontaneous and voluntary action of a group is to be thus drawn. When one or more members of any group become conscious of the nature of the group to which they belong, and of its relations to other groups, and, so distinguishing, place ends before them to be reached, or actions to be performed, by the group, as more desirable than other ends or actions which might be chosen; in other words, when the group or some of its members seek to modify the action of the group as a whole; then the action of the group becomes voluntary instead of merely spontaneous, becomes volition guiding spontaneous action. There are no actions which do not fall under one or the other of these two heads; and this distinction between spontaneous and voluntary action is therefore exhaustive, and leaves no further class of action unaccounted for. This change from spontaneous to voluntary action is also a further distinguishing of groups in the society or group in which it takes place. Those members of

the group who entertain the purpose of modifying its action are themselves formed into a new group within it by the very circumstance of this common purpose. If it were a single member only who formed the purpose, he would be equally distinguished from the rest in virtue of it; and if it were the entire number of members, they would have clothed the group itself with a new function, and would stand towards other groups in a double instead of a single relation, would be virtually two groups instead of one. The two kinds of action may be best distinguished by calling one force, the other power, and speaking of the spontaneous forces and the voluntary powers of society. The distinction itself is the most fundamental and important one in practical politic, or policy, since, when we come to the consideration of what is feasible and practicable as well as desirable, one most important branch of feasibility consists in the amount and kind of spontaneous forces which the legislator or administrator, who is the organ of the voluntary power, can reckon upon to second him, or must count upon to fail or oppose him, in adopting and carrying out the purposes which he wishes to have effected by the collective action of the community.

4. All the groups formed by interests simple or complex in the spontaneous action of society thus tend, by the mere development of intelligence, to organise themselves into subordinate groups; the three material groups and the three spiritual groups, for instance, as well as those smaller ones which they embrace. But all these are embraced by the concrete, empirical, historical groups, which are composed by their combination and superposition; the

family, the race, the nation, for instance; and thus within these historical groups, and incessantly modifying them, proceeds the same analytic and synthetic action, producing further organisation in the mass of historical groups themselves.

5. There are two main movements or relations to be considered in this organisation, the internal and the external, the relation of the parts to each other and to the whole, and the relation of the group itself to other groups. Let us begin with considering the action of the spiritual and material powers as operating between group and group. With regard, then, to these relations, whether the groups are themselves nations or groups within nations, the moment at which, by a newly developed organ, a group begins to exercise a voluntary action on other groups is the moment of its actuation by new motives, by the addition of interests of rivalry and ambition, reflective emotions, to those interests, whether direct or reflective, which actuate it already. It makes no difference what is the character of the group, whether spiritual or material; the organ which expresses its volition in respect to other groups must make, not only the material, but also those among the spiritual interests of the group which are founded in emotions of comparison, distinct objects of its volition. The ever recurring argument in justification of this is: the purposes of our group, our nation, our party, are good and for the benefit of mankind at large; therefore, the more power we possess, the better for those interests. It is a case of the general law, that strength is the de facto condition of an interest existing, the nature of the interest the justifying condition of the strength which supports it. But the question whe-

ther, in any particular case, the acquisition or consolidation of power is really justified by the interests which it professes to support, must be judged by considering the true nature of those interests, and the true relation between them and the supporting power. It may happen that the success of the power in question, in the objects of its ambition, may be the very circumstance which is to change its character as a supporter of the interests on which it professes to be founded. This is one of the cases in which names and professions most often conceal the nature of the things which they are employed to signify.

6. The new organ, exerting the will of the group as a whole, is in the case of a national group called the sovereign, and the nation a state. The terms, sovereign and sovereign state, are usually applied only to nations which are habitually and de facto independent, or not subject to any foreign power. But the office is the same, in point of nature, in the case of any group whatever; whatever is the purpose of the group as a whole, its governing organ is the organ of that purpose, and to that extent the sovereign of the group. Other groups can look only to this organ for its expression and enforcement. It must not be supposed that the sovereign of a group provides only for the material interests of the group. On the contrary it was shown, in the preceding paragraph, that motives of ambition were imported into the group, even though not included in its original purposes, by the mere fact of its organisation under a sovereign. The purpose of the sovereign is the promotion of all its interests, material and spiritual alike, the interests of all its sub-groups, in their several degrees; otherwise it would not be the sove-

reign of the whole. Hence there can be no greater mistake than to distinguish the so-called temporal and spiritual powers by assigning material interests to the one and moral interests to the other. The spiritual power when organised under a sovereign aims at material as well as moral, the temporal at moral as well as material interests. Call if you like the Church, the Bar, the Press, literary and scientific societies, guilds of artists, and so on, spiritual powers, but remember that they are also, and indeed chiefly, temporal powers, organised groups aiming at the promotion of their professed spiritual purposes only under condition of the prosperity and power of their societies themselves. Spiritual interests alone, or in their logical purity, have no home in groups organised under governing organs. Here is the cause of the eternally renewed antagonism between interests and groups which are really spiritual, on the one hand, and already organised societies called by the same names, on the other; the cause why newly proclaimed truths must make their way over the bodies of organisms which have once embodied the principles of those very truths. The mere development of knowledge, in one case with, in the other without, the clogging interests of an organised group, inevitably produces this antagonism in its onward progress. It is a problem for history, to show how this organisation of spiritual interests combines with the tendency to take names for things, with the permanence of external habits and symbols, compared to the feelings they are intended to express, in short with the easier comprehension of images than of emotions by the majority of men, to produce the full amount of resistance to the light exerted by societies called spiritual, when once they have been established and organised.

7. The governing organ or sovereign of every group provides on the other hand for all the interests, whether spiritual or material, of its members or subjects. There is no difference in this respect between the so-called temporal and spiritual powers. The distinction between such so-called spiritual and temporal powers as Church and State is an empirical distinction; the names are good as denotations, but false as connotations; the organised church is not more a spiritual power than the state, the state not more a temporal power than the church. The truly and purely spiritual power has no organisation under a governing body of any sort. The temporal power in its true sense exists wherever there exists such an organisation. The difference, therefore, between the modes of action of the spiritual forces and the temporal or rather the sovereign power, in respect to other groups, is very striking. The spiritual and material interests, it will be remembered, distinguished groups from each other, as spiritual and material groups or societies, in the spontaneous stage (§ 68. 8); but on passing into the voluntary stage, on the organisation of these groups under sovereigns representing their entire will, this distinction is replaced by a new one, that between the temporal and spiritual powers, as now defined in their true and logical sense. The spiritual power is or contains all those interests of a reflective emotional nature which are not provided for, or provided for insufficiently, by the temporal power, the sovereign of the group. Where its arm is too short, its touch too coarse, its vision too weak, to penetrate, there the spiritual

power steps in with its instinctive judgments, its imaginative purposes, its subtily communicated intuitions. Individuals are its organs, and individual character its source of power. It permeates all groups however hostile; where men are, there it is found, de jure supreme; it binds together those whom the temporal power would keep asunder. (La Mennais has expressed a similar thought, and drawn a similar distinction, in the preface to his translation of the Divina Commedia, as I have seen, since the above paragraphs were written, from an article in the Fortnightly Review, Jan. 1st, 1869, p. 24.)

8. I express no opinion whether or not the formation of a new spiritual power (so-called), such as Auguste Comte has aimed at founding, is probable, or whether or not it is desirable, questions which are beyond the scope of this work. Were such a power to arise, it would in my opinion offer only another instance of a temporal power characterised, from some of its functions, as spiritual, although its action might be on the whole beneficial, or even indispensable to the continued moral progress of mankind. The same law would then begin to come into operation, as in the case of former spiritual powers; that is, the true spiritual power would again be found in individuals as well without as within the organised hierarchy. Indeed Comte himself appears to admit almost as much when he speaks of "l'esprit universel de critique sociale," in those invaluable pages which he devotes to a sketch of the present condition of society, and to laying the foundation of a regenerated order, I mean the latter half of his 57th Leçon, Cours de l'Phil. Pos. vol. vi. Every enforcement or establishment obtained for morality by organising public

opinion is obtained at some cost of its freedom, that is, of its spirituality; and this loss of spirituality is the greater the greater the potency with which opinion enforces it.

9. Between states the spiritual power exerts itself in International Law. This is its province and its creation. International law is above sovereigns and sovereign states, but its de facto enforcement comes from its free recognition by them, as the law of a spiritual sovereign. Two features are the distinguishing characteristics of international law; it is distinguished from ethical or moral law by its commanding only overt or transeunt actions, although its scope contains immanent actions also, in common with all law as shown in § 84. 1, 2; and it is distinguished from other laws of overt action by the fact of its duties being all duties of imperfect enforcement. It is subordinate to the moral law, and must conform to its aims, and it must be established by temporal and national sovereigns, and derive its de facto sanction from their power. But when it is said that the aims of international law are governed by the moral law, it does not follow that all the duties of individuals are imposed upon nations by morality. Those duties which require personal affection, for instance, actions which can only flow from love, cannot be required of states, because they have not the single consciousness which alone feels this interest; a state as such can feel no love to another state as such, for love is a personal feeling between single individuals; a state therefore cannot be commanded to do acts of love, without being commanded to feel not only an immanent emotion, but an immanent emotion only possible to an individual. Acts

of benevolence and alliance are all in this kind that can be commanded, for these are feelings which every individual of a state can feel towards every individual of other states, without personal intercourse with them. Justice again is as universally possible as benevolence. Justice and benevolence are therefore the general or all-embracing duties imposed by morality on international law.

10. In the action between groups in the same state, the only difference to be observed between their duties and those of nations is, that they are governed and limited by the laws imposed by the sovereign of the state. Where these laws are silent or unenforced, there the conduct of group to group is governed in its overt acts by morality, is the subject of a kind of international law between the groups. A company or association for any purpose, within the state, is bound to observe rules of honour, equity, and benevolence, towards other companies or individuals. Morality takes up their conduct where the law of the state leaves it. And the same moral law, which is the de jure fountain of state law itself, is also the de jure fountain of that law which governs actions of smaller bodies of men too minute or too subtil to be regarded by legislative enactments applicable to the whole nation. Public opinion supplies the sanction of this intersocial law.

11. It is ideally possible, that the whole group of sovereign states which compose mankind may in the course of time develop an organ which shall represent them all in matters of international law, a tribunal invested by common agreement with power sufficient to enforce its decrees between state and state. If this should ever take place, and to what-

THE LOGIC OF POLITIC. 141

ever extent it takes place, international law would still not lose its two characteristic features. The states which had come to the agreement in question would become members, in certain judicial matters, of a federation; and their international law would to that extent become a constitutional one. If they so far coalesced as to form a single sovereign state, the only law having the two characteristics in question would be constitutional law, law within the state commanding duties of imperfect enforcement, but duties consisting in overt acts.

12. We enter here on the second branch of the enquiry, that of the action of the material and spiritual powers within groups and not between them, as proposed in paragraph 5. Since every group is broken up into subordinate groups or into individuals, and both are objects of the positive law of the state, the action of the spiritual power within groups has been sufficiently treated of, for the purposes of logic, in what has been said of the action of group on group in paragraph 10. The spiritual power as such has no direct and immediate action except on individuals; its office is to form public opinion to demand reform and improvement in existing de facto laws, and to lay by the same means the foundation of de jure validity of international and intersocial law. Intersocial law however having been sufficiently treated, the only action of spiritual power remaining is that which is manifested in the state as a whole, that is, in constitutional law; while, since the action of group on group within the state, so far as subject to law not intersocial, is governed by the positive law of the state sovereign, in adding the treatment of the positive law of the state (see § 90) to that of

its constitution we shall have completed the examination of the whole subject.

13. The constitution of a state (to speak first of cases where it is unwritten) grows up pari passu with that process of evolution and conflict of forces which determines, from time to time, the group or groups who are the sovereign of the state. The principles appealed to and acted on in this conflict, defined partly by the laws actually made in consequence of them, and partly by the ends to which they are perceived to tend by the most intelligent members of the state, are the constitution of that state; and thus the constitution grows up side by side with the sovereign, existing actually at every moment of history, and existing ideally, or as the perfection of the political action of the state, in the minds of statesmen and philosophic historians. The constitution may be defined as the law of harmonious development of all the forces and powers of a state; the idea of the constitution as the final or perfect condition of the state under this law, or of the law exemplified in the state, now imagined only, but imagined as capable of realisation and in order to be realised. The constitution is thus a work partly of spontaneous partly of voluntary action of the nation, having its foundations in the former, its modifications in the latter. To the state it is a law of nature which may be conquered by obeying it. Yet the true nature of the constitution and of its idea is perceived only by the spiritual not by the temporal power, by the sovereign only so far as the individuals who compose the sovereign are men of statesmanlike insight and volitions. Consequently there is no tribunal which can enforce the constitution by punish-

ing its infringement. Yet more and more of the true nature of the constitution may be known from time to time; and this knowledge be more and more widely spread. Public opinion is the only tribunal which can enforce constitutional law, and this it will do more or less, precisely in proportion as it has the knowledge of what the constitution is, and the will to aim at its fulfilment. For the distinction between this and constitutional law in another sense, namely, the law prescribing rights and duties to different members of the sovereign, see Austin's Province of Jurisprudence, p. 228, 2nd edit.

14. The establishment of a written document as organic law, as in the case of the Constitution of the United States of America, makes no difference with its two characteristics as constitutional law. The constitution of the United States is properly called by the writers in the Federalist "a limited constitution;" it is limited in being a particular form, a particular conception, of the constitution of those states, adopted out of that law of natural and ideal development which governs them, adopted soon after the time of their actual combination in the war of independence, and determined by the state of their knowledge to the best of their ability as a law which they would all agree to obey. A written document can no more exhaust the political constitution of a state, than a written book can exhaust the physiological constitution of a race. That stage of constitutional development reached at the time, by the United States, was arrested, written down, and voted, in order to prevent retrogression and secure union; it was reasonably hoped that, once tried, its incontestable benefits would assure its permanence. But

it is still a law enforced by the same persons as it is enforced upon; it has legal validity, de jure as well as de facto, only so long as those who have to obey choose to enforce it. The only difference between a written and an unwritten constitution is this, that in the former case a new function is added to the ordinary functions of the Judiciary, the function of interpreting and applying a written constitutional code. All positive law is an arresting and fixing of commands already supposed to be sanctioned by morality, a making good the moral ground already won in order to secure further progress; but constitutional and international law are not arrested and fixed in an equal degree with the rest, because the sovereign who establishes them, imposing them only on himself, enforces them by no punishment. To adopt Austin's expression, they are not law in the full sense, but positive legal morality. In the actual progress of mankind from law to morality, from external observances to internal duties, from legal bondage to moral freedom, these codes of positive legal morality stand mid way and prepare further domains for inclusion in morality. The sovereign is morally bound to observe and promote the constitution, with his best abilities, and in that which is to him its truest meaning.

15. The spiritual forces in any nation or state thus find their embodiment and become powers, not in any group or groups of men, but in constitutional and intersocial law, and between states in international law. Both as forces and as powers they reside in individuals, not in groups; but as powers they exist in the shape of definite doctrines and maxims held in common by many individuals, and

enforced by the opinion common to them, that is, by a public opinion. All groups of men on the other hand, whatever the interests may be which constitute them as groups, are, when they act as powers, exert a collective action, or exercise the volition of the group, homogeneous with the temporal power, as it is called, the sovereign power in a state. It now becomes the question, how the sovereign of a state is determined, what powers are those which from time to time become the organs of the state sovereignty. It has been already said, that this process of determination goes on pari passu with the development of the constitution. The organs or groups exercising the sovereignty are organs not only of the nation as consisting of groups, but also of the nation as developing its constitutive law. But the motive power in the determination of the organs of sovereignty is found only in the interests which animate the different groups composing the nation, and in the force which these groups exert in giving effect to those interests. It has been shown that the logical division of these groups gives, 1st, the three groups of labourers, profit-capitalists, and interest-capitalists, and 2nd, the three groups of churchmen, men of science, and artists. The mixture and superposition of these logical groups produce others with which history is more familiar; such, for instance, as landowners, bankers, merchants, manufacturers, farmers, retail dealers, skilled labourers, agricultural labourers, mechanics, unskilled labourers; clergy, lawyers, literary men, men of science, artists, educators; military men, both officers and privates, naval men with the same distinction. It is from the power exerted by these groups, and from the alliances formed between them, that results the choice of the sovereign, or organ representing the nation as a whole, and forming it into a sovereign state. But this power of the groups consists chiefly in means to supply or provide for the felt necessities of the time, whether their own or those of other groups. The need for defence from foreign nations and the pleasure taken in military adventure are two concurrent sources of power in the military group. Similarly the means of providing for religious wants of the community and the pleasure in establishing a religious cultus are concurrent sources of power in the clergy. It may often be the interest of several groups to favour each other's development. In that case they would tend to share the state government between them. They would naturally take the lead of groups which possessed less means of supplying the necessities of the time; and these other groups would be content to have their necessities so provided for. The felt necessity of providing for settlement of disputes between men or between groups, for the public administration of justice, would be another want which some group or other would find itself in a better position than others to supply; power or wealth already acquired is that which puts a group or an individual in such a position; and the pleasure of acting in that manner, together with the honour and other recompences attending it, is the motive for doing so. Hence a group of lawyers would become incorporated in the sovereign organ.—This brief sketch will be sufficient to show what is meant by saying, that the sovereign is determined by the mutual interest and relative power of groups.

16. An instance showing the operation of groups and interests in obtaining for themselves a share in the sovereignty, and developing the constitution of a state, may be found in the history of Rome, from the expulsion of the Kings to the unity of Italy under Roman power after the defeat of Pyrrhus, a period of about 250 years, described by Dr. Mommsen in the three first Chapters of the second Book of his History of Rome. He distinguishes three chief elements in the evolution. The first was the struggle for limiting the power of the magistrates; "this struggle was carried on within the burgess-body. Side by side with it another movement developed itself—the cry of the non-burgesses for equality of political privileges. Under this head are included the agitations of the plebeians, the Latins, the Italians, and the freedmen, all of whom—whether they may have borne the name of burgesses, as did the plebeians and the freedmen, or not, as was the case with the Latins and Italians—were destitute of, and laid claim to, political equality. A third distinction was one of a still more general nature; the distinction between the wealthy and the poor, especially such as had been dispossessed or were endangered in possession. * * * On these distinctions hinged the internal history of Rome, and, as we may conjecture, not less the history—totally lost to us—of the other Italian communities. The political movement within the fully-privileged burgess-body, the warfare between the excluded and excluding classes, and the social conflicts between the possessors and the non-possessors of land—variously as they crossed and interlaced, and singular as were the alliances they often produced—were nevertheless essentially and funda-

mentally distinct." Dr. Dickson's Eng. Translation, Vol. i. p. 269. ed. 1868.

17. When the sovereign government is established and organised, and its different functions distributed to different permanent bodies or individuals, recognised as permanent offices although the individuals filling them may change, still the same law continues to operate. Public opinion concerning the constitution has been formed, a line of public policy adopted, both in home and foreign matters, as well as the sovereign itself organised. The law then manifests its continued operation, not by new groups of forces in the nation becoming powers in the government or sub-organs in the sovereign, but by the change of men required by any apparently important change of measures. The transition from the Carolingian to the Capetian dynasty in France, as described by M. Guizot in his Civilisation en France, Vol. iii. p. 286, is an instance. One cause of a change in policy requiring a change of men is the distrust which the men representing the new or rising policy feel for the men who represent the old or vanishing policy; a distrust founded on two facts, 1st, the force of habit which must tend to make the old men act in the old ways, 2nd, the interest which they will feel in restoring the old state of things, as most obviously bound up with their own renown. The same cause, namely, the dislike to break with the old connection of ideas and throw themselves heartily into the new policy, acts also upon the representatives of the old; and this must tend to make them withdraw from active life and repose on their old laurels, awaiting the judgment of posterity.

18. The continuance of the same law is shown

again by the course which revolutions take in the modification of the parties who carry them forward. M. Guizot furnishes another instance in point, by his admirable exhibition of such modifications in the English Civil War under Charles I., in his Histoire de Civilisation en Europe, Leçon 13ᵐᵉ. "Trois partis principaux se montrent dans cette puissante crise; trois révolutions y étaient en quelque sorte contenues, et se sont successivement produites sur la scène. Dans chaque parti, dans chaque révolution, deux partis sont alliés et marchent ensemble, un parti politique et un parti religieux; le premier à la tête, le second à la suite, mais nécessaires l'un à l'autre; en sorte que le double caractère de l'événement est empreint dans toutes ses phases." These three parties were those of legal reform, with its religious adjunct, the party of church reform within episcopalian limits; of political reform with its Presbyterian adjunct; of republicanism with its Independent adjunct. Now the stand which the King made against the first party gave the preponderance within it to the second, with which it had to ally itself; the continued resistance of the royalists transferred the preponderance again in like manner to the third party; and the men of the third party remained in possession of affairs, on the victory which they had gained in common. The successive appearance of the three parties was due to the successive changes in public feeling and public opinion; it was the state of this feeling and opinion from time to time which gave the preponderance to each policy in turn; and in this feeling and opinion the men were not separated from the policy. The changing or developing course of public opinion and feeling, expressed by the growth of one party, the decay of another, is the real determinant of who are the men thrown into power by revolutions; and this by determining the policy in favour, and by the necessity of fixing on the ablest organs of that policy. The men can do nothing but take advantage of this changing course of public opinion, which they can do little to guide. Had the King succumbed at the beginning of the struggle, Cromwell could never have been Lord Protector.

19. The perception of the benefits of a settled government, a perception which is part of public opinion and feeling, is of course one of the strongest causes of its establishment and maintenance. This feeling of benefit is so strong, that an enormous amount of misconduct and failure in any long-established government is often required to overcome it; all established governments resting also upon interests of many subordinate groups, to whose members they assure a settled and desirable career. If any great interest is neglected by an established government, two remedies are open to it; it may either endeavour to have its interests regarded by the existing government, or it may endeavour to obtain for itself a larger share in the organisation of the sovereign power. The sovereign is constituted by the transformation of spontaneous forces into voluntary powers; it is the organisation of those powers. To allow a force to constitute itself as a power, that is, to organise itself, outside of the sovereign organism, is to create an imperium in imperio, dangerous and revolutionary in proportion to the force which is thus converted from a friend into an enemy. Such a revolutionary state of things appears to me to exist in this country at the present day. We are in the midst

of the struggle for incorporating the working class, the great bulk of the people, into the general organisation of the country. They, however, feel more strongly the desire for removing the various inconveniences which burden their industrial and social condition than the desire for political incorporation. From these motives they have not only begun but have carried to a great length the formation of a political organisation of their own, the system of Trades Unions; political, not because it was formed for the purpose of acting on the general political organisation of the country, but because it is already of itself such an organisation of the classes included in it, and must in time act as such upon the general organisation of the country, from which it is excluded. Now the Representation of the People Act, 1867, is an endeavour to incorporate the working classes into the general political organisation of the country; but its success, though ardently to be desired, is still problematical. It has to contend with a partial political organisation, an imperium in imperio, already constituted, with one which is conformable to the views of the classes embraced by it; while these classes on the other hand have hitherto manifested indifference to the general political organisation to which they are invited to accede, and to many at least of the political conceptions upon which it is based. The strength of the Trades Union system, as a political power, is derived from the general social and industrial discomfort of the classes which it organises; the question is, in what way this discomfort will be removed, or, failing that, in what way the force generated by it will find its outlet. Our present Parliamentary constitution seems to me, therefore, to be in a very critical position. But it must be remarked, that its rival, the Trades Union system, is itself of the same genus, a mode of government by as well as for the people, according to a distinction now about to be mentioned.

20. Sovereign governments have two ways of meeting dangers of the kind now contemplated, either to incorporate with themselves the representatives of the force or interest which is unsatisfied, or to provide for the satisfaction of this interest by measures of their own. To these two modes of redress for unsatisfied interests correspond two theories or systems of government, to one or the other of which, or to a combination of both, all actual governments will be found to belong. The first is the system of government by as well as for the people, a system which in small states may take place by direct interposition, as was the case at Athens, and at Rome in early times, but which in larger countries requires representatives elected by the people, as in England and the United States. The second is the system of government by a person or group of persons, as the committee of the people, governing in the name and for the interests of all, but without any considerable concurrence on the part of them or their representatives; of this France is perhaps the most prominent instance. The one system may be called, for brevity, Representative, the other Imperial. The difficulties of the latter system, compared to the former, consist chiefly in the separation between government and subjects, so that powerful interests may be neglected, and therefore may be becoming revolutionary, without this fact being attended to by the government; especially since the government must always be suf-

ficiently strong to repress minor outbreaks of discontent; and then, when the outbreak itself comes at last, it is so much the more violent, as in the first French Revolution. Its advantages are unity and continuity in the administration, so that a better administration, a speedier adoption of beneficial measures, may be expected. When a majority drawn from all classes and interests must first be convinced of the justice or expediency of any great measure, it must usually wait a far longer time for its adoption than when only a single man or a few men, of equally upright intentions, have to be convinced. But on the other hand, a great principle once adopted by a representative government, there is less danger of retrogression, since the long discussion of it must have served to secure its permanence in the habitual opinions of all the classes included in the representation.

21. The system of government prevalent in any country is the most important part of what is included in the term Constitution. The physical circumstances, the national character, the position relative to neighbouring nations, the events of its past history, and the habits of thought, feeling, and action, which those events have fostered, are the simultaneous or successive causes of the constitution of any state, and, as the chief part of the constitution, of the system of government therein established. To change from one of the two opposite systems of government to the other would be, in most cases, to run counter to the constitution of the state, to abandon its principles and its idea; and, since habits which have taken centuries to form cannot be changed in a generation, the endeavour to do so would, in most

cases, be to aim at the impracticable, and to introduce contradiction and anarchy into the state. Modify the practice, engraft improvements, but maintain the principle which is coeval with the state itself.

22. It remains to analyse the functions of government, abstracting from the system to which it may belong. The spiritual power is not organised in the form of groups of men, but of laws and ideas; individuals are its organs, their beliefs are its embodiment. All shapes are assumed by it, all domains permeated, all functions performed. No analysis, no classification, of its functions can be given beyond the analysis and classification of the functions of the individual. But the organ of the sovereign power in a state, since it exercises its functions by the appointment of separate individuals or groups to perform each of them, requires analysis and classification. This can be no other than that of the functions of voluntary redintegration in the individual; and for two reasons; first, that nothing else in the last resort can render the actions of men in groups intelligible, and we are therefore compelled, for the sake of knowing social and political functions, to compare them with, and see what relation they bear to, the functions of consciousness; otherwise they would be to us unreasoning functions, like those of inanimate objects. And secondly, that, every action of a group consisting of actions of the individuals composing it, and these being all complete actions by themselves, (see par. 3), there would be no sense in which the action of the group could be said to be a single voluntary action, unless the actions of the individuals composing it represented each one element or strain of a single concrete voluntary act, the other elements

or strains being abstracted from, and represented by the actions of the other individuals. It is, therefore, not a fanciful analogy between an individual and a body politic that is here relied on, but the essential unity of nature between the two, the body politic being an aggregate of individuals.

23. It is clear that all the action of government is included in practical reasoning and the transeunt actions consequent upon it. But these transeunt actions, strictly taken, are not the objects of our enquiry. It is not the action of muscle on pens and paper, telegraphs, steam engines, guns, and so on, that is the object of discussion. This action enters into practical reasoning and into the action of government only so far as it is known, that is, as an object of reasoning; the actions themselves are events in the domain of physical science. It is the reasoning process itself, as the determinant of these known events, which we have to do with. If then we turn to the analysis of practical reasoning given in § 56. 6, we find it thus distributed:

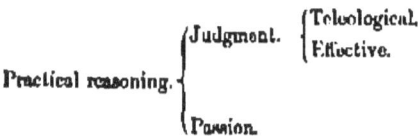

Now all judgment is, as shown in §§ 54-56, a balance of interests. If the feelings are preponderant over the intellect, the balance is struck by the preponderating feeling, and the action is one of passion; if the intellect preponderates, the act is one of judgment. But in a group of men deliberating about a common course of action, the feelings are represented by individuals; each individual becomes the organ

Book II.
Ch. III.
¶ 69.
The voluntary organisation of Society.

of an interest; and there may be interests of intellect or judgment, as well as interests of feeling. The balance of interests determines the decision of the group; and it is plain that one or more interests may be so strongly felt as to carry all before them, overpowering the interests of judgment. In this case the act of the group will be an act of passion; in the opposite case, one of judgment. But there is no function set apart for acts of passion in government, since it is recognised as what it is, a weakness and an evil in a deliberating group to be carried away by passion, which is only too likely to manifest itself, without artificial aid. The only functions established in government are the two functions of judgment, judgment of ends, and judgment of means to ends already determined; teleological and effective judgment. The boundaries of these two functions may be differently drawn, in respect to the acts and objects included in them; but the division will always be made at this point, always fall between acts and objects considered as ends and acts and objects considered as means. That is to say, the only ultimate division of the functions of government is into legislative and executive functions. The same persons may, it is true, often be found uniting both functions, but the functions are nevertheless distinct; and it is a maxim of sound policy, at least in all states organised on the principle of government by as well as for the people, that these functions, and the judicial function as well, should be kept in separate hands. See The Federalist, Nos. 47 to 51 inclusive.

24. The judicial function is properly a branch, though a most important branch, of the executive. It is the application and enforcement of the laws

made by the legislative; but it is a function of reasoning and of judgment, discriminating what cases really fall under particular laws, what laws are applicable to particular cases; and, in civil matters, what the claims of two or more suitors are, under the provisions of established law. The functions of the executive not included in the judicial may properly be called administrative; they consist in giving the orders requisite to carry out the ends, the modification of the old laws, determined by the legislative, and in appointing officers to fulfil these orders. The collecting and disbursement of the revenue, the support and direction of the army and navy, and of subordinate governors generally, form the largest part if not the whole of these functions. The table of functions of government, then, stands thus:

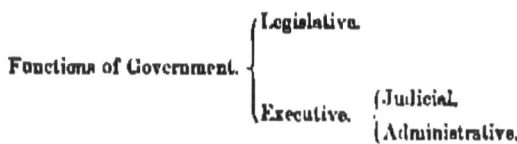

25. Leaving the judicial function of government to find its place in the following §, the action of the legislative and administrative functions must be here considered. This is in reality nothing more than a continuation of the same action which we have hitherto been analysing; the course taken by the government when formed is, like its formation, determined by the conflict of interests and the preponderance of one or some among them. And this is true under both systems, Imperial as well as Representative.

26. This may be shown from passages in the history of France, in respect to the former, the imperial,

system of government. The line distinguishing legislative from administrative functions is a varying one; administration being the carrying out aims already chosen, or the adapting of means to ends in government, measures which in one country are classed as legislative in another will be classed as administrative, and conversely. The system of government for but not by the people has the necessary consequence of making almost all measures appear administrative, all measures, that is, which do not make a change in the main functions of the sovereign itself. In government by as well as for the people, on the other hand, many most minute regulations are classed as legislative, the administration being confined to their actual carrying out, by appointment of subordinate officers, and by directing their conduct in detail. English Acts of Parliament, for instance, often contain a mass of minute regulations, which in France are matters of administration. Acts of Parliament are our Bureaux.

27. This premised, it is easily seen that the influence which parties or interests exert in effecting a change of measures must be exerted, in the one case within the legislative body, in the other upon the administrative body and from without it. This latter mode of action is seen in the history of the early States General in France. M. Aug. Thierry in his Essai sur l'Histoire du Tiers Etat, Chap. ii., having given an account of the States General of 1355 and 1356, of the resolutions passed by them and accepted by the king, and of the speedy dissolution of their power; and having pointed out that this was the moment from which the social history of France, complete in its elements, flows forward in a single stream; pro-

ceeds thus: "Voilà pour la société; quant aux institutions, la royauté, dans sa prérogative sans limites, les recouvre et les embrasse toutes, hors une seule, les états généraux, dont le pouvoir mal défini, ombre de la souveraineté nationale, apparait dans les temps de crise pour condamner le mal présent et frayer la route du bien à venir. De 1355 à 1789, les états, quoique rarement assemblés, quoique sans action régulière sur le gouvernement, ont joué un rôle considérable comme organe de l'opinion publique."

28. Another instance to the same effect is found in the joint action taken by the University and the Municipality of Paris, in the year 1413, and their forcing from the king the Ordonnance of May 25. In three months the Ordonnance was annulled. M. Thierry, having given the account of these events, in Chap. iii., says at page 70, speaking of the language held by the Municipality, "C'étaient là de nobles paroles dignes d'annoncer la grande charte de réforme, œuvre commune du corps de Ville et de l'Université; mais, cette loi administrative de la vieille France, il se trouva des hommes pour la concevoir, il ne s'en trouva point pour l'exécuter et la maintenir. Les gens sages et rompus aux affaires n'avaient alors ni volonté ni énergie politique." But these efforts were not without their effect; the substance of the reforms demanded and prepared by these efforts of public opinion was realised later by the ministers of Charles VII., taken for the most part from the Tiers Etat. "L'esprit de réforme et de progrès qui, en 1413, avait brillé un instant et n'avait pu rien fonder, parce qu'un parti extrême en était l'organe, reparut, et modela sur un plan nouveau toute l'administration du royaume, les finances, l'armée, la justice et

la police générale." page 74. The ordonnances to which M. Thierry here refers date from 1439 to 1460, the year before the accession of Louis XI.

29. Turning now to the case of government on the representative system, the debates and conflicts upon public measures are subject to the same law; that is, their issue is determined by the strength of conflicting interests. Take for instance a question of the present day, which perhaps is not even yet finally decided, the question of appointment to offices by competitive examination. Examination was the interest of the increasing middle class, patronage of the class already in possession of the appointments. Discussion of the merits of the two systems was the mode in which the strength of the two interests was tried. Each party tries to make out a case; each party is convinced of the merits of its own case; the triumph of the strongest interest is apparently the triumph of reason and of the true merits, just as the conflict of interests is apparently a conflict of arguments. But why this distinction into real and apparent, real motive and apparent discussion? For the same reason that each interest is reasonable in the eyes of the person feeling it, namely, that every emotion has its inseparable framework, and that communication between individuals by words is a comparison of frameworks. But while we insist on this logic for all cases of debate between parties, while we look upon parliament, for instance, as the arena for trying the strength of interests much more than for weighing reasons, it must not be forgotten that one important element in the strength of every interest is the reasonableness of its framework, its provable conduciveness to the general benefit. To fail in

"making out the case" is to palsy the strength of the interest, because the interest is thus shown to be incompatible with the interest of the country. It becomes less honourable to maintain it; its supporters diminish both in number and in vigour; and the victory remains with its opponents.

30. It is requisite in the next place to examine the groundwork of a phenomenon which is found in the political action of all free nations, the general distinction into and opposition between two political parties, under whatever names they may appear, the party of conservation and that of progress, the right and the left in political assemblies. Whatever may be the particular interests, represented by particular parties or groups, these are all pervaded by, and have a constant tendency to group themselves under, two general directions, one which presses for advance, innovation, or improvement, the other which resists and criticises all such attempts. What are the ultimate causes of this phenomenon?

31. The first and most obvious cause is the natural alliance between interests which have already obtained a position in the state, as established interests, between the various satisfied classes, against an alliance equally natural between interests and classes which are as yet inadequately established and satisfied. This forms the groundwork and nucleus of the two parties round which individuals rally, according as their personal interests lead them. The attractive influence of the conservative party is exercised on individuals by their finding a personal career open to them in business or in professions as they are at any present time constituted; their attention is turned away from political improvements, and fixed

upon the means of making the best they can for themselves of institutions as they are. Those on the other hand who find a less satisfactory personal career in institutions as they are seek to change them in those points where they are most incommoded, and thus gravitate to the party of progress. This is the natural and spontaneous mode of formation of the two parties. But there are other members belonging to each who have, as it were, taken service with them, making political action with one or the other party their profession, and seeking to advance in their personal career by means of the political services which they render to their party. They are a kind of Condottieri of political warfare; except that they rarely change their side.

32. But the formation of the two parties is not yet fully described. The main line between them is drawn by satisfied and unsatisfied interests; but with this line coincides another of an entirely different character. This is the distinction between the two intellectual dispositions, active and sluggish, drawn in § 62. Intellects that are naturally active are always in practical matters on the look-out for improvements, always suggesting some change, always aiming at some end. These fall naturally into the party of progress, unless either their aims, being mainly personal, are satisfied by institutions as they are, or their affections are already engaged in favour of some great public interest already established; in neither of which cases is their intellectual activity directed to political improvement. An active intellect, when unbiassed by personal ambition and unoccupied by a special party object, and thus set free to aim at the general public advantage, becomes as a

rule, and with the exception stated in the following par., a member of the party of progress. The active intellects which belong to the conservative party are, as a rule, intellects whose activity is not directed to the general improvement of the nation, the special aim of politic, but to some minor purpose which is subordinate and may become obstructive. The sluggish intellects on the other hand fall naturally into the party of conservation, from the mere force which is exercised over them by habitual images and established ways of thought.

33. But the formation of the two parties is not even yet quite exhausted; a further distinction is observable between them; and it must be remarked that each distinction, being a distinction between traits of character, is a distinction of motives, that is, of the motives which may lead particular persons to belong to either party. Within the active intellectual disposition there are two modes of thought, described in § 63 under the names of the constructive and the accumulative; the former of these gravitates to conservatism, from the wide, organising, statical, view of political action which is natural to it; the latter to liberalism, from the equally natural desire to keep constantly aiming at the next improvement in prospect. Only the elite of the conservative party become conservatives from possessing this constructive tendency of thought; but it is the bulk of the liberals, of those at least who belong to the satisfied classes, that is probably drawn to the liberal party by the prevalence of the accumulative. At the same time, this distinction affords an explanation of the often observed fact, that liberals themselves tend to become conservative with increasing experience; a

circumstance which cannot be entirely and in all cases explained by the cooling of youthful enthusiasm, or by the increasing dominion of habit. It is a very different conservatism from the ordinary kind which is either founded upon constructive modes of thought, or which, being so founded, has taken up liberalism into its own nature. Mere conservatism has no ideal but order, mere liberalism none but progress. A certain union and interpenetration of both, whichever of the two names it may bear, an union which has for its ideal both ends in combination, is requisite for perfect statesmanship; but such statesmanship would with difficulty win the appreciation of a popular assembly.

34. Finally must be considered what may be called perhaps the vital principle of nations, that which determines, or to which is attached, their rise, progress, and decay. The life of nations has been often compared to the life of animal or vegetable organisms; a most misleading comparison. It is rather to the life of character in individuals, the rise, progress, and decline, of the functions analysed in Book i. Chap. iv., that the life of nations should be compared. We have seen in that Chapter the importance to the individual of what was called a career, § 72; the same circumstance is all-important to nations, in order not indeed to the existence of a national life, but to its being a healthy and vigorous one. As the character of an individual rises and expands with the aims which he sets before his ambition, and declines in energy and dignity when, from whatever cause, no purpose worth living for remains to him, so a healthy national life is first kindled by the perception of some great national purpose, is kept

alive at its different stages by the unfolding of some new goal to be reached, and declines when, from causes either in its own organisation or in its relation to the nations around it, no further prospect is opened which as a nation it can hope to realise.

35. It is not only in nations that this law holds good; every group voluntarily formed is governed by it. As shown in parr. 1-3, every organised group or party is formed for a certain end or purpose; the common end brings its members together into a group and determines its constitution; the end attained or proved to be unattainable, the group dissolves; the end modified or supplanted by a new end requires the group to be differently organised. A career proportioned to their powers is therefore all-important for the healthy vitality of societies, large or small; a society outliving or renouncing its general aim as a collective society becomes eo ipso disorganised, a mere congeries of minor societies, groups, or even individuals, living for their minor or even only for their personal aims; the power of the nation is then exerted merely to secure the enjoyment of its several members, the classes or individuals who compose it. And according to the strength and permanence of the old organisation, supposing it incapable of finding a new career on the exhaustion of its old one, will be its force in repressing the formation of new organs informed with new life.

36. It is seldom that nations have no career open which a bystander can discern; the difficulty is for them to find one proportioned to their forces, one which sufficient numbers of the nation can discern and organise themselves to attain. The only career offered may be beyond their powers either of appre-

ciation or of volition; that is, they may want statesmen to discern it, or spontaneous forces of which statesmen can dispose. The struggle for existence in early stages of national life, and in later the ambition of conquest or of commerce, compel a nation to put forth its powers of endurance and activity; it is when a career is no longer forced upon it by circumstances, but must be adopted if at all by an effort of will, that the great trial comes whether the nation can renew its youth, or whether the elements of the next stage of history will spring out of its dissolution. Rome, for instance, was unequal to the great career which her conquests had opened for her, the career of incorporating into an organic whole the nations included in her empire. She perceived and attempted the task, but failed to cope with it owing to the advancing decay of her internal organisation; and, on the dissolution of the Empire, a society, foreign to the state, but which had silently grown up as an imperium in imperio within its limits, the Christian Church, was found alone occupying a suitable position, and possessed of sufficient strength, to take up the glorious and difficult inheritance.

37. Nations count their age not by ancestry but from the era of their foundation; from the time when they have shaken themselves free from the organisation of the past, and laid new bases for the future, that is, when they have entered on a new career. The United States of America, though inheriting the experience of England, are a young nation because entering on a new career, with institutions framed in anticipation of it. To organise the Union is the career immediately before her. India may one day spring to a new national life from an impulse re-

ceived from her British conquerors. The states of
Western Europe may open for themselves a new
career by the attempt to combine into one great re-
public, according to Auguste Comte's magnificent conception. Wherever a new career is entered on by
a nation, there a new organisation arises, a new life
begins, and the powers of all its members are braced
by the reaction, and strung to loftier effort.

§ 90. 1. It is requisite in the next place to attempt the general classification of Law itself, considered as the body of commands imposed by the
sovereign on the people of a sovereign state. The
formation of the sovereign and its organisation, its
gradual development out of the spontaneous forces
of society, have been already given; and it has been
shown generally in what manner a Constitution is
formed, pari passu with this development, of which
in fact it is the law or method. The classification
of the positive law of a state, in relation to the organ
imposing and the groups or individuals obeying it,
will complete the sketch of the whole subject. Law
generally, being command of transeunt or overt action, is first distinguishable into commands of perfect
and commands of imperfect obligation or enforcement. The former alone are positive law. Constitutional law, which is well called by Austin positive
constitutional morality, being enforced solely by public opinion both on sovereign and on people, is a part
of the latter. International law is another branch
of commands of imperfect enforcement; and both
together are excluded from positive law, which alone
is now to be examined. (See § 89. 9-11). When
the sovereign actually and habitually enforces obligations which would otherwise belong to constitu-

tional or international law, they become eo ipso parts of positive law, having thenceforward a perfect obligation or sanction. The increasing enforcement of constitutional and international laws by sovereigns is one process by which morality increases its dominion, by transformation into positive law, by laying behind it in its progress a field where its dictates are now enforced by sanctions; while the increasing conformity to constitutional and international law on the part of sovereigns, in obedience solely to public opinion, without giving them a positive and habitual sanction, is a recognition that there is a moral above any legal code, a spiritual above the sovereign power; being in fact a recognition of the supremacy of Law itself, in its widest sense, as the true sovereign, instead of the personal organs who are from time to time its ministers.

2. Constitutional and International law thus excluded from the survey, the question arises, in what way to classify the commands, that is, the acts and forbearances commanded by positive law. In the first place, every command imposes a duty or obligation on the person or persons to whom it is directed; and the person or persons towards whom the duty or obligation is to be performed are invested with a corresponding right. The acts and forbearances commanded by law are duties in the persons on whom, rights in the persons towards whom, they are imposed. The question is, whether to seek the principle of a first classification in the nature of the acts and forbearances themselves, or in their incidence, that is, in the classes of persons on whom or towards whom they are commanded. This requires some preliminary observations.

3. There is no more philosophical suggestion in Auguste Comte's writings than that in which he urges, that Law should be approached and its object-matter arranged from the point of view of duties, and not from that of rights. (Cours de l'Phil. Pos. Leçon lvii. Vol. vi. p. 454, ed. 1864.) And this is entirely in harmony with a dictum of Austin, whose invaluable work on Jurisprudence has given me the clue to all that I may be enabled here to advance. In a marginal note printed at page 485, Vol. ii. he says: "Law (or the Science of Law—Jurisprudence) cannot be expounded without dividing it into parts. The division most in use is founded upon an enumeration of the several sorts of Rights; but, inasmuch as right correlates with obligation, an enumeration of the several sorts of Obligations would be just as good a basis for a division. Both Right and Obligation (*i.e.* legal right and obligation) being creatures of Law, the notion of Law (or of a politically sanctioned Rule) ought to be placed in front (or to be made the *punctum saliens*) of a division."

4. Law, then, by one and the same command imposing duties on one person and conferring rights on another, it is open to us to consider it as consisting either of a collection of duties or of a collection of rights. It will be shown farther on, that the former method alone has the advantage of harmonising law with ethic in a single logical system, (par. 53), and so is to be preferred on that ground; but the preference may also be justified on grounds more decisive. Rights, as Comte clearly saw, cannot be taken as ultimate or indecomposable phenomena in law; they require, because they admit, analysis; and this analysis is into the duties, the acts or forbearances, im-

posed on other persons, the claim to which constitutes the rights. In order to define any person's right, recourse must be had to the acts or forbearances imposed on other persons. Names of rights are "second intentions," the "first intentions" of which are the duties into which they are analysable. To take rights and not the corresponding duties as the ultimate phenomena of law is to stop short of a complete analysis, and to make "entities of abstractions."

5. That Comte was correct in referring the conception of rights to that of will (Politique Pos. Vol. ii. Ch. i. p. 87), is made evident by the following passage in von Savigny's great work, the System des heutigen Römischen Rechts, Book ii. § 52: "Von dem nun gewonnenen Standpunkt aus erscheint uns jedes einzelne Rechtsverhältniss als eine Beziehung zwischen Person und Person, durch eine Rechtsregel bestimmt. Diese Bestimmung durch eine Rechtsregel besteht aber darin, dass dem individuellen Willen ein Gebiet angewiesen ist, in welchem er unabhängig von jedem fremden Willen zu herrschen hat." And again in § 53, in arguing against the admission into law of the so-called Urrecht, or Rights of Man, he says: "indem z. b. Eigenthum und Obligationen nur Bedeutung und Werth für uns haben als künstliche Erweiterung unsrer eignen persönlichen Kräfte, als neue Organe, die unserm Naturwesen künstlich hinzugefügt werden." The conception of duties being a further analysis and explication of the corresponding rights does not seem to have occurred to him. He argues indeed against basing Jurisprudence upon the conception of Wrongs, or violation of rights, which he truly says would be beginning with a negative no-

tion, with one which presupposes the positive notion of rights capable of violation. But if the conception of rights is logically prior to that of wrongs, so also that of duties is logically prior to that of rights; duties offer a deeper foundation as well as a more complete analysis. If legal commands are to be our "punctum saliens," rights are conferred only by commanding duties; duties are commanded immediately, rights derivatively; and to know what are the rights of one person you must ask what are the duties of other persons, for the rights have no other definition.

6. So far then is made good; the acts and forbearances commanded are to be considered as duties, not as rights. But this does not help us to distinguish duties from each other, or to arrange them into classes. To do this it is requisite to attend to the persons commanding and the persons commanded. This will afford at least a primary division of laws, the members of which may then be examined afresh for further distinctions. Looking back to the history of law, it is found to arise from the combination of the sense of justice with a de facto power enforcing it; (see § 33. 2). But wherever there is such a de facto power there is a virtual sovereign; and the two most elementary kinds of justice we can imagine are, therefore, that which the sovereign enforces on individuals towards itself, and that which it enforces on individuals towards each other. Accordingly we have two main branches of positive law:

1. Obligations towards the State, called State or Public Law.
2. Obligations of private individuals towards individuals, called Civil or Private Law.

7. The persons towards whom the obligations are imposed are thus the ground of our primary distinction. But, inasmuch as the infringement of obligations is visited with penalties, which are the sanction of the obligations, each class of obligations brings with it a class of penalties; or in other words, the class of penalties depends on the class of obligations. "The difference between Crimes and Civil Injuries, is not to be sought for in a supposed difference between their tendencies, but in the modes wherein they are respectively pursued, or wherein the sanction is applied in the two cases," says Austin, Vol. ii. Lect. xvii. Yet this is not precisely true, in my opinion; it is not the mode in which the injuries are pursued, or in which the sanction is applied, but the persons towards whom the obligations are enforced by the sanctions, which is the circumstance distinguishing the commands of criminal or public from the commands of civil law. It is because the persons are different that the modes of pursuit and punishment are so. The sovereign is invested with the persona of the community at large, and the rights which belong to the community, or the duties owed to the community by individuals, are coincident with those obligations, those acts and forbearances, which the sovereign enforces towards itself. So far from regarding, with Austin, absolute obligations as obligations without correlative rights (Lect. xvii. Vol. ii.), I hold that these obligations are correlative with rights in the sovereign as the representative of the whole community, being obligations imposed towards as well as by the sovereign; and am thus enabled to reject this apparent exception to the otherwise complete correlation between rights and duties. Since

all laws enforce overt acts by positive sanctions, and all aim at some benefit, the person benefited by the law must necessarily be invested with a right. He may choose to forego the benefit, but he cannot help being clothed with the right. The reason which forbids us to attribute legal duties, in the strict sense, to the sovereign, namely, the inefficiency of a merely self-inflicted sanction, does not apply to legal rights. The sovereign is the source of all obligations, and therefore those which it imposes on itself are merely moral, or of imperfect enforcement; but those which it imposes on others are legal, or of perfect enforcement, notwithstanding that some of them are imposed by it on others towards itself.

8. It is the conception of Law as the body of commands imposed by a sovereign which leads us to begin with distinguishing in it the two branches, Public and Civil, since these are the two main branches into which the commands themselves are divided in their practical enunciation and application. But it must be observed that this is a distinction between legal institutions, Rechtsinstitute, to borrow von Savigny's terms, and not between legal relations, Rechtsverhältnisse; that both the branches are equally and alike founded in a general logic of the science of jurisprudence, consisting of distinctions between Rechtsverhältnisse, or legal relations generally, which I propose to examine in connection with the second branch, that of Civil Law. The Logic of Jurisprudence is a classification of legal relations generally; but while civil law, from its greater complexity, is not intelligible without this logic, the simpler relations between sovereign and subjects, belonging to public law, are easily understood by themselves, al-

Book II.
Ch. III.

§ 90.
Analysis and
classification
of Law.

Public Law.

though they fall under the logic as cases of legal relations between Persons. (See par. 23). The advantage of this arrangement is, that we gain some insight into the nature of law in its practical shape, as command imposed by a political superior, before approaching it from the abstract side as the logic of legal relations.

9. The next question concerns the distinctions arising within public law itself. It is clear that many, if not all, of the obligations contained in it are owed towards private individuals, as well as towards the state, that it is only by injuries to private persons that the state is injured. Wherever there is a duty imposed directly to the state, there is a public law and a public obligation; but this does not hinder the same duty being also due to private persons. The persons towards whom the duties are imposed help us therefore no farther in distinguishing the laws from one another. The next distinction, within the class of public laws, must be drawn from differences in the persons upon whom the obligations are imposed. The state imposes duties towards itself, but it imposes different duties upon different persons. In the first place it imposes some duties upon all classes of persons alike; in the next it imposes special duties upon special classes, classes which are constituted as distinct from others by the imposed duties themselves. These special classes have thus two kinds of duties; and their special duties may be towards other individuals as well as towards the state. When any persons are thus singled out and laden with special duties, imposed upon them by the sovereign power, they become invested with some part of the power of the sovereign itself, as its organs or instru-

ments; they stand midway between it and the mass of subjects, owing special duties to both, and having special rights in the shape of special submissions imposed on the mass of subjects towards them in that character.

10. The branches of State or Public Law appear accordingly to be two:

1. General, or General Penal Law,
2. Special, or Administrative Law.

The first commands forbearances almost exclusively, the second commands acts as well. In the first we have the acts which every individual, in his private capacity, is forbidden to do towards other individuals; in the second the acts which officials, of any kind, are bound both to do and to refrain from, as well as those acts which individuals are bound to do and to refrain from towards officials. The second therefore includes all those parts of the machinery of government, sometimes characterised incorrectly as Constitutional Law, which consist of the duties, rights, and functions, of the special organs of the sovereign power itself, whether these organs are of great or small power and dignity. For instance, the rights, duties, and functions, of the Houses of Lords and of Commons, of the Crown, of the Judiciary, as well as those of jurors, magistrates, police, soldiers, revenue collectors, in short of employees of every description, are equally included under its provisions. The power of the sovereign collectively enforces the duties, which embody these rights and these functions, upon each of its special organs, whatever may be its rank or importance. Each organ has a code of duties, and a code of rights consisting in duties imposed on other persons, or other organs, to which it is legally bound to conform; it is only where these codes cease, or become indefinite in their provisions, that Constitutional Law begins; it is only where they are extended or transgressed by a de facto power that Constitutional Law is altered. The maintenance of the Constitutional Law means the tacit exertion of the collective power of the sovereign in enforcing the observance of administrative law. The legal development of the Constitution means the gradual changes introduced into administrative law, in accordance with the spirit of the constitution, by the public organs of the sovereign already established for that purpose. And in this working of the machinery of the state, the true sovereign is embodied not in this or that organ, the Houses, the Crown, or the Judiciary, but in the Law itself, which is common to them all, and which only their collective power can enforce;

> " A matchless form of glorious government,
> In which the sovereign laws alone command,
> Laws, 'stablished by the public free consent,
> Whose majesty is to the sceptre lent."

11. The general branch of public law is that which enforces acts and forbearances, but chiefly forbearances, on individuals or groups of individuals towards others, in their private or unofficial capacity. The distinction here available for further classification is derived from the importance of the act or forbearance commanded, the injury done or threatened by violation of the command, or, in other words, by the gravity of the offence. General penal law falls thus into two classes, commands constituting and punishing Crimes, and those constituting and punishing Misdemeanours. As already observed, the state is

injured in these cases only by and through injury done to individuals; but this does not prevent the injury being really done to the state. State officers are the proper persons to set the law in action, in order to enforce these obligations. Nevertheless, the double incidence of the injury opens a door for the state, if it sees fit, to allow the individual who is injured to perform the office of the public or state prosecutor. But this alters nothing in the nature of the commands, or in the penalties attached to them; they are defined by the person to whom they are owed in the first instance, the sovereign; and the sovereign's rights are not destroyed by the care of enforcing them being committed to private persons. But when the same acts or forbearances are owed at once to the sovereign and to private persons, they are unavoidably included twice over in the system of law, once as part of public, once as part of civil law. They have or may have two distinct kinds of consequences, the one in the shape of a public penalty, the other in that of damages for a civil injury; and these two consequences are not necessarily of equal gravity. An injury may be of very slight criminality, and yet inflict very heavy losses, or it may inflict but small loss and yet be of a high degree of criminality; as, for instance, forgery of securities to a small amount. When an individual enforces the law in such cases, he may do so either on the ground of a civil or a public injury. In the latter case he virtually steps into the place of the sovereign, foregoing for the time the reparation due to himself; in the former he enforces the reparation which the civil law attaches to the civil injury. The penalties for public offences are inflicted by, and if money fines

BOOK II.
CH. III.
§ 90.
Analysis and
classification
of Law.
Public Law.

are paid to, the sovereign; those for civil injuries are reparations made to the private individuals injured. Thus not only may the same act or forbearance form a part of civil as well as of public law, but also its commission or neglect, whether prosecuted by the sovereign or by an individual, may be attended with two kinds of penalties, civil damages or state-inflicted punishment. We may see from this how impracticable it would have been to derive the primary division of legal commands from a consideration of the acts and forbearances commanded, apart from the persons towards whom they are imposed.

12. The two branches of public law, namely, General Penal Law and Administrative Law, may either be made into two distinct codes, or thrown together into a single code. In the latter case they will form its two main divisions; and to both alike, and in either case, the distinction between greater and minor offences, crimes and misdemeanours, will be applicable. The Penal Code of Louisiana is an instance of the latter method. By Art. 76 of that Code: "There are two divisions of offences, establishing distinctions drawn, the one from the degree of the offence, the other from its object. By the first division, all offences are either *Crimes* or *Misdemeanors*. By the second, they are *public* or *private* offences." The latter distinction is the one employed as a basis of classification, and all offences are arranged under fifteen general heads of public, and six of private offences. But it is immediately added, in Art. 81, that this division of offences "is intended only for the establishment of order in the arrangement of the code; each offence will be hereinafter particularly defined and illustrated; and no act or

omission is an offence, which does not come within some one of those definitions as they are explained and illustrated."

13. This is an instance of the true method of legal classification; the principles of distinction are first laid down, then the particular commands, duties, and penalties, enumerated, and lastly these are classified by reference to the principles of distinction. The two extremes are thus harmonised by the classification, without it being attempted to evolve either of them out of the other. Were it attempted to evolve the commands and penalties out of the principles of distinction, a complicated and artificial system, unfit for daily use, might be expected to result; while it would be almost impossible to educe true principles of distinction from the mere consideration of an immense mass of commands and penalties.

14. The great practical requisite either for a code or for a system of uncodified law is, that its divisions should follow those into which the acts and events fall, to which it is to be applied; so that the treatment prescribed by law to each act should be found under its own head in the code, without having to compare several heads and construct, out of their conflicting prescriptions, the law applicable to the case. The law should be as completely distributed as the acts of life, and the artificial classification of the one should be conformed to the natural classification of the other. This is much more nearly attainable in Public than in Civil law; but the principle should be the same in both; and the ground already won, in examining the classification of the former, will supply the clue by which to attempt that of the latter more complicated case.

Book II.
Ch. III.

§ 90.
Analysis and classification of Law.

Civil Law.

15. The essential difference of Civil Law from Public consists in this, that it has not only to command and forbid certain acts, which it may define for itself, leaving all other acts alone, but has also to permit as well as command and forbid; and therefore to regulate all possible acts of human life, to declare and define what acts it will recognise as legally valid for the purposes proposed by the doers of them; what legal effects follow the doing or neglect of particular acts upon the respective rights and estates, not only of the parties to them, but also of third persons; what characters and properties are attached to persons and things from different circumstances, such for instance as birth, age, and locality. All possible circumstances and events of life are to be dealt with by civil law; it cannot exclude from its purview by excluding from its definitions; and for this reason, that the sovereign itself is not a party but a judge between parties, and both sides must have justice done them. The sovereign is a party in public law, and fixes its own rights, the duties of others, beforehand; whatever it omits expressly to command or forbid it is supposed to permit. But in civil law it is precisely this line between the parties which must be drawn afresh in every debated instance; a permission accorded to one party is a permission denied to the other; the extension of rights on one side is a diminution of rights on the other. The great purpose of civil law is to give effect to the intentions of men so far as they are just, and to ascertain and enforce justice between them, where these intentions are in conflict. It must therefore lay down rules to regulate the whole of life.

16. It is a consequence of this greater extent of

field, that the enactments of public law depend in a great measure upon those of civil. Before the infringement of rights in property, for instance, can be treated as a penal offence, those rights in property must be defined, and then their intentional violation can be punished. There is indeed one additional circumstance here, which makes the case more complicated, namely, intention and the proof of intention; so far public law is more complicated than civil; but, on the other hand, the right of property and its intentional infringement once shown, public law has no more to do than to punish the offender, while civil law has to ascertain and enforce the various rights and duties which may be the consequences of his act. For instance, a sale, though fraudulent on the part of the seller, may give rights in the thing sold to bona fide purchasers, who then have rights as against the original possessors, whose rights have been fraudulently infringed. Fraud then is a less complicated matter in public law than in civil, notwithstanding that intention to defraud is involved in the question, and apart from its depending partly for its definition upon the rights and duties created by civil law; for public law makes abstraction of all the legal consequences of acts, except so far as they affect the position of the agent towards the sovereign. Everything else belongs to civil law.

17. Notwithstanding the greater extent and complexity of the undertaking, the problem in civil law is of the same nature as in public. It is to enumerate and classify the commands, acts and forbearances commanded, in other words, the Obligations imposed, in such a way that they shall be immediately applicable to any case which may arise in

*Book II.
Ch. III.
§ 20.
Analysis and classification of Law.
Civil Law.*

ordinary life, calling for a decision between conflicting claims. Each act in daily life stands in a manner separate from others, and has a history, causes and consequences, motives and results, of its own. A man mortgages his land by one instrument, and makes a marriage settlement by another; he agrees to sell Consols by one instrument, to purchase railway stock by another. Each of these transactions belongs to a separate series of events; each should be regulated by provisions under separate heads in the code of law. Thus there are two conditions to be fulfilled by any code of civil law; one, that it should be distributed in accordance with the natural classification of the acts and events of life; the other, that it should take the form of commanding Duties, not of establishing Rights; that its commands and prohibitions should be addressed to those who are to obey them, not to those who are to profit by them.

18. In the foregoing remarks is already contained the cardinal distinction which is, before all others, applicable to Law as a part of human voluntary action, the distinction of it into a science and an art. The science is known by the name Jurisprudence; the art is shown principally in the enactments of the legislator as carried out by the machinery of the Judiciary. But the art and the science deal with the same matter, and traverse the same ground; the science being occupied with its analysis and classification, the art in employing the knowledge so obtained in the construction of a system of enactments in a form suitable for practical application. The legislator and the judge speak to the people, the scientific jurist speaks to the judge and the legislator. Nevertheless the domains of the art and of

the science are not exclusive, but the former is in some sort contained in the latter. The scientific jurist has to consider not only the general principles of the science, but also the particular codes or systems of law, which are from time to time and place to place enacted; not only the logic of the subject, but also the code in connection with the logic, its position towards it, and manner of dependence on it. The practical part of law, the code or system, is one branch of the whole science of jurisprudence.

19. This distinction between law and jurisprudence, between the historical de facto commands and the science upon which they are based, being once clearly drawn, a further distinction in the science rises into view. The science, which is jurisprudence, is then seen to be applicable to all systems of law alike, having both a general and most abstract part, common to all, which may be called the Pure Logic of Jurisprudence, and several special parts or branches, according as from this are deduced the several systems of jurisprudence which are the theories, or abstract counterparts, of the several national codes, or systems, of positive, institutional, concrete law. Jurisprudence is the applied logic of law; and there is yet a more abstract and completely general logic of jurisprudence itself. Law offers a new instance of a branch of human activity becoming more completely organic, more clearly distinguished into theory and practice, abstract side and concrete side, as time and practice develop it.

20. The distinction between law and jurisprudence, and the consequences which result from it, are the feature which perhaps most needs illustration at the present day. The distinctions of the logic of

jurisprudence have usually been adopted as the divisions of codes. There is not only no necessity for such a practice, but it is one which, if uncorrected by a salutary inconsequence, would introduce confusion into the codes where it should prevail. The Institutes of Justinian, for instance, founded it is said on those of Gaius, are distributed under the three heads of Persons, Things, and Actions. (Inst. Just. Lib. i. Tit. iii.) Now Persons and Things seem to belong properly to the logic of the science, but Actions to the practice. There arises, besides, the much debated question, to which of these three heads Obligations belong; obligations constituting, in Justinian's Institutes, a separate department, treated at great length, interposed between Things and Actions. Hence some rectification of this distribution has been frequently found requisite by jurists; in particular, von Savigny, in his work already cited, § 59, redistributes it as follows: Family Law; Property Law, containing both law of things and law of obligations; and Actions, or Verfolgung der Rechte. Divisions similar to this of Justinian's, and founded upon it, prevail in many modern Codes; for instance, in the Code Napoléon, Liv. i. Des Personnes: Liv. ii. Des Biens et des différentes modifications de la Propriété: Liv. iii. Des différentes manières dont on acquiert la Propriété. Here the different modes of acquisition take the place of Actions, a circumstance in which may be seen the effect of the distinction, to be drawn out farther on, between the static and dynamic modes of enquiry, in which there is placed, to use von Savigny's terms on another occasion, "neben der stabilen Seite ihrer Natur auch die bewegliche Seite derselben." (§ 59.) So also the Civil Code of Louisians has three Books, with titles just the same as those of the Code Napoléon. The Draft of Code proposed for adoption to the State of New York goes back again to the old nomenclature, without however being much different in substance. It has four Divisions: Persons; Property; Obligations; and General Provisions applicable to the three former.

21. The secret of these modifications, the possibility of substituting Modes of Acquisition for Obligations and for Actions, is found by attending to the distinction between static and dynamic logic. Persons and things belong to the former; modes of acquisition, obligations, and actions, to the latter. Now the Romans had completely classified the two portions of the statical branch, persons and things; but their analysis had not mastered, but only touched, those of the dynamical. "La méthode romaine avait discerné et classé ces deux premiers éléments; * * * Mais la déduction s'était arrêtée là; elle n'est pas complète. * * * le droit n'est pas encore engendré. Il manque la cause efficiente, la cause génératrice, la cause qui fera naître, qui transmettra de l'un à l'autre, qui modifiera, qui détruira les droits. Ce troisième élément, le voici: 3° Les événements, les faits, les actes de l'homme, juridiques ou non juridiques: ce qui comprend l'idée du temps, du lieu, de l'intention, de la forme, toutes choses qui entrent dans la composition des faits et des actes humains." (M. Ortolan, Explication des Instituts de Justinian. Généralisation. Titre Préliminaire, iii.) The branches of the dynamic logic are then two, according as the acts are "juridiques ou non juridiques," one containing all those acts and events which modify property and personal relations without the intervention of a

court of justice, the other those modifications which that intervention introduces.

22. When we apply this distinction to the one first mentioned between the science and the art of law, it appears at first sight as if the practical intervention of the legislator and the judge comprised only the fourth of the four divisions now introduced into the science; the three first divisions belonging to the science alone, as facts already existing, provisions already made by positive law and decisions upon it. Persons, things, and modes of dealing with property, seem to belong to the science; actions to the art. But this is far from being the case. The intervention of the judge alone may extend indeed only to this fourth division; but that of the legislator is coextensive with the whole range of all four divisions. He has before him indeed existing law as the basis of his work, but he may modify any part of it, and in any way. The four branches of the logic, two statical, Persons and Things, and two dynamical, Modes of Dealing and Actions, lie before him as a framework for better grasping in his mind the matter he has to deal with. The question is, whether his Code or System of Law, addressed to the people, shall follow these same distinctions which the jurists have adopted in addressing their instructions to himself.

23. The distinction now insisted on, between the logic of jurisprudence and the law as enunciated by the sovereign, corresponds to and coincides with a distinction laid down by von Savigny as the basis of his system, namely, the distinction between Rechtsverhältniss and Rechtsinstitut, §§ 4, 5, of work cited, (see par. 8). A Rechtsverhältniss is a legal relation

between parties, and may be broken up into the rights and duties which exist between them reciprocally. But this is always founded upon a Rechtsinstitut, that is, an established legal institution or law, which may be expressed by the sovereign in several forms, of which the highest or most general is a legal rule or maxim, Rechtsregel, the next a statute or Gesetz, the lowest a judicial decision or Rechtsurtheil. He speaks too in § 7 of "die unzweifelhafte Thatsache, dass überall, wo ein Rechtsverhältniss zur Frage und zum Bewusstseyn kommt, eine Regel für dasselbe längst vorhanden, also jetzt erst zu erfinden weder nöthig noch möglich ist." This seems equivalent to saying, that a Rechtsverhältniss is a conception abstracted from, or gathered out of, practice and positive law, whether customary or statute, that is, out of the fact of a Rechtsinstitut, with its derivatives, Rechtsregel, Gesetz, and Urtheil, which existed first in order of history. Under Rechtsinstitut he sums up and characterises positive laws as facts of history; under Rechtsverhältniss juristical conceptions, rights and correlative rights, springing out of the study of those facts and those laws. Hence quite consistently he maintains, in accordance with Austin's conception, that the proper form of all law is the form of command, Gebot; because it springs from the highest power, and its effect is to enforce obedience. But he immediately adds, to obviate the possibility of misconstruction, "Dadurch entsteht indessen ein Missverhältniss zwischen dem Gesetz und dem Rechtsinstitut, dessen organische Natur in jener abstracten Form unmöglich erschöpft werden kann." § 13.

24. Side by side then with the logic of jurisprud-

ence, with its four heads, two static, two dynamic, there stands the system of laws as they may be expressed by the sovereign for the guidance of the people. This latter is law in its de facto institution, in its historical shape. Jurisprudence is the abstract handling of its provisions, and the comparing them to the simple scientific conceptions which are contained in the logic. The jurist has to understand, and render intelligible to others, the laws which are contained in the statute book; but it is not his duty as a jurist to urge reforms, repeals, or new enactments, in the sole view of the benefit to result to the community. This is the duty of the statesman, whose office is therefore more comprehensive than the jurist's, involving the jurist's in itself. It is important that the study of jurisprudence should be pushed to its utmost limits, or, in other words, that the logic should be carried to the greatest possible perfection of organic simplicity. It is the Organon of Law. Now it has been already remarked, that to adopt the divisions of the logic as those of the Code or Statute Book may be injurious to the usefulness of the latter; but it is no less true, that to do so may be injurious to the perfection of the logic. For, in order to render its distinctions available for the code, they must not be pushed to their consequences, nor exhibited in that complete interdependence which is their nature. Hence it becomes no one's interest to follow the study of jurisprudence into the ultimate distinctions of its analysis; enough is thought to be done when those distinctions are exhibited (though falsely) as ultimate, which are available as practical distinctions of the code.

25. What then is this Logic of Jurisprudence; how far can it be logically carried; and at what point

should we have to stop short, if we were to adopt its distinctions as the practical divisions of a Code? The four heads already given are the basis or outline of the logic; and, when we ask how far we can carry them, that is, in other words, what they are in their ultimate simplicity, the first observation which occurs is this, that they are not so many divergent branches of law, each covering ground of its own which is not covered by the others, but that they are so many aspects of the whole law, each incomplete in itself, but when completed producing the other three out of itself and out of its own fund of conceptions.

26. To begin with, What is a Person? A person is a creation of law, the subject of rights and duties. Every command supposes a person, or subject, on whom it is imposed, and a subject towards whom it is imposed; a duty is created in the first, a right in the second; and the two persons are defined by the duties and the rights thus imposed. Person means legal character. For instance, the law recognises the legal relation of Father and Son; a father is a person who has certain duties imposed on him towards his son, and towards whom the son has certain other duties imposed on him reciprocally. The duties of the father are the rights of the son, the duties of the son the rights of the father. Such reciprocal rights and duties constitute the legal Status of the parties. The difference between Person and Status is that between part and whole; two persons have one status between them; a father and son have each the status called the status of father and son. In other words, person is the name for the individuals, status that for the legal relation which subsists between them. Two persons at least are requisite to any status.

Book II.
Ch. III.
§ 90.
Analysis and
classification
of Law.
Civil Law.

27. There is no need to introduce here the distinction between natural and legal status, or between status and contract, any more than, in speaking of persons, to advert to the distinction between natural or physical and legal persons. These are distinctions in the history, the historical growth, of law, not in its logic. Natural persons and natural things are extra-legal matter, with or upon which legal conceptions are occupied, and which enable each of the four cardinal legal conceptions to produce the other three out of its own fund, as remarked in par. 25. The logic knows only legal person and legal status; that is its starting point. Whatever natural objects, persons or things, may be adopted or recognised by law as its objects, it is not the objects themselves but the objects as recognised that are before the jurist. They become legal objects when they are taken up out of nature; what they were before is entirely indifferent. Thus, status may arise either by natural events, or by contract, or by a mixture of both; father and son are an instance of the first; master and servant of the second; father and legitimately born children of the third.

28. The neglect of natural or physical persons in the logic of jurisprudence may be illustrated by a corresponding feature in that more general logic which is metaphysic. Just as metaphysic begins with the analysis of perceptions, in their nature, without first asking after their origin or conditions of existence, while psychology begins by laying down these conditions arbitrarily, a percipient and an object to be perceived (which are here the counterparts to the natural or physical persons in law), before proceeding to the perceptions; whereas in truth it is

only by analysis of perceptions themselves that percipient or object can be understood or defined; so in law the true method begins with the obligations, the commands of acts or forbearances, as that which alone can explain, as of itself involving, the existence of persons invested with a legal character, or of things invested with legal attributes as objects of possession.

29. The same conceptions apply to Things. Here also we find legal notions still entangled by the nomenclature which has descended from times when the logic was not yet distinguished from the history of law. Things meant originally in law things natural or physical, objects of possession by persons natural or physical. It was a great step when things were distinguished into corporeal and incorporeal, and a further step when " rights" were included among the latter. But to maintain such distinctions as ultimate distinctions of the pure logic of law would be to burden it with past incompletenesses, to confound the distinction between logic and history, a vain endeavour to systematise anarchy. The logic knows nothing of things corporeal and incorporeal; it is a distinction of practice, a distinction for the Code, and only so far forth for jurisprudence as this gives back again those practical distinctions in an abstract shape.

30. Thing in logic means the object or substance of a right or duty, the benefit which a person enjoys in consequence of obligations imposed on others, or which he is under an obligation to confer on them. The proper term for things is Estates. A right of dominion or possession, jus in rem, good against all the world, is the estate a man has in the corporeal

Book II.
Ch. III.

§ 30.
Analysis and
classification
of Law.

Civil Law.

or incorporeal thing possessed; it is in him the correlate of the obligations imposed on other persons. It may be broken up into the several obligations imposed on all people alike, such as forbearances to interfere with the owner's enjoyment of it by stealing, destroying, trespassing, falsifying documents of title, and so on. So also the mass of rights which a man has, his right to his good name, to liberty of person, to dress and title of office or rank, consist in corresponding prohibitions to interfere with them addressed to others. What remains over and above these in the right is nothing but the pleasure or profit the man may reap or think he reaps from its enjoyment. Now these pleasures or profits, even in their specific differences, can plainly afford no ground for legal definition; they are heterogeneous to law, not capable of measurement or valuation by third parties. When we ask *what* such and such a right, such and such an estate, consists in, the answer can only be given by the legal obligations imposed on other persons. The specific pleasure or profit in rights or estates, the specific extension of a man's natural powers, or the artificial scope secured to his will, (to recur to von Savigny's expressions), is as much, and in a very similar manner, excluded from the logic of law, as value-in-use is from the logic of political economy, which has directly to do only with value-in-exchange.

31. The duty to abstain from all molestation of a person dealing with anything, on the part of all other persons generally, is the permission to him to deal with it as he chooses, that is, it is his right of property in it. On the other hand, the obligation on him to forbear injury to others is a restraint on

his dealing with it entirely as he chooses, as, for instance, to set up a nuisance on his land, or to fire a barrel of gunpowder in the street. Particular rights, *jura in personam*, consist in commands addressed to particular persons to do or to forbear particular acts, as, for instance, not to desert, but to maintain, wife and children, which is their right to companionship and maintenance; to perform contracts express or implied; to fulfil obligations springing from wrong or from construction of law. Now "every right is a right *in rem*, or a right *in personam*;" Austin, Lect. xvi. That is, every right is founded on obligations incumbent either on all men alike, or on particular men only. The whole field of rights is covered by this distinction.

32. By the logical conception of Estates all barrier is broken down between the supposed branches of law of things and law of persons, and both are shown to cover the same ground, to be two aspects of the same thing. All rights are estates in the subject of them, whether they are large estates or small, parts contained in wholes, or wholes containing parts. Rights to have certain acts performed by certain persons at certain times, for instance, to have deeds exhibited which make part of the title to a purchased farm, are estates in the logic of law; there is a certain definite interest secured to a man by an obligation imposed on other persons. Personal rights, as, for instance, to good name, to companionship, are equally estates by the same rule. The servant has a certain estate secured by the obligations of the master, and the master by those of the servant.

33. The largest kind of estate in civil law is the Dominium of Roman law, a majestic conception. But

it requires the previous natural or extra-legal separation of the thing or object over which the ownership is to be exercised. Starting from such a separate object of ownership, all smaller estates may be classified by their relations to dominium, which may be called, in the first place, an universitas of jura in re. To have some rights but not all in the particular object is to have rights in re but not dominium. If these rights, whether some or all, are good against all the world, they are also rights in rem. But to have a right or rights as against some persons and not others is to have rights in personam not in rem, notwithstanding that these rights are rights in re. Wherever there is a smaller estate carved out of a larger, if the larger estate is a physically separate object, there is jus or jura in re, meaning by re the larger estate. And the owner of the smaller estate may own it against all the world, or have jus in rem with regard to it, just as much as if it were a dominium. But he has also jus in personam against the owner of the larger estate, a jus which consists in the obligations on that owner to do or to abstain from such acts as secure or prevent his enjoyment of the smaller estate. He has both jus in rem and jus in personam, on the ground of his smaller estate, the particular person requisite to support the jus in personam being already determined by the ownership of the larger estate. Dominium, then, gives of itself no jus in personam; it is an universitas of jura in re et in rem; and these include no special obligations. It is only when they are infringed or threatened that jura in personam can be derived from them.

34. Here becomes visible for the first time the connection between Estates and Actions. Every es-

tate, large or small, and whether it consists in rights to possess or in rights to have acts performed, is of itself a right, or collection of rights, good against all the world. But other secondary estates or rights may be derived from it. These secondary rights are those which are necessary either for its establishment or for its protection. All such secondary rights or estates are jura in personam; for it is only from particular persons that the acts requisite to the establishment of estates can be demanded, or that the infringement of estates can proceed or threaten to proceed. Hence, while all estates are good against all the world, the practical enjoyment of them must be secured by action against the particular individuals, from whom their establishment may be demanded, or by whom they are infringed or threatened. A right of action is therefore a jus in personam, this person being defined either by his infringing or threatening to infringe a legal estate, or else by his neglecting to perform acts to which he is bound for the establishment of one.

35. The Obligations of Roman law, or, more generally, rights to acts and forbearances of particular persons, not immediately to the possession of a particular thing, may be considered as consisting in particular services, or particular forbearances, carved out of the dominium of a master over the person of a slave. All conceivable acts and forbearances on the part of the slave are the object of this imaginary dominium, which never could have existed de facto in its whole extent, but which may be imagined as an universitas of jura in persona, out of which the jura in personam, all the special obligations to do, to forbear, or to perform anything, which may be

Book II.
Ch. III.

§ 90.
Analysis and classification of Law.
Civil Law.

created by law or by contract, may be conceived to be carved, although the universitas has no de facto existence. Indeed the same may be said of dominium over things; since none is so complete as to carry the right of use and abuse to all lengths, as in the case of the barrel of gunpowder. There are always some obligations which limit it.

36. Status are to persons what Estates are to things; that is to say, they are characterisations of the functions which persons perform. But there is this difference, that, whereas estates are defined by the acts and forbearances due to the owner from others, status are defined as well by those which the person characterised by the status owes to others as by those which others owe to him. For instance, an estate of full possession in land consists in numberless acts and forbearances of others, but it does not give the owner a right to use it to the public detriment, e.g. to erect a public nuisance on the land. The owner, in respect of the land, has a status defined by the acts and forbearances imposed on him as well as by those imposed on others; but the former acts and forbearances are not part of his estate. It is true that the status in this case is merely that of a simple citizen; the other persons sharing in the status are the community at large; if the owner of the land had certain fixed duties, as owner of that kind of estate, then he would have a more particular status, one defined by the duties owed to and owed by him, in respect of his kind of estate. Again, when status is defined by duties owed to and duties owed by a person, there must be a connection between the two classes of duties; for otherwise he has no single definable status in respect to them; he

bears not one but two characters. It is sometimes laid down that these duties, owing and owed, must be continuous or habitual, and also general or defined by their kind; as, for instance, by Austin, Vol. iii., Notes to Table ii. p. 171. If you hire a person, he says, to do some single service, this does not create the status of master and servant; it must be a contract to render a series of services indefinite in number. But it is obvious that a series of acts or forbearances defined by their general kind is but a complex of single acts or forbearances of the same general kind. When such a series is sufficiently determinate to be capable of a general description, the person or persons bound to it are clothed with a status, that is, assume a certain legal character, in virtue or as a compendious description of the acts and forbearances owing and owed. The reason of the thing extends to all characters which may be borne by persons or groups of persons, even when depending on single acts or forbearances, whether past or promised. A man hired to do a single act has the status of a servant, the hirer that of a master, for that single purpose. The logic of acts and forbearances extends much farther than to the explanation of those aggregates of them only which have been already erected into a recognised legal status; it extends to any status which may be formed on the same principles. The various status, or legal characters, borne by persons or groups of persons, are therefore so many species or genera in legal classification, represent so much ground won by legal science, made good against indetermination and obscurity. And the same may be said of estates. When a status or an estate has arrived at a fixed definition, it may be known by certain marks; and to prove that any particular person or estate has one of these marks is to fix him or it with the other characteristics of the status or estate. The terms belong to the order of knowledge in the science of jurisprudence, and are modes of evidence or proof of particular acts or forbearances being legally enforceable.

37. So far as to the two heads of the statical branch of the logic; it will take less time to make out the same case for the two remaining heads, Dealings and Actions. When von Savigny had established his distinction of civil law into Sachenrecht, Obligationen, Familienrecht (reines und angewandtes) and Erbrecht, Book ii. § 58, he found himself under the necessity of preluding their exposition with a "general part," containing exposition of matters more or less common to all of them. There are, he says, several aspects of Rechtsinstitute, (Seiten ihres Wesens), which are common to many of them, and form a sort of General Part (Allgemeiner Theil) of the whole subject; "Dahin gehört hauptsächlich die Natur der Rechtssubjecte, und insbesondere ihrer Rechtsfähigkeit: ferner die Entstehung und der Untergang der Rechtsverhältnisse: endlich der Schutz der Rechte gegen Verletzung, und die daraus hervorgehenden Modificationen der Rechte selbst. Es giebt in der That kein Rechtsinstitut, in welchem nicht die Erörterung dieser Fragen nöthig und wichtig wäre." Indeed the whole of his great work, the System, consists, as we have it, in nothing else than this General Part, together with a disquisition on the Conflict of Laws. The special exposition of the other branches is not found in it, but was reserved, by a change in plan, to be carried out by separate monographs.

38. Now the two first of the topics here mentioned belong properly to the law of Persons; the two last however are nothing else than the two heads of the dynamic branch of the logic of jurisprudence. And it is clear that the ways in which estates and status originate, in which they are modified, that is to say, divided, devolved, diminished, attacked, defended, or finally cease to exist, cannot be treated otherwise than in connection with the estates and status themselves. A modified estate or status is a new estate or status. The modification stands between the old and the new; and if no estate or status exists at either end, there is no modification, for there has been nothing to modify.

39. Here again we are restricted to those circumstances, events, acts, and omissions, which have legal significance or legal consequences attached to them; just as we were to legal persons and legal things. But the law may either appoint certain formalities or instruments, of its own accord, as methods of dealing with estates and status, or it may attach certain consequences to natural events, or events otherwise extra-legal, such as death, or going beyond seas. The exclusion of natural persons, things, and events, from the proper domain of law corresponds, in civil law, to the exclusion of all acts from the cognisance of criminal law, except those which are positively defined in order to be commanded or forbidden.

40. But if this third head of the logic is closely connected with the two first, still more closely if possible is it connected with the fourth. Legal decisions, when delivered in conclusion of Actions, are at once the bond and the test of validity of all the other parts; it is by them that estates, status, and

Book II.
Ch. III.

§ 90.
Analysis and classification of Law.

Civil Law.

modes of dealing with them, are regulated, in order that they may be so assured as to be able to stand the test of enquiry, if they should ever come before a court.

41. Here it is that the nexus between all the four heads is most clearly seen. After the distinction between the different kinds of estates and of status comes the question, whether such and such a person, the plaintiff, has such and such an estate or status. This can only be ascertained by an examination into the acts, events, and circumstances, by which that estate or status is alleged to have arisen. That is to say, matters belonging to the third head are required to be proved, in order to show the existence of matters belonging to the first and second. These acts, events, and circumstances, are the essential matter in the whole case, its de facto history; it may happen that they show, not the estate or status which either the plaintiff or the defendant alleges, but some other, different, greater or less, estate or status. The acts and events, however, which have actually taken place are that which determines what the estate or status of the parties really is, that by which the decision ascertaining them is governed. Thus the estate and the status not only rest logically on an analysis into acts and forbearances, but questions both about their nature and extent and about the entitlement of A or B to them are in actual discussion reduced to the questions, what acts and events have taken place, and in what circumstances, and whether these have been acts and events recognised, permitted, or enjoined, by the law.

42. There is another bond between the fourth head and the rest. Whenever the law allows a man

to come before the court and entertains his suit, he is said to have a right of action. This right accrues in certain cases already defined and provided for by law. Now this right itself is a species of estate, in the wide sense now attached to the term (see par. 34). Actions, therefore, as founded upon rights of action, might logically, though not conveniently, be treated as a subordinate portion of the head of Estates.

43. Actions were divided by the Romans into two main kinds, actions in rem and actions in personam. This must not be confused with the distinction of jura, into jura in rem and jura in personam, which is the distinction between rights or estates good against all the world and those good only against particular persons. Actions, or the methods of establishing and protecting rights, of enforcing obligations, the rights to which Actions are all jura in personam, are distinguished on a different principle; both kinds of rights or estates may be maintained by both kinds of actions, in rem and in personam, according to the kind of danger with which they are threatened. When a particular act or forbearance, or series of acts or forbearances, is required for the purpose of defence, then there is actio in personam; some person or persons are required to do or to refrain from doing something, e.g. to exhibit a deed, to make a conveyance, to confess judgment, to surrender a claim. Whenever, in short, the estate or right sought to be established is not capable of separation or transference, there the reason of the thing suggests, that the method of enforcing and maintaining it should be by an action in personam; for to secure acts or forbearances in dealing with it is the only way in which its enjoyment can be secured to the rightful owner.

Where, on the other hand, the whole estate or right claimed can be made over to the claimant, there the proper method of maintaining it is by an action in rem, for the possession of the estate itself.

44. Finally it must be remarked, that we are not to expect the abandonment of the term Rights, and substitution of the term Duties, in common legal parlance. The plaintiff, or person who feels aggrieved, will always require some phrase by which to express the state of things as they ought to be in reference to his own interests, and he in every case will be the person who sets the law in motion to bring about the result he desires. It is the law that must decide on these rights by the consideration of the corresponding duties which constitute them, the law that must correct the plaintiff's view of his rights by their analysis, the defendant's obligations. These two views are to be conciliated in the following manner. Rights, it was said in par. 30, consist of two parts, enjoyment, and the security given to it by acts and forbearances enforced on other persons. Enjoyment consists in acts or states of mind; the habit or possibility of frequent recurrence of these acts or states is what is meant by the enjoyment being secured. Now the enjoyment of anything may consist in two things, first its use and possession, secondly its exclusive use and possession; to use a property and to be alone or not interfered with in its use; to enjoy the benefit of another person's act and to be the sole person benefited by it. This distinction is applicable to all classes of rights, not to corporeal possessions only, as enjoyment of land with power of excluding trespassers; but also, for instance, a patient has a right to the skill of his physician, though not exclu-

sively; a client to the skill of his advocate, and that to the exclusion of the opposite party to the suit; a wife to the companionship and, in certain points, the exclusive companionship of her husband. This logic of user and exclusion, then, seems wide enough to secure the full consideration of the plaintiff's claims, notwithstanding that these are to be judged of as consisting in the duties imposed on other persons. The intention and spirit of the duties enforced must be regarded, in order to secure justice between the parties; and this intention is made definite by its two purposes, user and exclusion, being pointed out. The practical questions which the judge puts, in applying the law to any event, are two: Does it destroy or threaten the enjoyment,—does it destroy or threaten the exclusiveness of the enjoyment,—intended to be secured by the command of the law, or by the legal acts of the parties? Obligations are imposed to secure benefits; they must therefore be judged, not by their letter alone, but by a reference to the purpose for which they exist.

45. The logic of jurisprudence seems now to have been handled sufficiently for the present purpose. Its basis at least has been given. But this must not be mistaken for an attempt at a complete sketch or outline of the whole of jurisprudence; (see par. 19). Jurisprudence itself is nothing less than a picture in the abstract, a picture conceived in general terms and distributed under logical categories, of the concrete commands or laws which are the body of a perfect code or statute book. Jurisprudence is the applied logic of law; the sketch here given is but the foundation of this, the logic, as it were, of jurisprudence itself. In order to complete the structure, it

would have to be developed into a body of organic distinctions, upon which the principles and maxims could be founded, which in their turn would become the basis of the practical commands of the code. To give a single instance for the sake of illustration, the distinction between what was void ab initio and what was only voidable, in certain events, would have to be given, and applied to status, estates, and transactions; the different kinds of events by which different transactions were voidable would have to be assigned; and the general reasons for the doctrine in each case given. Such a general and abstract mode of treating the whole body of law could alone secure among lawyers a conception of law as an organic whole, a conception requisite to unity of purpose and consistency of treatment in establishing or interpreting the different provisions of the statute book. But to enter upon such a development of the subordinate distinctions of jurisprudence would be to enter upon differences in the systems of law established in different countries. The logical outline here presented is common to all alike, consisting as it does in conceptions involved in every system of jurisprudence.

46. I come now to the form which the Law should take in the mouth of the legislator speaking to the people. Usually, it has been already said, this form has borrowed its divisions from the distinctions of the logic of jurisprudence. But this has only been done, and can only be done, by an arbitrary distribution of matters under those heads, in order to keep separate, for practical application, the laws relating to distinct classes of rights and distinct classes of acts, which fall with equal logical fitness under all

four heads of the logic. A different distribution is now to be attempted, but at the same time one which will not depart far from those at present in vogue, which it is presumable have been found to possess sufficient practical fitness, or they would not continue to secure the adhesion of codifiers.

47. The principles upon which is made the distribution of matters in public law are, first, their bearing upon the administration or upon private individuals, secondly, their greater or less degree of gravity and importance (par. 12). The second alone is of a nature to serve as a guide in the distribution of matters in civil law. But civil law embraces all matters of ordinary life, and not only those acts and omissions to which penalties are attached by the sovereign. Gravity and importance must therefore mean something different in this case from what they mean in that. We have before us a long and heterogeneous list of relations and transactions between men, each practically separate from others, which we might content ourselves with simply enumerating. But for the sake of order and intelligibility it is advisable to arrange this list in an order founded upon some principle, which shall give to each class in it a position corresponding to the importance with which the transactions and relations belonging to it are usually invested in the view of mankind. The principle of distribution must therefore be drawn from some ethical and general view of social matters.

48. Nothing appears to me so suitable for this purpose as the distinction, established in §§ 23 and §§. 3-9, between the direct and reflective emotions. This divides life into two great portions, the so called "material" and "moral" interests; the former the

groundwork and basis of the latter. Accordingly I should distinguish all legal provisions which aimed at regulating solely material interests, matters of business, property, and dealings with property which had exchange value alone as their purpose; and make of these the first great group in the arrangement. The other main group would then contain those legal provisions which aimed at regulating relations and transactions in which a moral aim predominated, notwithstanding that material interests were also involved, as they would be in all cases. All legal transactions and relations have a common nature, as being valid in law, and all are founded upon and involve material interests. Accordingly, the laws of my second group do not relate to transactions founded upon moral interests alone exclusively of material, which is impossible, but to transactions in which moral interests are motives superinduced upon material interests; the legal character of the transactions, and documents evidencing them, remaining just as strict and just as valid as in those arising from purely material interests. A deed of gift, for instance, in consideration of marriage must be construed just as strictly as any other legal document; a knowledge of the conditions affecting legal documents generally is presupposed, before coming to the consideration of those which especially affect legal documents emanating from moral interests. Pure exchange value transactions may be set apart in a class by themselves; but transactions which have a moral purpose always may, and in most cases do, involve an exchange value transaction also. These complex cases are the object of the second main group of laws.

49. Each minor class of legal provisions would

then contain not only the definition of the persons and estates created, or capable of being created, but also of the acts and events, the deeds and formalities, creating, modifying, and extinguishing them, and also of the actions and rights of action springing from both. Each separate relation and transaction in life would then find the whole law relating to it under a single minor head of the code or statute book; so far at least as the variety of aspects in each separate transaction or relation would permit; for it is clear that any transaction may belong to several heads, as, for instance, a sale of land may belong to the head of sale, and also to the head of bankruptcy; in which case two heads of law might have to be compared. But no possible arrangement of any code can entirely escape from this necessity; all that can be done is to distinguish the aspects and classify the transactions under each.

50. The two main groups, each containing a list of minor classes, would then be these:

1. Laws regulating material interests,
2. Laws regulating material and moral interests.

The Law regulating material interests would contain all matters which are so called matters of business, such as, buying and selling moveables and immoveables; letting and hiring; mortgage, loan, and pledge; shipments, bailments, insurance; notes, bills of exchange, and dealings with currency; principal and agent in business matters; partnership; bankruptcy; railway legislation, so far as generally fixed; to which others may easily be added. The Law regulating material and moral interests would begin with those matters which stood nearest to the highest class in the foregoing group; it would comprise, for instance, the laws relating to master and servant; advocate and client; physician and patient; trustee and cestui-que-trust; guardian and ward; Family law, marriage, divorce, children, settlements; succession and devolution of property; wills; corporations for intellectual or moral purposes, churches, schools; and so on.

51. I do not of course profess to give even the heads of a code; all I aim at is to illustrate my meaning as to the general principle of distribution. Such a distribution would form a sort of ascending scale, in which the laws regulating material relations and transactions would be supposed to govern those regulating moral ones, except so far as modified by the provisions laid down as exclusively applicable to these. Such a distribution would have the advantage of offering a ready-made framework for future legislation; each new law, according to its scope and purpose, would find an already existing body of laws to which it could be appended. When any subject required special legislation, railways for instance, the laws made from time to time would form a kind of special code within the general code, extending it in a particular direction. The code or statute book would thus reflect the actual life of the nation, and furnish us with a firmer grasp over our actual condition.

52. A code or statute book moulded not on the distinctions of the logic, but on some distinctions or other drawn from ethic or from daily life, would seem also the best adapted to express law in the form of command. Such and such are the transactions which we permit to have legal validity, the sovereign would

in effect say; such and such are the obligations which they impose, the rights which they confer; such and such will be their effect when brought before a court. It is no longer exposition of a science, but publication of a precept. And in such a form it is most readily capable of comparison with the moral law, with the conceptions of right and wrong which the subjects, to whom it is addressed, may from time to time entertain. The civil and the public law alike would thus speak the language of a sovereign; and both, by taking duties and not rights as their text, would suspend law on the same principle as ethic. This, which was mentioned in advance in par. 4, as an additional merit of the method advocated, must now be briefly shown.

§ 90. Analysis and classification of Law.
Civil Law.

53. A law of "rights" will not harmonise with ethic. There are no moral rights, in the sense of claims, as rights are understood in law; a moral right in ethic is an absurdity; and for this reason, that it is conscience which determines and sanctions moral right and wrong, and does so by commanding and forbidding the man himself, the Subject of conscience; it has no dominion over another man's conscience or acts; consequently the supposed moral rights must be duties commanded by another man's conscience, and the man who claims them cannot feel their moral validity; when their validity is felt, it is and can be only in the shape of duties, not of rights. This may serve to explain a phenomenon which must often have struck minute observers; many rights, so called, seem to lose their validity by the very fact of being claimed and insisted on. For instance, women are entitled to a peculiar courtesy and deference in society, but this depends solely upon the duty of cour-

tesy felt as such by men; a demand for it on the part of women, appealing either to a "right" in themselves as women, or to public opinion, destroys the very thing which is demanded, the essence of which is freedom, to be given from a feeling of duty. The acts may be enforced, but the courtesy is destroyed; and how can that be claimed as a right which is destroyed by the claim being made? Courtesy is a moral duty on the part of the renderer, but not a moral right on that of the receiver; whenever it is enforced, it is courtesy no longer. The same line separates the Law from the Gospel; the law, as law, from the law of liberty and of love. The revelation of this latter, in religion, deposed the former from being religion; the essence of religion consists in the worship being freely given, not claimed as a legal right, nor enforced by legal penalties. God makes no demand to be worshipped; were he to do so, he might be a temporal, but could not be a spiritual sovereign. The only demand is the duty felt and enforced by conscience. I conclude, therefore, that Law and Ethic have in common the conception of duties, but not that of rights.

54. There still remain two branches of law to complete the entire picture, the law of Procedure and the law of Evidence; the procedure which is adopted as a rule by the different courts of justice, and the rules of evidence which they require in proof of the matters on which their decision is demanded. A title to property, for instance, is properly speaking the evidence which can be given of the right to it, or, what is the same thing, of the existence of the obligations which constitute the right. All legal forms, such as those of legally valid documents, rest

ultimately upon the evidence required by courts of justice, in proof of the rights and obligations intended to be created and secured by them. Procedure again is the mode which the courts prescribe for the purpose of bringing disputed matters to a simple and clear issue. Procedure and evidence are therefore the regulation of that judicial action upon which all other legal relations and transactions depend for their sanction and validity. This is their connection with the rest of the legal provisions, whether of public or civil law.

55. On the other hand, procedure and evidence, being rules laid down for the guidance of the judiciary, are branches of public law. They are the method of dealing between particular organs of the sovereign and subjects of the sovereign. Themselves a part of public law, they are distinguished from the remainder of it by being the portion which regulates the intercourse between the people and the judiciary alone in its judicial capacity. The procedure of the judiciary is subject to no other supervision but its own, except by a recourse to "positive constitutional morality," a change in constitutional law in the strict sense. There must be a final authority somewhere; and this final authority is found in the methods and principles adopted by the judiciary for regulating its own procedure.

56. It has been maintained by Austin, Lect. xliv., that Public Law itself is a part of the Law of Persons, being a law of status, namely, the status of subordinate political superiors, their reciprocal relations to the subjects with whom they deal. It is no doubt true that the conception of such a status depends upon the conception of status generally; and so much

as this follows from what has been above insisted on, namely, that the logic of jurisprudence embraces all acts and relations of life. Hence public law as well as civil depends on the conceptions and distinctions of that logic. But it does not follow that public law should be treated as a branch of civil law, because both are dependent on the same general logic.

57. Here is applicable the distinction, above insisted on, between the code or statute book, containing the laws as addressed to the people, and the logic of jurisprudence as the instruction acquired by the legislator and judge. (See parr. 8. 23.) It saves us from the embarrassment of having to classify public law as subordinate to civil law at one time, and as coordinate with it at another. The logic of jurisprudence is common to both; the codes are coordinate streams from the same source. Were the logic and the civil code identical, public law could not be separated from civil, and, not being separable, must then be made a subordinate branch of it. Convenience, however, as evidenced by universal practice, seems to demand that the law laid down by the sovereign for subjects to observe towards the community at large, and towards itself as the representative of the community, should be kept separate from the law laid down in regulation of the dealings of individuals with each other. The practice of the Roman lawyers will thus be retained. "The Roman lawyers," says Austin, Lect. xliv., "divide the *corpus juris* into two opposed departments:—the one including the law of political conditions, and the law relating to crimes and criminal procedure: the other including the rest of the law. The first they style *jus publicum*, the second they style *jus privatum*."

58. It is accordant with this view, that to each of the two main branches of Law should be attached a side branch, containing the law of procedure and evidence. This is itself a part of public law; but, since it relates only to those organs of the sovereign which form the judiciary, it is distinct from the rest of public law on the one hand, while, on the other, it is the guardian both of that and of civil law. This classification will perhaps be better seen in the subjoined tabular arrangement:

TABLE OF THE GENERAL CLASSES OF LAW.

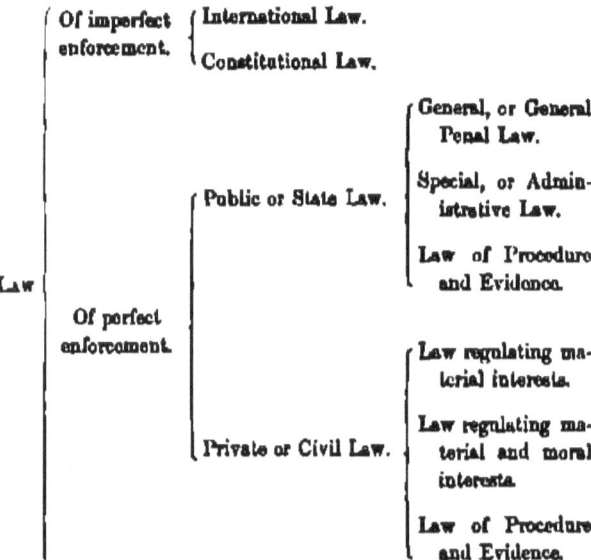

§ 91. 1. The analysis which has hitherto occupied us will find its natural conclusion in some remarks on political action from the practical point of view, that which is adopted necessarily by any one about to act with the purpose of ameliorating the actual condition at any given moment. In other words, the analysis of political action and of its different branches is now to be completed by the consideration of Policy, or action directed towards some definite end, at the moment of its adoption.

2. The general divisions of policy are accordingly the same as those of the branches of action; and these have been already given in the classification of law. Six branches have been distinguished, namely:

1. Administrative; Penal; Material; Material and Moral;

2. Constitutional; International.

The statesman may be considered as leading a column of advance on each of these lines; he has a policy to recommend in each of them. His point of view is general, all-embracing; and in this respect the same as the critic's. Justice and Liberty, which are the statesman's final ends, the purpose at which his policy aims, are the criteria of the critic, the tests by which he judges the policy.

3. The establishment of these ends or criteria leaves us still very far from a rule of policy in immediate and particular cases. One thing only is clear, that the extreme generality of the ends involves an equal generality in the persons or objects whom the policy must embrace. Since there can be only one justice and one liberty, for otherwise the purity of their character would be attainted, there can be only one community among whom they are to prevail. The results of statesmanship must tend to the unifi-

cation, not only of particular states, but also of the whole human race, including also together with it all beings, however low in the scale of organisation, to whom the conceptions of justice and liberty are applicable. One vast family is thus formed, compared to which states and federations of states are but transitory institutions, a family which, always and from the first existing potentially in the common features of human nature, has its actual realisation reserved as the goal and crown of all political endeavour. The ideas of justice and liberty are not only final ends and ultimate criteria of action, but they mark out the limits of the community which is its field or object. There is a logical unity in this procedure which seems wanting in Bentham's mode of defining the ethical community as consisting of all sentient beings.

4. Putting together the two conceptions now reached, namely, the ultimate ends and the community in which they are to be realised, we may attain some further conception of the characteristics of that final state of society. It must be a society in which shall reign the perception that the interests of every member are not only compatible with, but also conducive to, the interests of every other member and of the whole; in which there shall be full and final renunciation of war as a means of settling disputes, and the irrevocable adoption of some impartial tribunal in its stead; in which therefore mutual confidence shall take the place of distrust and suspicion; in which every member shall find a career open to its activity, in harmonious cooperation with others, under a general organisation of the whole.

5. But in order to this result, in order to each

primary member of the whole community, that is to say, each State, being in harmony with the rest, it must be first at harmony within itself; the larger result can only be realised in proportion as the smaller one is attained, and the progress made towards both must be simultaneous. The activity of groups and classes within each state must be so organised and combined as to leave none without a legitimate career, which is liberty, none without the satisfaction of its reasonable expectations from other classes, which is justice.

6. The ends of justice and liberty, as realisable in each state, are then the cause, or conditio existendi, of justice and liberty as realisable in the community of states; and conversely, these ends in the whole community are the final cause and the justifying reason of the same ends in each state. The realisation of justice and liberty in the whole community is the remote or negative condition of a true policy; that is to say, whatever measure does not harmonise with these ends is to be rejected. The realisation of justice and liberty within each state, on the other hand, is the positive condition of a true policy; being nearer it can guide the action of statesmen more determinately, subject to the negative condition above stated. And we shall see that this narrower and more determinate condition, positive in respect to the final ends of the whole community, becomes itself negative in regard to the still more determinate ends of constitutional and legal policy.

7. The true glory of nations consists not in the material power or wealth which they have possessed, but in the services which they have rendered to the whole community of which they form a portion, in

the part which they have played in the general progress of civilisation, in their career as a development of the best mental and moral characteristics with which they are endowed. Their relation to the rest of mankind, to the nations which are their contemporaries, as well as to those which have preceded and to those which will follow them, is the decisive circumstance by which we constantly, as a matter of fact, form our opinion in judging their character and assigning them their place of honour. So also it is with the policy of statesmen; a reference to the whole community of mankind decides our opinion of the greatness of an Alexander, a Cæsar, a Charlemagne, a Richelieu, a Cromwell, a Washington, a Napoleon. Those policies are enduring in their effects which are conformable to the great purpose of promoting justice and liberty among mankind; no step taken in this direction, no ground won, is ever entirely lost; the nation which, under the guidance of a statesman who has made this his aim, has achieved a success, however partial, may like an individual cease to exist, but it finds its true successors in other nations and other statesmen, who take up the inheritance, conduct its cause to victory, and keep alive the memory and the glory of the states and the statesmen who have been their predecessors in the struggle.

8. The rule of international policy therefore is, that it should be conformed to justice and liberty as negative conditions, the advantage of the state itself being the positive or guiding condition. The first or positive duty of a statesman is towards his own state; it is only when he cannot direct its policy in conformity to these higher but negative conditions, as he himself conceives their requirements, that a

statesman is bound to retire from the service of his state, as a function no longer compatible with his duty as a man. But in pointing out justice and liberty among mankind at large as the criteria of international policy, difficulties of a casuistical nature are unavoidable, as they also frequently are between individuals. Without pretending to have a solution ready for all cases, the conception already given of justice seems capable of removing one class at least of these difficulties.

9. So long as the final state of mutual confidence and security is unattained, and in proportion as it is unattained, so long will the necessity and the justification exist for keeping the means of defence unimpaired, and on a level with the means of attack. This is the only but sufficient justification of defensive war and the maintenance of armies, of the occupation of military posts on foreign soil, and so on. So also between individuals, the Christian precepts as to not resisting evil can only be carried out by means of a simultaneous advance towards obeying them, on the part of all men alike; for they are equally binding on all. But over and above such questions as these, there are others which are often felt to embarrass policy, when accepting the obligation of strict justice.

10. Now justice is ascertained only by the adjustment of claims founded on the contrary expectations of the parties concerned (§§ 31-33). Between individuals these claims have been to a great extent adjusted, and positive law is the acknowledged arbiter of disputes. But between nations, not only there is no common and sovereign law, but the claims of the parties have but very partially adjusted them-

selves. To apply rules of justice between individuals to questions arising between states, and to treat nations as if they were individuals and not aggregates, would be to enforce not justice but a nominal and artificial counterfeit, justice being nothing absolute, but consisting in the perception of justice by the parties concerned. If the analogy of individuals is employed, it must take individuals in what is called the state of nature. Suppose two savages, one having abundance of food, the other starving; it will not be felt by either to be justice, that the former should refuse to give food to the latter, but that the latter should receive food in return for some service or other, even though he should compel this transaction by force. He may say to the other, You have conquered this food from the forces of nature; now conquer it from me. The relative powers, brute or natural forces, of the two men must not be neglected in estimating their claims to the food, that is, their expectations from which justice will result; justice between them is not the same thing as justice between men living under an established law of property; it is one with it in point of nature, but it is justice forming, not justice formed. Similar is the case between nations, except to the extent which already recognised international law or morality provides for. Beyond these limits justice between nations is still in process of ascertainment, and the statesman is not the organ of what justice will consist in, but of what his nation now perceives or thinks it to consist in. The state and the statesman are both bound to do this justice; they can be bound to no other. Bystanders may and must criticise both their conceptions and their conduct; this is part of the action of the spiritual power upon them. But it is a fallacy in the criticism when nations are treated as individuals with equal rights, as it is called, independent of their relative powers.

11. Let the following serve as an illustration. In the late War of Secession in America, many of the advocates of both sides appealed to the Constitution of the United States, on the one side as showing that the States had given up their independence as states on entering the Union, and on the other as showing that they entered the Union only as sovereign and independent states. Justice as founded on an express contract was thus appealed to on both sides. But this was entirely beside the mark. Actual secession destroyed the unity of the only sovereign who could enforce the constitution, and the question, as between the remaining and the seceding states, returned to the position it was in before the acceptance of the Constitution. But the history of the Union from its establishment to the secession of the southern states had altered the position and the expectations of the parties concerned. In 1787 there was a strongly and generally felt necessity for union; the constitution was the method, the terms by which it was effected, the means, among others, of securing it, not supposed of course by any sensible person to be infallible. Whether any body of States would have been justified in establishing the Union by force in 1787, it is superfluous to enquire; since it is clear that none would have had the power to do so. But in 1860 the advantages of upholding it were more strongly felt than ever by the Federalist States, while they found themselves also in a position to uphold it by force. Were their expectations of an united

America to be defeated, the work of eighty-eight years to be undone, by the secession of an interest which they had made constant sacrifices to retain in the Union, sacrifices the entire fruit of which would thus be lost? The Federalists had, I think, justice in demanding that the southern states should remain in the Union, and, having the power, they had also the right to enforce their demand by arms. I do not say that the seceding States had not also a fair show of justice for secession; but that the case was one which could not justly be settled by the analogy of individuals equal before the law; in which justice itself required a consideration of the expectations and the relative material power of the parties; but in which unfortunately these claims could not be settled except by an appeal to arms, not because either party were deaf to justice, but because their relative strength, one element of the justice, could not otherwise be ascertained.

12. Relative power, geographical and economical position, previous sacrifices and efforts, present necessities and cherished expectations, are elements which enter into the conception of the justice of demands which one nation makes on another; they are the constituents of the nation's judgment of what is right, and ought also to be so of ours in criticising a nation's judgment and conduct. When a submission and transaction between two nations is thus compelled by the stronger of them, the terms of the transaction are not matters of favour but of justice, not concessions granted by the stronger to the weaker ex benevolentia, but the price paid for the submission on larger points. The true interests of both contracting parties require justice to be aimed at in the con-

cessions of the stronger as well as of the weaker party. If union between the two states is the concession demanded by the stronger, justice in the concessions made in return for it, in the measures of the government imposed on the weaker, is the surest guarantee of stability. It may often happen that the best interests of states are promoted by a sacrifice of their autonomy, partial or even total. No policy, for instance, could have done more honour to a statesman of any of the United States, than the policy of combining it with others in the Union, after the War of Independence. A similar condition of things may one day arise for the States of Western Europe, interposed as they will be between the Empires of Russia and North America, each a match for their united strength. The perfect autonomy of his country is by no means a sine qua non of a true statesman's policy.

13. Passing from international to constitutional concerns, the same harmony between the classes or groups which compose a state is required, both by the purpose of rendering the state a concordant member of the community of nations, and by the ends of justice and liberty realisable within the state itself. The reasonableness of the first of these two orders of considerations is shown by the fact, that where a powerful class in any state is justly discontented with its social and political condition it finds allies in the corresponding class in other states, and brings the governments of these states into collision with its own; thus dividing the community of states into two parties, the anti-revolutionary, in which the different classes are as yet in harmony, and the revolutionary, in which the discontented classes are

threatening to be in the ascendant. This was the origin of the arming of the hereditary governments of Europe against France at the beginning of the Wars of the Revolution, at the close of the last century.

14. Social and political injustice within a state, even when the class which primarily suffers from it is not the moving cause of disturbance, is again in another way the cause of disunion between states, namely, by establishing conflicting interests between them. No one, for instance, doubts that the spreading institution of slavery in the southern states of the American Union was the chief cause which made disruption inevitable in 1860. The interests of the ruling classes in the southern states were bound up not only with slavery but with its progressive increase, and their hopes fixed on its final supremacy over the whole continent. This was radically inconsistent with the interests and hopes of the northern states, founded on the principle of freedom in labour, as in all other modes of activity. One or the other system must succumb if the Union was to be preserved. The preservation of the Union being the fixed purpose of that side which ultimately proved victorious, slavery was doomed to extinction, and doomed with increasing certainty in proportion as their victory became assured. Nevertheless it was only the prolonged resistance of the South which brought out into clear light this necessity. Had the South yielded at once to re-incorporation, the deep-seated cause of disruption would probably have been permitted to continue, but only to produce a similar disruption at some future time. A difficult and prolonged struggle was needed in order to fix the atten-

tion of the victors on the true cause of the suffering which the struggle entailed on them, as well as to inspire a sufficient effort to eradicate it.

15. Turning to the consideration of justice and liberty as realisable within the state itself, these ends become negative or limiting criteria of constitutional action. They cannot be positive or guiding criteria, because the different parties, classes, or interests, are not agreed as to their definition; only what is not compatible with justice or with liberty can be clearly seen and excluded from the aims of politic. The spontaneous force exerted by each great class in the state is the measure of the political power which it can justly claim; and therefore the first necessity for a statesmanlike adjustment of these claims is a clear view of the true history of the national and constitutional development, compared with that of other nations, in order to attain a sound conception of the point at which the nation at present stands, and of the course which it may be expected to pursue; to modify which for the better is the immediate purpose in question.

16. It need hardly be said that, in the view of the ablest politicians, the immediate problem now in process of solution by the states of Western Europe is the incorporation of the proletariat, or working classes, into the social and political organisation of their several states. The delay of this solution is rendering our condition unstable and revolutionary, a condition to which if anything could open our eyes, at least in this country, intent as we are on personal interests or party politics, it would be the comparative indifference to direct constitutional action on the part of the working classes, mentioned in § 89, 19,

together with the progressive organisation of these classes for combined action throughout Europe by annual international congresses. The statesman's aim should be to discover, and then to satisfy, the just claims which these spontaneous forces of society, now transforming themselves into powers, may make on the powers which have hitherto divided the government between them. It will probably be found that these claims are rather of a social than a political character, not a claim to share in the government but a claim to be governed well, a claim to have their interests made as essential a condition of government as those of the governing classes have been made hitherto. But such a claim would be a far harder one to satisfy.

17. The problem is the same in principle as we have found it to be between nations. The people, stung by social inequality and the pressure of social burdens, will say "Now reckon with me." The upper classes say in their contentment "Old things are just;" the people say "We are uneasy," and "The earth hath he given to the children of men." Now justice cannot be altogether, as they say, on the side of the upper classes and the old institutions; for institutions are just only so long as they flow from and respond to needs; and they have a tendency to remain established after these have ceased to exist; then they begin to be unjust, satisfying the needs of one party only, those who find their account in their maintenance. Prolonged discontent is itself a proof of injustice. Justice lies in the transaction,—in the incorporation of the lower classes with the upper, in the transformation of the institutions so that both classes find them easy and fair; so that both may find

a career open to them, a life which is worth living, a life of moral and intellectual advance.

18. This problem is the same, whichever system of government, imperial or representative, may prevail. "L'élévation continue du tiers état est le fait dominant et comme la loi de notre histoire," says M. Aug. Thierry in the Essai already quoted. This is paralleled in England by the advance of the Commons. But we must not be blinded by the general and vague terms, Tiers Etat and Commons. These have now broken up and developed themselves into two very different classes, in consequence of the progress of industry, wealth, and population. It is only the capitalist class of the Commons or Tiers Etat which has become truly incorporated into the national organisation. The labouring class is still seeking incorporation; and the mode of that incorporation is the practical point in question.

19. When in the next place we try to figure to ourselves the shape which a government must take, in order to fulfil the conditions now laid down, and at the same time bear in mind the two general kinds under which all governments fall, the imperial and the representative, (§ 89. 20), it seems evident that the government required must belong to neither of these with strict exclusiveness. On the one hand it must reject the habit of ruling by means of party conflicts, which belongs to the representative system, as incompatible with a permanent direction of public affairs founded on fixed principles of action, and incompatible also with the combination of the best trained and most enlightened rulers in the work of administration. On the other hand it must reject the exclusion of the subject population from partici-

pation in the free choice of their rulers from time to time, as incompatible with the full development of individuals as citizens, by restricting their thoughts and their energies to domestic and industrial concerns. The problem is to combine the principle of selecting inferiors by superiors, as the best guarantee for special fitness in the agents selected, with the principle of electing superiors by inferiors, as the only guarantee for the work being performed in the interest of the latter, in this instance the people itself. Just as, in all minor matters, the judge of any work is the person for whose use it is destined, while the training of the agents or producers of the work is in the hands of those already skilled in it, so also, in the comprehensive work of government, the final ratification of policy, the final acceptance or rejection of its agents, should be effectively in the hands of the governed, for whose benefit the government is carried on, while the designation and training of the agents selected should be in the hands of the already skilled agents, the government itself already existing.

20. The principles of the imperial and of the representative systems must thus be combined, in whatever modes of government are accepted as final. Separately the two systems can only be regarded as tentative approaches to a satisfactory system. The representative system, as we see it in this country, is but a crude attempt at government in the full sense of the term, however elaborately it may have become organised as a mode of regulating the various personal and party interests into which the nation is broken up. As government it is a government of amateurs. Still it has the merit of keeping the country together, government and people of a piece.

And it is precisely this connection, this free interpenetration of thought and aims between people and government, which is severed by the imperial system. What is wanted is the free and active concurrence of all the citizens in the work of government, without injury to its efficient and intelligent administration.

21. Government has for its function to direct the action of the whole community in all the several departments of its activity; it is to the community what the function of practical reasoning is to the individual. The members of the government constitute the organ of that function. But however these members may have been selected, and to whichever of the two systems the government may belong, the practical questions which have to be decided are always amenable to the final criteria of justice and liberty. This reference to the ends or criteria is entirely independent of the form of government, or of the stage at which its development has arrived.

22. Practical questions are always questions for individuals; it is for every individual, who takes any part in public affairs, to consider what the conduct of the body with which he acts ought to be, in order to determine what he ought to contribute to make it. Individuals have to decide wholly their own, partially the conduct of the state; they have to decide, but for the good of others, and as representing others. The conduct of the state is collective, but its conscience as well as its motive is distributive. The result of its conscience being distributive is not to release it from the obligations of morality, but to impose conduct dictated by the morality of one interest or party upon others, according as one or other

is predominant or in a majority. The dominant party, which determines the collective action of the whole, is not released from moral obligations; but there arises for it the further question, how far it is justified in overriding the moral convictions of the parties or interests which are in the minority. "The action of man in the State," says Mr. Gladstone in his Chapter of Autobiography, page 58, "is moral, as truly as it is in the individual sphere; although it be limited by the fact that, as he is combined with others whose views and wills may differ from his own, the sphere of the common operations must be limited, first, to the things in which all are agreed; secondly, to the things in which, though they may not be agreed, yet equity points out, and the public sense acknowledges, that the whole should be bound by the sense of the majority." The question then is how those things, in which the whole should be bound by the sense of the majority, are to be distinguished, whether by members of the majority itself or by critics outside.

23. The much-debated question as to the proper limits of the functions of government is thus opened. One extreme view is to restrict these functions to the protection of person and property; the opposite extreme to extend them to the establishment of all spiritual interests whatever. It may be laid down, however, that neither the origin nor the scope of government is decisive of the limits of its functions; that is to say, neither the supposed ἀναγκαῖον or minimum of government, such as must have existed in any government even at its origin, is to limit the benefits which government may become capable of conferring in more advanced societies, nor is the

scope of its action, which is coextensive with that of morality (§ 84. 1), to impose upon it functions equal with its scope. The benefits which are practically found attainable by its means are the only consideration which points out the proper limits of its functions. We are thus brought back to the question in the shape in which it was presented in the preceding paragraph. The question as to the limits of the functions of government is only this question over again, in a more general and abstract shape; for, before we can say what general classes of measures are within the proper competence of government, we must have some decisive experience of what kinds of action may properly be imposed on a mass by the will of a majority, or of its organs.

24. Greater definiteness may be given to this mode of stating these questions, for to attempt their solution by advocating any particular policy would be beyond the purpose of the present work, by recalling the four remaining heads of internal law and internal policy. These are the administrative; penal; material; material and moral heads. Every direction given by government to the action of the community or of its members, in any matter, takes the shape of a law or a command, more or less temporary, more or less special, falling under one or more of these divisions. For instance, sanitary regulations belong partly to the first, partly to the last of them; taxation to the first and third; education, marriage, and devolution of property, to the fourth. A satisfactory government must be in possession of the best knowledge attainable on all subjects which immediately relate to human activity. It must be able to draw the line between interfering and abstaining from in-

terference, and, when it decides for the former, must be in a position to interfere for the best advantage. Its aim ought to be not to supersede but to guide and increase individual effort, individual intelligence and morality.

25. Finally I would remark that, since the ends or criteria of justice and liberty are final, and not always capable of immediate application, the means which may be adopted to realise them must be distinguished from the final state to be attained by those means. This applies more especially to liberty, as being less determinate than justice. By liberty is meant not freedom of one person from the control of others, but the freedom of his reflective modes of consciousness from the predominant influence of the direct modes, whether this influence is derived from his own passions, or from his fears and hopes from other persons. (See §§ 73. 23, and 82. 2). It may often happen that to set a person free from influences of the latter kind is only to subject him more completely to influences of the former. In other words, so long as the final state is unattained, there is a certain educational function in government, a certain discipline to be exercised by it; and this not only in penal matters, but in all the branches of legislation; a function which cannot be laid aside without disregarding the moral end and scope of government, without restricting it to material purposes alone. The laws upon which the civil institution of marriage rests are an instance. To give the support of law to any contracts whatever, irrespective of their purpose, would prima facie be a policy in accordance with liberty; but if the effect of such a policy were to endanger marriage as a practical custom, an effect

which might reasonably be apprehended, the tendency of the policy to favour true liberty in the end would very justly be doubtful. Government therefore cannot escape from the necessity of forming a definite view of the moral ends which it ought to pursue, and of the degree and mode of interference with individual conduct most conducive to those ends. And this in fact forms the highest and most difficult problem of policy.

26. To adopt an expression of Coleridge, every advance in spiritual life leaves a dead law behind it, at once destroyed and fulfilled. Wherever love is, there law is fulfilled; where love reigns, law ceases. The ethical writer has nothing to do here but to repeat and generalise St. Paul. What he declared in the case of the Jewish law being fulfilled in the Gospel of Christ is true of all law in relation to morality, the law of love, of liberty, of conscience. Law arises out of the midst of morality, is added to morality, in consequence of transgressions of the conduct dictated by, or of the conflict of other motives with the motives of, conscience and love, τῶν παραβάσιων χάριν προσετέθη. Whenever these transgressions and this conflict shall cease, the undisturbed reign of conscience and love begins again, law ceasing with the transgressions and the conflict. Conscience resisted is law, unresisted is liberty. The same is true of international as of civil law, of law between classes as between individuals, of law in matters so-called self-regarding as in matters regarding others. The furthest aim of statesmanship therefore, the ideal of its activity, is to prepare the way for the dominion of conscience in every individual, and for the union of men into one great family, bound together by

brotherly affection; to hasten the time, far distant though it may be, when

> "liberated man,
> All difference with his fellow man compos'd,
> Shall be left standing face to face with God."

CHAPTER IV.

LOGIC OF THE PRACTICAL SCIENCES.

Biron. More sacks to the mill! O heavens, I have my wish!
Shakespeare.

§ 92. 1. WHEN we look back upon the course followed up to the present Chapter, in order to prepare our next spring, we find that we have been constructing an Art of life. Practical science, with its logic, is another name for art. The distinction between art and science is not a separation, but a distinction of aspect in one and the same thing or object-matter. That which is science in its nature, in its results earliest and latest, is art in its process. The method of discovery is art. Art is the discovery of means to ends, the discovery of the comparative importance of ends, no less than the application of the means to the ends, or than the choice between the ends themselves. For, on the one hand, the application of means to ends is the discovery of means to apply them, or of the method of application, so that the actual muscular movements, the ultimate steps of all in the process, are the only part of art which is not science, and these are under the guidance of volition

and reasoning; and, on the other hand, the choice
between ends is a discovery of their practical importance, either true or apparent. The sameness of art
and science follows immediately from the analysis of
voluntary redintegration, which, in all instances of
it, contains inseparably the two elements of emotion
and framework, of matter and form. All reasoning
is choice; its motive power consists in the general
pleasure of harmonising framework or form; just as
that of the reasoning called practical consists in the
pleasure of harmonising specific pleasures. Reasoning therefore, both speculative and practical, is art in
respect of its motive power or its process; but inasmuch as it is reasoning, or conscious volition aiming
at the true as well as moved by the pleasureable, it
is science. There is no science to which this does
not apply, however independent of human effort, or
even human existence, it may appear, astronomy for
instance. We seem to have gradually discovered pre-
existing facts; but the discovery has been an invention, the system of the heavens a construction, of
science; the method has been art, the result science.
So also in what are commonly called arts, engineering
for instance; practical engineering consists in the
discovery of facts of nature, the comparative strength
and durability of materials, wood, stone, iron, and in
different shapes, solid or cylindrical, of their malleability, of the firmness of different soils, of the pressure of water, and so on. The skill employed in the
discovery and arrangement of facts like these, and in
the directions given to workmen in consequence, is
of the same nature as the skill, called manual, which
makes one workman excel another in executing those
directions; that skill of hand which is so valuable

consists in the complete guidance of the hand by perceptions, and the complete accuracy of those perceptions.

2. Yet the metaphysical distinction of aspects in this case, as in so many others, becomes the ground of an empirical distinction; that class of phenomena in which one aspect predominates being named after that aspect, and the other class of phenomena after the other. Accordingly we find some classes or branches of science named arts, and others sciences. And it follows that there is no art without its corresponding science, no science without its corresponding art. The empirical distinction between art and science is drawn by a reference to the metaphysical distinction between them as aspects, art being the process, science the stage started from and the stage reached by the process; and in the following way. Whatever is already acquired or known is science, the advance into the unknown, that is, further acquisition, is art, the application of means, drawn from the already acquired knowledge, to the end, as yet only vaguely designated, of future knowledge. Art is founded on science and advances to science, its constructions become science, and serve again as material or foundation for art. Again, the direction is given by science, by the 'end vaguely designated;' the end in view commands the application of means, that is, directs the art, while the means are supplied by the already acquired science. Practical science, as distinguished from speculative, is that which begins by fixing and precisely designating the end to be attained, and proceeds by discovering the means and materials, and finally the mode or means of applying them to the end, that is, by directing the art. Speculative science,

keeping the end in view, but vaguely designated, proceeds by using the means and materials in any or all ways consistent with that vaguely designated end, further knowledge of the object-matter in question. Art occupies the intermediate position in both kinds of science, practical and speculative; but practical science begins by determining the τέλος, speculative by determining the means and materials; practical science commands and directs art by definite aims, speculative by indefinite; practical science begins by establishing a hierarchy of aims, or τέλη, speculative by establishing a hierarchy of general propositions concerning not wishes but facts of nature. Science never knows beforehand where she will arrive; practice always knows it, if she arrives at all. When, therefore, we are dealing, as in the present Book, with practical science and its logic, the empirical distinction between science and art is the distinction between enquiries which determine the comparative importance of ends and enquiries which determine the means to ends already adopted or fixed.

3. To turn now to another distinction, between the sciences and arts themselves. Metaphysic proper, or in that part of it which deals with the formal element in consciousness, has no art corresponding to it but pure logic, the method of voluntary redintegration in its purest or most abstract shape. ("Time and Space" § 66 ad fin.). But in its larger acceptation, when taking into consideration Feeling in all its varieties, as well as form, metaphysic becomes ethic, and its practical branch becomes a logic of ethic or of practice, a determination of the most general principles which ought to guide, as well as of those which actually guide, conduct; it becomes a con-

struction of a hierarchy of aims, combining yet distinguishing for that purpose both their de facto and their de jure validity, both those which guide and those which ought to guide practice, practice being the choice of what is most desirable out of what is feasible. Completeness and accuracy in picturing the facts and feelings, the phenomena, of human nature, embraced in its analysis, are that which enables a logic to lay claim to validity as an ultimate guide to practice or conduct. Where the logic of practice stops, where its general rules cease to determine details, there science ends and art begins. The whole field of human action is enclosed by the science, but no part is fully cultivated; this can only be done by art, that is, by science in progress, making further application of the results of history, practical logic, physiology, and physical laws. But there is no class of phenomena, no branch of enquiry, no art so mechanical, no science so abstract, which does not fall under the practical legislation of ethic; because there is no kind of feeling, whether sensation, emotion, or passion, which is excluded from the survey upon which the logic of ethic is built. The aim or end of every art and every science is judged by ethic, that is to say, is held relatively or positively good or bad, deserving to be pursued or neglected, commanded or forbidden, on ethical grounds, inasmuch as these aims or ends find their place in the hierarchy of aims, of which the logic of practice consists. Thus it has been shown that politic is subordinate to ethic, and both to the general laws of human choice and action which were called the logic of practice. But under either politic or ethic, or partly under both, must fall every aim and endeavour which man can propose to himself, and every tendency of which, if spontaneous, he can become aware. Relatively to other branches of effort, ethic and politic are architectonic; to one or both of them it belongs to prescribe conduct in any other, narrower and more definite, branch of action, leaving it always to every branch to pursue its own peculiar methods and aim at its own peculiar purposes, so far as they do not clash with the essential ends of the higher and larger sciences of practice. (See on the relation of Art to practical science Mr. J. S. Mill's System of Logic, Book vi. Ch. xii. 6th ed.).

4. All branches of knowledge therefore may be regarded alike either as speculative or as practical, according as we consider them from the point of view of the object-matter with which they are concerned, or from that of the aims or tendencies which they are pursued in order to satisfy. But there is a class of sciences which, from the circumstance of their aim being fixed once for all, coinciding with the circumstance that their object-matter is best examined objectively, are properly distinguished empirically as speculative and not as practical; the desire of knowledge supplies the aim which makes them practical, but the distinctions within this general aim are derived from the object-matter itself. This class contains all the physical sciences in the largest sense of the term, including mathematic at one end of the list and physiology or biology at the other. Those pursuits which are commonly called arts are founded on these sciences; their results are the materials or means of the several arts and manufactures. Fixed and definite aims or wishes make these arts practical, as the general indefinite desire of knowledge makes

the speculative sciences so, which are their foundation; but the whole detail of the arts consists in the knowledge of laws of nature, results belonging to and comprehended under some one or more of the physical sciences. Between these two extremes, speculative sciences and arts which are their detailed application, there lies another class of sciences which are sciences of practice. Wherever human action is the object-matter of enquiry, there is or there may be a science of practice; for enquiry into human action includes enquiry into the relative strength of motives in consciousness, the relative value and validity of feelings and aims, the mode of action of these motives as shown by history and experience; all which things require a subjective treatment, as the only means of analysing correctly the object-matter, and as alone supplying the distinctions between one branch of the enquiry and another. These sciences of practice are the subordinate sciences to the general or architectonic sciences, ethic and politic; and they are distinguished from the speculative and physical sciences, with their dependent arts, by this, that human action is the object-matter dealt with as well as the power dealing with it; or that human action is the end as well as the means.

5. Each of the subordinate sciences of practice so determined has both a speculative and a practical branch or department. Just as the physical sciences, as shown in the preceding paragraph, supply the detailed knowledge in which the arts consist, or, in other words, have their practical departments in the arts which are their applications, so each science of practice, which differs from physical science only in having conscious human action for its object-matter,

has its practical department in the art of action which is founded on the laws discovered by it, and the logic of which is the logic of that science. The logic of the art, or constructive practice, is the result of the analysis given of the phenomena by the corresponding science, or speculative department of the art. The logic connects the art of action, the branch of practice, with the science of action, or the practical science, its speculative branch. This has been exhibited already in the present work; Book i. contained the analysis of the phenomena of action generally; Book ii. has contained the logic of practice generally, of ethic and of politic, general laws of general actions, founded on that analysis. We have now to consider the more special sciences and arts of action subordinate to the architectonic arts of action, ethic and politic. The practical branches of the different special practical sciences, in distinction from those dependent on the physical sciences, may be called arts of action, as distinguished from arts of knowledge.

6. When we ask what these special practical sciences with their corresponding arts of action are, it is clear in the first place that any class of emotions, or any group of functions, may be the object-matter of such a science and art. For instance, the religious emotions may have a special science or branch of enquiry devoted to them, and the corresponding art of action will be the establishment of a cultus, or system of religious practices. Every developed religion has such a system; but since the cultus depends upon the formation of the religion itself, the universal religion of mankind, being as yet the religion of the future, has no cultus yet finally formed. Cultus is the art of action, corresponding to the practical sci-

242 LOGIC OF THE PRACTICAL SCIENCES.

Book II. Ch. IV.

§ 92. Practical Sciences and Arts of action.

ence, theology, the object-matter of which consists in the religious emotions, with their inseparable object, God. Every practical science has its basis in some distinct department of human emotional activity, from which it draws its conceptions, and in which it finds its motives of enquiry. Theology was originally undistinguished from philosophy generally, as was shown in § 88. 13 et seqq.; but with the development of character there comes also a development of science, and each department is then distinguished from the rest and placed upon an independent footing. The effect of this development is not to destroy but to renovate theology, by assigning it its proper place and its proper function, as the science of the religious emotions and their inseparable object or objective aspect.

Criticism and Fine Art.

7. Again, the phenomena included in poetic imagination have a special science, but one as yet in a very imperfect state, existing in literature, not organised into science, usually known as criticism. The phenomena of poetic imagination have not hitherto been analysed and described with sufficient accuracy to admit of a logic, or practical science, being founded on them. The scattered intuitions of critics are tending no doubt to this result; and on this account I have been led to pay particular attention to the analysis of these phenomena, as well as to those of religion, in Book i. Poetry the art is far ahead of criticism the science. The arts of action subordinate to poetry, standing as they do nearer to arts of knowledge, from dealing with phenomena of sensation rather than of emotion, are in a more advanced condition; that is to say, the rules of criticism, their science, are more completely established. Such arts,

for instance, are those of metre and rhythm, of structure and division of poems, and even of the employment of images, metaphor, and simile, the play of fancy, and rules of rhetoric. The effect of this or that metre, stanza, strophe, rhyme, or alliteration, on the ear; of the combination of this image with that, in fancy and in rhetoric, upon the understanding or critical taste; are matters admitting of more ready measurement and agreement than the effect of imaginative and emotional expression upon the imaginative and emotional temperament of the hearer. The same holds good with the other fine arts; the laws of harmony in music, of composition in the plastic and pictorial arts, are more subject to admitted rule than what is called the inspiration of genius, which means the emotional and imaginative character of the artist evidenced by his work. The science of criticism, and that science which corresponds to the art of cultus, have also an historical aspect or branch, and may be considered as special portions of history or historical science. The same is also true of those sciences and arts about to be mentioned.

8. There are other sciences which are more advanced. One is the science of the motives and feelings acting on men disciplined in masses; its corresponding art of action is the Art of War, under which head the scientific branch has been included. The need for defence and for the means of exerting power felt by organised states, against the corresponding powers of other states, is the practical foundation of the science, and the cause of the existence of armies. The whole art of war consists in effecting, the whole science in discovering the conditions of effecting, one

general purpose, namely, to reduce an enemy to submission by operating on his fears. The means by which courage, energy, and material forces, are increased in one army, and those by which they are decreased or destroyed in the other, whether these means consist in morale, physical strength, supply of food, weapons, tactic, or strategy, are the object-matter of the science to discover, of the art to apply. The science is practical, and the art an art of action.

9. Diplomacy is another practical science and art of action. It is the art of conducting the public intercourse between States. It requires in the diplomatist a knowledge of the operation of motives and their relative strength, not in a general or merely speculative manner, but as they exist in the character of the rulers of the particular states and under the particular circumstances in question. This knowledge being requisite is what makes the science a practical one; the knowledge which may be called preliminary, such as legal, historical, economical information, as well as the knowledge of the circumstances of the states concerned, is not constitutive of the science of diplomacy, though most requisite to success in it. The art of diplomacy is the application of this knowledge; it is like the art of conversation, bringing point after point to bear upon the person with whom you are conversing, yielding one and pressing another according to the end in view. Diplomacy is indifferent to peace or war; it may be used for all purposes, and of course may be made either to support or to obviate the need of war, by gaining the same ends at less cost, or by agreements to the common advantage of both states.

10. The foregoing arts or sciences bear all of

them a special character; but far more general is the one now to be mentioned, although it may be broken up into several subordinate less general branches, the art or science of Medicine. The art of preserving the body in health cannot possibly be separated from that of preserving the mind in health; the two branches into which all human effort may be divided, as determined by their ends, mens sana in corpore sano, are mutually dependent and reactive on each other. No disease of body but is evidenced sooner or later by some disease of mind; no disease of mind but depends on some disease of body as its immediate or proximate cause. And not only so, but there are many diseases of body which cannot be reached, in order to a cure, but by operations directed upon the mind, by restoring mental ease or cheerfulness, or otherwise acting, as it is said, upon the imagination. Not that the states of consciousness so introduced, or so modified, are as such the causes of the cure, but the nerve states and nerve movements so introduced or modified, upon which these states of consciousness depend, and from which they are named, according to what was said in § 57.

11. Equally general is the art or science of education. In considering the true outlines of this great subject, the first distinction to be drawn is between training for any special purpose, or calling in life, and training the faculties generally, or, as it is sometimes expressed, educating man as man. The special purposes of the former branch of education may be of all degrees of generality compared to each other; it matters not, for the present distinction, whether the training is for a manual trade, or for business, or for a lawyer's career, or for an artist's, or for

a politician's or statesman's; all alike are excluded from that general education which consists in training the faculties common to all men alike, and giving them that harmoniously organised development which is independent of the special walk in life, and a high degree of which in all members of society, whatever their rank or calling, is the great object of attainment for humanity.

12. In the next place, this general education must be still farther restricted. In one sense education never ceases but with life; but in the practical sense of a systematic education applicable to men in masses, it is only up to a certain, though of course varying, age that it can be carried on. In speaking of education, therefore, general education for the young is what is intended. What are the principles upon which this practical science or art ought to be founded? The confusion of general with special education seems to me to have chiefly hindered us hitherto from attaining a clear insight into this point. The divisions of general education, as now defined, must be taken from the broad distinctions of Character. Education is the training of character, the strengthening of the power of self-control, the organised development of the different tendencies and dispositions of which the character is composed, an analysis of which was given in Book i. Chap. iv. Education ought to be varied so as to suit the varieties of character in different individuals; each variety has its own line of development, each has its own limits to the modifications which can practically or profitably be introduced into it; but the main divisions and ground plan of education will be common to all.

13. The general aim of education accordingly is

to promote the active powers of the mind in each of the main divisions in which they may be displayed, and to harmonise these directions of activity with each other. The crude empirical distinction between action and speculation is entirely useless here. Activity is shown not separately, but involved in the two main directions of activity either predominantly intellectual or predominantly emotional, or in a direction where both elements are present in equilibrium. The three great branches of general education are, accordingly, the intellectual, emotional, and æsthetic; all of which must be carried on more or less simultaneously, and with reference to the progress made in each. In the intellectual branch, the chief means and mode of general training of the intellectual powers consist in the study of language, for this offers the means of directing the attention to precision of thought, by comparing the different shades of meaning attached to different forms of expression, and by comparing the different modes of expressing the same or similar meanings by the idioms of different languages. The second great means of general intellectual training is the study of history, that is, the history of human culture at different eras and among different nations. In order to this, some knowledge must be gained of the physical world, and of man's position in it; that is to say, some knowledge of mathematic and of physical science is indispensable, as a condition of historical knowledge. Besides which, both mathematic and physical science stand on ground of their own, the former as a general training of the reasoning powers, the latter of the perceptive. Four modes or objects of study are thus distinguished in the intellectual branch of education;

BOOK II.
CH. IV.
§ 92.
Practical
Sciences and
Arts of action.

Education.

language, history, mathematic, and physical science, at least in some department of it. It is superfluous to point out how closely this branch, in all its modes, is connected with æsthetic culture, the second great branch of general education. This consists in training the powers of poetic imagination, which begins, or has its earliest foundation laid, in the pleasure taken in beautiful objects of sight, beautiful sounds of voice and musical instruments, and in the learning to produce them; a part of the training which seems adapted to the very earliest period of life at which any education can take place. Most children either draw, build, or sing, naturally and spontaneously, and advantage should be taken of this disposition, as the first groundwork of education. Thirdly the emotional tendencies, the moral and religious feelings, should be simultaneously trained and developed; and this is not the less an educational process that it depends chiefly on the example of the educators and of elders generally, and on their conduct towards those who are being educated. Instruction in dogma or mythology is not moral or religious education, though, like instruction in everything else, it may be made its vehicle; it is, if anything, a part of intellectual education. The aim by which emotional education is defined is that of strengthening the good moral emotions, and forming a habit of subjecting the inferior ones to their control.

14. Such is an outline of a general education which would be in accordance with the metaphysical analysis attempted in the foregoing Book. It is the minimum of what general education must contain, to be a general education at all; a minimum determined by reference to the different functions in the

character. It is the foundation for preserving and farther developing the *mens sana*, to which medicine furnishes the complementary condition, *in corpore sano*. Such an education ought to be within the reach of every member of the human family, not in the meagre miserable degree in which it now falls to the lot of the immense majority, but in a degree much nearer, at any rate, to that in which the most cultured classes at present enjoy it. Then and not till then will the mass of the population be competent judges of the political conduct and policy of their rulers, not indeed in the character of skilled politicians, but as those persons who are judges of any work for whose use or benefit it is destined (§ 91. 19). For even in this kind of judgment there are degrees of competence, and those are most likely to be dissatisfied with results who are ignorant of the obstacles which may have opposed their realisation, or which may still prevent the realisation of better.

§ 93. 1. General philology or the science of language is also a practical and not a speculative science. Its object-matter, language, is a phenomenon of human action guided by motives, and determined by the wish or need to express, retain, and communicate, states of consciousness. The distinctions in language are or may be as numerous and subtil as those in consciousness; the phenomena of both equally varied. The motives which have led men to choose this sound rather than that to express a feeling or a thought, this or that grammatical form to express this or that relation of thought, or mode of connecting images and feelings, — motives of ease in pronunciation, of euphony, of pleasure or clearness in imitation, as in onomatopœia, of pleasure or relief in expressing strong feelings by loud or emphasised sounds, and so on,—motives which we may observe still at work in modifying language,—these and such motives as these, being many, and varying in their action upon different individuals and races, and upon the same at different times, are that which makes the science a practical one. The art of action, founded on this science, consists in applying its discovered laws to modify and improve speech; an art certainly which is not capable of exerting very much influence upon language, owing to the comparatively small number of those who are capable of exerting it scientifically, language being formed and modified by the united but inartistic efforts of masses of men; but which nevertheless is of some effect already, and may become more effective when its principles are more commonly established. (See, on the subject of this and the two following paragraphs, Prof. Whitney's remarks, in his Language and the Study of Language, Lect. ii. English edit. Trübner). It might even have weight in accelerating and guiding the establishment of a common language between races now speaking different ones, and thus removing one of the greatest obstacles to unity of interest between nations.

2. Some persons argue from the small power which individuals can exert over language, or from this together with our ignorance of the first steps in its formation, that the science is one of the same order as the physical sciences, a speculative not a practical one. Its laws, it is said, are as much beyond our power to alter as the laws of physical nature; they depend upon the constitution of the organs of voice; the connection of which with thought is perhaps in-

scrutable, and the effects of which are only seen in languages which we never discover in the act of first formation, but always in act of re-formation or modification. Considerations like these do not appear to me conclusive against holding the science of language to be a practical one. Practice means, not that the phenomena included by it are entirely due to volition, but that they are phenomena making part of the same conscious agents who exert the volition. This is the case with the phenomena of language; the spontaneous actions of the vocal organs, dependent upon physical structure and function, and so far falling under physical science, are all of them modified and guided by volition before becoming language; and those of them that are not so modified are not language. Language means sounds expressing feeling or thought. The spontaneous connection of vocal sounds with feelings and images, caused by the transmission of some stimulus from the central nervous organs to the nerves of the organs of voice, is the ground and material which, when perceived, attended to, and guided by purpose, that is, when it has become volitional from being spontaneous, becomes language. A definite sound is then and thus appropriated to a definite feeling or image. To trace these steps, the earliest purposes or volitions, in connecting sounds with images or feelings, whether they are the same in every language, or different in different families, or races, is precisely the problem of the Origin of Language. And if this is true of language at its origin, it is a fortiori true of it at every subsequent stage. From beginning to end the science of language is a practical science, resting indeed upon, but not confounded with, the physiology of the organs subserving it, which is a part of speculative science.

3. The view which renounces seeking the determining causes of language in voluntary human action, since there is no other assignable source of its determinations, would present us, not with a science, but with a history of language or of languages. A classification of the phenomena as accompanying or succeeding each other would be all that could be reached. It is, I suspect, this historical aspect of the study which those have had in view who would parallel this with the physical sciences. The certainty and invariability of the phenomena of language; their comparative immunity from alteration by caprice of individuals; their dependence only or chiefly upon causes acting over large masses of men, such as the opening of foreign commerce, conquest, emigration; the analogy between the development of languages of different stocks; the similarity between early and late developments of languages of the same stock; are phenomena which make the laws of language seem like those of physical growth and structure, while at the same time they are all phenomena which may be included in the history, without being included in the science, of language.

4. Language being the expression of consciousness, we should expect it to exhibit phenomena with distinctions corresponding to those of consciousness. To trace this correspondence belongs to the science of language, not to the mere history of it. The generality of the phenomena of language, that is, their coextensiveness, potential at least, with consciousness, a coextensiveness which they share with the objective world, is the circumstance which justi-

fies, and indeed compels, their treatment by direct application of distinctions discovered in consciousness by metaphysic. The actual steps in the growth and development of language depend on the actual course of the volitions which guide it; the logical analysis of its phenomena statically, at any or all stages of its growth, can only be discovered by the distinctions applicable statically to the feelings and images which are the content of these volitions. And accordingly it is found that the whole of the phenomena of philology fall, in its actual treatment by philologists, under the two heads of etymology and grammar; etymology comprising whatever relates to the grouping of sounds into syllables and words, and grammar whatever relates to the correspondence between the perception and the sign, and between the sequence of perceptions and that of signs. Etymology thus contains the laws of composition and decomposition, of roots, affixes, prefixes, infixes; and grammar the distinctions, 1st, of the parts of speech, as they are called, 2nd, of their structural changes corresponding to the general structure of thought, and 3rd, of the changes in structure of sentences and periods corresponding to the transient changes in the flow of thought.

5. The whole of the phenomena is included under either head, but from a different point of view in each. Etymology is dominated by the consideration of the matter, the sounds, of language; grammar by that of the form, the time and space relations which different sounds are appropriated to express. Etymology traces the decomposition and recomposition of the forms of sound, the syllables and words, of a language, discovers the history and sequence of these

changes, including those due to changes in thought and feeling expressed by them, as well as those due to motives of ease and satisfaction in pronunciation, and of accuracy and euphony in sound. Its materials are gathered from the history of language, which it endeavours to reduce to science by discovering the motives of each change or class of changes. Grammar, on the other hand, considering the relations of sounds to the feelings and thoughts expressed by them, regards its phenomena statically, taking a language to examine as it exists at any one time; and is throughout logical and analytical in its method, science not history; the history of grammatical development falling properly under etymology.

6. The grammatical distinctions and structure of a language reveal the distinctions and structure of thought, the logic, which has become the ruling framework of the mind of the people speaking it. Hence the doctrine established among philologists, that it is the grammar and not the etymology which distinguishes one language from another; the race which imposes its grammar on a mixed language spoken in common by two or more races, not the race which introduces the greatest number of its own words, is the race which is held to impose its language on the others. Different families and races have different logics, in the sense of the term just employed; some give more prominence to some relations or forms of thought, others to others; some distinguish accurately and minutely, others vaguely and with less minuteness. But in attempting to establish a general framework of logical distinctions as a test applicable to the grammars of different languages, by which we may judge of their relative grammatical

fulness and precision, we must approach the question from the side of consciousness, and its metaphysical distinctions, just as has already been the case in distinguishing etymology from grammar. The distinctions of grammar must be founded on distinctions in the formal element of consciousness, or on observed relations between states of consciousness, which ultimately depend on such distinctions.

7. Grammar is the theory of the functions of sounds, that is, of sounds as expressing meanings. But in what does the meaning of sounds consist? In the images and feelings attached to them. How attached? By habitual connection between sound and meaning. Here is the point of connection, the common source, from which flow language and logic. An articulated sound uttered is prompted by a meaning in the brain; the same heard recalls by association the same meaning, in the same or another brain. The act of utterance, and also the impression of hearing, is an additional, but closely connected, phenomenon, which gives fixity to the meaning which would otherwise be less recognisable and more vague; it ascertains the meaning. From the close connection between the nerve apparatus of speech, and that of hearing, with the brain, the seat of meanings, comes the special aptitude which spoken and heard language has to serve as the expression and support, the ascertainer, of thoughts and feelings. Now Logic is the regula of the sequences in meanings, that is, in thoughts and feelings; Grammar the regula of sounds and language. Grammar is the logic of language. But both depend upon the laws of redintegration and association in thoughts and feelings.

8. Grammar then being the theory of the func-

BOOK II.
CH. IV.

¶ 93.
Philology.

Parts of
Speech.

tions of sounds, its first province is to distinguish sounds into classes corresponding to the several kinds of function to which they are applied; in other words, to distinguish the several parts of speech. And first, what is the distinction in thought which is expressed by the distinction of noun and verb? Or in other words, what are the functions of thought which these two classes of words are the means of expressing? It seems to me to be the distinction between an object considered statically and one, perhaps the same object, considered dynamically; an object fixed in thought, sundered from what is before and after, and an object moving or acting. The first depends ultimately upon space, since a portion of time is sundered from time before and after it only by applying to it the logic of space, a surface seen simultaneously; any event may be considered statically, and the name for it as so considered is a noun. A similar event, object, or thing, considered in action, or moving onward in time, is a verb in language. The verb does not express action or movement alone, nor even this or that particular action; it expresses an object acting or moving. A verb is a noun in motion, a noun is a verb at rest. The selection and appropriation of forms of sound to express these functions of thought, or different modes of perception, in different languages, are questions for etymology; but for etymology taking into account causes or motives of both kinds, logical as well as material.

9. The same word, according to its modifications, or relative position among others, serves either as verb or as noun, indicates either an action taken statically, e. g. the infinitive in Greek, the participle in English, or an object taken dynamically, thus

making a verb of a noun, as, in English, mark, a noun, is also the verb mark, to set a mark upon a thing. So also participles are formed from nouns, e.g. hoofed, horned, meaning furnished with hoofs or horns. Participles arise from an abstraction of the dynamical function of their verbs and a generalisation of these functions for any objects indifferently; the dynamical quality of the object, which the verb expresses only as involved in its object, is separated from this and set free to combine with other objects, as a particular quality or mode of action appearing in or exercised by those objects. Participles are to verbs what adjectives are to nouns; but the qualities expressed by the former are dynamical, modes of action; those expressed by the latter are statical, fixed qualities either of sensational, emotional, or intellectual nature, which in combination with others compose the statical object expressed by the noun substantive. Adjectives are words used to express the qualities composing or inherent in remote objects of perception; which are the chief of those which are expressed by nouns substantive. But any quality taken by itself, yet always in some form of time and space, is a complete object, and may be the object expressed by a noun substantive. The distinction between nouns substantive and adjective is, that the latter express qualities as requiring union with others in a remote or independent object; the former express the same qualities as objects already complete or independent. Participles are for verbs, in this respect also, the same thing as adjectives for nouns, only that the qualities are dynamically not statically taken. Here again it is a question for the etymologist to find how far, and by what combinations of sound, these further distinctions in the statical and dynamical functions of thought have been effected by different languages.

10. We must not expect to find in language separate sounds expressing time or space apart from feeling, or feeling apart from time or space; empirical or complete objects, being the earliest in the history of consciousness, must be the earliest things expressed by words. Time and space relations between two or more empirical objects, or states of consciousness, being expressed by words, these words may afterwards be generalised so as to express the same or similar relations between any objects, or states of consciousness, indifferently. And these words may either remain separate, as in the case of prepositions and conjunctions, or may be conjoined to other words, as case and tense endings; while the same relations may be expressed by other means in other languages, as for instance by insertions or vowel changes within the principal words, or by changes in the position of the words in the sentence.

11. The distinction between the statical and dynamical modes of perception gives the distinction between noun and verb; that between denotation and connotation (in Mr. J. S. Mill's use of the terms) gives the distinction between pronoun and noun. The pronoun simply denotes or designates, abstracting from the qualities, or connotation, of the object denoted. The meaning of pronouns is position in space or time; hic, iste, ille. When emphasised, so as to convey meaning, this is done by a recalling of some part of the connotation, or qualities, of the thing or person denoted. I, thou, he, are purely

denotative; emphasis alone recalls the qualities of the persons indicated.

12. Demonstrative pronouns attached to nouns are definitive of them to a certain extent; they are then called articles. A noun without any article attached denotes its whole connotation, the whole class indicated by its name, but in an entirely abstract, indefinite, manner, leaving it undetermined, and to be gathered from the context, whether one, several, or all instances of the thing are meant; as in the line from The Ring and the Book, Guido, 634,

> "And the Pope breaks talk with ambassador,
> Bids aside bishop,"—

as if he had said 'an ambassador for instance,' 'a bishop for instance.' The noun becomes what may be called an aorist noun; and this form of its use may be compared with that of the aorist tense in Greek verbs to signify repeated or habitual action, indefinite only in point of the precise moment of past time to which it is referred; as for instance in Hesiod's description of the Muses on Helicon, Theogonia, 5.

> καί τε λοεσσάμεναι τέρενα χρόα Περμησσοῖο
> * * *
> ἀκροτάτῳ Ἑλικῶνι χοροὺς ἐνεποιήσαντο
> καλούς, ἱμερόεντας· ἐπεῤῥώσαντο δὲ ποσσίν.

With the indefinite article, as it is called, the noun denotes one of the class named by it, but does not indicate which; with the definite article, it denotes one, and which one, in time or space position, of that class.

13. All pronouns refer to some thing or person with qualities or connotation. When it is intended to refer to this connotation and to add something to

it, so as to connect an image which is coming with one which is past, even though the past image is as yet entirely provisional, a denotation expressed solely by a pronoun, then this past image is expressed by a relative pronoun. The relative pronoun expresses movement just as much as the verb does; but with a further distinction, namely, movement from one thing to another; it carries on the thought by connecting what is going to be said with what has been said, and expressing a sameness between the two, id quod, hoc illud. The noun itself may have been previously given, or it may be given only subsequently. Hence the use of the relative in questions; since when you ask Who? What? you ask for a further connotation of an object or person already in your mind. Whatever can be treated as a noun can be denoted by a relative pronoun, and conversely; position in time and space, for instance, modifications of things and actions; and accordingly there are relative adverbs, where, when, and relative adjectives, qualis.

14. In pronouns first appears the cardinal distinction between object and subject. The pronoun of the first person is the denotation of the Subject, of which the whole subjective aspect of things is the connotation. Ego is the pure denotation of the subjective aspect. All other nouns and pronouns are objective to the speaker; but the distinction of the second person from the third depends upon the prior distinction of the first from the second and third together, that is, from objects as such. Those objects in which consciousness is recognised, or which are recognised as the seat of consciousness, the centre of a subjective world, are addressed or spoken of in the

second person; the use of the second person is the expression of this recognition. Besides pronouns, verbs are the only parts of speech which have persons; for verbs alone can distinguish the speaker from things objective to him. The verb is that part of speech which expresses the continuance of action in time; and when this action is part of the very chain of thought and feeling to which the speech itself belongs, when the action is self-describing and so far as it is self-describing, the verb is in the first person. The verb in the first person is the grammatical form which expresses the identity of the agent spoken of and the agent speaking. The distinction of the subjective and objective aspects is thus found in the distinction of the first from the other persons in pronouns and verbs. But this distinction is farther elaborated in the use of verbs and their adjuncts, as will shortly be shown under the second head.

15. The distinction between chief and subordinate conditions, between the qualities of objects or actions and the modifications of these qualities, is expressed by means of adverbs, which may properly be called modal particles. The modes of which things are susceptible are innumerable; hence there are adverbs of all kinds,—adverbs of place, of time, and of quality; and hence the usual derivation of adverbs from adjectives, as

"A being darkly wise, and rudely great."

Hence also the degrees of comparison attach to adverbs as well as to adjectives. Adverbs modify only verbs, participles, and adjectives, taking the latter term in its true functional sense of words used to express qualities or properties of objects, the objects themselves being understood; for substantives, in the usual empirical sense of the term, are certainly modified by adverbs, as 'some gentlemen mostly barristers crossed the Channel,' where it is clearly not the verb which is modified by the adverb. The words 'mostly barristers' are functionally an adjective, applying to the substantive 'some gentlemen.' Adjectives are the modals of substantives, adverbs of adjectives, participles, and verbs.

16. Relations of place and time, and that as well in subjective as in objective order, give rise to two classes of words expressive of them, prepositions and conjunctions. When the relation is one of equality, that is, when both the members are treated alike and have the same thing affirmed or denied of them, we have the simple conjunctions, and, or, neither—nor. 'John and James' is very different from 'John with James.' But when one member of the relation is named first, and then the others brought into connection with it, two classes of words arise according as the relation is statical or dynamical, that is, between things treated statically or as nouns, or between things treated dynamically or as verbs. In the first case these words are prepositions, in the second conjunctions. 'Ora pro nobis;' here the prayer is treated as a whole, and its relation to its object given statically by the preposition pro. 'Orandum est ut sit mens sana;' here the dynamical movement of the prayer itself is given, the motive animating the prayer expressed, by connecting the two verbs by the conjunction ut. It must however be remarked, that the names of the parts of speech are names for functions of words, not for the words

themselves; and that consequently the same word may be employed in several functions, now as preposition, now as conjunction. For instance, 'when' is both conjunction and relative adverb corresponding to 'then;' its relative nature enables its use as a conjunction; see par. 13, where the movement involved in relatives was pointed out. So also 'before,' 'after,' are either prepositions or conjunctions according as they are employed; e. g. 'before sunset,' 'before I go home.'

17. The second province of grammar contains the methods in which the classes of words, distinguished in the first province, are modified and connected so as to express trains of thought and feeling, that is, chiefly, inflections and syntax. Verbs, for instance, in the first place are distinguished into kinds, as neuter, transitive, frequentative, inceptive, having active, passive, middle voices, and so on. Nouns have certain forms to express diminution and augmentation. The rules of construction of sentences, the concords as they are called, belong here, together with rules for government of cases, that is, for connecting the inflections of nouns which express the different relations of their objects to each other.

18. As nouns are either inflected or modified by prepositions in order to express the statical relations of their objects, so verbs have tenses, or are compounded with auxiliaries, in order to express the dynamical relations of the actions named by them. The whole of past, present, and future, time is thus included in grammatical survey, and distinguished into epochs, applicable to all events of whatever variation in actual length. For instance, our English distinctions of imperfect, perfect, and pluperfect, time coordinate

Book II.
Ch. IV.
§ 93.
Philology.
Inflection and Syntax.

past events in a series, starting from the present moment; a present moment, however, which is entirely undetermined as to its length. Thus the imperfect 'he ran' describes an action in a past time, merely past because distinguished from present; it is a past aorist. The perfect 'he has run' is more definite, implying a connection with what is now going on. 'The creation of the earth effected a considerable change in the condition of the universe' is one thing; 'the creation of the earth has effected a considerable change in the condition of the universe' is another; the latter implies that this change is still existing; the use of the perfect lights up the picture with a present interest, and this present moment reaches back to the definite instant in which the creation of the earth was completed; from that instant to the instant of speaking becomes one vast present time. The pluperfect goes farther back still, that is, it implies a perfect or imperfect between it and the present. 'He had written a book,'—you immediately ask When? This must be at a time previous to another already past action.

19. The principal verb in the sentence gives the time to which all the other times are referred; 'I was unable to do it if I had wished;' where the pluperfect 'had wished' indicates a time previous to the imperfect 'was,' and the present 'to do' a time then present. The form 'I could not have done it if I had wished' must mean 'It is impossible as I now know (causa cognoscendi) that I should have done it if I had wished;' where 'could' is a conditional present, the same as 'can' in point of time, but indicating a condition on which it depends. Compare 'I cannot if I wish' with 'I could not if I wished;' and

'I can if I wish' with 'I could if I wished;' where 'can' and 'cannot' express the mere facts of ability and inability, 'could' and 'could not' the dependence of these facts on some condition; the time in both cases being the same, namely, the immediate future counting from the moment of speaking. So with the future, 'When I shall have travelled' indicates the close of a period which is itself entirely future; and this double future becomes a proper vehicle for expressing a double uncertainty,—'Quis tulerit Gracchos, &c.?'

20. The distinction between the subjective and objective aspects is expressed in inflection and syntax by many devices, chiefly by the distinction of the moods in verbs. The indicative mood expresses fact undistinguished from opinion or feeling about it, without distinguishing the two aspects; the present and preterite of the indicative mood are those which alone are thus entirely undiscriminative of the two aspects; the future tenses of the indicative, shall or will, and shall or will have, already admit of the expression of different degrees of uncertainty, different modes of subjectivity; and these tenses accordingly should be considered as forming a link between the indicative and conjunctive moods, while all the remaining purely verbal forms would conveniently fall into one class, as branches of the conjunctive mood, or the mood expressing different modes of subjectivity, or ways of regarding objects as distinguished from the objects themselves, or in their purely objective aspect.

21. Pure commands, λίγε τὸ ψήφισμα, and pure wishes, μὴ γένοιτο, should then be classed apart as expressing a subjective condition of mind in its great-

est possible abstraction. These stand at the opposite end of the scale, as it were, to the present and preterite indicative. There is no purely objective form of speech, as there is nothing purely objective in thought; the most purely objective form of speech is that which draws no distinction between the two aspects; a pure object is an absolute, its existence an illusion. But between these two extremes, between the undiscriminative indicative and the pure imperative and pure optative, lie the different degrees and modes of discrimination, belonging to the future indicative and to the different branches of the conjunctive mood.

22. The moment we leave the firm ground of direct assertion of a present or past fact, we enter upon that of uncertainty, conjecture, hope and fear. The conditions or causes of a future fact require to be taken into account in making a statement concerning it. Accordingly we find in some languages, for instance in our own, the means of discriminating conditions in the simplest statement in future time; and the means impose the necessity of doing so, for we must use either 'shall' or 'will' in the indicative future, and then leave it to the context, or to the emphasis, to take back the distinction if we do not wish to insist upon it. 'Will' is applicable wherever the action is to be represented as moving from the thing or person himself without constraint, 'shall' when it is to be represented as the result of some condition or powerful motive, and hence is employed to indicate certainty of effect. 'I shall rise at daybreak,' that is, I know I shall, or, some cause, e. g. my present resolution, will act as a bond upon me; but 'I will rise at daybreak' is a present resolution simply, or,

if spoken to another person, a promise. 'Shall' describes the action ab extra, 'will' ab intra. 'It will rain tomorrow;' 'will' because the weather is uncertain matter. 'The parcel shall go off tomorrow;' 'shall' because its going may be certainly provided for. Hence the future with shall is an imperative, 'you shall' 'you shall not;' the determining condition lying in the will of the speaker. An equally strong will in the speaker himself is expressed by will, 'I will' 'I wo'nt.' The forms 'I shall' 'I sha'nt,' spoken in contradiction to commands or wishes, imply an unreasoning determination not a reasoning choice, obstinacy not firmness. It is in cases where the distinct expression of volition and necessity is less obvious that the confusion in the use of 'shall' and 'will' is most frequent. 'I will thank you to stand out of my light' is not correct, unless it is meant as a command; if it is meant as a request, it ought to run 'I should thank you;' for then the thanks are a matter of course; while 'I will thank you' implies 'I mean to have to thank you,' that is, 'you shall.' The same holds good in the third person; 'he will thank you to stand out of his light' is a command in shape of a message; but a request 'he would thank you' is correct. Why 'would' in the third person, 'should' in the first? Because in speaking of another you speak of him as acting spontaneously, in speaking of yourself you speak with certainty. So also we say 'I shall die,' but 'you and he will die,' in a matter where the certainty is equally great, in order to soften the expression. 'Shall' and 'should,' implying certainty arising from constraint, are always avoided in speaking of others, unless this certainty is the thing intended to be expressed. 'One would hope so,' 'one would think so,' 'as Aristarchus would say;' but 'I should' in all these cases is correct; 'I would hope so' means 'I should like to hope so,' that is, I would if I could, if external conditions allowed me; but 'I should hope so' means I should hope so on some grounds if there were not counter reasons; where the distinction is between two classes of external conditions, not between external and internal.

23. But the most important of all the methods of distinguishing the subjective from the objective aspect is the use of different branches or tenses of the conjunctive mood. The moment we leave the ground of direct assertion, in which the two aspects are undistinguished, we find two directions open,— the expression of a fact as uncertain, either in itself or as dependent upon another fact, and the expression of a feeling or an opinion. Both are fundamentally the same, and both are accordingly effected by the same means, the use of forms of the verb which may best be classed together as branches of the conjunctive mood. When motives are assigned as final causes; when reasons are given for an opinion; when details are indicated as uncertain, the general tendency or result only being expressed, e. g. 'sunt qui dicant;' when probabilities are stated as such; when the opinions or sayings of others are reported; and doubtless in many other cases which might be mentioned; these characters are given to the statement by means of the conjunctive mood. The general principle is, that an impression on the mind is to be expressed as distinguished from the impression which either might have been produced on others, or would have been produced if the truth had been known.

24. Other means are at the disposal of language for contributing to the same effect, for instance, the distinction of the two kinds of negatives in Greek, οὐ and μή, and their derivatives. Participles, when placed in prominent positions, usually have a meaning either explanatory of what has gone before, or limiting it to an hypothetical case; whence comes the well-known rule of translating, to amplify the Greek and Latin participles, by an 'if' 'though' 'at least' and so on.

25. The expression of the distinction between causa cognoscendi and causa existendi is to some extent provided for by the means already described, but yet it would be well if some more readily applicable sign could be brought into current use, like shall and will for instance, so as to make speakers attentive to which of the two they mean, and to supply hearers with a means of detecting the confusion at once where it exists. As it is, the words Why and Because cover both meanings alike. So also there is no reason why first and second intentions should not be distinguished by appropriated forms of speech; but the evil of confusing them has not yet made itself sufficiently felt. General terms contain another source of ambiguity which there are no ready means at present of clearing up. 'Humanity' for instance means either 'all men' or 'all men so far only as they are distinctively men;' it means either the empirical whole or the logical concept of mankind. To point out these distinctions in conversation involves, in the present state of language, immense circumlocution, not from the difficulty or abstruseness of the notions, but from the want of a distinct notation of them by language. Yet they are not

distinctions which belong to a special subject, like mathematical or chemical distinctions, for instance, but are involved in all matters of common discussion. We are able to indicate by slight changes in form, or at least in tone, whether we are reporting the opinions of others; we have invented inceptive and frequentative verbs, diminutive and augmentative nouns; why should we not invent similar forms to distinguish logical from empirical objects, reasons from causes, things as they are to us from things characterised by their relations to other things?

26. The third province of grammar, indicated in par. 4, contains whatever may fall under the term Style, the more transient modifications of speech by trains of consciousness, the more flexible details within the limits of the general rules of inflection and syntax. There is a style which is peculiar to each language, depending partly on its inflectional and syntactical structure, partly on the genius of the people working onwards upon that basis; and it is within this general style, or genius, of a language that the style of particular writers moves and develops itself. Some languages arrange their sentences in what may be called an accumulative way, the main clause first, the subordinate clauses afterwards, branching out from the main stem and from its larger boughs; others have a constructive or analytic style, in which the main verb comes last, and not till reading to the end of the period is light thrown back upon the meaning of the whole. German is an instance; a German period is like a Hegel's Logic on a small scale, as it were a box containing smaller boxes within it, and these again the same; so that the whole is not only organic, but the com-

prehension of the whole is prior to the comprehension of the parts.

27. Some languages again lend themselves with greater readiness than others to a varied and perspicuous style, a rapid flow of minute distinctions without circumlocution or repetition. For instance, the French particle of comparison 'que,' equally applicable to express 'as much as' and 'more or less than,' gives French a great advantage over English in point of style, as in a sentence which I take from De Tocqueville, "avaient toujours été aussi, et je pourrais presque dire, plus inconnues qu'elles pouvaient l'être."

28. Some languages again have made more approach than others to the distinction of concepts from percepts, mentioned in par. 25; and have on this account a great clearness and precision of style. Latin for instance can and often does use its neuter plural adjectives as concepts. Bona, magna, divina, mean things so far forth as they are good, great, divine. French in the same way has the use of the article, le vrai, le beau, le bien. Opposed to this feature of style is the analytical distinction of abstract qualities from the concrete objects to which they belong. In Greek abstract nouns we always think of this abstract quality, in Latin abstract nouns always of the concrete phenomena in which it is exhibited; φιλία from φίλος is the feeling of friendship, amicitia from amicus is the state of being friends. The turn of mind which analyses percepts produces a different style from that which holds fast concepts; language of the first kind keeps us steadily in face of the facts, language of the second kind substitutes for them our already current generalities. It makes us think we know the subject, whether we really know it or not.

29. The style of writers in a language must move within the limits imposed by the general style of the language itself. For instance, Mr. Browning's style, in poetry, is a constant wrestling with the difficulties which the English language offers to the combination of brevity and rapidity with clearness and fulness of thought; elliptically suppressing relatives, articles, prepositions, auxiliary verbs, and 'to' in infinitives; and thus continually having to trust to the context to show whether a word is a verb, noun, or participle, which without the usual complement of particles is especially difficult in a language so little inflected as the English, and where the same word is so frequently both noun and verb. This dependence of the syntactical construction upon the context, together with the constant use of the figure known as πρὸς τὸ σημαινόμενον, that is, the referring to a meaning which is involved, but not expressly stated, in what has gone before, compels the reader to be constantly interpreting the parts by the whole instead of the whole by the parts, and constitutes, as it seems to me, at once the peculiar difficulty and the peculiar beauty of Mr. Browning's style.

30. There are two ways of interpreting the meaning of sentences, either by their purely syntactical and inflectional structure, or by the context, as it is called, which determines what syntactical structure is intended, when this would otherwise be doubtful. Spoken language has this immense advantage over written, that it can call emphasis into play to explain its meaning. It is the art of writing so to arrange the clauses and words of sentences as to show where the emphasis would be laid in speaking them. All sentences lay down one image or notion

at the beginning, and proceed to superinduce another upon it, or to modify it in some way or other; the terminus a quo is properly called the subject, the terminus ad quem the predicate, of the sentence. The Greek language had the power of indicating the subject by the addition of the definite article. The English has to trust to position or to emphasis, by which it indicates not the subject but the predicate of the sentence, the new thing intended to be said; as was pointed out by Abp. Whately in his Logic. 'Prayer wins *heaven*,' that is, it is heaven that is won by prayer; '*Prayer* wins heaven,' that is, it is prayer by which heaven is won; 'Prayer *wins* heaven,' that is, it is a conquest that prayer effects. Some writers use stops to indicate pauses in the pronunciation, and thus insert them often without any regard to syntax; for instance, a comma between nominative and verb. The proper use of stops is to distinguish the logical or syntactical clauses of a sentence, or the several members of an enumeration; for, since they must be used for purposes of this kind, it is confusing to use them also to indicate mere pauses of the voice.

31. It is to this third province of grammar that the distinction between verse and prose belongs. When mere differences of accent, emphasis, and quantity, with their derivatives, metre, rhythm, cadence, rhyme, and alliteration, are employed to express feeling, or to impress different degrees of importance in what is said upon the hearer, there arises a certain style in the language so modulated, distinct from mere prose or speech of common life as being more adapted to solemn occasions, by the expression of emotion along with thought. The first literature would probably

be metrical; in later times only would a literary or cultured prose be produced, a style, however, which would be no less susceptible of harmony and elegance than the more regularly modulated metrical style. The beauty of style in prose depends, first, upon its having a logically symmetrical structure of thought to express, and secondly, upon its expressing this structure with precision and perspicuity. No style can be good in point of form which is not supported by a full command of the syntactical contrivances of the language, and none in point of matter which does not rest on a similar command of its vocabulary. The matter of style is the thought or meaning to be expressed, the form is the language expressing it; and this language again may be distinguished into the same two branches, which are its matter and its form, namely, the vocabulary and the syntax employed in its composition. No language without style; and, since language is, potentially at least, coextensive with consciousness itself, we may see in this the justification of the well-known aphorism 'The style indicates the man.'

§ 94. 1. Another science is that of Political Economy, which has taken its place among acknowledged sciences more decisively than perhaps any other branch of practical science. See Mr. J. S. Mill's System of Logic, Book vi. Chap. ix. § 3. I shall make no apology for treating this subject, in this and the two following §§, at greater length than might perhaps seem at first sight appropriate to a general enquiry into the theory of practice. The reasons which weigh with me for doing so are of two kinds; first, in order to show the connection between this, the most completely constituted, branch of practical science and the general body of the practical sciences, to incorporate it as a stone already hewn and carved into the entire building, which can only be done satisfactorily by showing at some length its community of distinctions, principles, and method, with theirs; and secondly, in order to derive for the distinctions, principles, and method themselves, a new justification, by exhibiting their applicability to this science. I do not profess to be a discoverer in political economy, but merely attempt to arrange truths which I consider already established in such an order, and to organise them in such an interdependence, as to exhibit the connection of this science with the rest, and the value of the principles and distinctions common to all, in a true light.

2. It is admitted on all hands that, in whatever way political economy may be conceived, it is subordinate to the general sciences or arts of ethic and politic; that its results are not alone decisive of the merits of political, still less of moral, action; that when it has discovered how wealth is acquired, how most abundantly acquired, and how it tends to be distributed in consequence of the process of its production, the further questions, as to how far it is right or prudent to follow these methods strictly, how far to modify them for the sake of other advantages, are questions which fall under a larger and more general science. It is then within these limits that the organisation of the art and science of political economy is to be considered.

3. The art and the science of political economy are properly defined by the action which is their object-matter, namely, the acquisition of wealth, or of commodities having exchange value. Sometimes

it is defined as the science " which treats of the Laws which govern the relations of Exchangeable Quantities," Mr. Macleod's Theory and Practice of Banking, Vol. i. Introduction, 2nd edit. This is good so far as the science or logic of political economy is concerned ; but it leaves out of consideration that political economy is a practical science, and includes an art as well as a science ; in which view its object-matter must be defined by some action, as well as by the objects, and their laws, with which that action is concerned.

4. Others would define political economy by its supposed single motive, the desire of acquisition. The desire of acquiring wealth, it is said, is not indeed the only motive actuating men in their dealings with it, but it is the predominant motive ; it may be isolated and its results studied, as if it were the only motive, on condition of taking into account at last the concurrent motives by which it is modified; especially since, in the most important classes of dealings, those of industry and commerce as a business, it is this motive which acts almost alone, at least with only its inseparable antagonists, love of ease and enjoyment of wealth already acquired. According to this definition, political economy would contain two branches ; one in which it would be an abstract science, examining the action and results of a single motive, artificially isolated for the purposes of enquiry, the other in which this action and these results are combined with those resulting from the action of other motives, which vary according to the circumstances of each nation, each class of possessors, and each individual. Such is apparently Mr. J. S. Mill's conception of the science.

5. This mode of organising the study of political economy is radically different from mine, and in my opinion unsound. The supposed isolation of the motive of acquisition is a chimera. We have no test or measure of its strength but in composition with other motives. It has always at the least two inseparable antagonists, the motive of taking one's ease, and the motive of enjoying unproductively wealth already acquired. In every case, and in every individual, these two motives in composition with it help to determine its strength; and this strength is different in every individual and in every case. We must therefore begin by assuming a certain normal degree of strength in the motive of acquisition so modified and determined, before proceeding to examine its action. But how ascertain this normal degree of strength? How calculate its strength in one individual compared to its strength in another? The answer, I suppose, must be, By the quantities of wealth which we see individuals acquiring. But these quantities depend, undoubtedly, upon many other circumstances as well as the strength of their desire of acquisition, such as natural powers, physical and intellectual, natural products or facilities offered by countries where the men live, mines, timber, harbours, and so on. If we put these aside, under the phrase cæteris paribus, and suppose men to be set on acquiring wealth under equal conditions but with different degrees of energy, depending on different strengths in the common motive, we must still examine first the concrete cases of acquisition in which this motive appears to be the predominant one, that is, the operations of industry and commerce. In other words, we must begin our enquiry

with isolating, not a motive, but a class of concrete operations, as the immediate object of enquiry. Abstracting then, first, from natural powers in the men and facilities offered by circumstances, and secondly from concurrent motives of action, we may arrive at some estimate of the normal strength, and its various different degrees in different men, of the remaining motive of acquisition. But it is evident that this motive is a residuum, not a known force with which we begin the enquiry, or which can be laid at the basis of a deduction. It is known only by means of a previous knowledge of other circumstances, and other motives depending on them. It is clear therefore, that, although we may characterise the enquiry into the express operations of trade and industry as an enquiry into the action of the abstract motive of acquisition, the enquiry itself, or as I should express it the object-matter of the enquiry in its first intention, consists in examining the phenomena of this class of operations, without any especial use being made of the motive of acquisition. The strength of this motive is x, an unknown quantity, which does not ascertain but is ascertained by the analysis of the operations in question. To lay this motive at the basis of the abstract branch of political economy is a fiction, an instance of mistaking the character, or second intention, of a thing for the analysis or nature of the thing itself.

6. I return, then, to my original definition of the science by the acquisition of commodities having exchange value. This definition gives the limits and the characteristics of the whole. Two things are involved in the term 'having exchange value;' first, the commodities in question are material as distin-

guished from spiritual, because they must be capable of being sundered from other commodities in order to be separately valued, and of being passed from one person to another in order to be exchanged. I do not mean that they must be corporeal, that is, visible and tangible, but that they must be capable of a distinct and separate existence; the act of teaching, for instance, is a commodity having exchange value, the act of teaching one person a science and abstaining from teaching it to any one else is another, which would probably have a higher value; but the knowledge which enables a man to do the act of teaching is a spiritual commodity which cannot be separated from the man nor valued in exchange. So again a character for honesty is non-valuable and non-exchangeable; but the acts which a man may covenant to do, as to enter into another's service, have an exchange value all the higher in consequence. It is like the fertility of a field, the right of using which is the more valuable in consequence of this inseparable quality. In short, all exchange value is founded on some value-in-use; but all value-in-use, by itself, is excluded from the consideration of political economy. The second consequence from the definition 'having exchange value' is, that the only actions in pursuit of wealth immediately and exclusively belonging to political economy are dealings between men. The best way of ploughing, of cropping, of shearing, the best kind of machinery, of material for manufacture, the best climate, the best soil for particular crops, the best iron, timber, and so on, in short everything that relates to the dealings of man with nature alone, may serve as the foundation or subsidiary knowledge to political economy, but is excluded from the science itself; for instance, the law that the increase of product from land tends, beyond a certain point, to decrease in amount with additional labour and capital bestowed (Mr. J. S. Mill's Principles of Pol. Econ. Book i. Ch. xii. § 2) is not strictly within but subsidiary to the doctrines of political economy. The same may be said of the doctrine, or fact, that all capital, all means of further production, consist in saving, or are the result of self-denial in abstaining from consumption; a doctrine which is true whether the capital saved is intended for exchange, as in making advances to labourers, or solely for employment by a solitary hunter or trapper. These are cases of knowledge to be elsewhere acquired, being extraneous to political economy just in the same way as the knowledge of the laws of the land or countries traded with is; as for instance, the law of debtor and creditor, or the course of history which has determined the existence of a landlord class in England.

7. If then, instead of defining political economy by the supposed isolated motive of the actions which are its object-matter, we define it by those actions themselves, that is, by the act of acquisition, instead of by the desire or motive of acquisition, everything becomes clear, logical, and homogeneous. The action of acquisition may have many motives, all of which are included in the scope of the science, along with the action which they prompt and guide, but only so far as they prompt or guide it. The act of acquisition limits the motives; the things acquired, commodities having exchange value, limit the act of acquisition; and these commodities, acts, and motives, are together the object-matter of the science.

These motives, and the reasoning about them and about the means of satisfying them, the balancing and deciding between them when they conflict, these constitute the voluntary action which is the material or object-matter both of the science and of the art of political economy; the laws, principles, and governing distinctions, in these actions and reasonings are its logic, theoretical branch, or science; and the practical rules which may be deduced for guiding conduct towards the attainment of any desired end, that is, the acquisition of the most desired commodities, constitute its art. The acquisition of the greatest possible quantity of exchangeable commodities is not the purpose or τέλος of the art of political economy, but the acquisition of such commodities and in such quantities as we may most desire to have. What and how much we may most desire to have is to be decided extraneously, and falls under the scope of politic and ethic, not of political economy. Were it contrariwise, political economy would not be subordinate but superior to those larger arts, which is admitted on all hands not to be the case; while if the aim of political economy were to acquire the greatest possible amount of wealth, as in its abstract branch it would be if the science were defined by the motive of acquisition, it would be independent of ethic and politic, so far as that abstract branch of it was concerned, and the logical coherence of the three sciences would be so far disturbed.

8. Motives in political economy hold precisely the same position as the different kinds of value-in-use. They are in fact the subjective aspect of value-in-use. Whatever has value-in-use, utility, or pleasure, supplies a motive for its being acquired; the perception

of a value-in-use is the motive for acquiring the thing perceived to have that value. When it is said that the motive of acquisition, apart from other motives, is the motive proper to political economy, the only motive of which it takes cognisance, it is meant or ought to be meant, that all or any motives leading to acquisition are its motives. The confusion of this with the wish to acquire by itself, the wish to have a thing because having it is the means to enjoy it, is a confusion of the effect with the cause; in other words, it is to confuse the action resulting from motives with those motives themselves, treating them as a single motive because the act is single in which they result. It is true that the wish to acquire may become a special motive by itself, as it was shown by Tucker that the desire to possess coin is a result of translation, from association with the pleasures which the possession of coin procures. But in this sense the desire of acquisition is one motive among many, leading as others do to the action of acquisition, but very insignificant compared to the rest; the action of acquisition gratifies this wish as it does all others; and it is not in this secondary character, as gratifying a desire of acquisition, that the action of acquisition enters into political economy, but in its character of an action gratifying all wishes indifferently. Acquisition is the single channel into which all motives are gathered up, and through which they operate, as it is the single means by which all pleasures, all enjoyments of values-in-use, so far as dependent on wealth, are procured.

9. But what is the connection between the art and the science of political economy, and whereby is it sustained? The art consists in making desirable

exchanges; and the immediate knowledge requisite for this is the knowledge of the values, or prices if estimated in money, of different commodities and services; of their probable fluctuations in the near future; and, as the key to this, of the causes which specifically operate in raising or lowering the prices of different articles. To possess the art thoroughly and in its full extent it would therefore seem requisite to possess the knowledge of the laws of prices, as well as of their actual state, and current transactions in the business world. But this would be impossible without a knowledge of the history of prices, of their changes in the past as well as in the present, and also, it must be added, of other modes of human action, with the comparative strength of the motives on which they are founded, which come into collision or combination with the actions of acquisition and exchange, and modify their results. To trace the laws which govern this complex action of society, in their effects upon that part of it which consists in acquisition and exchange of values, is a part of the science which may be called its dynamical branch; and the logic both of the statical and dynamical branches would have to be laid down, before the science of political economy could be considered to be complete. It is however only the logic of the statical part of the whole subject that can be sketched here. The dynamical branch with its logic contains the principles upon which the practice or Art of political economy immediately depends; an art which, as distinguished from the science, it would perhaps be well to name Economical Policy. Political economy would then be reserved as the name of the whole subject considered as a science, having its pure logic as the statical, its applied logic as the dynamical, portion of it; and economical policy the name of the whole subject considered as an art, or practice flowing, mediately from the pure, immediately from the applied logic, that is, from the principles of the dynamical branch. The connection between the statical and dynamical branches will be again touched on before quitting the subject. (§ 95, 96.)

10. The laws of values or prices, then, upon which their phenomena depend, are that part of the art which connects it with the science. This is the ground common to them both; but the statical part of the logic contains only the most general laws, the most general organic distinctions, which serve to distinguish and connect the different classes of exchanges, and to trace the different elements which compose the value of the commodities exchanged. This statical part is entirely analytical; and it is from its application to the facts and history of prices, in connection with general history and other modes of human action, that the general laws of exchanges in the dynamical part would result. History would supply the facts, the dynamical logic their explanation; history the material for induction, and facts for the verification of laws; the dynamical logic the principles and theory to be verified. The general laws of values or prices are the common ground where the logic and the history meet, and in which they ought ultimately to show concordant results. But the statical logic is the foundation of the whole enquiry.

11. It is, then, only with the statical logic, its general distinctions, methods, and laws, that I profess to have to do here; and with this only so far as may be necessary for the purposes explained in

par. 1; even this, I fear, will occupy more space than may to many seem proportionate to the rest of the book. What then is the first organic distinction in the object-matter? It must be observed that the actions are dealings between men, and in this respect similar to the object-matter of the science last examined, namely, language. The exchanges between men may be distinguished from the means by which they are effected, just as the sounds of language from the thoughts and feelings which they express and communicate. This distinction seems to arise from the very nature of the case; and in political economy we find it quite as applicable as in philology. Commodities are broadly distinguished by it into two classes; on the one side is that commodity which is the universal purchaser, the means of exchanging all the rest; on the other are the other commodities which it purchases.

12. Founded on this broad distinction between the commodities arises a distinction between two branches of the logic; the first containing those distinctions and laws of value which are of universal applicability, valid whether money is used to purchase and exchange other things or not; the second containing those which flow from the nature and use of money, as universal purchaser and means of circulation. Two aspects of the logic are thus disclosed, for the entire phenomena might be treated from either side. But in the first we have laws and distinctions of a more general nature than any which are peculiar to the second; and under which those of the second may be shown to fall, as cases or instances of them. It is requisite to begin with the more general; but these in their turn will, in one way, depend upon the

laws and distinctions arising in money; namely, the modes of value belonging to them will be estimated and expressed in money value, that is, as prices, as in a language which has become current and intelligible.

13. Or the same division may be reached by another way, namely, by adopting Mr. Macleod's threefold distinction of exchangeable quantities, in his Theory and Practice of Banking, Chap. i. § 3. into commodities, services, and debts. The first branch of the subject will include commodities and services, the second debts. The distinction between commodities and services will be found of the greatest importance in the analysis of the first branch; the difference in nature between these two kinds of exchangeable quantities gives rise to differences in the mode of their remuneration, and in the requirements of the persons who are their holders.

§ 95.—

"You can't eat your cake and have it too."
Old Proverb.

I.

1. To begin with the first and general branch of the subject, what are the principles and distinctions governing the reasoning about acquisition, or, in other words, what are the first outlines of the logic of political economy? So far as I am aware, De Quincey's Logic of Political Economy, which together with his Templar's Dialogues is professedly an exposition of Ricardo's doctrines, is the only work in which these principles and distinctions are exhibited with an adequate perception of their importance as the dominant principles of the whole science.

The logical centre of the whole subject is the nature of Exchange Value. The most usual method of treating the subject is to begin with commodities generally, their mode of production, the division of labour, so as to produce them better, their distribution among different classes of the community, the elements of their production, land, labour, capital, and so on, before entering on the question of exchanges. The wealth, it is said, must first exist before it can be exchanged, and we ought to see how it exists, and what are its characteristics, before entering on the dealings of men with each other in respect of it. (See Mr. J. S. Mill's Principles of Pol. Econ. Book iii. Chap. i. § 1). But this is to enter on questions subsidiary to political economy. It may be the best method, for practical exposition, to begin with these subsidiary phenomena; but political economy is not entered on until the dealings of men with men in respect to wealth are treated. Wealth in the wide sense, commodities having value-in-use, are of two kinds, those which are acquisible from nature only, and those which are acquisible from man as well as from nature. Those of the first class have values-in-use only, those of the second have exchange values as well. But the dealings of man with nature alone can hardly be the object of political economy; they are subject to the laws of ethic, for these embrace all human acts, and to those of politic, so far as they have results bearing on other men. But political economy, being subordinate to politic, considers property to be already established, everything which can be separately possessed to be already provided with a possessor, or at least with a possible legal claimant, a claim which may have its

Book II.
Ch. IV.
§ 96.
Statical logic of exchange.

value and its price. Only within the limits of legal possession, though indifferent as to who the possessors may be, indifferent to systems of private or systems of Communistic property, is political economy possible; consequently all acquisition within its limits must be from man as well as from nature. Now all commodities having exchange value include, as a cause of that value, some value-in-use; consequently their value-in-use has to be considered as a part of the whole question of their exchange value. See the admirable distinction between the two senses of the term value-in-use, one in which it is opposed to exchange value, the other in which it is opposed to D as the other element which, together with it, composes exchange value, in De Quincey's Logic of Pol. Econ. Chap. i. Sect. vi. The term 'exchange value' is that adopted by Mr. Mill, as an improvement on the clumsier 'value-in-exchange.' If now value-in-use, or commodities acquired from nature alone, were taken as the starting-point, or logical centre of organisation, the science would come out logically as a science of the whole doing and working of man, as a science of practice generally.

2. Similarly it may be said of labour, by which man wins or appropriates values-in-use from nature, that alone it has nothing to do with political economy. Like value-in-use it is only as a cause of exchange value that it belongs to the science. As there is no exchange value which is not founded on some value-in-use, so there is none which is not founded on some labour, be it only the easiest labour of appropriation or preservation. In these two opposite causes of exchange value lies the connection of political economy with the outer world of natural phenomena

and their laws, which are the condition of its existence and the limit of its powers. As such causes they must never be lost sight of; forget them, and political economy drifts anchorless as a cloud. We may begin with them if we choose, but it must be for the sake of applying them to the analysis of exchange value; while, if we begin with the analysis of exchange value, the logical method, we must carry it up to its causes in the outer world, and end with labour and value-in-use, as the ultimate foundations upon which every instance of exchange value rests, as the basis of the supervening fluctuations. Applying therefore the old distinction between nature and history, I take the nature of exchange value as the centre of the science, and starting point of the enquiry.

3. The elements in analysis of exchange value are these two: the value-in-use of the commodity in question, which is called U, and the difficulty or obstacles to its acquisition, called D. Both elements, U and D, are taken subjectively, that is, as they are estimated by the parties to the exchange; and this is true of all their subdivisions. The purchaser has his estimate of U, and so has the seller; the purchaser has his estimate of D, and so has the seller. Now the elements of U may be any of the innumerable satisfactions possible to man. But the elements of D vary according to more fixed conditions. These may be all summed up as the U of the seller or possessor of the commodity, its value-in-use to him, either to enjoy or to reserve for a better market; which clearly makes or sums up the D of the buyer, the obstacle which he must overcome if he wishes to purchase. Every exchange is thus a balance between

U and U, the D of the purchaser consisting in the U of the seller, while the D of the seller consists in the U of the buyer decreasing or vanishing. It is well however always to speak from the point of view of the purchaser or acquirer, when speaking of U and D, in order to avoid confusion. Then, and from this point of view, the existence of some kind and degree of U, or estimated utility, is necessary to every exchange; without it or below it no commodity would command a price, even at the minimum of D; and beyond or above it the maximum of D will fail to enhance the price. U therefore, from the acquirer's point of view, is the condition sine qua non, D the limiting or determining condition, fixing the point in U at which the acquisition is made, the estimate of the exchange value of the commodity, that is, the price, if reckoned in money.

4. From the acquirer's point of view, D is always the governing or limiting element of the value. D consists in the resistance offered by the seller, but it is caused by various considerations, or is determined by different elements at different times, according to the nature of the commodity in question. There are two heads under which all cases may be brought; the first is where the commodity is unique, or stringently limited in quantity or number; the second where it may be multiplied indefinitely by increased application of labour and capital. The first head includes only those cases where the price is fixed by the varying estimates of the value-in-use of the commodity, and by the consequent resistance of sellers in comparison with the insistance of purchasers, the quantity of the commodity being fixed; the second head includes the cases where, besides or

beyond this, the varying degrees of difficulty in acquiring the commodity from nature modify the resistance of sellers, the quantity of the commodity being variable. And this second head again falls into two branches, according as the difficulty of acquiring the commodity from nature, or the fluctuations in its supply from time to time, are the predominant element in the D of its exchange value. We have thus three classes of exchanges; 1st, where the D consists entirely in the scarcity or uniqueness of the commodity; 2nd, where it consists chiefly in the difficulty of acquiring it from nature, but is modified by the temporary fluctuations of supply and demand; 3rd, where it is based upon the difficulty of acquiring it from nature, but chiefly determined by the quantity which is from time to time demanded compared to that which is from time to time supplied.

5. The first class of cases is by far the simplest. The commodities belonging to it form a very small part of the whole comprised in political economy; the consumer's prices of them are not business but fancy prices, depending on fashion and taste. De Quincey's musical box on Lake Superior is a perfect instance. Speculation is entirely excluded from these cases of exchange, because, if the commodities in question were procured with a view to sell them for a profit, D would then depend upon difficulty of production, and a minimum price would be fixed by the cost of production and bringing to market. Such cases would fall at once under one or other of the two remaining classes. Works of fine art, old china, rare books, wine of famous vintages, are among the chief commodities of the class, but not as offered for

sale by regular dealers in them. Two cases of exchange belong to it; either there are several intending purchasers, or there is only one. In the first case, the competition of the purchasers is what constitutes the D, the difficulty of attainment by any one of them; the seller's knowledge of this competition enables him to insist on a high price, which rises till it reaches that point of the joint U of the purchasers where only one purchaser continues to have an U at all, the others dropping off as the price increases. The resistance offered by the seller is the D; this continues until the seller is afraid of its exceeding the highest U of the purchasers, beyond which there would be no bargain. The value is thus measured off on U by the action of D; it consists in the U of the actual purchaser, but is determined by D, the knowledge which the seller has of the various estimates of U by the intending purchasers. In the second case there are only two persons bargaining, one purchaser only. Here the D is still fixed by competition, for the seller himself stands in the place of a purchaser, and brings his U into competition with that of the other party. If the purchaser does not offer a sufficiently high price, he will purchase it himself, that is, keep it unsold. It is still D which fixes the price, when a bargain takes place, in virtue of this competition of the seller himself.

6. I am aware that De Quincey considers, in these cases, U as the determining and D as the determined element, and not vice versa; and it is true that the estimates of value-in-use are that which is operative. But the estimates of value-in-use are made by both sides, and are common to both; it is not the U of the buyer but the U of the seller which determines

the price, or, if the U of the buyer, yet this as estimated by the seller; that is to say, in the exchange, when U and D are distributed to buyer and seller, D is the determinant, although it consists in an estimate of value-in-use. Besides which it may be remarked, that the U of the last purchaser is not exhausted by the price at which he purchases; if the seller were to hold out longer, the price might rise still higher, and it is only the fear of the seller that it will not do so which forces him to conclude the bargain. This however exhausts ipso facto the whole D; D ceasing measures off a portion of U; and not U a portion of D; since the whole of U is not measured by the price arrived at. There is thus uniformity in the operations of all three classes of exchanges, for it will be seen that, where D depends on difficulty of production, D and not U is the determining element.

7. The second and third classes of cases of exchange, differing only in the degree of influence exercised on price by difficulty of production, may be treated together, so far as the principle constituting them, and distinguishing them from the first class, is concerned. They include exchanges of all commodities which are producible at pleasure by a proportionate expenditure of capital and labour, the quantities of which therefore are variable, and the supply open to competition among producers. It is not necessary at this moment to enter upon the further distinction between commodities of this kind, into those producible in amounts which preserve an equal ratio to the additional capital and labour expended and those producible in amounts whose ratio to the additional labour and capital expended is continually decreas-

ing. This distinction will find its proper place farther on (par. 64).

8. The producibility of commodities at pleasure by a proportionate expenditure of labour and capital, rendering their supply variable, and admitting of competition among the producers or holders of them, gives efficiency to the element of difficulty of production, expressed as cost of production, in determining their prices. It enables us farther to analyse the exchanges of them, in their U and D elements, and to distinguish in the resulting prices two parts, one due to the difficulty or cost of production, which has been called the natural price, the other due to the fluctuations of supply and demand at different times and places, which results in oscillations about the natural price, and together with it, or on its basis, composes the market prices at which the commodities are actually sold from time to time.

9. To begin with the concrete market price or value of a commodity of this kind. U is still the determined, D the determining, element in its value. But the case is complicated in this way. In the first place, U is not only the value-in-use estimated by the purchaser for himself, but the value-in-use to manufacture or employ in industry, or the exchange value to sell again, where the prices in future markets must be taken into account. D again is complicated in a similar way; it consists not only in competition of purchasers, but also in competition of sellers, which tends to diminish it. The sellers come into the market with as strong an interest in selling as the buyers in buying. Hence the interest and competition, known to both parties, and corresponding to the competition among buyers, combine with it in de-

termining D, the difficulty of attainment. Added to this is the distinction in D arising from the variableness of supply. As in every exchange there must be some value-in-use, as the sine qua non of U, so in every exchange of commodities of the present kind there is a sine qua non of D, an element of difficulty which fixes a minimum, below which the exchange value cannot permanently fall without causing the commodity to vanish from the market. This sine qua non is the labour of production, measured and expressed by the cost of production. The competition of producers, the supply being variable, is directed to diminish this cost, so as to enable them to offer the commodity at the lowest price, which must cover this cost, including their profits, or remuneration for placing it in the market. The effect is to distinguish in the total or market price a minimum amount, or part of the price, below which the commodity, ceasing to be remunerative, will cease to be produced.

10. D, thus determined and thus distinguished into its two elements,—competition among purchasers compared to competition among sellers, and cost of production,—marks off on U the point at which the exchange is effected, the actual price of the commodity. U and D gather up the purchaser's knowledge on one side, the seller's on the other, and through these estimates the exchange is effected. The price itself by the same means becomes distinguishable into the basis or minimum, fixed by cost of production, and the oscillations about that basis, which can never fall permanently below it to any extent, and never rise permanently above it to a great extent, without in the first case stopping the production, in the second

bringing additional producers into the market, and so reducing the excess of price. These oscillations about the natural price are due to competition between purchasers compared to competition between sellers, that is, to demand compared to supply. The market price as a whole is determined by the quantity demanded compared to the quantity supplied; but it may be analysed into component elements, natural price determined by cost of production, and oscillations about that basis due to variations in the supply and demand. And we must accordingly distinguish between two senses of the term 'supply and demand,' the one when it means the determinant of market price as a whole, the other when it means the determinant of oscillations about the natural price, which are but one element of the total market price.

11. I wish now to apply to this analysis the distinctions pointed out in § 94. 6; whereby the perfect harmony between them will become apparent. The analysis began with stating the thing to be analysed, the market price of commodities producible at pleasure and therefore variable in quantity. The two elements of this market price were then distinguished, natural price and the oscillations about it. This analysis leads us to ask the conditions which regulate the two elements; and the first element, natural price, is determined by the physical laws which limit production, laws of nature extraneous to political economy, which determine the acquisition of commodities having value-in-use from nature alone. This is a condition limiting man's power of production generally, and consequently the production of commodities having exchange value. The relation of natural price to market price is now evident; it is

not only an element in its composition, but that element which depends on laws of nature extraneous to political economy. Market price anticipated is the final cause of production; production is an efficient cause of market price; and the difficulty of production, which is itself measured and expressed by cost of production, is the measure of the energy with which this efficient cause operates upon market price, appearing as that part of it which is called natural price. Treating then, as we have done, all exchanges as dealings between men, governed by final causes, and beginning accordingly with market price as the result, and the anticipated result, of those dealings, we may characterise them all, in the first place, as cases of a relation between supply and demand, inasmuch as they are cases of transaction between suppliers and demanders. In this view we may say universally, that a commodity is not demanded because it has been produced, but that it is produced because it is expected to be demanded. The market price is the first thing to be considered in treating exchanges as voluntary actions or matters of practice. But this treatment of the case brings us in the next place to the conditions imposed by nature upon such production, to the roots which exchanges have in the world extraneous to political economy; and here it is found that one part of market price is fixed by nature, namely, the part answering to the labour or difficulty of production, expressed and measured by its cost.

12. It is the more necessary to insist upon the distinction between the final cause of production and the natural difficulty or cost of production, because the latest opponent of Ricardo's theory of value, Mr.

Macleod, seems to have become so from neglecting it. He sees no difference between the anticipated market price regulating "the greatest cost of production that can be afforded" (Elements of Pol. Econ. p. 114) and its regulating the cost of production itself. True, it regulates the action of men on the condition of a given cost of production, but it cannot regulate this condition itself, which is imposed by the resistance offered by nature to human energies. And, since this resistance may be overcome to an indefinite extent by additional energy being expended, while the energy expended may be measured as cost, the cost becomes a distinguishable part of the price, which must be of that amount at least, in order to be a motive for expending the energy and producing the commodity. The cost of production is a cause contributing to determine the motive, as well as the motive a cause contributing to determine the production.

13. While therefore with Mr. Macleod, and indeed I believe with all political economists, for Ricardo's system contains nothing to the contrary, it may be laid down as the first and universally valid law of exchanges, as matters of human practice, that, in order to fix the value of any commodity, there is requisite a certain relation between the quantity supplied and the quantity demanded, it must be maintained at the same time, that this relation itself depends upon conditions, extraneous to the science of political economy, which have a definite effect upon the supply, which definite effect is distinguishable in the value under the name of natural value or price. This distinction is a further analysis of the market price, as well as a further analysis of the relation be-

tween the supply and the demand. That the value or price of anything arises in a certain relation between the supply and demand of it may be called the first law of political economy, because it is the most general fact concerning exchanges; a law or fact which can only be analysed farther by going back from the nature, or first analysis, of exchanges into their conditions or causes, which are then seen reflected in the further and more complete analysis. And this regress into their conditions lays bare the distinction between commodities producible at pleasure, and therefore variable in quantity, and commodities unique or stringently limited in quantity, and therefore such that their cost of production is no longer operative on their price. Ricardo's law of value is as universal in its principle as that on which alone Mr. Macleod insists; but since it is a law founded on a further distinction in the object-matter embraced by the other law, namely, the distinction of commodities fixed and commodities variable in quantity, the results which it affirms of the one kind of commodities it necessarily denies of the other; which is a very different thing from its being, as Mr. Macleod seems to suppose, (page 125), applicable only to one kind of commodities and not to the other. While therefore the two laws are equally universal they are not inconsistent, but, in political economy, Ricardo's law, that the quantity of labour is the sole efficient cause of value, with its corollary, that cost of production determines natural price, is a further explication and analysis of the law, that supply and demand is the sole regulator of value; for the latter treats exchanges solely as matters of human practice and volition, while the former treats them as conditioned also by laws of nature extraneous to political economy.

14. There are only two opinions which can be held respecting natural price, either that it is, as here maintained, a real component element of market price, or that it is a term mistakenly applied to a mere average price, deducible from a sufficiently long series of exchanges, which is the opinion held by Mr. Macleod, Elements, p. 210. Since I am writing on political economy in connection with metaphysic, I may perhaps be allowed to illustrate this difference of opinion by one which is still under discussion there. Time and space in perceived objects are held by some metaphysicians to be mere abstractions from the objects themselves, and their apparent universality and necessity to be nothing more than consequences of our having, as it happens, always perceived objects, in relation to each other, in sequence of time and juxtaposition of space; and this opinion corresponds to that which maintains the part of price in question to be a mere average, abstracted from a series of fluctuations. The opposite opinion, that this part of price is a real component element in market price, corresponds on the other hand to the opinion, which I myself maintain, that time and space are real elements in every perceived object itself, however minute, and can only be inferred, generalised, or abstracted, from experience, because they are first perceived in every such portion of it.

15. Let us now see what sort of a law this law of supply and demand is. The law that demand tends to call forth a supply to satisfy it, and that supply tends to be equal to demand; and farther, that the quantity supplied compared to the quantity demanded

at any particular place and time is that which regulates the market price; or, to express the latter part of the law in the more elaborate words of Mr. Macleod, Elements, p. 100, that "Price varies directly as the intensity of the service rendered, and inversely as the power of the buyer over the seller;" is not a law analytic but only descriptive of the phenomena which it embraces. It is a law which "reigns but does not govern." It tells us that prices tend to rise with an increase of demand or a decrease of supply, and vice versa; and it tells us that an enhanced price will tend to stimulate, a lowered to check, supply. But it does not tell us what proportion the changes in price will bear to the changes in supply and demand which are supposed to cause them, or, in other words, to what extent a change in the relation between the quantities demanded and supplied will cause a change in the price which results from it. See on this point Mr. J. S. Mill's Principles of Pol. Econ. Book iii. Chap. ii. § 4. And also Mr. W. T. Thornton's proof of the nullity of the law of supply and demand, as an analytic or explanatory law, in his work On Labour, Book ii. Ch. i. Supply and demand is but another expression for the operation of exchange itself. It regulates price in the same sense as the act of exchange regulates it. That is to say, it is a description of the phenomena which are to be regulated, rather than of the law which regulates them. Whatever the proportion between supply and demand may be, whatever causes operate to raise or lower price, whether combination, monopoly, legal intervention, taxation, intimidation, or protection in any shape, the law of supply and demand holds equally good, for all such causes operate upon price only by changing the proportion between them. It is one of those unfortunately famous "immutable" laws of political economy, which we are continually cautioned not to violate, although their immutability consists in nothing else than in the impossibility of violating them. This however is but saying, in other words, that it is a description and characterisation of the phenomena in general terms, or terms of second intention; a description which needs a further analysis, but does not itself supply the means of giving one. Such a further analysis is supplied by Ricardo's law of value, and by the corollaries which may be deduced from it. But one side of this distinction, the oscillations of market price about natural, has not yet been reduced by observation to a classification sufficiently established to be admitted into a logic of the science. It remains therefore only to follow the thread of natural price, which will be found to exist in the case of all commodities and all services, the supply of which is not stringently limited but may be increased or diminished at pleasure.

II.

16. The whole difficulty of production may be included in the words Quantity of labour; the differences in value between any commodities depend upon the different quantities of labour required to produce them. But differences both of degree and kind of irksomeness must be considered as included in the general expression, quantity. The difficulty consists in the irksomeness; and this irksomeness or quantity of the labour is that which hinders a man from acquiring commodities by labouring. We are here on the solid rock of human nature and human

motives. The question of analysing the difficulty of production is therefore the question of analysing the different modes and degrees of labour. Now here the term labour is used as an equivalent to the term difficulty of production; there is another sense in which it is used as opposed to Capital, and shares with capital in composing the difficulty of production; just as the term value-in-use had two senses, one as the contrary to, the other as a subordinate element in, exchange value (par. 1). In this latter sense, quantity of labour remunerated by wages, and capital remunerated by profits, compose the total difficulty of production measured by cost of production.

17. Before proceeding to the second sense it is requisite to dwell somewhat on the first or undivided sense of the term labour. As no distinction is here introduced into labour, beyond that of different kinds or degrees of irksomeness, so it is also with the labourers; the producers generally are undistinguished into labourers and capitalists employing labour. Here the fundamental and most general proposition, first established by Ricardo, is this: that the natural value of any commodity depends upon the quantity of the labour producing it, including in quantity degree and mode of irksomeness, which quantity is measured by the natural value of the labour; and not upon the value of that labour, or the amount of commodities which that labour will purchase, meaning by value in this case the market value of labour from time to time. To confound or neglect this distinction is to confound the distinction between nature and history, between what a thing is, or is measured by, and what it causes or is caused by. The quantity of labour

is the cause of the value of the commodity produced by it; that commodity is equal in value to any other commodity produced by an equal quantity of labour; but both these commodities are greater in value than the labour which produced them. The labour produces a value greater than its own. Here we come again to the solid rock, in this case to the physical laws of increase in natural products. It is often said that labour is a commodity like other commodities, and so it is in the sense of being exchangeable for them; but it is not so in the sense of having, like them, its value dependent on the quantity of labour producing it; for it is not produced by labour, it is labour itself, an ultimate source of value.

18. When we take labour in this general sense, embracing the total difficulty of production, we find the same distinctions applicable to it as to all commodities under the second head of exchanges (par. 7). It has both a market and a natural price, and its natural price is governed by its difficulty of production. But here we come to the circumstance which is the source of most of the confusion between quantity and value of labour. This difficulty of producing labour consists in the estimate of men, the lowest amount of commodities for which they will consent to labour. In every employment there is a minimum of the labourer's requirements, sometimes this minimum goes as low as the bare necessaries of existence, sometimes includes many comforts and luxuries as well. But in every case there is a minimum of requirement, and this minimum is the natural value or price of the labour. Labour then produces commodities, but the expectation of commodities produces, calls forth, or causes, the labour. But the

commodities expected are the value of the labour; and therefore it seems that there is a lower depth beyond labour, and that the ultimate cause, in analysis of the conditions of value, is value itself.

19. We are indeed at the lowest point of the analysis, for this value, the natural value of labour, is at once the cause and the measure of the quantity of labour which it purchases; the cause and the measure of labour are identical. It is, however, because the labour is a voluntary act of a conscious agent that there is this identity between cause and measure, because it is a final cause that is here the efficient one. And because of this identity we may take henceforth the natural value of labour, which measures its quantity, as a term convertible with it, while it offers at the same time the convenience of being itself measureable by other values. We obtain an expression for quantity of labour in terms belonging to political economy; that is, we express it in terms of value.

20. But now to point out a distinction which has hitherto been overlooked, and the neglect of which enables the confusion above spoken of to arise. We see well enough why there should be that confusion, let us now see why there need not be. When it is said that the commodities expected are the value of the labour, and that this value is the cause of the labour, abstraction is made of the value of those commodities in other commodities. It is not their value as against other commodities, but the value of all commodities alike that is in question; and therefore the value which is the ultimate cause, in analysis of the conditions of value, is not value as fixed by the fluctuations of supply and demand, not market value

of commodities, some of which must fall if others rise and rise if others fall, but a value of commodities generally against labour alone, that is, a value-in-use, an estimated motive of action, which as value-in-use, or motive, causes the quantity of labour given for it, while it also measures it as exchange value. All that is done, in the above proof that value and not labour is the source of value (par. 18), is to show the point and the mode in which value-in-use becomes transformed, in political economy, into exchange value. And it was shown that value-in-use and physical conditions of increase were the two roots by which political economy is founded in the conditions of the outer world, and on which its exchange values depend. The natural exchange value of labour depends on the value-in-use of the commodities obtained by it, compared with the counteracting cause, the irksomeness of the labour.

21. Equal exchange values are therefore always the product of equal quantities, or equal degrees of irksomeness, of labour. But this does not constitute labour an invariable measure or standard of value; for the labour is not capable of being measured by itself, any more than values-in-use are; it is not the thing that measures, but the thing that is measured by, the exchange values which are its causes.

22. To come now to the second sense of the term labour, that in which it is opposed to capital, as one of the two constituents of difficulty of production. Just as it was a difference in commodities which caused us to divide them under the two heads of exchanges, namely, into those which are and those which are not again producible by additional expenditure of labour, in par. 4, so here the difference between labour itself

and commodities employed by labour in further production is the ground of distinguishing the one as labour, the other as capital. Those who contribute labour alone are now called labourers, those who contribute capital alone, with only so much labour as the management of the capital requires, are now called capitalists. The returns to capital are called profits, which, it is true, include the wages of management, but which may most conveniently be opposed, under the name of profits, to the wages of labour alone, if it is borne in mind that the kind and degree of this labour of management must be considered, in estimating the profits for which a capitalist will consent to contribute to production. In the same way a certain capital is contributed also by the labourer, if he works with tools belonging to himself; but in this case too, though the value of the tools must be considered in his wages, the effect is usually so small that it may safely be abstracted from.

2J. The true distinction between capital and labour, capitalists and labourers, must be drawn, not from the labour and capital themselves, but from the remuneration for them, and from the mode of its receipt. Profits are in one sense a reward for skilled industry, the labour of management, and this distinguishes them from interest, which is the return to the capital alone exclusive of this labour. In this sense profits are of the same nature as wages. But the difference is, that wages proper, as distinguished from profits, whether paid for skilled or for unskilled labour, are a fixed and previously agreed on amount between employer and employed, while profits are an unfixed and uncertain residuum, namely, the remainder of the Price, or gross profits, after payment of the wages. When the employed are paid by a percentage on the gross profits, they may in one sense be said to be sharers in the business, and to be paid by profits not by wages. The percentage may be fixed, but the sum of gross profits on which it is reckoned is uncertain. Still the agreed percentage is wages and not profits. The amount the labourers will receive may be called profits, being paid out of the gross profits of the whole business and varying with their amount; but with respect to the employer's share of the price it is a fixed amount, and the agreement made with him as to the rate of payment, the percentage on the gross profits, is subject to the same laws as if a definite sum were named, as in the usual case. A definite agreement with the employer as to remuneration makes that remuneration wages; an uncertain residuum, left between that agreement and the price, is alone properly to be called profits. The question now is, what modifications are introduced by this division into the results of the general law, that the natural value of commodities depends upon the quantity of labour producing them.

24. Now here we come upon a very remarkable circumstance, found in all cases where, as in England, labourers and capitalists are distinct classes. Just as the term labour has two senses (par. 16), so also capital. Capital in the first of these two senses is the parallel of labour in the first sense; that is, it includes the whole difficulty of production. The second sense is that which has been already explained, as opposed to labour in the second sense. But as to capital in the first sense, it has been shown in par. 18, that the cause producing la-

bour is wages; labour being the cause of production
of all other commodities, wages are the cause producing labour itself, that is, maintaining its agents
and inducing them to work. Now all wages are paid
by capital, and all capital is expended in wages; (Mr.
J. S. Mill's Principles of Pol. Econ. Book ii. Ch. xv.
§ 5). In other words, capital is coextensive with
wages, another characterisation of the value of labour. Again, the returns to capital are profits; but
the returns to capital consist in the price of the commodities produced, all of which is in the first instance
paid to the capitalist employing labour; that is, the
returns to capital, or profits, consist in the very same
thing in which the returns to labour, in the first
sense, consist; the same price of the goods produced
remunerates and causes the employment of both the
total labour and the total capital. Consequently we
have in labour and capital, in the first sense of the
terms, not two things, but one thing in two aspects;
labour the thing producing commodities, capital the
value of that thing; and again, in the commodities
of which capital consists, we have the cause producing
the labour, of which capital is the value. Capital in
its first intention, meaning certain commodities, is
the cause producing labour; in its second intention,
is the measure or value of that labour. The commodities called capital have two functions, one in
which they operate as motives to labour, the other
in which they measure its value.

25. As capital has two senses, so also have profits,
which are its remuneration; the returns to capital in
the first sense are gross, in the second net, profits.
The gross profits are the price of the commodities
produced; the net profits are that portion of the

price retained by the capitalist after paying the wages of his labourers and providing for the repair or replacement of his stock. In net profits must be reckoned the different degrees of risk in different employments. Risk is an incident in capital corresponding to different degrees of irksomeness in labour; the return for the one is higher wages, for the other higher net profits. Both circumstances may be abstracted from in considering the rewards of labour and of capital generally, since they affect only the relations between wages in one trade and wages in another, profits in one trade and profits in another, leaving the relations between wages and profits generally unaffected. There is however this difference between the two cases, namely, that risk, which by itself would be reckoned to net profits, causing the capitalist to demand a higher price, may be in many cases covered by insurance; in which case the risk, if the expression is allowable, is capitalised, that is, the sum paid for insurance is added to the capital advanced, requiring replacement out of gross profits, and bearing, like the rest of the capital, a corresponding addition to net profits. The advantage is, that this addition to net profits is both fixed by rule and comparatively small, instead of fixed by guess and therefore comparatively large. When risk is covered by insurance, therefore, we may reckon the insurance to capital, and leave, so far, no difference in point of risk, or net profits, to abstract from.

26. Now since the problem before us is to determine the elements which govern the price, or value, of commodities, so far as that price depends on difficulty of production, and the price is another name for the gross profits of those commodities, we have

to determine what governs the natural amount of
gross profits. When we approached from the side
of labour, the answer was the quantity of labour;
when from the side of capital, the answer is the
wages of labour. But neither answer is sufficient,
because we want to know, not how the determining
elements may be characterised, nor that each may be
characterised in terms of the other, but what they
are in relative amount, what the amount of each is,
when the whole is really analysed, that is, divided
into capital which is not labour and labour which
is not capital, or, in other words, when capital and
labour are taken in the second sense, as the two constituents of difficulty of production.

27. In this sense, the value of labour is determined by the requirements of the labourers; and
similarly net profits are determined by the requirements of the capitalists; and both together fix the
natural or minimum value, in the long run, of the
commodities produced. This is the ultimate ground
beyond which we cannot go, the solid rock of human motives. It is usual to say that the net profits
which will content the capitalist are determined by the
average rate of profits in his business, and that this
average rate is maintained by the flowing of more
capital into employments where the rate is rising
and likely to rise, and its withdrawal from those
where it is sinking and likely to sink. But this accounts only for the libration of oscillations about the
natural amount of net profits, not for the natural
amount itself. The natural amount depends upon
what the great majority of capitalists will be content with; and a single individual has no power to
alter this amount, not because it is not determined

by human motive and volition, but because his single volition is impotent against that of the vast majority. He has no choice but either to be content with those profits or to withdraw from business. A parallel to this has been seen in the case of language; language depends upon the combined and accumulated volitions of a nation, but a single individual, who himself contributes to determine it, has but an infinitesimal power of altering the language spoken; he must either speak as others do, or submit not to be understood (§ 93. 1-3). The same applies to the wages of labour as to net profits; the requirements of the majority determine what each individual must be content with. When therefore we approach the question from the side in which labour and capital are divided, two elements of difficulty of production are found to be fixed. Labour alone is measured by wages, capital alone is measured by net profits; and the average amount of wages on the one side, and the average amount of net profits on the other, are two at least of the constituents which make up the total cost of production, gross profits, or price, so far as these depend on difficulty of production.

III.

28. A distinction must now be mentioned which has caused much confusion from not being clearly grasped and kept firmly in mind, that between the amount and rate of values. When a commodity or a service is exchanged for others, amount is exchanged for amount, and there is here no question of rate. But when an amount is divided into two or more portions, each portion, which is itself an amount, bears a certain proportion to the other or others, and

to the whole amount divided. This proportion is
the rate. Thus when gross profits are divided into
wages and net profits, each portion has a rate both as
against the whole and as against the other portion.
If the whole amount increases or diminishes, the
amount of each portion may increase or diminish
without any change in their rates, and similarly the
rates may change without any change in the whole
amount. So it is also with interest for money, and
with rent of land or hire of goods. The amount paid
as interest, rent, or hire, is usually expressed by the
proportion it bears to the amount lent and borrowed;
and this proportion is expressed by considering the
amount as divided into quantities of 100, and expressing the amount paid as so much per cent. So
it is also with prices. These are already rates, portions of the whole mass of commodities and services
balanced against other portions. The price of any
commodity is its value in other commodities indifferently; if it rises, there must be a fall somewhere
among them; if it falls, a rise somewhere. A general rise of values, or of prices (abstracting from the
commodity, money,) is an impossibility, for it would
be a general change in rates, at the same time that
all rates remained unchanged. Prices therefore, as
the term is usually taken, are the same thing as rates,
whether rates of wages, of profits, of rent, hire, or
interest. They are amounts paid for other amounts,
both being portions of the same total amount, the
commodities and services in the world at large. And
it is the increase of this total amount of the world's
wealth which alone can enable the amounts enjoyed
by different classes of its owners to increase without
alteration in their rates, that is, without lessening

the amount enjoyed by one class compared to another.

29. Let us now follow up this analysis, and use these distinctions in applying them to the cases where labour and capital are employed together in production; whereby it will be seen what consequences flow from differences in the relative amounts of capital and labour employed, and from differences in the kinds of capital itself; and also the connection between the natural values of commodities, labour, and capital, that is, natural prices, wages, and net profits, and their market values will be more clearly seen. Production in every instance takes place by the employment of some capital with some labour; but this capital has itself been produced by other capital and other labour, and this other capital again in the same way; and thus, though we come invariably to the same elements of analysis, we come upon them always in varying proportions, and also, as will be seen, giving rise to varying values. It is not enough to point out the two elements in value of commodities, we must also point out the effects which flow from their different natures.

30. In order to escape as far as possible the embarrassment of this perpetual implication of capital with labour, we may begin by supposing a case in which no capital is employed except for the payment of wages; the payment of wages itself cannot be eliminated without reversing the hypothesis of a division between capitalists and labourers. Suppose, then, that labourers are employed to produce a machine out of materials which may be had for nothing. Here the quantity of the labour, including the employer's, gives the value of the commodity produced,

the machine; and the whole difference between the wages paid and the value of the machine is net profits, remuneration for advancing the wages, and management. The wages only have to be replaced out of this value, which is gross profits, the price of the machine if sold.

31. Suppose now that the instruments and materials for the construction of the machine had a value, and were supplied by the capitalist. In this case their value, as well as the wages, has to be replaced out of gross profits. The replacement of consumed capital and of wages is all which can be required out of gross profits; whatever remains is net profits. We have then to distinguish three things in the natural amount of gross profits or price: the replacement of wages, the replacement of consumed capital, and the net profits; and of these the first depends on the minimum requirements of the labourers, the second on the varying or market values of the commodities consumed, the third on the minimum requirements of the capitalists.

32. It is then the commodities consumed in production which, by their varying or market prices, introduce the greatest fluctuations into the price at which the supply of any commodity can be offered. The minimum requirements for wages and for net profits change but slowly, and the natural price of the commodity, so far as dependent upon them, would change but slowly also. But the natural price of the commodity is exposed to fluctuations, arising in its supply, from changes in the market price of the commodities consumed as capital in its production; while its market price depends on these causes, operating on the supply, compared with the

demand for it, which may change in two ways, first, from changes in the taste, fashions, or purposes, of the public; secondly, from the changes in the supply itself, and the price at which it is offered. Thus the market price of any commodity consumed as capital is an element in the natural price of the commodities produced by its means, and at the same time a cause of fluctuations in its market price about the natural price so fixed. It is then almost impossible to estimate how much in the market price of any commodity is natural price, and how much is due to fluctuations about it, because the market price of one commodity is an element in the natural price of another; all we can say is, that the natural price contains at least two elements which are comparatively stable, namely, the minimum requirements of labourers for wages, and those of capitalists for net profits.

33. We may however draw a further distinction in the market price of the commodities consumed as capital; distinguishing between permanent variations in that price and temporary variations in it, independent of their amount. The amount of variation will of course have influence upon the price of the commodity produced. But, great or small, it is clear that it may affect the price either for a long or only for a short time. The lowest price for which a commodity can be permanently offered is perhaps the best expression for its natural price; and, if we assume this definition of it, we may abstract from the temporary variations in the market price of the commodities consumed in its production, as having no influence upon its natural price; only those variations which continue permanently at a point once

reached are thus to be counted as elements in the natural price of the commodities produced; and we shall find that the same distinction is applicable also to fluctuations in wages and net profits (see par. 40).

34. It must now be remarked that the elements in natural price are all elements in the price of the supply, independent of the demand; they are elements in the price at which the supply of the commodity can be permanently offered. And since the market price of any commodity may vary either from changes arising in the supply, or from changes arising in the demand, it will be well, in the first place, to consider changes arising in the supply alone, abstracting from those arising in the demand. The distinction between these changes coincides with the distinction between changes which affect the natural price and changes which affect the market price, or between changes which affect the price at which the supply can be permanently offered and changes which affect the price which is actually obtained.

35. When we consider the price at which the supply of any commodity can be offered, and the elements which contribute to fix that price, abstracting from the demand for it, we find that these elements are three, the wages, the price of the commodities consumed as capital, the net profits. Of these the price of the commodities consumed as capital, which must be replaced out of gross profits, enters directly and inevitably into the price at which the commodity can be offered. If raw cotton has been consumed in manufacturing calico, and raw cotton rises in value, a larger sum than that for which it was purchased must be set apart from gross profits in order to replace it, and a smaller sum if it

falls. This larger sum cannot be taken from wages or from net profits, because it would cause workmen to leave the trade in the first case, and capitalists in the second; and this would happen only in case a less quantity of manufactured cotton was demanded, a supposition which is now abstracted from. The price at which manufactured cotton is offered must therefore rise; and this rise will not attract more labourers or more capitalists into the trade, because the price is required to meet an expense peculiar to that trade, which does not increase either wages or net profits.

36. In wages two cases may be distinguished. If the rise or fall of the sum paid as wages by the capitalist is required for the payment of a greater or smaller quantity of labour than before, which is a change affecting the particular commodity produced and not others, then the sum so paid regulates gross profits or price in the same way, and for the same reasons, as a change in the value of consumed capital does. These two cases may then, from this point of view, be classed together. If, secondly, the requirements of the labourers in a particular trade rise or fall from a temporary scarcity or abundance of labourers, or from a temporary scarcity or abundance of capitalists engaging in it, or from a change in the requirements of the labourers in that particular trade alone, which is a change in the value of labour in that trade, this may either affect the price at which the commodity can be offered, or it may affect the amount of net profits, in the one case attracting in the other driving capitalists from the trade. If we assumed that net profits were unaffected, the change in wages would necessarily affect

the price; but, since the price could only be affected by means of a corresponding change arising in the demand, and we are now abstracting from such changes, the other alternative only remains, namely, that a change in wages is compensated by a change in net profits. An increase or decrease in the quantity of labour affects price, an increase or decrease in the value of labour affects net profits, which is Ricardo's law.

37. To turn now to the third element, net profits, some of the remarks about which have been already anticipated. A rise or fall in net profits in a particular trade, not owing to a rise or fall in the price of the commodity from a change in the demand for it, cannot affect the price at which the commodity is offered; because competition prevents the capitalist from raising the price in consequence of a demand on his part for larger profits; the rise of price may be the cause but not the effect of such a rise in net profits. Every such rise in net profits must therefore be at the expense of wages.

38. Taking the three elements in turn, the results are, that the permanent requirements of capitalists for net profits enter into the price at which a commodity can be offered, but not the fluctuations in these requirements, which in all cases are compensated out of wages; secondly, that the permanent requirements of workmen for wages enter into the price, but the fluctuations in them, affecting the market value of labour from time to time, are compensated out of net profits; and thirdly, that the market price of the commodities consumed as capital enter into the price in all cases, and are never compensated out of either wages or net profits. But

since it is only the price at which a commodity can be permanently offered which constitutes its natural price, it is only those changes which are permanent, among the changes enumerated as entering into price, which can be held to enter into or determine its permanent or natural price. That is to say, a temporary change in the value of commodities consumed as capital will change the market price but not the natural price of the commodity produced, but a permanent change in their value will affect the natural price; and a temporary fluctuation in wages in a particular trade, though, if a rise, it may be paid out of a price increased in consequence of an increasing demand, and may therefore fall on price and not upon net profits, is no element in the natural price of the commodity produced. And net profits are in a similar position to wages.

39. But let us now reverse the process of enquiry, and, leaving the analysis of the price at which a commodity can be offered, begin with the demand for that commodity, with its market price as subject to changes originating in the demand for it. In other words, let us suppose the demand for some commodities to be altered, as it will almost certainly be if the supply can only be offered at an altered price, which is one source of change. Changes in taste and fashion, or new purposes prevalent for a time, such as war, are causes operating on demand, independent, as to origin, of the price at which the supply can be offered. But from whatever cause the change in demand arises, it affects the market price. An increased or diminished demand will operate to raise or lower the market price of the particular commodities in question. If it lowers them, a smaller sum

will have to be divided between wages and net profits, assuming replacement of capital consumed to require the same sum as before, that is, the commodities so consumed to be unaltered in price. But this fall in wages, or net profits, or both, cannot go beyond the minimum of their natural amount, without causing production to cease; and at that point the supply will begin to be diminished. So on the other hand, if the demand raises prices, a larger sum will have to be divided between wages and net profits, thus raising their amount; this larger sum coming out of the market price of the commodities, and eventually calling forth an increased supply of them.

40. The great struggle between labourers and capitalists consists primarily in the constant pressure, one against the other, of the permanent requirements of wages and net profits in dividing between them the gross profits or price of the produce. But secondarily there is superinduced upon this another conflict for division of the gross profits as affected by fluctuations in the market price arising from changes in demand. But since there is no clear line between temporary and permanent changes, either in price of commodities, or in wages, or in net profits, but a change which appears at first likely to be only temporary may turn out to be permanent, and vice versa, all changes which raise wages are, as a rule, resisted by capitalists, all which lower them by workmen. Habit is that which makes a requirement, either of the capitalist for net profits, or of the labourer for wages, which at first may have arisen out of a temporary rise in gross profits, divided between the two, assume a character of permanence, and enter into the minimum amount for

which either will consent to give his labour or his capital. And a steady increase in culture and refinement on the part of the labouring classes is a cause constantly at work to make enlarged requirements on their part become habitually necessary and permanent, or to make, in other words, a higher amount of wages for the same amount of labour become fixed as the natural value of labour.

41. Both net profits and wages are remuneration for services not for commodities; wages wholly, and net profits in that part of them which is distinguished from interest, a distinction to be drawn farther on (see § 96. 87); and in this they are together distinguished from the commodities consumed in production. But the cost of production, in all its three branches, depends on human desires and the strength of human volitions, the latter of which may be increased indefinitely by combination and organisation among those whose interests are similar. Causes of this as well as of a physical kind contribute to the result, the prices at which commodities can be offered. How erroneous then is the language of those who speak as if exchanges were governed by laws as "inexorable" as those of inanimate nature, in their relation to the persons whom they govern, and hold out "Supply and Demand" like a Medusa's head to turn into stone those volitions of which it is itself nothing but the brief collective expression. The laws are known only so far as the volitions which they express are classed and estimated; the laws of wages, for instance, being unknown until the strength of the volitions to combine and insist on terms, among masters and among workmen, has been first taken into account. The root of this error, over and above

the natural tendency to make entities of abstractions, seems to lie in treating political economy, a science of human practice, as if it were a science of physical and inanimate phenomena, the opposite error to that, argued against above, of treating it as if it were exclusively concerned with human practice, without being conditioned by physical laws.

42. The higher the natural value of labour, and of that kind of it which is remunerated by net profits, or of either of them, in any country, the higher pro tanto will be the natural price, or the price at which can be permanently offered those commodities in producing which it competes with other countries. Unless it can apply greater skill, or procure its commodities consumed as capital cheaper, the country where wages and net profits are permanently the highest will not be able to produce those commodities, in competition with other countries where they are lower. The commodities consumed as capital may however be rendered cheaper by improvements in manufacture and economy in working them. Intelligence and skill are therefore an influence counterbalancing the operation of a continued rise in the natural value of labour; and this is no doubt the only mode in which that rise can be counteracted, as it is the only one in which a friend of the true interests of mankind can wish that it should be. The increase of the natural and permanent remuneration for labour enables the labourer to rise to greater culture and refinement, leaves his mental powers greater scope for activity and development, and thus not only raises his moral condition, but also provides a fund of mental power which is certain, in a great number of cases at least, to be applied to that which most

interests him, the work upon which he is engaged, and to bear fruit in more intelligent work or invention of superior processes. The attempt, on the other hand, to keep labour from rising to higher natural and permanent values must be unsuccessful in the long run, for it is fighting against the inherent tendency of nature to better its condition; while, if it succeeded for a time, its success would be purchased by the loss of the increased intelligence and mental power, which are the only secure basis not only of national greatness but also of national wealth.

43. The same analysis as that hitherto applied is applicable also to the commodities employed as capital in every stage of production, to the machinery, buildings, and raw materials, as well as to the commodities produced by their means. These are commodities when purchased by the capitalist to be employed as capital, and have their value determined by the same elements, and in the same way, as the value of the commodity which he will produce; that is, their value in each case may be distinguished into natural and market value, the one affected by the permanent or natural value of labour and amount of net profits, and by the market value of the capital consumed, when this market value is permanently at the same amount; the other affected, not by any fluctuations in value of labour and amount of net profits, but by temporary changes in the market value of the capital consumed, and by the demand for the commodity itself, the supply of which is thus affected. And in the last stage of all, where no commodities having value are consumed as capital, which is the rudest state of production, the value of the commodity produced is determined by the two elements

only, value of labour and amount of net profits; which is the stage which was assumed as the starting point of the enquiry in par. 30.

44. The main outlines of the analysis being now complete, it will be well to cast a glance back and endeavour to draw some general conclusions, as well as to fill up the picture with some further distinctions. The three elements of production have been distinguished as capital, or commodities consumed or employed in new production; skilled labour of management accompanied by risk, remunerated by net profits; and rude or less skilled labour, remunerated by wages. The price of the commodities produced has been shown to depend on causes operating through these three elements of production, in conjunction with other causes operating through the demand for the commodities produced. Let us examine each of these elements in conjunction with changes in the demand; and first with respect to the capital, or commodities employed in production.

45. The first circumstance to be considered is the following. All capital, it has been shown, is expended in the payment of labour; and we may consider the difficulty of production as expressed either by the capital expended, which must be remunerated by profits, or by the labour expended, which must be remunerated by wages. Adopting the former of these expressions, a new distinction in capital must be drawn. Capital is either fixed or circulating. Fixed capital consists of those commodities which are not entirely consumed in the production of new commodities, and the profits of which therefore are not entirely paid by the price of those commodities, but in part by the successively produced commodi-

ties in which they are employed. Circulating capital consists in those commodities which are entirely consumed in the new production, and the profits of which must therefore be entirely paid by their price. Wages and raw materials are a part of circulating capital; machinery, implements, buildings, land, are a part of fixed.

46. Since the entire profits of fixed capital have not to be paid out of the first returns to production, the price of the commodities so produced will be lower than the price of commodities produced by an equal amount of circulating capital, the entire profits of which must be paid out of it. And, in proportion as the capital employed is fixed capital and not circulating, the price of the commodities will be lower, as compared to those produced by an equal amount of wholly circulating capital. If 50 labourers are employed at £50 per man to produce cloth, the price of the cloth will be equal to the wages of 50 labourers, £2500, and net profits, say at £10 per cent. £250; together, £2750. The capital is returned together with net profits. But if a permanent machine, which produces an equal amount of cloth, and costs the same sum as the labour of 50 men, that is, £2500, is employed in producing the cloth, then the price of the cloth will be only £250, since no replacement of capital will be necessary, but the capital continues to exist in the machine itself, the value of which, £2500, may be realised by its sale. The replacement of consumed capital is all that has to be deducted from price, or gross profits, before satisfying net profits; and it matters not whether the capital is consumed in paying wages or in replacing consumed portions of instruments or materials.

47. But there is no kind of material capital so durable as to require no replacement or repair. In proportion as the repairs required are considerable, in proportion as total consumption is approached, as in the case of raw cotton consumed in making calico, in that proportion will the price of the commodities produced by employment of fixed capital approach the price of commodities produced by an equal amount of circulating, whether consisting in wages of labour or purchase of commodities. In all cases alike, the prices of the commodities produced will be equal to the wages, net profits, and replacement of capital; the only difference now pointed out consisting in this, that in different kinds of commodities the requisite replacement varies in the time over which it is spread.

48. From this we may conclude that the larger the proportion of circulating to fixed capital employed in any production, the greater will be the influence exerted on the price at which the commodity produced can be permanently offered by the market value of the commodities consumed as capital and by the natural or permanent rate of wages, compared to that exerted by the natural or permanent rate of net profits; and conversely. The greater influence of the rate of net profits, in the converse case, depends on time. The longer the time elapsing between the expenditure of the capital and the sale of the produce, the greater must be the return in net profits. If I spend £1000 in one year on the construction of a machine, and only at the end of the next year bring commodities produced by it to market, and net profits are at £10 per cent., the net profits must be reckoned, not on £1000, but on £1100, the sum

which is composed of the accumulated net profits of the first year added to the capital. In other words, a rise in the rate of net profits adds to the amount of capital which requires replacement, and therefore to the price necessary to support the replacement and the net profits on the whole. A fall in the rate of net profits lowers the required replacement, and therefore price, by the same rule.

49. Under the foregoing distinction between fixed and circulating capital we have seen some kinds of capital and labour classed together, and opposed, in their effects upon the price at which the produce can be offered, to the labour and risk which is remunerated by net profits. Under the following distinction we shall see the two kinds of labour classed together, and opposed to commodities distinguished into the two classes of those consumed in further production and those consumed unproductively; and this distinction is one of far greater social importance. Without changes in demand, and consequently in price, wages and net profits, it has been seen (parr. 36-38), will vary inversely if at all, what one loses the other will gain, supposing the third element of production, capital, unaltered. But there is always a certain number of commodities the price of which admits of being raised, if only producers are aware of the opportunity; and these commodities give a foothold for a rise in wages and net profits simultaneously. Employers and labourers may then be regarded as always on the watch to raise prices, wherever this can be done without reducing the quantity of produce demanded. Consumers on the other hand are always on the watch to obtain the commodities which they consume as cheaply as pos-

sible. Now the price of commodities consumed in further production has been already shown to come out of the gross profits of that production; it is in the long run, that is, supposing the production to be kept up, replaced out of those profits, whether it is high or low (par. 35). If productive consumers, as a body, pay more for the commodities they consume in production, they will, as a body, receive more for the commodities which they produce. It is out of the prices paid for commodities unproductively consumed that the remuneration ultimately comes for their production in all its branches, and at all its stages. The demand of the consumer so far as he consumes unproductively is the reservoir out of which all increase of price is ultimately supplied. In other words, the remuneration for present labour of all kinds comes out of the accumulated results of past labour, now in the hands of unproductive consumers, or, more accurately, of consumers so far as their consumption is unproductive. A rise in that remuneration can only be met by a rise somewhere or other in the aggregate prices which unproductive consumers, holders of previously acquired wealth, are willing to pay for certain commodities. The commodities productively consumed being abstracted from, as having their price, whether high or low, provided for in the manner above described, the demands of present labourers, for remuneration of present labour, are left face to face with the means or wealth of unproductive consumers, consisting in accumulations of past labour.

50. This distinction, between labour skilled and unskilled on the one side and commodities on the other, is a very prominent one in a new school of

economists, and already we may see that it lies at the basis of the great economical and social changes which are in progress. "The labourer," says Mr. Harrison, in the Fortnightly Review, No. xiii. p. 50, "has not got a commodity to sell, because what he seeks to do is not to exchange products, but to combine to produce." The former view of economists was, that labour was a commodity bought and sold in the labour market, the price of which was determined by the amount of circulating capital, the "wages fund," on the one hand, and the number of labourers on the other; a theory which was a corollary of the doctrine of supply and demand in its old or untenable form (see par. 15). It was assumed that the wage fund was, at any given time, a fixed amount, all of which would be, and more than which could not be, expended in the employment of labourers. This fund constituted the demand for labour, the number of labourers constituted the supply; and the rate of wages depended on the proportion which which these two quantities, the supply and the demand, bore to each other. Two sources of variation, however, were here left out of the account; first, that the expected amount of gross profits determined the amount which an employer would be willing and able, by borrowing if necessary, to throw into his business; second, that, the less the portion of these gross profits, when realised, which went to replace the wages paid to labourers, the larger would be the share of them remaining as net profits, and vice versa, so that, if the labourers were content with lower wages, the employer would spend as revenue what otherwise would have been spent as wages. It was true that, at any given time, the sum actually spent in wages was a fixed amount, but it was not true that it was fixed before being spent or agreed to be spent; the agreement between masters and men was the very thing that fixed it (see remarks in par. 41); so that the wage fund could not, without logical error, be called the fund "destined" to the payment of wages. See Mr. Longe's able Refutation of the Wage-Fund Theory, published in 1866. The wage fund theory is thus an instance of the fallacy of the cart before the horse, precisely similar to the logical blunder pointed out in § 79, which defines the motive of conduct as the motive which contains the greatest pleasure, whereas it is only by its being the motive of conduct that we know which or what pleasure is the greatest, and must consequently reverse the order of definition.

51. According to the former view of economists, then, an employer bought labour as a commodity, and, using it as he used fuel, iron, or horses, competed with other employers by endeavouring to produce more cheaply and abundantly. So long as the labourers were unable to combine, and employers could deal with them man by man, this mode of industry and the theory which reflected it held their own. But with combination of labourers organised as it now is, and still more as it inevitably will be, it becomes impossible to treat labour as a mere commodity, and its true character as an ultimate agent of production comes to light. The unlimited competition of employers against each other is finished, by the necessity they will be under of supporting each other against the dictation of the labourers; a result which has been ably indicated by Mr. Thornton in his work On Labour, Book iii. Chap. iv.

52. But this result will not be produced without a further result following, one also pointed out by Mr. Thornton; labourers and employers will not stand organised as two bodies without also, and in proportion as their internal organisation advances, organising themselves also in such a way as to "combine to produce" for their common advantage, in other words, to effect the much longed for "organisation of industry" as a whole. The two classes of labourers, employers and employed, will therefore place as high a value as they can on their commodity, present labour, estimated in the only other kind of exchangeable wealth, namely, commodities which embody the results of past labour. In other words, we come back to the distinction with which we started, that between commodities which may or may not be employed as capital on the one side, labour, superintendence, and risk, on the other. We may already see the germs of this combination in the boards of arbitration between masters and men, which would have no logical standing-ground were it not in the interests of increased and improved production common to both parties, as well as in the various successful attempts to establish cooperative societies and partnership of labourers in profits. The terms of combination can only be settled by considering the common end which both parties have in view; so much however may perhaps be said beforehand, that these terms will include a comparatively stable rate of wages, not liable to the fluctuations of the goods market, as well as higher average rates than at present. Wages will be calculated permanently on the basis of the average gross profits of a trade, and the temporary fluctuations in these gross profits, whether

large or small, will be thrown upon the capitalist's residuum or net profits, whether the capital is owned by one, or by many, or by the labourers themselves, who would thus bear a double character.

53. It may appear at first sight that a contradiction is involved in saying that an increase in value of labour means a corresponding decrease in the value of commodities, since the remuneration of the labour of production consists only in the value of the produce when sold; and, if this falls, the value of the labour must, it would seem, fall along with it; while, on the other hand, if we assume that labour and its products really rise in value, this seems to contradict the well established law, that no general rise or fall of values, and no general rise or fall of prices (supposing no change in money), are possible; since, it may be thought, a general rise in labour, that is, in all industries, would produce, if it could take place, a general rise in values, that is, of the products of all industries, which, unless merely nominal, or only in the money they are reckoned in, is an impossibility. Both the apparent contradictions, however, are dissolved, the rise in labour is shown to be real, and also not to involve a general rise in values, by drawing the distinction between commodities used in productive and commodities used in final or unproductive consumption, and by attending to the coincidence of this distinction with another, which will be drawn more fully farther on (par. 79), between the part of total income which is spent as revenue and that part of it which is spent as capital. It is commodities finally or unproductively consumed which are both purchased by revenue and also, by this exchange, replace the commodities consumed in

producing them, and pay the wages of labour, at every stage of their production. If the wages of labour generally rise, these commodities of final consumption will rise also, that is, more commodities must be given for them, and larger amounts of revenue will be required to command the same amount of them as before. The consumers of these commodities, and every man is a consumer of them to some extent, will pay more for them in other commodities which they already hold (and the holder of money is really a holder of commodities). And to whom do they pay it? to the series of producers; and for what purpose? to be employed partly in unproductive but chiefly in productive consumption. But it was shown, in par. 35, that the value of commodities consumed in production enters into the price of the product, whatever that value may be; if this value falls, the price of the product falls pro tanto; if it rises, the price pro tanto rises. The increase of value therefore in commodities, assumed to be caused by a general rise in the value of labour, need not be supposed to cause a general rise in the value of commodities, but only in the value of commodities of final consumption, purchased by revenue; these and these alone will rise in value; more must be given by ultimate or unproductive consumers to those who expend their labour in producing them, in remuneration not for the commodities they have consumed but for the labour they have bestowed, the higher value of the commodities used in productive consumption being paid in the first instance by the productive consumer, and ultimately restored to him by the price of the finally consumed commodity purchased by revenue. The change thus effected is a change in the distribution of values between two classes of persons, or more accurately between persons in two characters, that of labourer or productive consumer, and that of enjoyer or unproductive consumer; the commodities which are consumed in production are replaced by the value of the commodities produced, and remain unaffected by the change in the value of labour. The rise in value of commodities productively consumed is a nominal or rather a compensated rise; but the labourers are benefited, without any such compensation, at the expense of those who hold commodities alone without labouring, for a larger amount of these commodities must now be given for the same amount of labour as before. And the general result of this tendency to a rise in the value of labour, as distinguished from that of commodities, will no doubt be to draw the owners of larger and larger realised fortunes into industry, where they may obtain the rewards of labour as well as the remuneration for the use of commodities employed as capital; inasmuch as it tends to lessen the value of fixed or nominally equal amounts of previously accumulated commodities or realised fortune; thus contributing to the universal prevalence of the industrial life. And here we have the answer to a question which has no doubt already suggested itself, namely, Whence comes the value to furnish the supposed general rise in labour? It comes from the additional labour of those who will now begin to earn profits, where before they earned only interest, the number of purely unproductive consumers being lessened, and that of consumers who are productive as well as unproductive being increased. The labour will be attractive because it is remunerative.

54. This result may be expressed as a rise in the natural value of labour, in both its kinds, as measured in or purchased by commodities previously produced. These commodities fall in value; but it is only one part of them in which the fall is real or uncompensated, namely, that part which is consumed unproductively or as revenue. In the other part, the commodities which are consumed as capital or productively, the fall is compensated by the value of their produce, ultimately consumed unproductively. The kind of commodities which must necessarily fall in value if all other commodities and services, or labour, rise in value, so as to escape the contradiction involved in a 'general rise of values,' has been thus pointed out, namely, the results of past labour, as well as the mode of its separation from the rest, as a different class of commodities. The division which each producer or receiver of income makes between what he consumes unproductively and what he consumes productively is the division between the two classes of commodities, one of which falls in value while the other remains unaffected.

55. To test this conclusion let us suppose a general rise in the natural value of labour to have taken place, although of course it can only be a gradual and piecemeal change in actual practice, a change always in progress and never complete. Let us take two articles of final consumption as representatives of all. A hat which exchanged for a pair of shoes, before the rise in the natural value of labour, will exchange for the same after it; but both hat and shoes will exchange for a larger money price than

before, that is, will require a larger amount of that command over commodities generally, conferred by money, to be given in exchange for them. This, I am aware, will be regarded as equivalent to saying that the hat and the shoes, now standing for all commodities, have not risen in real but only in nominal value, or money price; for it will be argued, if the hat will not command more commodities than before, as it will not if it only commands the shoes, it cannot have risen in real value. This conclusion, however, is only drawn by overlooking the distinction between revenue and capital, and between the results of past and those of present labour.

56. The question then is, how the distinction is drawn between the results of past and those of present labour. And here it will be seen in what way money as a means of exchange, substituted for barter, is a condition enabling this distinction to become practically operative, not by means of any change arising in the quantity or value of money itself—change of a kind which is here entirely abstracted from—but by enabling us to measure, and distinguish between, kinds of commodities which are otherwise inextricably intermixed. The part of income which a man spends as revenue and that which he spends as capital are distinguished by him only as money amounts; now, if all money prices rise, and at the same time a money amount which is spent as revenue commands less in commodities or services than before, while one which is spent as capital commands the same as before,—which it has been maintained may be the case by means of the compensation in the raised price of the produce,—then it is possible for this general rise in money prices to be in one part

real, in the other part nominal, without any difference between the amounts which commodities command in commodities.

57. In money a new commodity is introduced, whereby other commodities are divisible into amounts different in kind from the amounts into which they were divisible before. So to speak, they were before divisible mechanically, they are now divisible chemically as well. All commodities as soon as sold and exchanged for money become, as money in the hands of the seller, or as an entry to his credit in his banker's books, representatives of past instead of, as before, representatives of present labour. The act of exchange is the moment of their separation. And this is the meaning of the expression at the beginning of par. 54, " commodities previously produced." These commodities exist henceforth in the shape of money amounts. A man brings a hat to market, representing his present, as yet unremunerated, labour; he sells it, and the money represents his remunerated, or past, labour. That money amount is a command over commodities generally; it is, as Mr. Macleod most forcibly explains (Theory and Practice of Banking, Chap. i. § 9, and elsewhere)—DEBT. Now, if the commodities, or any part of them, rise in value, the command over them of a stated money amount falls in value. It is a certain amount of command over commodities generally, a certain amount of debt owing to him, that the seller of the hat has received in exchange for his commodity; and it is a part of the same kind of command, or debt, that the receiver of an income distinguishes into that which he will spend as revenue, in purchasing commodities of final consumption, and that which he will spend as capital,

in producing commodities to employ in production again.

58. Now all spenders of revenue spend a part of this general command or debt; and this general command or debt is the new commodity, introduced by money, which falls in value as all the previously existing kinds of commodities rise. Although, therefore, hats and shoes do not rise as compared to each other, they do rise as compared to the existing amount of command for them, or debt owing by them on exhibition of money, or to that amount of the results of past labour which is or may be set apart for purchasing articles of final consumption. If then possessors of income wish to enjoy as much of these commodities as before, they must set apart a larger amount than before out of their income, as revenue, thereby decreasing what they would otherwise set apart as capital. All the commodities of final consumption are in the hands of productive consumers, all the command over them, or debt owed by them, in those of unproductive consumers. And on the one hand, it is of real importance to the unproductive consumer whether his stated amounts of this command command much or little, because his command has cost him labour, and is labour in its remunerated result; on the other hand, it is of equal importance to the productive consumer, because his commodities have cost him labour too, and are the means of its remuneration.

59. The command or debt, money, is the market for commodities and services. Certain portions of these commodities, while in the hands of their producers, are virtually the property of the commanders, at least they have been produced with no other pur-

pose than to become so; and the same also is true of any portion of the command itself, namely, that it is virtually the property of the producers, and for the same reason. More commodities and services are produced and kept at demand, in proportion as a larger demand is anticipated, in order to meet it. Hats are not produced in order to be exchanged for shoes, nor guineas for guineas. Each kind, hats and shoes on one side, and guineas on the other, have been produced to exchange for the other kind; each represents real labour; the hats and shoes labour which has not, the guineas labour which has, had its remuneration fixed. That a hat will only command a pair of shoes, a pair of shoes only a hat, after as before the supposed rise in value, is no more inconsistent with that rise than that a guinea will command no more and no less than a guinea. The unproductive consumer, unless himself also a producer, has no means of counterbalancing a general rise of prices; he has no labour or commodities to sell in his turn. His command over commodities consists solely in the amount of money for which he parted with his own commodities at some previous time. If then commodities generally rise in money price, and there is no change arising in the money itself, the rise will be a real though gradual transference of real as well as nominal value from the unproductive consumers to the labourers, whether employers or employed.

IV.

60. We come now to a distinction in capital which opens a new field of enquiry, the distinction between capital owned and capital borrowed. Capital bor-

rowed is that kind which has now to be examined. It may be of two kinds, commodities themselves to be employed in production, and money to be employed in the purchase of such commodities. The return or price paid for the use of money lent and borrowed is Interest, and this is a subject which cannot be examined here, but falls under the second branch of political economy. (See § 96. 81 et seqq.). Commodities borrowed and lent may be conveniently divided by the foregoing distinction between fixed and circulating capital; and the price for fixed capital will then be properly called Rent, that for circulating Hire. See Mr. Macleod's Elements of Pol. Econ. Chap. ii. Sect. ii. As Mr. Macleod points out, rent and hire are high in amount, in proportion as the capital for which they are paid is perishable and likely to be restored in deteriorated condition from use.

61. Interest, rent, and hire, of borrowed capital must be paid for out of the price of the commodities produced, just as wages and net profits are. It is clear that interest can never bear so large a proportion to capital as net profits do; for these include the remuneration for risk and labour of management, and, if any one could obtain the same returns for lending money at interest as by employing it himself, he would never be at the trouble of engaging in trade. The owned capital which a man employs in his business he usually charges with, or considers liable for, interest to himself, at a certain rate, as if it were borrowed money on which it was paid to a lender; and by this means ascertains for himself the pure profits of his business, the pure remuneration for his skill and good fortune in its management.

Rent and hire on the contrary are not estimated by a per centage, but are gross amounts paid for the use of commodities in the mass.

62. The case of rent seems to be the only one that calls for examination. All fixed capital when borrowed is paid for by rent; but there is one kind of rent which has obtained a special title to the name, the rent paid for the use of the inseparable qualities of land used in agriculture. There is hardly any case in which the rent paid consists solely of the remuneration for these qualities; in almost all it is combined with rent of buildings, fences, and so on; so that what is called the Theory of Rent must in the outset be restricted to this special component of the whole sum paid under that name. With this restriction, the theory of rent follows from Ricardo's theory of natural value; and I shall hold myself dispensed from doing more than here stating it, having already offered what reasons I was able in support of that theory.

63. The rent paid by a farmer for the use of the inseparable qualities of that land which produces either more abundant crops than the worst land under cultivation, or an equal abundance with less labour, is paid out of the price of the crops, but has no effect in raising or lowering that price; and for this reason, that the corn grown on the worst land, or on the better land with a greater expenditure of labour and capital than was before requisite to produce the same quantity, fixes the price of all the corn, under whatever condition grown. It is evident that this additional expenditure of labour and capital, or this additional cultivation of inferior land, would not have taken place had there not been

an imperious demand for a greater quantity of corn;
and therefore the corn produced does not constitute
a supply which is in excess of the demand. This
being so, there is no reason why the corn grown at
less expense, or under more favourable conditions,
should bear a lower price than that grown under
conditions less favourable. There will then always
be a surplus in the gross profits on the corn grown
under the more favourable circumstances, and this
surplus is rent. "Corn," says Ricardo, "is not high
because a rent is paid, but a rent is paid because
corn is high; and it has been justly observed, that
no reduction would take place in the price of corn,
although landlords should forego the whole of their
rents." Rent in short is a distinct kind of value,
traceable by analysis to the laws of production from
land, and exists quite independently of the question
what class of men are or become its owners.

64. Here we come to that distinction between
commodities which was mentioned in passing in par.
7, namely, between commodities producible in equal
additional quantities by equal increase of labour and
capital expended and commodities producible only in
diminishing quantities by equal increase of expenditure.
Agricultural produce belongs to the latter class,
in consequence of the physical laws governing production
from land; the result being that, while land
bears a rent, rent does not affect price. The circumstance
too, that the greater part of necessaries
consists of agricultural produce, equal additions to
which are only procured by constantly increasing applications
of labour and capital, has the effect, in a
progressive state of population, of raising the natural
value of labour in all employments, that is, of raising

the natural rate of wages; a rise which will only necessarily be compensated by a fall in net profits in those cases where prices cannot be raised upon the consumer, or a larger demand created for the produce (par. 36).

65. The theory of rent is therefore an exemplification of the doctrine already insisted on, that the physical laws of production, the obstacles which nature sets to acquisition, are the ultimate determinants of the value of commodities exchanged between man and man. The action of man, determined by the strength and kind of his desires, is limited by, and has to conform to, the physical conditions of satisfying them; and in whatever commodity, or at whatever point, a physical difficulty in acquisition or obstacle to satisfaction occurs, at that point and in that commodity an exchange value is created, and political economy begins. Supply and demand, including the modes in which and the conditions under which they are equated, is the whole of political economy; and all limitation in supply comes ultimately from nature, just as the supply and just as the demand themselves do. Every limitation of supply, however, in presence of a demand, is the creation of an exchange value.

V.

66. There is a class of exchanges founded on an empirical distinction in actual practice so important as to merit a separate examination, the class of exchanges constituting International Trade. The conclusions hitherto reached are of universal application, being applicable to all mankind generally, taken as a whole, and to every nation taken as a separate whole;

but they undergo certain modifications in consequence of the separation of different climates by distance, and of different nations by distance, language, laws, and customs of life. These modifications must now be taken into account; and in doing so it will be well to distinguish, at the outset, two aspects of the subject, first, the exchanges between any two nations as wholes, in which the exports as a whole are the price paid for the imports as a whole, and vice versa; and secondly, the machinery by which these exchanges are effected, that is, as broken up into single exportations paid for in money to the individual exporting the goods, and single importations for which the importer pays in like manner. The first way of looking at the matter will give the general and abstract treatment of the case, and will furnish the characterisation of the processes described in the second way of looking at it, which in their turn will furnish the analysis and verification of that general characterisation.

67. And first under the first aspect. When commodities produced in one country are exchanged for commodities produced in another, the cost of production is still the minimum, or natural value, below which the market price cannot permanently fall. But while this cost of production consists in the price of the commodities consumed as capital, in the price of labour, and in the amount of net profits, in the producing country, the market value of the commodity produced consists, not in the commodities for which it will exchange in the producing country, but in those for which it will exchange in the foreign country to which it is exported. It must exchange for such an amount of foreign commodities as, when

sold by the original producer in his own country, will give him at least an equal remuneration to that which he could have obtained by the same cost expended in producing commodities for home consumption. And the same rule applies to the foreign commodities which he receives in exchange for his exports. Their value consists not in the commodities which they could command at home, but in those which they can command abroad, that is, in the commodities which will be exported to pay for them, and which when received must sell for a price equal at least to replacement of capital, wages, and net profits, a price which might not have been obtained if the commodities originally produced had been sold at home. The cost of production depends upon the home markets, but the remuneration for producing depends, first, upon the foreign markets for the produce, secondly, upon the home market for the foreign commodities imported in exchange. The effect of the separation of countries is therefore to interpose a new link between production and remuneration, namely, the foreign commodity, first bought by and then sold for home products. Two markets instead of one must be taken into the account.

68. From this follows this singular result of international trade, that a commodity may be imported from abroad notwithstanding that it might be produced at a lower cost at home than abroad. (See Mr. J. S. Mill's Principles of Pol. Econ. Book iii. Ch. xviii.). For it may be paid for by commodities which at home have cost less in producing than the commodity itself would cost. It is therefore cheaper to import than to produce it, although it is dearer to produce abroad than it is to produce at home.

The foreign producer obtains commodities which are the cheapest to us to produce, paying for them by commodities which cost him less to produce than the price for which, in his markets, the commodities imported from us are sold. The condition of foreign trade is, not that the commodities imported shall be produced at a lower cost in the exporting than in the importing country, but that the commodities imported shall sell for more than the cost of production of the commodities exported in return. The advantage or disadvantage of foreign export trade, at any particular time and place, depends upon the sum which we receive for our exports compared to the sum which we have spent in producing them, and not compared to the sum which we pay for our imports; while the advantage or disadvantage of a foreign import trade depends, not upon the sum which we pay for our imports compared to the sum which we receive for our exports, but upon the sum which we pay for our imports compared to the sum which we receive for the productive use we make of them.

69. It is evident therefore that each country finds its greatest advantage in devoting its labour and capital exclusively to the production of those commodities which it can produce the most cheaply compared to foreign countries; and in buying with them foreign produce of all descriptions which it can produce less cheaply, even although it may be able to produce some of these more cheaply than foreign countries. The natural conditions, extraneous to political economy, such as soil, climate, neighbourhood, raw produce, government, and manners, go a long way towards deciding what kinds of production are

the cheapest, and therefore the most advantageous, to different countries. The tendency of advancing industry is to introduce the principle of division of labour into international transactions; and the more complete the fusion of mankind into one vast family, by breaking down the artificial barriers of diverse laws, manners, languages, weights and measures, currencies, and so on, the more pronounced will this separation of industries become, depending as it does on the natural barriers which cannot be removed. But there must always remain a great number of productions in which the differences of cost of production, though depending on such irremovable natural barriers, are too small to effect the cessation of their production in one place and its removal to another. There will always be a large variety of industries in every country, in which no interchange will take place, notwithstanding the slight difference of advantage in favour of one country over another; such differences being too small to cover the cost of carriage.

70. The minimum price or return received for an exported commodity is fixed, it has been seen, by its cost of production. The maximum price or return for it, the upper limit of oscillation in its market value, is fixed, in a similar manner, by the cost of production, in their own country, of the commodities imported in return for it. The consideration of this point will bring us to the question of the machinery, the particular exchanges, by which international trade is effected, which is the second aspect of the whole subject.

71. Country A exports goods to country B; their minimum aggregate price must be sufficient to cover

their cost of production in A. But what is their maximum aggregate price, the maximum which B can afford to give for them? It must consist of the goods which B can export and sell to A, at prices sufficient to cover their cost of production. These goods are the price paid to A by B in return for the goods sent to B by A; and the highest aggregate prices for which they sell in A form the maximum aggregate price of A's exports; just as the highest aggregate prices for which A's goods sent to B will sell in B are the maximum aggregate price of B's exports. The lower, therefore, the cost of production in B, the greater is the quantity of goods it can afford to export, and therefore the greater are its means of purchasing from A. In other words, the cost of production in B, which fixes the minimum price which B can afford to receive from the sale of its imports from A, fixes also the maximum quantity of goods which B can afford to send to A in return; and the price for which this quantity will sell in A is the limit above which the price received by A, for goods exported to B, cannot rise. The cost of production in each country fixes the maximum quantity of goods which can be given for the commodities imported from the other; and the money price which they fetch, when sold in the country which imports them, is the purchase money of the commodities which have been exported in return for them. In other words, the cost of production in the exporting country determines the quantity of goods which can be profitably exported, the markets in the importing country determine the price of those goods to the importer.

72. Here then we reach a distinction between

quantity and price of goods imported and exported which carries us over into the question of the actual machinery by which international trade is effected. It is through the prices received for exports compared to the cost of production, and through the prices realised by sale of imports compared to those given for the imports, as separate transactions, that the merchants in the two countries know what transactions are likely to be advantageous to them; the aggregate of which transactions constitutes the international trade which has been characterised as a purchase of exports by imports between the countries. Let us endeavour to connect these two aspects together. The prices oscillate, between the limits above described, according to the demand of each country for the productions of the other. An increasing demand is a demand for a greater quantity than before; the price rises in consequence. How is this price paid? By offering goods for export at lower prices, in order to reach a larger market, and obtain a greater sum of money. The country which demands more raises prices on itself; it has to export more in quantity than before, and therefore to lower the price at which its exports are offered. The country which demands less obtains, therefore, foreign goods at a lower price and in greater quantity. The demand of consumers, the U of the acquirers, is the operative element in determining market values, in international trade, between the limits, either way, fixed by cost of production; and this overcomes the D, the resistance of the sellers, at the point where the cheapness of the goods, which the buyer offers in exchange, induces him to take a quantity sufficient to pay for the goods now demanded by the buyer. And this is the difference between the two cases of international trade and trade between individuals; in the latter case the acquirer overcomes D by offering a larger amount of goods or of money for the goods which he demands, while in the former he overcomes it by offering to sell goods at a cheaper rate, in expectation of having a greater quantity of them demanded in consequence; that is, he offers a greater quantity, not directly, but indirectly by lowering the price. If a greater quantity is not demanded in consequence, then he either diminishes his own demand or exports in return some commodity which brings him in no profit.

73. We may now pass to the second aspect of the subject, the actual mechanism of the trade, adopting the trader's point of view, and beginning with the changes which arise in demand, on consideration of market prices as they may exist at any one time. Not only does the general expression 'the country' mean, not an individual person, but the producers and traders of the country, but also each of these individuals singly does not, as a rule, export goods for which he receives payment in other goods, but he exports goods for which he receives payment in money, by bills payable or discountable in his own country, as single and separate transactions, or he imports goods for which he pays in a similar manner. Bills are drawn against goods exported, and bills are drawn against goods imported, which bills are exchanged against each other; thus enabling us to characterise the transactions as exchanges of goods against goods.

74. Now it is the state of prices to which the producers and traders of a country look, when con-

Book II.
Ch. IV.
§ 95.
Statical logic
of exchange.

sidering what commodities it will be profitable to export or produce for exportation. When the prices of any kind of goods abroad are sufficiently high to cover the cost of production and of carriage, they are produced and exported; when the quantity demanded is greater, the price will rise, and they will be produced and exported in greater quantity; this however raises the price of them at home as well as abroad, for, if the price was not raised at home, the merchant who purchased them of the producer would alone make the increased profit, by purchasing at the former low price. Producers and traders keep exporting all goods which bear a price abroad sufficient to cover their cost of production and carriage, and those goods most which bear the highest price and are most in demand. Those goods alone cease to be exported the price of which falls below the cost of production and carriage. Similarly in the country traded with; its producers and traders keep producing and exporting all goods which bear a remunerative price, and those the most the price of which is highest, from their being most in demand. The lower limit to exportation on either side is fixed by cost of production in the exporting countries.

75. If however the demand for goods at high prices ceases in one country before the corresponding demand ceases in the other, there will be importers in the latter country, where the demand still continues, who have to pay for the goods imported without being able to find goods to export at remunerative prices; the bills which are drawn on them for payment of the goods imported will be of greater amount than the bills which they can draw, or purchase when drawn, upon importers in the

country where the demand has ceased. This effect however is not produced until the traders and producers, in the country where the demand still continues, have sought to follow up the decreasing demand in the other country by offering goods at decreasing prices, down to the lower limit of cost of production, in hope of reaching a demand for a greater quantity at those lowered prices. It is only when this limit is reached, without a greater quantity being demanded in consequence, that the total amount of bills, drawn on the country where the demand continues high, becomes greater than the total amount of bills drawn on the country where the demand has diminished.

76. When this is the case, those importers, in the country where the demand continues high, who have to meet the bills drawn on them, and are unable to find bills on the other country to pay them with, have to transmit not goods but bullion, in payment of the bills drawn on them for the goods they have imported. Bullion becomes the commodity exported to pay for import of goods. But bullion is a commodity on the export of which the trader makes no profit; which is evident from this, that if the producer or trader sent goods which would sell, in the other country, for the amount of his debt, he would obtain the difference between their price and the expense of their production, that is, he would obtain the net profits; but when he sends bullion (unless bullion itself is a product of the country) there is no difference between the value of the thing sent and the debt which it pays. The transmission of bullion therefore shows, not only that the country to which it is sent has ceased to increase its demand

for the commodities of the country which sends it, but also that the maximum price of imports, which the country sending bullion instead of sending goods can pay with a profit on the payment itself, that is, on its exports, has been reached; for the commodity now exported in return for goods is a commodity which cannot sell for more in the country to which it is sent than it costs to procure it in the country which sends it, unless it is a product of that country. In other words, the cost of production, in the importing country, of the commodity exported in return for its imports fixes the maximum of price at which it can afford to import without having recourse to money or bullion payments. (See further with reference to bullion, § 96. 76).

77. The transmission of bullion in payment of an international balance is therefore the final stage in the oscillation, upwards or downwards, of market prices between any two nations, and indicates a state of trade which will normally be followed by a diminished demand on the part of the country which exports the bullion. The most advantageous state of commerce is one in which the transmission of bullion is entirely avoided, because in such a state, though the two countries may divide the advantage unequally, according to the demand of either compared with the demand of the other, yet there are no exchanges on which net profits are not reaped by the exporting country. International trade is therefore most advantageous to all concerned when the exchanges are to the largest amount, without the limits of oscillation in market prices being reached in either direction, and consequently without any transmission of bullion.

78. We are thus brought back to the statement made in par. 69 as to the mode of judging the advantage or disadvantage in exporting and importing. The export of goods must be profitable on the whole; that is to say, it must at least repay the cost of production of the goods exported; for otherwise it would soon cease to be carried on. Its returns may be left to the care of the individual traders, for, if they find their profit in it, it is clear that the country must do so too. But an import trade which is not supported or balanced by an export trade of goods, but which has to pay for its imports by the export of bullion, will be profitable no doubt to the individual traders, for the same reason as in the other case; but it does not necessarily follow that it will also enrich the country. If bullion is exported to meet imports of commodities to be used in productive consumption, the country will no doubt be the richer for the transaction, notwithstanding that we make no profit on the export of the bullion itself. But if the imported commodities are commodities of final or unproductive consumption, not being necessaries of life which must be supplied in the same quantity from some source or other, then the importers may be benefited by their sale, but the country not enriched, because it will have expended its wealth in the purchase of indulgences, that is, commodities of final and unnecessary consumption. It is the use to which the imports are put, in such a case, that determines whether the importation is, economically speaking, advantageous to the country. Both limbs of international trade may be profitable in the case of imports of goods met by exports of goods; but it is only importation that can be, where

§ 95. Statical logic of exchange.

the corresponding export consists not of goods but of bullion.

VI.

79. In order to complete the examination of the first branch of political economy we must return to the general point of view from which we departed in considering international trade. The prices or values of commodities have been to some extent analysed into their component parts or elements. A distinction of prices must now be introduced, founded on the different purposes for which they are paid, or, in other words, on the different modes of consumption. Capital has already been opposed to labour, but the term has another employment in which it is opposed to Revenue. (See par. 53). Let us take the term Income to signify the sum which may be spent either as capital or as revenue, or partly as both. Revenue, then, is that part of income which is spent in unproductive consumption, capital that spent in productive. It is clear that this division is exhaustive; all the wealth in the world must be either revenue or capital; for it must be either consumed or hoarded, and, if consumed, then either productively or unproductively, and if hoarded, this is equivalent to unproductive consumption so long as the hoarding lasts.

80. The only motive for consuming productively is to be able to consume unproductively hereafter. Productive consumption is labour, unproductive is enjoyment. Consequently unproductive consumption is the reward of productive, and the portion of wealth consumed unproductively is that which purchases, and is purchased by, the portion produced by productive

consumption. Revenue is the demand, not for capital, but for the commodities produced by consuming capital.

81. The men dividing their incomes into revenue and capital cannot be so simply divided into two classes. There are not two classes, one of productive and not unproductive consumers, the other of unproductive and not productive. There might indeed be men who were the first, namely, such unskilled manual labourers who should consume no more than was requisite to repair the waste of their frames and keep themselves in good working order. There might be men who were the last, namely, pure spendthrifts and pure paupers. But between these two classes lies the vast bulk of mankind, namely, men who spend their incomes partly productively partly unproductively, partly as capital partly as revenue.

82. The industrialist who spends capital or labour in production clearly sets apart one portion of the total resulting income to replace his consumed capital, the other portion to consume unproductively as revenue, in buying house, food, clothing, and luxuries. So much of this so-called revenue as is strictly necessary to maintain him in health of body and mind may be reckoned as replacement of capital; since it is requisite to the superintendence of his capital, or to the application of his strength in labouring, that he should be able to work; but this portion cannot be actually divided from the whole of what he spends, or from that portion which is mere luxury.

83. So also the man who is said to "live on his means" sets apart one portion of his total Having each year as capital, and the rest as revenue; he lends his money, goods, or land; and the interest,

rent, or hire, is that portion which is his revenue. His money, goods, and land, are employed as capital in reproduction; the interest, hire, and rent, are consumed as revenue.

84. Thus out of the total Having or Income of each year,—if we break up the total into yearly periods for the sake of convenience,—one part, capital, is set apart to provide the total income of next year; and all income arises solely from capital so employed. In looking to the mode in which revenue arises, we find that it comes solely from capital, being a part of income, which itself has no other source. Capital productively consumed is the parent of the revenue of one year, and of the capital of the next; the capital of that next year the parent of the revenue and capital of the year following, and so on.

85. The gradual increase of revenue from year to year comes out of the gradual increase of capital; and the capital of each year is increased by saving out of income; that is, by setting apart out of the total income a larger part than is requisite for the mere replacement of the capital producing it, a saving which can only be made by leaving a smaller sum, that year, than would otherwise be left for revenue; smaller, that is, than it would have been but for the saving, but perhaps not smaller than the revenue of the preceding year, since the capital may have produced a larger total income. The larger the capital the larger the income; and the larger the income the larger may be both or either of the two parts of it, capital for next year and revenue. Revenue can only permanently increase by permanent additions being made to capital; the two increase pari passu; and the capital is the parent of the revenue.

86. It is clear therefore that capital is necessary to revenue. But the converse also is equally true, namely, that revenue is necessary to capital, by being the demand for its products. Now in what sense is revenue the demand for commodities produced by capital? And would those commodities lose their value if there were no revenue to purchase them with? These are questions which concern the most fundamental principles of political economy.

87. It may be stated in the first place that the term unproductive consumption, the expenditure of revenue, is sometimes used in a sense in which the consumption is not wholly unproductive. The money paid for the luxuries consumed goes to swell the total income of several productive consumers, to replace their capital as well as to furnish their revenue. That is to say, A. B. C. produce commodities which X consumes unproductively; the exchange between the two parties is a source of income to A. B. C. and a source of revenue to X. But the income of A. B. C. is partly at least capital employed next year. It is the other limb of the exchange, the revenue of X, the commodity he consumes, which is consumed unproductively. But if X were a productive consumer as well as A. B. C., if the commodity he purchased of them were consumed as capital, then both limbs of the exchange would be employed as capital productively; and the result next year would be an income increased by the savings of X, as well as by those of A. B. C.

88. The X of this illustration must not be taken as a representative of the class who "live on their means." This class is liable to be confounded with those who spend revenue and consume unproduc-

tively, instead of spending capital and consuming productively, merely because the way in which their capital is usually invested, permanent investment in land, stock, or shares, gives returns in the shape of rent or interest, and thus their whole annual apparent income has already, when it comes into their hands as revenue, been diminished by subtraction, from the whole real income, of that portion set apart as capital for next year. Being permanently invested, the capital has not to be deducted and set apart by them each year; they receive only the revenue. To the extent of their investments this class is a class consuming capital productively, just as much as the classes actively engaged in industry. Revenue, however separated out of total income from capital for next year, is revenue in the strict sense, if it is a portion of income unproductively consumed. The rich farmer, ship-builder, contractor, manufacturer, merchant, and so on, spends as much revenue unproductively as the rich landowner or fundholder. X therefore means every possessor of an income, quatenus a spender of revenue.

89. But now as to revenue being the demand for products of capital; suppose X to spend no revenue, but, buying only what was necessary for bare subsistence and health, to reduce his unproductive expenditure to a minimum, and to employ his total income as capital, productively; would that destroy, or at all diminish, the demand for products of capital? Certainly not. The kind of commodities demanded would be changed; only such would be demanded, and consequently in the long run produced, as could be employed in further production. Jewellery, for instance, might not be produced, but

more of such things as machinery for cotton-spinning instead. The wealth of the world would be enormously increased by the change; because both sides of the exchange spoken of in par. 88 would now be employed as capital, instead of only one. The employers of capital would make their own market, X would have become included in the class A. B. C., and class X would cease to exist.

90. But if X were to cease unproductive expenditure without substituting productive; if he were to hoard or annihilate his revenue, not transferring it to capital, which would be the case if he bought no articles of luxury at all, but received his interest or profits and then threw them into the sea—(and the sea is a first-rate place for hoards)—the demand for products of capital would be greatly diminished; for the obvious reason, that a large part of existing wealth would be destroyed, a large part of the already realised products of capital. In this case both limbs of the exchange spoken of above would have become unproductive.

91. We have then three cases of employment of income:

1. where it is consumed unproductively as revenue, the exchanges having one limb unproductive, the other productive;
2. where it is consumed productively as capital, the exchanges having both limbs productive;
3. where it is destroyed, the exchanges ceasing, which in point of wealth is the same as both limbs being unproductive.

92. It is not therefore an unconditional truth

that revenue is the sole ultimate demand for the products of capital; there might be a demand just the same, though for different kinds of products, if that portion of income usually spent as revenue were to be spent as capital. And in this case enormous additions would be made to the world's wealth. But as things are, as human nature is actually constituted, revenue is the sole ultimate demand for these products; it is a contingent truth, conditioned on a fact in human nature, which is this, that man seeks present enjoyment to a certain extent and not beyond, the precise extent being measured, in matter of wealth, by the proportion of income which he devotes to enjoyment one year, compared to the portion which he devotes to produce income for next year. It is a case falling under the general law of choice, that the comparative strength of conflicting motives, or conflicting pleasures, can only be known by the result, that is, by the pleasure which becomes the motive of the choice actually made. The capital set apart, and the labour of employing it, are the means of attaining an ultimate end; they are therefore mediate or subordinate ends only. And this shows the truth of the doctrine in § 94. 4, 5, that political economy cannot be defined by, or founded on, the single motive of acquiring wealth, even allowing that this motive should be taken as an artificially abstracted phenomenon, for the purpose of examination; but that it must be founded on all the actual motives of men, their desires of enjoyment of all kinds, so far as these are satisfiable by commodities or services capable of acquisition by exchange. If the motive of man was to increase his own wealth and the world's, and not to enjoy by spending revenue, then the only demand for the products of capital would be a demand by productive consumers as such. But since the reverse is the truth, since the sole ultimate motive of man is to spend revenue, and not to increase his wealth, it follows that the sole demand which gives value to the products of capital consists ultimately or originally in the demand of unproductive consumers. The demand for products to employ again productively is a demand derived from this ultimate one, as a demand for the means whereby it may be satisfied.

93. In other words, Trade exchanges depend upon General exchanges, the exchanges between dealers and dealers upon those between dealers and consumers. And the amount paid by dealers to dealers can never be greater than that paid by consumers to dealers; for the funds to furnish the former come out of the funds employed in the latter. Hence Adam Smith, in Book ii. Chap. ii. says: "The value of the goods circulated between the different dealers never can exceed the value of those circulated between the dealers and the consumers; whatever is bought by the dealers being ultimately destined to be sold to the consumers." The price of the shoes sold to consumers, for instance, paid by consumers to a dealer, pays not only that dealer for his capital and trouble, but a great many other dealers besides for theirs, the tanner, the grazier, the threadmaker, and so on; their capital and trouble being paid out of the capital of the shoe dealer, and he retaining for himself only the profits on his own capital.

94. Revenue, then, is the market for commodities produced by capital, and these lose their exchange value if no market can be found for them. Just as

the weapon of the savage loses its value-in-use if there remains no game which it can kill, so these commodities lose their exchange value if they lose the market which revenue supplies. But this revenue itself also consists of commodities produced by capital; it is that portion of them which is set apart for final consumption; and this portion is the market for the remainder. Here is the point which chiefly demands attention. Under an industrial system organised by means of a recognised currency or medium of exchange, the portion of commodities which is the revenue of particular persons is not separated from the remainder, but both together remain in the hands of dealers until purchased piecemeal, for present use, by the virtual owners, namely, those who have the command of them by possessing portions of the recognised currency. He who has and spends a revenue, say of £100, would, without such a currency, have to keep the commodities in which his revenue really consists in his own hands; and these commodities would be confined to such articles as he could himself produce. But this alters nothing in their nature as the market for the commodities which are set apart for productive consumption. Those dealers who deal in articles of final consumption are, as it were, the commodity bankers of the community, and are paid for their trouble by a command of commodities, part of which replaces their capital, part is consumed as revenue. All the commodities in the hands of such dealers taken together constitute the revenue of the community; of which the revenue of the dealers themselves is a part. The revenue of the community is distinguishable by its being in the hands of the dealers in articles of final consumption, but that of individuals is undistinguishable except by the sums of money with which each person commands those articles.

95. Just as market price is the thing to be fixed on as the starting point, when we are analysing exchanges statically, so in analysing them dynamically, that is, in considering the movement of exchanges from year to year, revenue is the starting point, being the fund out of which comes the remuneration for all employment of capital. Revenue however may be considered as composed of all the sums paid by consumers to dealers, at rates which are called general as distinguished from trade prices; it is to them that trade prices, together with the kind and amount of goods exchanged, have in the long run to conform; and by them that the success or failure of speculation is determined.

96. It is in the dynamical branch or aspect of political economy, which, it must be borne in mind, is also its historical aspect, that most of the great moot questions of practical importance arise, such, for instance, as most of those stated by Mr. F. Harrison in his admirable article on the Limits of Political Economy in the Fortnightly Review for June 15, 1865, " What are the laws of population? Are small farms or large farms best? Does the peasant proprietor thrive? Define the 'wages fund.' What decides the remuneration of labour? State some of the laws of the accumulation of profits. Give the ratio of the relative increase of population, and the means of subsistence. What are the economical results of direct and indirect taxation? of strict entails? of trade-unions? of poor-laws? and so on." Taxation and Free Trade, questions which usually form so

important a feature in treatises of political economy, belong to its dynamical not its statical branch. They are parts of economical policy, the art of political economy, the rules of which depend upon the different circumstances of different communities. Before any fixed course of economical policy can be adopted, principles must be established which involve an answer, one way or another, to questions of the kind just enumerated. But all such questions depend for their solution upon a knowledge of the comparative strength of different motives under different conditions; questions which consequently cannot be answered by a mere logic of political economy, but only by a knowledge of the laws of human practice generally and of the interdependence of all its several modes of activity. Before the dynamical logic of political economy can be attempted with anything like success, a much more detailed analysis than exists at present must have been made of the interaction of men in all branches of history; then perhaps we may be able by degrees to descend from the whole to a part, and establish one by one propositions which, when systematised, will form the dynamical logic of the science. Meantime, we can only signalise the place at which its logic as a whole is imperfect, and where immense discoveries are still remaining to be made. This however is no ground for dissatisfaction with the logic of values in the statical branch, so far as it may be held to be actually established.

§ 96.

> All' idea di quel metallo,
> Portentoso, onnipossente,
> Un volcano la mia mente
> Già comincia a diventar.
>
> Il Barbiere.

I.

1. We now come to the second great branch of the statical logic of political economy, Money as the means and measure of exchange. This branch is not only one half, but also one entire aspect, of the whole science, so that the whole of it might be treated as a question of money, without omitting any of its essential features. Money stands to exchanges as language to thought; it is the measure and the expression of value in all its possible analyses, and it is also the means of communicating values, as words are of communicating thoughts, in precisely measured portions and shapes. The mode of origin and adoption of money is besides an instance of the same process of consciousness as the mode of origin and adoption of language; each is a case of the volitional and conventional adoption, for a definite purpose, of objects and of modes of action offered in the first instance by spontaneously arising processes, such as, in the case of money, the use of tallies and other simple records of barter; and each grows in minuteness and complexity of device with the growth of that which it ascertains and communicates, namely, wealth in the one case, thought in the other. The comparison of words to coin has, then, a greater aptness of analogy than was probably contemplated by those who first drew it. Money is the causa cogno-

scendi, the evidence, of the values of exchanged commodities, as fixed by the exchange itself; and it is also the means of reckoning the U and D elements of that value, by each party to the bargain before he concludes it. It is a perfectly general instrument of calculating, expressing, and communicating values, indefinitely subtil and flexible. U, it has been shown, is the perception, the subjective aspect, of a value-in-use; a certain sum of money, the price of that value, is the name, sign, measure, and means of transferring and commanding it. The metaphysical distinctions of objective and subjective aspects, and of spontaneous and voluntary actions, are thus pre-requisites to a full comprehension of the phenomena of money; and a reference of the phenomena to these distinctions is the only guarantee that any comprehension of them is exhaustive.

2. In treating the first branch of the logic we have already used money as the measure of value, nor would it be possible to do otherwise consistently with being intelligible. The values of commodities are always estimated in money; money is their language, prices are their names. But now, in the second branch of the logic, we have to treat of this language itself; and the circumstance which gives this branch, money, its consistence as an independent subject, capable of being treated by itself, is this, that the mode in which money serves to effect exchanges between commodities is by being itself exchanged against each of them in turn, in separate transactions. It is no longer some commodities against others, but money against all, that is the object in view. Money is the universal purchaser, one commodity against all the rest. The point of view therefore is altered, from

that of the acquirer of commodities to that of the acquirer of money by means of commodities.

3. And here also is seen the logical necessity, in political economy, of making the foreseen result of transactions the starting point, of treating the subject as an Art, governed by motives, and its laws as laws of voluntary action. Just as the price of a commodity, paid when it is finally brought to market, determined the amount of remuneration to its several producers, and the anticipation of that price stimulated or depressed production, so also the value of that price, estimated in commodities of all kinds which it may purchase, is the remuneration for procuring the money of which it consists, the final cause of procuring money at all. A certain sum of money has a certain quantity of commodities or services as its value, and the procuring those commodities or services is the motive for procuring the money. As all production of commodities rests on the expectation of remuneration by exchanging them, so all production of money rests on the expectation that it will always command or purchase an equivalent value in commodities. All money therefore in its nature is credit, confidence in the purchasing power of an otherwise useless commodity; and for the same reason all money is debt, that is, it is commodities owing to the person who has money to pay for them, though of course not a debt legally enforceable.

4. Money accordingly is three things:
    1. The measure of value of other commodities,
    2. The medium of exchange of other commodities,
    3. A commodity possessing exchange value itself.

We may put out of the question the value-in-use and

Book II.
Ch. IV.
§ 96.
Statical logic of money.

in exchange of the precious metals for purposes of art and ornament, which is entirely irrelevant to this branch of political economy. In this capacity they are one commodity among others, and belong like the rest to the first branch. But the value-in-use of the precious metals as money is their serving as a measure of value and medium of exchange for other commodities; and this value-in-use is one ground, one cause, of their exchange value; it is their U element. But to constitute this exchange value the element D is requisite. This element is provided for by cost of production. The cost of production, since money is a commodity produced by definite quantities of labour and capital, is the D, and the services rendered as a medium of exchange and measure of value are the U. But here arises an apparent contradiction, which I do not remember ever to have seen noticed or clearly explained, in the functions of money. It is this: the exchange value, or purchasing power, of money has been said to depend upon its D, or cost of production, together with its U, or power of serving as a medium of exchange and measure of value; but its serving as a medium of exchange and measure of value *is* its purchasing power; it purchases that for which it is exchanged, the value of which it measures. In other words, its exchange value is at one time represented as the product of D and U, and at another as U alone, one element only of itself. How escape from this circle?

5. The solution is this: The U element of the exchange value of money is not the definite value of this or that particular quantity of money, but the power of rendering the service of measuring and exchanging values generally, a service not greater in

exchanges of a large than of a small amount. It is the D element, or cost of production of any definite amount of money, which gives to the money so produced its power of measuring and exchanging for definite amounts of other commodities; but without the general and indefinite U the D element would be powerless to give money any exchange value at all. Hence the contradiction is only apparent, arising from our falsely attributing to the U element of the exchange value, or purchasing power, of money a definite amount, which it only acquires from combination with D, the cost of production of a definite quantity of metal; in other words, from confusing two distinct senses of the symbol U. Mankind were desirous that the service of measuring and purchasing values should be performed, if any commodity could be found to perform it. The cost of production of money enabled it to perform the service, by not only giving money a common measure of value with other commodities, namely, the quantity of labour requisite to produce it and them, but also by giving it a definite value of its own on condition of a service being rendered by it, on condition of its having some U. (See § 95. 1). The U arises from an universally felt want, and is therefore universally operative when combined with D. Several reasons then concurred for the selection of the precious metals as the medium of exchange, such as their malleability, their durability, their divisibility, the comparatively slight variations in the quantities of labour requisite to produce equal amounts of them from time to time, and their containing the results of much labour in small compass.

6. The element D is essentially necessary to constitute the exchange value of money, and of every

particular portion of it; but it is not equally essential that the D should consist in cost of production, that the money should be one of those commodities whose natural value depends upon the quantity of labour necessary to produce them, and not one where it depends upon scarcity or limitation of the supply. But it is far better that it should belong to the former class. If its D consisted in limitation of the supply, this limitation must be either natural or artificial, and in either case a greater burden would be imposed on the volition of men than it could easily support, in the one case by their being compelled to accept, and accept with equal confidence, from some arbitrary source, the determination of values which are now determined by the physical laws of difficulty of production; it would throw upon U alone the functions of U and D together. If on the other hand the limit was fixed by nature, in the scarcity of the medium chosen as money, say for instance shells of a certain kind, it would on the one hand not have the expansibility of metals to meet the rapidly increasing commerce and wealth of the world, and it would be liable on the other hand to sudden and perhaps violent alterntions of quantity, since we could never be certain that some new store of such shells might not be discovered, whereby the relations of money to commodities would be altered. Again, if the limit was fixed artificially, suppose by the use of paper money issued by governments, who is there who could either be supposed capable of estimating the quantity required, or trusted not to exceed that quantity, if it were left in his power to issue? In either case the confidence in the purchasing power of particular sums of money would be lessened, and insecurity in all commercial transactions increased. All money is credit, confidence in the purchasing power of money, that is, in the readiness of other persons to give commodity value for money value. And this confidence has been the growth of ages, gradually strengthened by the habitual use of a commodity as money which it required real labour to procure, but probably founded originally in the effect produced on the imagination of men by seeing the use of the precious metals as articles of ornament and luxury.

7. A metallic currency is self-regulating; as soon as it becomes scarce in proportion to the commodities requiring to be exchanged, its value rises and remunerates the additional labour required to produce an additional quantity. No one judges how much money is required to perform the exchanges of other commodities; but as soon as a certain quantity of money, produced by a certain quantity of labour, will buy more goods than can be produced by an equal quantity of labour, some one will be found to spend the labour in producing money and not goods. And so long as money is being produced from the mines, so long will money be somewhat above its natural value, owing to scarcity having produced an oscillation in its favour above the natural value point.

8. All money is credit, and metallic money is that kind of it which is most invariable and most secure. A paper currency must therefore always have a metallic basis, that is, must represent some real amount of the commodity chosen as the medium of exchange. Under this condition it is possible to supersede the use of metal by paper to a great extent, and thus save

the expense of the more costly medium. "A currency" says Ricardo "is in its most perfect state when it consists wholly of paper money, but of paper money of an equal value with the gold which it professes to represent." This perfection however, like all ideals, is unattainable actually; since the only certain means of securing an equal value in a paper currency is by making it convertible into metals at the demand of the holder, a condition which supposes a considerable part of the currency to consist of metal. The precious metals having once for all been established as the universal purchaser, being themselves nothing but the most secure and invariable form of credit or of debt, all other forms of currency share the same nature and possess a value which varies with the confidence secured to them, from time to time, by the credit of the persons who issue them. Bullion, coin, notes, cheques, bills, book credits, and so on, are so many forms of Money, which circulate freely in times of confidence and speculation, but which are thrown out of use in times of distrust, and in inverse proportion to the security they offer,—notes in this country, notes and coin in others, and bullion in all, being the last to remain in circulation, the kinds of currency which no want of confidence has ever been sufficient entirely to invalidate, so firm are the imaginative bases upon which they rest.

9. But now more precisely to answer the question, What are the main kinds or forms of money? They will be found to be three. The process which established the commodity, metallic money, as the representative of other commodities or services does not stop there; the same motives lead to the establishment of some representatives of metallic money

itself; for money is the universal object of acquisition, and yet it is impossible, for the wealthy at least, to have all their wealth in the shape of money in pocket or cellar. Written or printed documents thus become to money the same thing that money is to other commodities; their possession gives a right to the possession of the quantity of money specified by them, against the persons who have issued them; the difference being that, while no one is bound to sell commodities unless he chooses, the issuers of documents representing money are bound to fulfil the contract they have entered into by issuing them. All such documents are securities for money, and rest on credit in the sense of belief in the ability of the promisor to fulfil his engagement. Credit means a believed promise to pay money at a future time, with or without interest for its use.

10. Of these documents there are many kinds, all depending upon positive law to define their character and secure their convertibility; for, as just shown, they all differ from money itself in being creatures of contract, not of universal and tacit convention. All money is credit, but some kinds of it consist in contracts, positive promises, to pay the metallic kind; they are credit by a double title. Hence the distinction between a metallic and paper currency.

11. But not all documents of credit are credit currency simply; many are this and something else besides, namely, a security not for money in hand but for money in prospect. There is a distinction to be introduced into credit currency itself, a distinction between those documents which are designed by the legislator to serve as substitutes for money actually possessed, to provide a more convenient and

less expensive medium of exchange for other commodities, which therefore constitute, together with coin, the national and legal currency of the country, and those documents on the other hand which are designed by individuals and permitted by the legislator to serve as representatives of money in prospect, that is, of credit in the ordinary sense of the word. The documents which compose credit currency are therefore distinguished by such marks as these, 1st, their being payable on demand and to bearer, 2nd, their being issued only by certain responsible persons or bodies of men who, in the opinion of the legislator, are likely always to be able to pay them in specie, for which certain conditions may possibly be imposed, such as are contained, for instance, in the Bank Charter Act, 1844. These documents may be called Public Credit Currency.

12. The third kind of money, the second division of credit currency, consists of documents which may be called a Private Credit Currency. They are promises to pay money by private persons, and comprise Deposits in Banks, and Cheques and Drafts which transfer these, Book Debts, Bills, and Promissory Notes, a class of documents which performs a far greater part of the exchange transactions of the country than is performed by means of both the former classes taken together. The amount of these documents fluctuates with the exchanges which they are required to perform, being created for the purpose of performing them, and being destroyed when the transactions which gave them birth are completed. "The amount of currency or circulating medium in any country," says Mr. Macleod, "is the *sum total of all the debts due to every individual in it.*" Theory

and Practice of Banking, Vol. i. p. 23. 2nd ed. And at p. 102 he says, "It is certain that 'credit' exceeds 'money' many times in this country, for whereas it is not supposed that the actual money exceeds £60,000,000, the credit in bills of exchange, and which is only one form of it, exceeds £400,000,000." In one sense therefore private credit currency is as much currency as Bank notes or metals; but the element of individual credit is much more important in this class than in public credit currency, just as it is more important in the latter than in metallic currency. There is a scale of security inversely proportioned to the use made of bare credit in the different classes of currency. Bank notes hold a middle position, and the controversy which raged so long as to whether they were money or not is one which cannot be settled by a single sentence, yes or no. So long as they are de facto convertible they are money; when once they cease to be convertible they become mere securities; for they are of the nature of securities, but securities so fenced as to have the value of ready money.

13. Nor is this distinction of money into three classes or kinds of currency, that is to say, Metals, Public Credit Currency, and Private Credit Currency, applicable only to particular countries; it is applicable also to the international concerns of the whole world. It is no special distinction but an universal one. The only difference is, that there is, at present, no class of documents which are an international Public Credit Currency, since there is no universal coinage, and no international government to establish the security of paper documents. International metallic currency consists of bullion, or, if of coin, of

coin taken at its bullion value; and international private credit currency of Foreign Bills of Exchange. The different national currencies are like so many different languages which need translating into other languages before their value abroad can be determined; but Bullion, which is the foundation of all alike, is the universal language which is everywhere current. The reason for these remarks will appear farther on.

II.

14. The different kinds of currency having been thus distinguished, the next question is to determine the different Functions of money, the different kinds of transactions in which it is employed. When we have obtained these, we ought to be able, by comparing them with the different kinds of currency which are employed in them, to discover the bearings on each other of all the various operations which are transacted by means of money. Now two functions of money are plainly enough deducible from what has been already said, namely, money of all kinds purchasing commodities or services, and money in some of its forms purchasing money in other of its forms; money in the goods market and money in the money market; having in the former a commodity value, in the latter a money value or price. But just as credit currency had to be distinguished above into two classes, public and private credit currency, so here also the money of all kinds in the money market has to give place to two functions, one where one form of currency is exchanged against other forms, to which function alone it will be proper to restrict the term Price of money, and the other where it pur-

chases, not another form of currency, but the Use of money or currency for a certain time, and pays for that use by Interest or Discount, in addition to returning the same sum at the time specified. Money promised to be paid at a certain time, with the addition of Interest then, in return for the same sum received now, or money promised to be paid at a certain time, in return for the same sum received with the subtraction of Discount now, is money purchasing the use of money, money in the Money Market properly so called, money which has not price, nor commodity value, but money value; which money value is great or small according as the rate of interest or of discount is low or high; great if the rate is low, small if the rate is high. Or conversely, the value of the money which purchases the promises to pay, that is, the securities, is great if the rate of interest or discount is high, and small if it is low.

15. It does not follow that only private credit currency will be used for these purchases; currency of all three kinds may be used to purchase the promises to pay with interest, that is, the securities; but the promises to pay, the securities themselves, must always belong to private credit currency, inasmuch as it is of their essence not to be money in hand but only money promised. Nevertheless, these securities themselves may be used, in the goods market, as currency purchasing goods, or in the money changer's market as one form of currency purchasing another form. Only in the money market proper, where money has a money value, they are not currency but its opposite, the thing that currency purchases.

16. This double character of the documents composing the private credit currency is the circumstance

which perhaps most of all wraps monetary matters in confusion. It is not to any difference in the nature of the currency in the money market that the difference in operation is owing, but to the difference of the functions which currency performs, in the one case buying currency or goods, in the other buying the use of currency, and leaving its repayment dependent upon that use, the use which is still to be made of it, upon its being used in a remunerative manner. All credit currency is a promise to pay money, but that credit currency which is discounted, or which purchases currency with interest, is a pledge upon future industry, and not upon profits already realised, unless that industry makes default. And all money, whether metallic or credit currency, which is purchased by interest-bearing securities is borrowed Capital, borrowed on the expectation of future profits. Not all credit currency, not all private credit currency, is borrowed capital; it is borrowed capital only if purchased by interest-bearing securities. The mode in which, the purpose for which, a credit currency is issued determines whether or not it is a creation of capital; and capital can only be created in the money market by being borrowed; the money capital which a man has of his own is not a new creation out of expectancies, but comes from profits already realised. So also are all those Deposits in Banks on which no interest is paid; it is true they are liabilities, but they are liabilities secured, not by future industry, but by the reserves, the portion of already realised profits reserved to meet them. Credit currency is based upon the reserves of bullion; credit currency which is capital is based upon the expectation of future profits.

17. Capital in the form of commodities can only come from profits already realised; it is that part of profits which is set apart for future productive consumption. When borrowed it must be borrowed from the same source. But when we turn to money capitals, we find that future industry can be anticipated and employed almost as easily as if its results were already realised. The invention of Money enables all the anticipated profits to be used in further production, as if they were already realised in the form of commodities. And this it does by the combination of the use of private credit currency with the circumstance, the principle of which was explained in § 95. 94, that all commodities whatever remain in the hands of the dealers until commanded by the holders of money; so that the expected demand rules the quantity of commodities produced, irrespective of whether this demand comes from money already realised or from money borrowed only on anticipation of future profits. But all these commodities purchased to be used as capital by borrowed money are to the purchaser borrowed capital, borrowed first in the form of money, and obtained in the money market by the creation of interest-bearing securities.

18. So far the mere invention of money allowed us to proceed in the creation of capital; but modern banking permits us a far greater advance. "The great modern discovery," says Mr. Macleod, Theory and Practice of Banking, Vol. i. p. 91, "is to make the debts themselves saleable commodities; to sell them either for ready money, or for other debts of more convenient amount, and immediately exchangeable for money on demand, and therefore equivalent to money." Before this, a man could lend his realised

profits in the form of money, and another man could borrow this money on the credit of his future profits to be realised by its use. He could use his expectations as if they were already realised capital. But now, by the modern system of banking, not only can he do this, but, while he is using the capital lent him on his securities, and the lender, to whom those securities are given, is using them as capital by discounting them at a bank, the banker also can employ the greater part of them again by giving a credit in his books for their present, or discounted, value, to meet which he has only to keep a small portion in reserve. The same capital is employed three times, once by the borrower in purchasing commodities, once by the lender in discounting his bill, and once by the banker who purchases the bill by creating a liability; the profits of the banker consisting in the interest, which he deducts as discount, when he creates the liability, and receives from the original borrower when the bill becomes due. "There are two classes of traders whose especial business is to buy these commercial debts. * * * The first class of these traders are called BILL DISCOUNTERS, *i.e. buyers of debts;* they buy these debts with money. The second class are called BANKERS; and they buy these commercial debts, by creating other debts payable on demand," namely, by creating Deposits. (Macleod, id. id. See also par. 89 of the present §).

19. Money in all its three forms, and in all its three functions, appears from what has been said to be a vast structure of wealth, the counterpart and purchaser of commodities and services, in all their forms, future as well as present. No portion of wealth here without a corresponding portion there;

no exchange here without a corresponding exchange there; in whichever of the two sides the creation, destruction, or exchange, may originate. Correlative however as the two structures are, the analysis, the organisation, of each is peculiar and independent. The wealth of commodities and services depends upon the wants and wishes and labour of men, and upon the laws of physical nature which govern the products of that labour. It is an outgrowth of the original possessions and the original skill of man. Money wealth is an outgrowth of one commodity only, the precious metals, and is built upon this foundation by means of credit. Forms and modes of credit are its logical analysis. Not what man has done but what man will do is the substance of this structure. It is not the present result of the past, but the present realisation of the future. Possunt quia posse videntur. But the question may occur, What is the real value of this money wealth, and still more of this credit wealth?

20. There is an axiom, true in its proper connection, but pernicious when taken alone, that the only use of money is to transfer commodities; that commodities are the only wealth, money but the instrument of transferring it; and it is true that this is its only value-in-use. We must connect this with the opposite truth, that the only mode in which this this transfer is effected is by money being exchanged against commodities in separate transactions. The resulting truth will be, that money is real wealth, a commodity having exchange value, and one which, at the present day, is essential to the existence of the wealth with which it exchanges. Without their market, the demand for them, these commodities

would be valueless, productive of no enjoyment, any more than gold and silver taken alone can be. The value-in-use of the commodities is gone along with their exchange value. It is only by their having exchange value, and by their being actually exchanged in consequence, that they can be enjoyed. But this exchange value is procured for them only by means of the money which they purchase, which is their immediate market, and which consequently has an exchange value itself.—Nothing would give me greater pleasure than to find my views in accordance with those of the present Professor of Political Economy at Oxford, Mr. Bonamy Price; and it is with unfeigned diffidence that I venture to criticise anything which proceeds from him; but I think that the cause of the difference between his views (see his Principles of Currency) and those which will be here maintained lies in his not sufficiently weighing the consequences of the mode in which the exchange of commodities is effected by money, namely, by money becoming itself a separate commodity in the two transactions into which, at the least, every exchange of goods for goods may be broken up, or, to use Mr. Price's own expression, by the 'substitution of double for single barter.' Money thus becoming a separate commodity, the equivalent in quantity of all the rest, becomes also subject to laws of its own, besides those which affect it as the purchaser of commodities, or which are based immediately upon its value-in-use.

21. It may seem as if the use of anticipated profits as capital, and still more the double and often treble use of it by advances on securities, is a creation of money capital which has no corresponding

commodity capital to be purchased by. But this is a
mistake arising from the distinctions of capital being
different in the two structures. True, all commodity
capital must be already in existence in order to be
used; while the money capital which buys it may
be built on anticipation. But the knowledge that
there will be a market, a demand, for so much commodity capital, a demand made efficient by creating
money on credit, has been already the cause of a
great part of this capital being produced, of so much
as was judged likely to satisfy that demand, that is,
to be sold remuneratively for the money in which
the demand consisted. The credit wealth founded
on expectation of the future has in fact doubled and
trebled the commodity wealth resulting from the labour of the past. It was neither the forces of nature
nor the energies of man that were in default, or
stopped short at a certain limit of production, but
the market, the remuneration, the motive for putting
those forces and energies to work. Credit represents
commodities, true; those of next year; it purchases
those of this, which are supplied in quantity to meet
the demand. And similarly, a great destruction of
credit capital, in the form of Deposits, Book Debts,
or Bills, is immediately felt in the check given to
production of commodities, from more having been
produced than will now meet with a sale.

22. Nothing can show more clearly than the
phenomena of money the necessity of building political economy upon the analysis of values, and of
making value the central point in the whole theory.
And it is, I believe, to Mr. Macleod that is due the
honour of having been the first to see, and to apply
to the phenomena of money, the truth that money

is "the *representative of debt*" in opposition to the older conception of its being the medium of exchange. (Elements of Pol. Econ. Chap. i. sect. 12-18.) He does not however, at least as I understand him, deny the truth of the latter conception, but its efficacy in explaining and analysing the phenomena.

23. The conception of money as the representative of debt, or of money purchasing and purchased by commodities in separate transactions, is a further analysis of the phenomena, which are only described in general terms, or in their general character, by the conception of money as the medium of exchange. The first conception is a definition of money, money defined in its first intention; the latter conception is a description of money, money described in its second intention. And there can hardly be a better instance than this, either of the distinction between first and second intentions itself, or of the superior efficacy of first intentions in explanation and analysis. The harmonising effect of the distinction is also here apparent; for two conceptions which appear to be in conflict, one of which at any rate it is sought to substitute for the other, are shown by the application of the distinction in question to be not only not conflicting but the logical complements of each other. Both therefore not only may be but must be held together, if a complete and harmonious view of the whole subject is to be attained.

III.

24. We come next to the consideration of the three functions of money in their order; and first of the function of money purchasing money, or the Price of one kind of currency in another kind. Here

we must first of all distinguish internal currency from international, for the different currencies of nations are like so many languages, each current within its own limits, each bearing a price when estimated in the currency of another nation, and all having one common basis and common measure, namely, Bullion, the value of which as against commodities is fixed by the relative cost of production of definite quantities of it and them, thus serving as the starting point, the unit of value, in estimating the price of bullion in currency, and of different currencies against each other. The weight and fineness of bullion are the real ultimate standard by which to test and measure all coinage values, and the price of different coinages in each other, because bullion is the only commodity which directly purchases all other commodities and coinages as well.

25. When bullion is coined it becomes price, the Mint price of the bullion itself. Gold coins, silver coins, copper coins, and notes, are modes of reckoning, not only the value of the bullion in commodities, but the price of the bullion in coin. Universal currency has necessarily as many standards as there are kinds of bullion, gold, silver, copper. But any particular country may adopt either all of these, or two of them, or one only, as its standard of currency. Supposing it, like England, to adopt gold only, then the gold coinage is the standard which is taken, instead of bullion, as the measurement of all other kinds of coinage and notes.

26. The adoption of a standard and the use of a currency, estimated by that standard and in its terms, not only changes at once the object of contemplation from universal currency to a number of particular

currencies, but also makes uncoined bullion itself a commodity among commodities, instead of being as before the universal purchaser of commodities. There cannot be two universal purchasers. If standard currencies are substituted for bullion as the universal purchaser, bullion must become one of the commodities purchased by them. Now standard currencies are adopted solely for convenience of transacting business; so long as this motive lasts will currencies be the universal purchaser, and not bullion. Nevertheless this further exercise of volition, this conventional adoption of standard currencies, cannot alter the natural law which makes bullion the universal purchaser; but must accommodate itself to that law as its condition of validity. The practical problem therefore for every currency is, first, to conform the value of the coins and notes which compose it to its own standard, and secondly, to conform that standard itself to the bullion which professedly affords it; in other words, to provide such a currency in coin and notes that the same amount of commodities may be purchased by a given sum of them as would have been purchasable by the bullion for which that sum professes to be a substitute. Thus the regulation of currencies, the regulation of the price of one kind of currency in another kind, and of the price of bullion in all or any of the rest, depends upon the comparison of their values in the commodity market; the value of bullion in the commodity market being the standard to which the value of currencies must conform; conforming thereby the price of every part of those currencies to every other part, all being estimated in bullion.

27. The first question, then, relates to the price

of bullion in coin; and here it will be sufficient for the purposes of logic to take a single metal, gold, as the subject of enquiry. A nation determines to adopt a gold coinage as the form of all legal payments. For this purpose it is requisite for it to fix two things, first, a standard fineness of bullion, second, a standard weight, or quantity of that fineness, in the coin which it establishes as the legal purchaser of commodities. Thus the English standard of fineness is 22 carats gold, 2 carats alloy, out of a total of 24; and 40 lbs. Troy of gold, of this fineness, are to be coined into 1869 sovereigns; thus making the Mint price of gold, of this fineness, £3 17s. 10½d. per oz. The Mint price of gold means the number of coins into which a given quantity of gold bullion is divided by coining it. The Mint price of 1 oz. of gold bullion is £3 17s. 10½d.; and that of 40 lbs. is £1869. (See Mr. Seyd's work, Bullion and For. Exchanges, Part i. Chap. xiii.).

28. Now here we are met, at the very outset, by a difficulty respecting the value of the coin and the bullion. It is clear that there is an advantage in having coin circulating instead of bullion, a value-in-use, or U, at least in the estimation of the nation which uses coin; it is clear also that there is a certain expense or difficulty of production, D, in coining. Coin in short is a manufactured article, and must on that account be of a greater value than the raw material, bullion, of which it is made. Why then is it so often said that coins can be of no greater value than the bullion which they contain, or, in Mr. Macleod's words, that "any quantity of metal in the form of Bullion must be exactly of the same value as the same quantity of metal in the form of coin"? The

difficulty may be cleared up as follows: To whom are coins more valuable than the bullion which they contain? To the nation at large, or to those individuals in it, who make use of the coinage. The service rendered by coinage consists in ascertaining the weight and fineness of the bullion, instead of leaving this to be done by individual buyers and sellers in each case of exchange. The value of the coin consists in the value of the bullion which it contains; the value of its being in the form of coin, and not of bullion, consists in the ascertainment of that value. If then we can separate the ascertainment of the value from the value itself, we can ascertain the difference between the value of the bullion and that of the same quantity of bullion coined. This can be and is done by making a charge for coining.

29. When the state coins bullion brought to it by individuals, three courses are open to it. It may either coin the whole of the bullion at its previously fixed standard, and return it to the bringer free of charge; receiving for instance an oz. of gold, it may return in coin £3 17s. 10½d.; or it may coin some of it into a less sum than £3 17s. 10½d., but preserve the same standard, while it retains a part of the bullion as its own remuneration; or thirdly, it may coin some of it into the full nominal amount of £3 17s. 10½d., and return it to the bringers, keeping as before the other part for itself. In the first case, the state takes upon itself the whole expense of coinage; in the second, it levies a mintage or seignorage; in the third, it not only levies a mintage or seignorage but at the same time debases the coin. Here we see the necessity of distinguishing, as was done in the preceding par., between the value of the form of coinage

and the value of the bullion in the coin, between the value of the ascertained bullion and the value of the ascertainment itself. The value of the form of coinage, of the ascertainment itself, is a real value added to the bullion; it exists as value, and must belong to somebody or other, somewhat in the same way as rent must; the state, who confers it, may retain it by levying a mintage or seignorage, not exceeding the expense of coinage, or may give it away to the holders of the bullion by coining gratis. But it is a value which cannot be deducted from the bullion itself, by giving a less quantity of bullion in the form of a nominally standard coin, without eo ipso destroying the very value which it is professed to confer, that of ascertaining the quantity and fineness of the bullion. There is thus a reconciliation of the apparent contradiction, that coinage adds a value to the bullion coined, and yet that the value of the coin is no greater than that of the bullion. The one is the thing itself, the other is the thing known. A coin of 122 grains of gold is not of equal value to 123 grains uncoined, notwithstanding that 1 grain may be the expense of coining; for when you come to compare them you must ascertain the 123 grains as well as the ascertained coin of 122. The value-in-use added to the bullion by coining is the advantage of being able to make purchases with it readily, and not the advantage of being able to purchase more goods. The purchase money of this value-in-use of coin, that is, the exchange value of the advantage it secures, is therefore separable from the coin itself, and is at the disposal of its creators, that is, of the state.

30. The people of any country bear in any case

the expense of coining; for, if the government makes no charge for coining, it comes out of the taxes; while, if a seignorage or mintage is levied, it falls first upon those who take the bullion and receive the coin from the mint, and secondly upon those who purchase it of them by commodities or services. For the use of a coinage, and of other kinds of currency founded on the coinage, all those who use it pay; which obviously includes all classes in the country. There is a real exchange value added to the bullion by coining it, and a real price paid for the advantage of coin. At the same time, it never purchases more commodities than bullion would do; not beyond the country, for there it has no currency; not within it, for there bullion has none.

31. While however the two methods of coining are indifferent with regard to the persons on whom the cost ultimately falls, they are not so in another respect. Gratis coining gives back coin equal in the holders' hands to bullion, neither more nor less; for they pay no more and no less for the coins than the bullion contained in them; the coins can be purchased for the bullion itself, and consequently can be sold again for the same price as the bullion. Mintage on the other hand distributes that value of the coined money which is over and above the value of the bullion, that is, the price of coining it, over every batch of coined money, so that the holders must have given more than the mere bullion for it, and consequently will require more than the mere value of the bullion if they part with it. The consequence of this would be felt in case of a drain or scarcity of bullion; for, under a system of gratis coining, coin would be as readily sent abroad as

bullion, being of no more cost to the holders, and the country would be coining money at the public expense only to have it sent abroad at bullion prices. The charge of mintage, then, is a means of keeping the coin in the country, for the use of which it is intended.

32. Comparing coin and bullion, the true price of one is just the same as that of the other. This is called the mint price of bullion, being that quantity of coin into which a given piece of bullion of a certain weight and fineness is divided. The market price of bullion, paid in coin, can never rise above the mint price without showing that the coin is depreciated. The market price of bullion may rise to any amount from scarcity, difficulty of carriage, and so on; but, when this price is paid in coin, either the coin is depreciated, or the coin also rises in value along with the bullion from which it is coined. The market price of bullion is a commodity price, though estimated in coin, and carries with it the commodity price of the pieces it is coined into; that is, in case of a rise, more commodities or services must be given for it, and more and equally more commodities or services must be given for them, unless the coins are depreciated. The purchasing power, or value in commodities, of both bullion and coin is increased.

33. Now here again arises an apparent contradiction. If more coins are given for bullion than those into which it is coined, this shows depreciation of the coinage. But how can the market price of bullion, as a commodity price, vary in any case from the mint price without being expressed in a larger or smaller number of coins, that is, without, in any actual exchange, requiring a different number of coins to be

given for it from that which constitutes its mint price? The answer must be given by referring to the distinction between money as the medium and money as the measure of exchange. The rise in the market price of bullion is a rise in its purchasing power, not its purchasing power over coin but over goods; accordingly it is estimated in or measured by coin, but not exchanged for coin; the coin rises also, and equally, in purchasing power. The bullion can only be bought by credit or paper currency, that is, promises to pay coin at a future date, or, if on demand, in the certainty of the demand not being made on more than a small proportion of the promises. And these promises will be for a higher sum than the mint price of the bullion. Thus the coin, if undepreciated, becomes a commodity purchased by currency, and that currency a paper one; just as bullion becomes a commodity purchased by coin, when coin is established as currency; for there cannot be two currencies, but, whatever is taken as currency, everything else becomes a commodity purchasable by it. The effect therefore of the rise in the market price of bullion, supposing there to be no depreciation of the coin, is to make paper become currency, and to throw the corresponding fall in the values of other things than bullion and coin upon the paper, as their representative for the time being. But the paper currency, in which the payments for the bullion are made, cannot be intended to be, or be capable of being, immediately converted into coin; for otherwise the transaction would defeat itself; no one would give, for coin or bullion, notes which he might be immediately called upon to pay with the same amount of coin or bullion that he bought with them. When, therefore, the market price of bullion, in an undepreciated condition of coin and of notes, rises above the mint price, this additional price is advanced upon credit, and paid in some form of private credit currency, or, if in notes, in notes which, it is known, only a small proportion of coin need be reserved to meet. The fall in the value of paper, in the case supposed, does not arise from insecurity or over issue of the paper, but from the fall of the commodities which are now contrasted with bullion and coin. If the fall in its value were permanent, continuing beyond the period of the exceptionally high value of coin and bullion, its diminished value would be a depreciation attaching to the paper itself, and arising from over issue or insecurity of credit. Coin conformed in value to bullion is the ultimate or permanent measure and purchaser of all other commodities; it is to the proportions between these two, coin on the one side, everything else on the other, that all particular values are referred as their standard. Fluctuations in these proportions, arising in one limb of it, coin, can be measured by the rise or fall in the value of paper, if this is otherwise unaltered. But a permanent change in the value of paper could not be owing to temporary fluctuations in the value of bullion or coin.

34. We are thus launched into the question of notes, the paper or public credit currency of a nation. Notes are the price of coin, as coin of bullion. They are therefore liable to depreciation from a double source; they may be a substitute for a depreciated coinage, and they may be depreciated as against that coinage itself. Depreciation arising in the notes themselves may be caused either by over issue, if

they are inconvertible, or by insecurity of credit in the issuers, if they are convertible. Inconvertible notes are properly called paper money; when convertible on demand into coin, they are not paper money but merely convenient substitutes for coin; and their legal convertibility is a perfect safeguard against an over issue. So far as the price of currency is concerned, convertible notes cannot be over issued, because no one is bound to take them in payment instead of coin. And here is one of the great fallacies of the so-called "currency theory." Because advances are often made in notes, and advances may easily be excessive when compared to the means of repaying them out of the returns to future industry, it was argued that notes might be issued in excess, although convertible on demand into coin. The accident of advances, their being sometimes made in notes, and not their substance, their being an advance upon credit, was fixed upon as the essential part of these transactions, and the attempt was made to limit the advances by limiting the issue of notes; thus not only not limiting in all cases the advances, but transferring the notion of over issue from the advances upon credit to the issue of notes against coin, turning a fact belonging to the money market into a conception concerning the price of currency, and confounding one of the most fundamental distinctions in monetary science. In support of the view here maintained it is only necessary to refer to the names of Mr. Tooke and Mr. Fullarton, its original propounders. Reference will again be made to this point when treating of the money market.

35. Coin itself can only be depreciated by being debased, not by being coined in excessive amount, for

all such coin, not required in the country, will bear its full bullion value in foreign transactions. Notes may be depreciated either from excessive issues, if inconvertible, or, if convertible legally, by insecurity of credit in the issuers; while, if they are not only legally but also de facto convertible, no depreciation can arise in them in the first instance. But a depreciation arising in either branch of the currency, either in coin or notes, may extend to the whole currency; for notes will represent the coin depreciated by debasement, and coin will be driven out of circulation by the use of a depreciated note currency, when the depreciation is caused by over issue. "In a perfect state of the coin, provided the exportation and melting of it be allowed, there cannot, it is evident, be an excess in the market price above the mint price of the metal, as measured in coin. It is possible, in such a case, that the coin may, even without a seignorage, be *more* valuable than the bullion; but it is hardly conceivable that it should be less valuable: if, therefore, in a perfect state of the coin, there be in general circulation bank notes which, by law or custom, pass current in all transactions; and if, under these circumstances, the market price should be above the mint price of gold—the whole of the difference would constitute the exact measure of the depreciation of the paper." Tooke, Hist. of Prices, Vol. i. p. 123. And for this reason, that the bullion would be paid for in those notes which pass current in all transactions; we should have the same case as was described in par. 33, except that the depreciation would be permanent and arising in the notes themselves. They would become the real currency of the country, the coin becoming a commodity like bullion, and like bullion profitable only for melting and exportation. Wherever, therefore, the issues of notes are unlimited, and yet the notes are inconvertible, they will drive out by degrees all the coin, whether depreciated or not, causing it to be exported or melted, or consigning it to secret hoards against a convulsion.

36. In the third kind of currency, private credit currency, it will be enough to take notice of bills of exchange. Foreign bills of exchange are between nations what the private credit currency is to the nation itself. In both cases one part of the currency liquidates and pays for another part. What the Clearing House is between the customers of bankers that the purchase, sale, and transmission, of bills of exchange is between nations. Those transactions which are settled by means of bills are virtually settled by an interchange of commodities. (See § 95. 74-78). It is only the balance of these transactions, the remainder due to one country by another, that must be settled by the transmission of bullion; and this is only sent when, for any reason, it has become unprofitable to send commodities which may be paid for by bills. The private credit currency of one nation also may be depreciated in respect to that of another, the bills of one nation worth less or more ready money than those of another, just as the credit of its merchants is worse or better; but there is no standard, nor any public means of ascertaining this, except the actual discount of the bills. This being premised, we come upon a new class of variations in the value of the coin currencies of different countries; variations which are introduced into the exchange of those currencies in consequence of fluctuations in the transactions carried on between the countries by

means of their private credit currencies. The variations arising from this cause, if we suppose the currencies otherwise in an undepreciated condition, may be compared to the oscillations of market price about the natural price of commodities, the undepreciated condition of currencies being analogous to commodities being at their natural price.

37. It is only between the currencies of different nations that the variations in question can take place. When two places have the same currency, and there is free and ready transmission of currencies between them, no room is left for supply and demand of currency to operate; debts are paid at once on becoming due. But between nations debts may in a certain manner accumulate, by the total balance of indebtedness of one country to the other increasing, without being discharged by payment of specie, notwithstanding that particular debts are paid both ways by bills from time to time. Between the arising of a balance of indebtedness and the remission of specie, depreciation of one currency relatively to the other will take place; and this is the well-known phenomenon of fluctuation in the rate of exchange up to specie point. These variations arise, therefore, in the goods market, and to trace their causes belongs to that branch of the enquiry. But their effects upon the price of currency in currency must be here stated. When the rate of exchange between two nations is either above or below par, this is an evidence that one of them is more largely indebted to the other, than the other to it, upon the transactions of all kinds that have taken place between them. The balance is due in coin or bullion, and the exchange is said to be unfavourable to the country which owes the

balance, and favourable to the other. There is a supply of coin or bullion, or, since we may suppose the currencies undepreciated from other causes, of money generally, expected to be imported into the one country, and expected to be exported from the other.

38. The metallic par of exchange is that quantity of coin of the two currencies which is exactly equal in bullion value. Between England and France this par is 25·22½ francs=20 shillings; and 15 10$\frac{1}{5}$ shillings=20 francs. The effect of an expected supply of francs, or their equivalent, in England is, that the price of francs in England, or estimated in English money, falls below this par; 20 francs at an exchange of 25·30 becomes worth only 15s. 9¾d., instead of 15s. 10$\frac{1}{5}$. Or, what is the same thing, 20s. becomes worth 25·30 francs instead of 25·22½ francs. By the same rule, when exchange is unfavourable to England, when there is a great supply of English money expected in France, the 20 francs become worth more than 15s. 10$\frac{1}{5}$, and the 20 shillings less than 25·22½ francs. These figures are taken from Mr. Seyd's work, Bullion and Foreign Exchanges, Part ii. Ch. i. Pars of Exchange. The state of things now described has of course no effect upon the price of English money estimated in English, or of French estimated in French.

39. To turn now to the effect upon the private credit currencies of the two countries, the bills themselves. Up to a certain point of indebtedness, no specie will actually pass from one country to the other in payment of the balance. It is clear that none would pass if the exchanges were at par; and the exchanges may vary also from par, to a certain point, without causing the transmission of specie. But in this case the difference or balance of indebt-

edness produces an effect upon the currencies; the bills which balance each other do so only by means of a greater value in bills of the one country being the equivalent for a less value in bills of the other, that is, by means of the same bill purchasing a larger amount of currency in the one country, and a less amount in the other. The greater or less amount of indebtedness has its cause in the general transactions of trade and of the money market between the two countries. Until specie point is reached either way, in the fluctuations of the rate of exchange, this greater or less indebtedness is accompanied by a higher price, in currency, commanded by the bills of the least indebted country in the other, and a lower price, in currency, commanded by the bills of the most indebted country. The country which owes most gives most for the other's bills, and that which owes least gives least. Nor is this a merely nominal advantage. "When the fluctuations were determined," says Mr. Goschen, referring to a case which he had previously described, "simply by the balance of trade, (within the limits of the specie point upon either extreme), the purchaser, when he bought cheap—that is to say, when he obtained a greater sum than usual in foreign coin for his own money—secured an actual advantage; this greater sum of foreign coin had an actual greater purchasing power." Theory of the Foreign Exchanges, p. 65, 3rd ed. But this, he shows, is only true where the cheapness of the bills is not *caused* by the depreciation of the foreign currency. On the contrary it is itself the cause of its temporary depreciation.

40. Foreign transactions of all kinds are settled in the first instance by means of bills. For con-

ciseness we may, with Mr. Goschen, speak of those persons who owe and those who are owed sums of money, in any two countries, as the importers and the exporters. The importers of one country, then, owe money to the exporters of the other. Suppose these countries to be England and France, and let us use letters to denote the men, e. g. F.I. for French Importer, E.E. for English Exporter, and F.B., E.B., for the Brokers who buy and sell the bills. We have then, in the first instance, the following scheme:

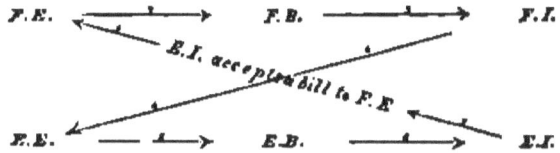

The first movement is that E.I. accepts a bill drawn by F.E. for goods. F.E. discounts it with a broker and receives payment. The broker sells it to F.I., who transmits it to E.E., to whom he owes money. E.E. discounts it with E.B. And E.B. presents it for payment to its acceptor E.I. Thus a single bill, an English bill, settles both transactions, that between F.I. and E.E. as well as that between E.I. and F.E.

41. But F.I. may settle his account with E.E. in the same way as E.I. did, namely, by originally accepting a bill drawn by E.E. Thus:

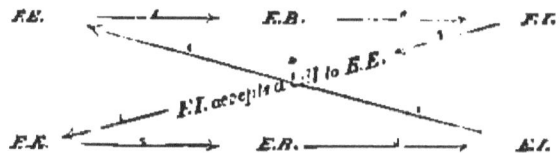

This bill also settles both transactions. That is to say, bills on England settle transactions, or debts, to an equal amount in both countries. So also bills on France. If therefore the bills upon France and the bills upon England were accepted to an equal amount, exchange would be at par, and the bills would exactly balance each other.

42. There cannot be more bills upon England bought by F.Is than are accepted by E.Is. Nor more bills upon France bought by E.Is than are accepted by F.Is.

43. But there may be more bills upon England accepted by E.Is than are bought by F.Is; and fewer bills upon France accepted by F.Is than bills upon England accepted by E.Is.

Or there may be more bills upon France accepted by F.Is than are bought by E.Is; and fewer bills upon England accepted by E.Is than bills upon France accepted by F.Is.

44. In the former case all the bills upon France will find a ready sale; in the latter case, all the bills upon England; for a certain number of the bills accepted will balance each other, leaving those beyond that number without purchasers.

45. In the former case, bills upon England will be at a discount, more being supplied than are demanded, and will fall below their nominal or par amount, in France; while bills upon France will be at a premium in England, above their nominal amount or par, more being demanded than are supplied. It will be enough to consider this case, an exchange unfavourable to England, without taking the opposite.

46. In an exchange unfavourable to England,

then, that is to say, when bills upon England have been accepted to a larger amount than bills upon France, the F.E. will get less from the F.B. for his English acceptance; he will be paid in a depreciated currency, the English bill, which is worth less than par in French money; but the F.I. who buys this bill will give less for it, and thus discharge his debt to the E.E. with less money. The E.E. again will find the bill which he receives at a discount, when he sells it to the E.B. But the E.B. will get the full amount from the F.I. who was the original acceptor. In other words, both English and French goods will be worth less in French money than in English; prices will have fallen, money risen in value, in France, as compared to England. But the advantage of this will be reaped by the French Importer; it will be a disadvantage to the French Exporter, as well as to the English Importer and Exporter. The advantage is reaped by the importers of that country the exports of which exceed the imports, and which has consequently more to receive than to pay, so far at least as the bills upon the other country are concerned.

47. But at the same time a premium will be paid for bills upon France in England, since there are fewer accepted than there are E.Is to bid, fewer than there are bills upon England accepted by E.Is. E.Es who hold bills upon France will get more, and E.Is will give more, for them. The F.Es to whom these bills are transmitted also find them at a premium, that is, they receive more for them, while they cost no more to the F.Is by whom they are finally paid than their nominal amount. So far, therefore, as bills upon the country to which the exchange is fa-

vourable are concerned, the exporters of both countries reap an advantage; and on the whole of the bills, upon both countries, taken together, it is the importers of the country to which the exchange is unfavourable who bear the loss of the depreciation of the currency of that country. The depreciation of the currency of the country which is most indebted is a real loss; for there is a lessening of its purchasing power compared to the currency of the other country; and this was the test given above of depreciation, namely, relative power of commanding commodities other than money.

48. Third countries have been hitherto abstracted from in this enquiry. If, for instance, England, though under a balance of indebtedness to France, had a balance of debts to receive from a third country, say Holland, bills upon Holland might be sent to France in discharge of England's balance, and thus the depreciation of English currency avoided. But this makes no difference in the principle which governs the action of international transactions upon the price of the different national currencies estimated in each other. Foreign exchanges, then, belong to all the three functions of money, by producing on the one hand these fluctuations in currencies, and on the other by depending on influences not only of trade in goods, but also credit or the money market, in which the price of money is interest. This latter dependence will be made more clear as we proceed. The analysis of any complex and concrete set of phenomena, such as the Foreign Exchanges, into the three functions of money, which combine to produce them, is the application of the logic, or the logical treatment of the phenomena in question.

49. But now the question occurs, to what extent will this proceed; to what extent will the balance of indebtedness between the two countries be accompanied by depreciation of the currency of the country which is most indebted? Accompanied, not discharged, by it, because, up to the point in question, the debt to be discharged is accumulating, being represented by the bills, on the country most indebted, which from time to time are unable to find purchasers in the country least indebted. It is the delay in discharging it which is purchased by, or finds its quid pro quo in, the depreciation. The answer is clear; it will proceed until specie is exported in discharge of the balance. If we suppose the balance of indebtedness to continue increasing, a point will be reached when so much must be paid that the bills representing it can no longer be retained, but are presented for actual payment. But what will be the cause determining this effect to take place; what efficiently determines specie point? The answer is—the rise of premium on Foreign Bills to such a rate that the premium alone is greater than the cost of transmitting specie; for no one will give a greater sum for a bill to discharge his debt than that which is equal to the debt itself together with the cost of transmitting coin to pay it. The same cause which originally produced the effect of depreciation in the comparative price of the currency, namely, the cost of transmitting specie, now operates in preventing further depreciation. And so long as the balance of indebtedness keeps the rate of exchange above specie point, so long the indebted country must keep exporting specie to meet that part of the balance which does not fall upon the currency.

50. As to what the specie points are, Mr. Seyd says (Bullion and For. Exchanges, p. 394) "we may assume as a general rule,

That when the French Exchange is at 25·10, it pays to send Gold from England to France;

And, when the Exchange is at 25·35, it pays to send Gold from France to England.

The Mint Par being taken at 25·22½, we have thus a margin of 12½ centimes, or ½ per cent. either way, and 25 centimes, or 1 per cent. between the two extreme points.

The ½ per cent. either way being absorbed by charges of Brokerage, transporting, realisation, and incidental costs, constitutes a natural bar to the more frequent interchange of shipments of bullion between the two countries."

51. When bullion is at last exported in payment of the balance of indebtedness, the further depreciation of the currency of the indebted country ceases. It is only between the departure from par and the reaching of specie point, and to the extent which that interval represents, that depreciation takes place. But what is the effect of the demand for bullion on the currency of the country where it is demanded for export? The price of bullion will certainly rise, but this will not necessarily produce any alteration in the relative price of the different parts of the public currency of the country, coin and notes. If coin is kept entirely free from debasement, and notes are kept completely de facto convertible, there can be no difference between them and bullion, but they will remain as before; coin being just so much dearer to export than bullion by the charge for coinage, or, as in England, by delays and expenses which are equi-

valent, and so much cheaper as, its fineness being already ascertained, the trouble of assaying the bullion is saved. Whence then the rise in bullion?

52. In the first place it should be remarked, that, in many cases, what is called the rise in price of bullion is only the additional sum paid for placing it at a certain spot abroad. The merchants who have to export bullion to France will pay, say, 20s. 6d. here for 20s. there, the 6d. being the cost of transmission, including profits of the transmitter, the price paid for its carriage. There is here no difference in relative price to the other parts of the currency.

53. But supposing an imperious demand for bullion to continue, and yet to be accompanied by no failure in the credit supporting the convertibility of notes, by no issue of inconvertible notes, and by no debasement of the coin; then the gold for export must be procured in one or both of two markets, the money market or the goods market, and in these either by an extension of private credit currency, which is borrowing on the returns to future industry, or by a sale of commodities abroad, perhaps at a great loss, or by what is the same thing as a sale of commodities, a sale of foreign securities, or a withdrawal of foreign loans. The gold for export will be purchased either by a cheapening of commodities, or by a cheapening of securities; that is to say, in the latter case, it will be attracted by offering a high rate of interest, that is, raising the rate of discount, in the money market. (See parr. 93 and 106).

54. Bullion in fact has a threefold, and only a threefold, function, a value or equivalent in three markets, and, if it is assumed to be restricted from

varying in one of the three, all its variations are eo ipso thrown upon its relation to its equivalents in the two others. Now by the fact that bullion, or coin at its purely bullion value, is distinguished from all other currency as the sole medium of universal exchange, the sole medium in which international balances are ultimately paid, it becomes, in reference to the rest of the currency, either a commodity among commodities in the goods market, or a commodity the use of which has value in the money market; it has no longer a price but a value, it becomes purchasable only by commodities or by credit. When in demand for export, its price is no longer, strictly speaking, price, but value; it is the value of the currency in which it is estimated, the value of the goods which purchase it. We thus return again to the universal point of view, from which we departed in speaking of the different currencies of particular countries, the price of currency in currency. But in doing so we enter on the second branch of the subject, the second function of money, its value in the purchase of commodities and services.

IV.

55. In the second branch of enquiry, the function of money purchasing commodities or services, the starting point is the same as in the first branch, namely, the value of bullion, depending on its cost of production, as against the value of commodities depending on their cost of production or on their scarcity. Two things are therefore to be noted, first, that we may make abstraction of the price of bullion in currency or of currency in bullion, treating all forms of money as of equal value against commodities

Book II.
Ch. IV.
§ 96.
Statical logic of money.

and against each other, and secondly, that we must begin with the distinction between the natural and market value of money as purchased by commodities.

56. It is sometimes said that the value of money depends on its quantity and rapidity of circulation compared to the quantity of goods and the number of times they are exchanged. Thus Mr. J. S. Mill (Principles of Pol. Econ. Book iii. Chap. viii. § 3) says: "If we assume the quantity of goods on sale, and the number of times those goods are resold, to be fixed quantities, the value of money will depend upon its quantity, together with the average number of times that each piece changes hands in the process. The whole of the goods sold (counting each resale of the same goods as so much added to the goods) have been exchanged for the whole of the money, multiplied by the number of purchases made on the average by each piece. Consequently, the amount of goods and of transactions being the same, the value of money is inversely as its quantity multiplied by what is called the rapidity of circulation. And the quantity of money in circulation is equal to the money value of all the goods sold, divided by the number which expresses the rapidity of circulation."

57. But this in reality tells us nothing. It expresses accurately in general terms the result of exchanges, taking the natural value and market value of money together; it is a description of the relations of money to goods in terms of second intention, just like that description of exchanges between commodities which consists in saying that supply will be equal to demand and demand to supply; and, as such a description, it is by no means without value. But

it neither tells us the cause of variation in the value of money, nor analyses that value into the elements in which the variations arise. The distinction which it takes in value, between the quantity of goods and number of exchanges, and between the quantity of money and number of purchases, is not a distinction into elements of value essential to a knowledge of its variations. For this purpose, those elements must be distinguished in which the variations exclusively arise.

58. A statement like the one quoted may have great value in fixing our general preliminary conceptions of the object-matter in question; but it has no value as an analysis of it. It comes merely to saying, that the money and its circulation is the equivalent of the goods and their circulation, with the addition, that the proportion between money and its circulation need not be the same as the proportion between goods and their circulation. Or, to put it in another shape, starting with the same assumption as Mr. Mill, if the quantity of goods and the number of times they are resold are assumed to be fixed, then the value of the money *as a whole*, the value of the whole quantity used, will be greater or less according as the same pieces are used less or more frequently. But it is not the value of the money as a whole which it is essential to know; in fact we begin with assuming it, since it must be equal to that of the goods which it purchases; it is the value of the particular portions, or coins, which compose it; and of these values we certainly want to know more than that they will be greater or less according as the whole value, of which they are parts, increases or diminishes. Prices of particular

Book II.
Ch. IV.
§ 98.
Statical logic
of money.

goods, and values of particular portions of money, have no dependence upon the proportion between money and its circulation compared to goods and their circulation. It is true that, if prices rise, goods and their circulation remaining the same, the money employed must have been increased either in circulation, or in quantity, or in both; and that if they fall, under the same supposition, the money must have been decreased either in circulation, or in quantity, or in both. But this variation begins in the particular prices, not in the relations which express their total results; these results so expressed are general truths which hold good whatever the particular values may be.

59. What, then, is the distinction indicating the elements of value in which the variations originate? That between the part of it determined by its natural rate and the part added to or subtracted from this by oscillations in the market rate. Here at last we are on firm ground. The natural value of money is determined by its permanent cost of production as compared to the permanent cost of production of each of the various commodities which it purchases. When its cost of production decreases, a greater quantity will be produced from the mines, the value of each portion of it will fall, and the prices of all other commodities will rise, supposing no change to have taken place in their cost of production. Where money is the cheapest to produce, there it will be the most plentiful; it is not cheap because it is plentiful, but plentiful because it is cheap; those countries are the first to feel the effect of the increased supply which are in most complete communication with the countries which produce it; prices being highest at the

mine's mouth. Thence it circulates through the world at large, raising prices in all places where goods or services are exchanged for it, until, as is said, it 'permeates all the channels of trade.' The full effects of a large discovery of gold will not be felt for many years; and the rise of prices which it tends to cause may of course be counteracted by a corresponding increase in the cheapness of production of the commodities or services for sale.

60. From the effects of such additional production of gold there is no escape. Since it is the universal purchaser, and the remunerativeness of its production depends on physical causes, namely, the comparative ease with which it can be produced, it must influence the prices of commodities, whether the holders of those commodities like it or not, whether the exchanges of commodities between themselves can be effected better or worse by the greater quantity of it. Particular values or prices do not depend upon the quantity of money compared to the work which the money has to do, the interchanges of commodities which it has to effect. This is the value-in-use of money, its general U, as explained in par. 5. The briskness of this interchange has no causal influence on prices; if it increases, more money or a greater use of the same money, will be required, but at the prices fixed by the relative cost of production of the money and of the various commodities. Were prices fixed by the quantity of money compared to the work which it has to do, namely, the interchange of commodities, we should then require to be told how, or by whom, this work is estimated and a certain quantity of money destined to perform it.

61. But whence spring the oscillations about this

natural value of money, which together with it constitute its market value? It is clear that they do not spring from any fluctuation in the demand for money, except so far as that demand is made efficient by the possession of commodities wherewith to purchase it. Money being the universal purchaser, all men everywhere wish for it, and 'the more they have the more they want.' For the same reason they cannot spring from the supply of money at any particular time or place being in excess or defect. It never is in excess or defect, compared to the efficient demand; it is at once supplied, at existing prices, to all who have commodities to give for it. It remains, therefore, that the oscillations in its market value depend either upon those temporary variations in its cost of production which originate in the process of production itself, or upon the variations in market value, from time to time and place to place, of the various commodities which it purchases, upon which depend the varying number and amount of exchanges which it is required to perform. Now the temporary variations in the cost of production of money are clearly a cause of oscillations about the permanent value fixed by its permanent cost of production; but the other source of variation now supposed will be found to have been already disposed of, in principle at least, in the remarks made about its natural value.

62. Let us then leave apart the temporary changes in the cost of production of money, as being an element which is undisputed in its market value, and turn to those changes which arise in the varying market value of different commodities, and consequently varying number and amount of the exchanges which money is required to perform. If any particular com-

modity is in great demand compared to its present supply, so that a great number of exchanges are set on foot by stimulated production, its market value will be high, the value of money purchasing it low, that is, it will command a high price; if in abundant supply but small demand, its price will be low, the money purchasing it will have a raised value. But these variations in the value of money are variations in it as the measure and medium of exchange, and not in its market value, as a commodity having exchange value itself, because they are changes which money shares with all commodities, except only those in which the change has arisen, and because by the market value of any commodity must be meant its value against all other commodities as a whole, just as in the case of its natural value. Changes in the market value of money, therefore, can arise only from temporary changes in its cost of production, and not from changes either in the cost of production, or in the market value, of commodities, by which some are affected and not all. The natural value of money, just like the natural value of other commodities, is fixed by its permanent cost of production relatively to theirs, and its market value by temporary changes in that cost relatively to temporary changes in theirs, taken as a whole. But the changes in price which come from increased or diminished cost of production, increased or diminished supply or demand, of particular commodities, producing changes in the number and amount of exchanges to be performed, are not changes in the market value of money, but only in the value of some goods in other goods expressed by money. In the money market however the case is different; there the market value of money means the value, not of money, but of its use for a certain time, that is, the rate of interest.

63. But the question may be asked, Since money measures values and effects exchanges between commodities only by being itself exchanged against them, portion for portion, how can a change in price be a change only in the value of commodities in commodities expressed by money, without being at the same time a change in the value of the money itself? The answer to this question brings us to the very knot of the difficulty, if difficulty there be, the turning point of the connection between money as a commodity and money as the measure and medium of exchange, between money in the goods market, where it has value, and money in the currency market, where it has price. It will be seen that two functions of money are inseparably involved in every single act of exchange, the act being indeed empirically indivisible, but logically distinguishable into its two elements and two functions; in treating which, therefore, the metaphysical conception of elements only logically distinguishable is the only available instrument.

64. Gold is one of those commodities which are capable of indefinite further production by a corresponding additional employment of labour and capital, commodities in which the market value is clearly distinguishable from the natural. Now just as the value-in-use of commodities, whose D consists in scarcity alone, must be measured by the purchaser against the value-in-use of reproducible commodities, before their exchange value can be estimated by him in money; for before he knows how much money he is willing to give for them he must settle how much

of reproducible commodities he is willing to forego in consequence; so the cost of production of gold determines the value of all the other forms of currency which represent a determinate amount of it. The value of coin, notes, and bills, is the value of the bullion which they contain or represent, minus the debasement or depreciation to which they are liable. A change in their value is a change in their price, that is, in their value as against bullion, and not in their value as against commodities. The basis of value in all of them is the value of bullion as against other reproducible commodities. But their quantity is indefinite and inexhaustible, at least it is restricted only by the limits of credit. When commodities are in existence, and require to be exchanged, money can be and is created at once and to any amount to effect the exchange, and is again destroyed at the close of the whole transaction. But the value of the portions of money thus created is fixed by the existing value of bullion together with the debasement or depreciation, if any, of the coin or paper representing it. Abstracting from this latter source of variation, the value of money is the value of bullion in reproducible commodities, independent of the quantity of the money used, or frequency of its use, and independent of the quantity of goods or number of exchanges between them. And this value it is which is said to remain unaltered, when the value of particular commodities changes without a change in the cost of producing the single commodity, gold. That commodity only, the cost of whose production has changed, has changed its value in other commodities, and in gold among the rest; the value of gold has changed only in relation to that commodity. The labour and the commodities employed as capital in producing it are the first things in relation to which it changes value; that is, it is a change in value between commodities and services, before it is a change in money value; or, in other words, it is a change in value of a commodity in commodities and services, expressed in money, quite independently of the circumstance that gold is included in the class of commodities, as against which it has changed, and notwithstanding that the two changes are equal to each other and inseparable, being, as they are, two functions of one and the same act of exchange, the purchase of goods or of services by money. When any commodity varies in its cost of production it varies in market value against all the rest which have not changed; the change in market value is said to be in that commodity in which the change has arisen, or in which the cause of change lies. When gold is among the commodities which have not changed, in the case supposed, its market value has not changed, notwithstanding that it has become more or less valuable than the commodity which has changed. The change is common to it with all commodities except this one, and its changed value is a measure of that general change, as well as a change in its own value against that particular commodity.

65. The proposition of greatest importance which results from this analysis, and which sums it up in a form suitable for application to practice, is the following: the money which is imported or exported from a country, except from the mines, additions from which source have their value fixed by cost of production, that is, all the money which is imported or exported in settlement of an international

balance, has no effect upon the value of commodities in money, or of money in commodities. Although when imported it is an addition to the quantity of money in the country, it does not raise prices, but is a part of prices which have been already raised, and raised not by an addition to the quantity of money in the country, or elsewhere, but either by an increased purchase of commodities on speculation, or by a more profitable sale of commodities already produced. It is a part of the market value of commodities in other commodities, measured by money, not of commodities generally in money as a whole; and therefore the increased or diminished quantity of money employed in the exchange of these commodities is the effect of changes in value between these commodities themselves, but not the cause of future changes in those values.

66. It may seem at first sight, that the amount of money which will be paid from abroad for any commodity has necessarily one part of it fixed by the natural, the other by the oscillations in market, value of money, that is, by the plenty or scarcity of money compared to commodities generally. But that this is not the case is evident from the account given above, par. 36, of the Foreign Exchanges. Ready money is not paid from abroad, as it is or may be paid at home, for commodities as they are bought; it is paid in the form of private credit currency, bills of exchange, which are balanced against each other, till the amount on one side exceeds the amount on the other to a certain extent determined by what is called specie point on either side; up to this point, the purchase of commodities by bills of exchange is a purchase of them by other commodities, not by

money. And here we must advert to differences, before abstracted from, between different kinds of currency; not however differences in the value of different kinds of currency, but differences in their mode of operation. The use of private credit currency in settling international accounts, irrespective of its value as compared to ready money, enables us to draw a distinction between that part of international purchases which is paid for by commodities and that which is paid for by money. Now, since no money, as distinguished from private credit currency and from commodities, passes between any two countries, until the total imports differ by a certain considerable amount from the total exports, therefore all the money that passes in settlement of such balances is a part of the whole payment for the commodities transferred, and moreover a part which does not arise except in consequence of a difference between supply and demand of particular commodities, and which must therefore be reckoned to belong wholly to differences in value between these commodities, and not to a difference in value between them and money.

67. That the foreign payments which are made by means of bills, balancing each other up to specie point either way, are virtually made by commodities and not by money might be shown from many approved authors on money and commerce. I will however content myself with the following citation from Mr. Wilson's Capital, Currency, and Banking, p. 218. "Gold is a commodity which is imported, like other commodities, only when it offers to the merchants the greatest inducements. As long as wool, or silk, or tallow, or any other commodity is scarce at home,

and offers a profit to import, no merchant will buy bullion; but when the stocks of all other commodities are so full, that the prices at home are such that it will not answer the purpose of the merchant to import them, then he has recourse to bullion as the most profitable return. So that bullion is never imported except when the stocks of other commodities are large, and their relative prices in this country and others such as will not remunerate the importer. Then bullion is taken as the best mode of balancing the Exchanges."

68. To turn the matter round, we may abstract entirely, in considering the causes and the effects of variation in prices, from the quantity of money as compared to the quantity of commodities and number of exchanges, because variations in quantity of money, from time to time applicable in the world to purposes of exchange, are variations which affect equally all commodities and services alike. And the case of money imported or exported, as payment of an international balance, has been shown to be no exception to this rule. Those changes of price and of value, which accompany such import or export, are not caused by it; and the effects also which follow those changes are caused by the changes themselves, and not by the greater or less abundance of money which accompanies them. Just as Mr. Tooke and Mr. Fullarton (see the latter's Regulation of Currencies, Chap. iii. p. 57 et seqq., 2nd edit.) maintained that an increase or decrease in the issues of convertible notes has no effect on prices, but is caused by an increase or decrease of business, or by a rise or fall of prices, so here the same is maintained of all currency whatever, except an additional supply from

the mines. For, if we suppose an additional issue of paper money, or inconvertible notes, the rise of prices from this cause will be solely due to depreciation, will come out of the diminished value of the paper as compared with currency in other forms, and not out of a diminution of the value of money as compared with commodities. There is however one way, one channel, through which the money imported or exported in payment of international balances affects indirectly the prices of commodities, a way which will presently be mentioned, and which forms the common element connecting the function of money purchasing commodities or services in the goods market with that of money purchasing debts or securities in the money market.

69. Abstracting however for the present from this influence, the causes which govern the market values or prices of commodities may be classed under two heads. The first consists of the relative quantities of commodities, expressed by their relative prices, existing at any one time; and the second of the speculative purchases and speculative production of commodities, induced by a more or less accurate calculation of profits, and a greater or less prudence in speculating, upon a consideration of those quantities and prices. The quantities and prices of commodities, at the end of any one period, are the result of the speculation founded on the knowledge of the corresponding quantities and prices at the beginning of it; and these quantities and prices are again the foundation of the speculation for the next period. Quantities and prices of commodities are first the condition of speculation, then the result of the speculation superinduced upon those quantities and prices

which were its condition. Though varying of course from period to period, they are relatively to speculation the known or fixed element, while speculation is the variable element, in the production of the quantities and prices of commodities which result from both together.

70. Now there are many causes which operate primarily only on the first of these two elements, on the quantities and prices of commodities, as the condition of further speculation. Many of these are most important, such for instance as good or bad seasons, the immense importance of which in affecting food, an article of prime necessity, was so clearly shown by Mr. Tooke in his History of Prices. War, new discoveries whether of materials or of markets, new inventions in manufacture or means of transport, any new direction given to industry by change of fashions or tastes, losses by accident or by fraud, are among the causes which directly affect prices and quantities of commodities, to which all further speculation must conform. They are in the position of conditions extraneous to the art of political economy, which as an art is properly restricted to the task of accommodating itself to such circumstances, and to the state of prices which are their result. The logic of the subject at least has nothing further to do with them; speculation is the thread which it has to follow.

71. Accordingly it may be said that future prices depend upon the amount and direction of speculation, and that speculation depends upon two things, first, the amount and kind of capital invested, second, the prudence or imprudence of the investment, which however can only be tested by the result. But here arises the distinction which carries us over into

the next branch of the subject. The amount of the capital invested by an individual industrialist is not limited by the gross profits or total income which he has already realised. He can raise money which will purchase capital, by pledging his expectations of future profits; and those to whom these pledges or securities are given may themselves raise money upon them, on the expectation, afforded by the securities, that they will be repaid by the original issuer, according to the description given in par. 18. There is a vast amount of material capital existing in the world, which has been produced only on the prospect of this demand for it existing.

72. When any one employs as capital materials or instruments purchased by the commodities which he has already produced, the capital which he employs is his own, but the moment that he employs as capital commodities purchased by his expectations of future profits, although these profits will be as much his own as those already realised, yet he necessarily procures them from the mass of capital just spoken of, which has been produced in prospect of a demand for it arising. The capital which he employs belongs to some other person, and he borrows it, or buys the use of it by incurring a debt. The line between an industrialist's realised profits and expected profits, employed as capital, coincides exactly with the line between his own and his borrowed capital. Not, of course, that he borrows the capital, which exists for the most part only in a purchasable not in a loanable form, but he borrows money and with it buys the capital. Just as a hatter sells hats for money and with the money buys shoes, so the industrialist sells securities for money and with the money buys capital.

73. Whence comes the money, and to whom does it belong? The money is an accumulation of real rights to commodities and services, but existing for the most part in the form of private credit currency, just as the security does with which it is bought. The difference is, that the security must be private credit currency, but the money may be currency of any kind. And the money belongs to private monied capitalists, to bankers, and to bill brokers, who are the owners of money which is intended to be employed in the purchase of securities, that is, employed in the money market. The mode in which these accumulations are formed, and the processes by which they are employed in the purchase of securities, fall properly under the third head of the enquiry.

74. But how does this money, these rights to commodities and services, come to be accumulated, and are they real values and real wealth? They certainly are real values and real wealth, and they are accumulated just in the same way and from the same causes which lead to the accumulation of the capital which they purchase. They are accumulated in consequence of the expectation that there will be a demand for them, a demand for money in the money market. The corresponding truth to this was shown, in § 95. 59 and 94, with respect to accumulations of capital; the same holds good with respect to money.

75. Three things are requisite to exchanges of credit for capital, namely, credit, money, and capital. The money is the medium and measure of exchange in this case, just as much as in the case of exchanges of commodities; and in both cases alike the exchange is effected only by money being exchanged first for one and then for the other, as if it were, what indeed

it is, an independent and separate commodity. A destruction of any one of the three members of the exchange is a loss of market for the other two, and consequently a loss of value until a new market is found. Not only the loss of credit by industrialists is a destruction of values and of wealth, but also a loss of banker's money is so. It equally destroys the market for the capital. Being therefore a real right to commodities and services, banker's money is real value and real wealth.

76. This being premised, what is the effect of an import or export of money as the balance of international transactions? It is only imported or exported in the form of bullion, or coin at bullion value; and it is only imported or exported instead of commodities, being less profitable than they would be in other circumstances, but more profitable as circumstances actually are. When imported it shows that there is already an abundance of commodities in the country, for otherwise commodities would come, and not bullion; bullion being a commodity which brings no profit in the goods market (§ 95. 76). Now if commodities came, they would go to increase the general fund of capital, to which that also belongs which is purchased by borrowed money; but when bullion comes, it increases the fund of money which purchases those commodities, and which is itself in turn purchased by securities. It increases the supply of money in the money market, instead of the supply of commodities, or of money, in the goods market.

77. In the money market it tends to lower the rate of interest, and thus facilitates speculation with borrowed capital. It has therefore a direct influence

on speculation, increasing it, and an indirect action on prices, by the demand for commodities produced by that increase of speculation.

78. Similarly, an export of bullion diminishes speculation by raising the rate of interest, and through diminished speculation tends to lower prices, by lowering the demand for commodities to be used as capital.

79. To return then to our thesis,—all prices depend on speculation, and not on the quantity of money; but there is one mode in which a change in the quantity of money,—namely, an import or export in payment of an international balance,—operates upon prices, namely, by operating first upon speculation.

80. The double function of bullion, imported or exported in payment of an international balance, is therefore the joint, or connecting link, between the goods market and the money market, and between the corresponding functions of money.

V.

81. The examination of the mechanism of the money market, and of the price paid for the use of money, or rate of interest, is the third branch of the enquiry, and will complete the whole subject. It was said in par. 37, that the bullion exported or imported was the balance of indebtedness between two nations on all transactions between them. What kinds of transactions are included in this phrase? Not only exchange of goods, but also such accounts as the following:

    Services, such as freight, and other carriage of goods,

Foreign Government Stock,
Shares in foreign industrial enterprises,
Subsidies, and Government Loans,
Tributes,
Expenses of travellers and employés.

In the case of stock, shares, subsidies, and loans, the entire principal sums go out of the country, and only the securities and dividends come back in return. Tributes, travellers' and employés' expenses, and services, go out of the country without any return in the shape of money; the services performed are the return for them, just as goods are in the case of a purchase and sale of goods. These are therefore cases of transactions belonging to the goods market, where money purchases commodities or services. That the commodity is an interest- or dividend-bearing security, in some cases, makes no difference in the nature of the transactions. The interest or dividends when paid are part of the commodity received in exchange. The rate of interest is another question, and the only part of these transactions which belongs to the money market.

82. The same distinction must be taken in corresponding transactions at home. Stock and shares are bought in the market for money, and these are dealings in commodities of a certain kind. The value of these commodities depends upon the rate of interest, but this rate itself is the only thing which properly belongs to the money market. So also in what is called by Mr. Macleod Mercantile Credit, where bills of exchange or cheques upon bank deposits are given by one merchant to another. These are advances of money, but the equivalent for them consists in the commodities or services rendered in return.

No money is paid for the use of money, the use of money is not bought by interest or by discount, until the bills are discounted by a banker. Then first they enter the money market.

83. In both foreign and home dealings in stock, shares, bills, and cheques, that part of the transactions, in which they are exchanges of commodities for money, and in which they depend upon the rate of interest, must be distinguished from that other part, in which they not only depend upon, but also in turn themselves influence, the current rate of interest, or price of the use of money for a certain time. The foreign exchanges were said, in par. 48, to belong to all three markets, or functions of money; their place in the currency market was there explained; their place in the money market depends upon the interest or discount with which the bills are originally purchased; and their position in the goods market is now clear, for not only is the exchange of bills virtually an exchange of commodities (par. 67), but the bills themselves are a new kind of commodities, bought and sold for the sake of the difference in their value at different places, at whatever rate they may have been originally discounted. To this function of bills belong all the operations included in what is known as the Arbitration of Exchanges, operations which are therefore excluded from the examination of the money market strictly so called.

84. The first question with regard to the rate of interest arises from the distinction between natural and market value. Interest has no natural rate in the same sense as commodities indefinitely producible have. It has an average rate, about which its market

rate oscillates; but this is not a natural rate in the strict sense, since it is not referable to any cause beyond the supply and demand itself. The average rate is an inferred result, deducible from the fluctuating market rate, not an element contributing to cause those fluctuations. We cannot therefore begin with determining the average rate, but must wait till the market rate and its fluctuations are at least to some extent determined, before asking what the average rate may be. But this market rate has limits, one of which is fixed by other circumstances, arising in another market, namely, the goods market. Its maximum is fixed by the rate of profits. The profits expected in particular enterprises fix the maximum which can be paid by the borrowers, for the purpose of those enterprises. (See § 95. 61). Since the profits in different trades, and in the same at different times, vary considerably, the maximum of the rate of interest will vary likewise. The minimum, on the other hand, depends entirely on the reward which owners of money will be content with, rather than either wait for better times, or spend the money as revenue, or employ it themselves in trade.

85. The limits of the rate of interest leave a wide scope for fluctuations, which arise from the supply and demand of money at different times, in different enterprises, and are reacted on again by the rate itself, there being possibly a supply or a demand for money at one rate, when there is no supply, or no demand, at another rate; just the same as in the case of goods. The other cause of fluctuation is the confidence felt in the borrowers generally, or in the different degrees of risk to which different enterprises are exposed, or the same at different times.

86. Within the limits which may be regarded as the pre-existing conditions of interest at all, the fluctuations owing to supply and demand stand to those owing to different degrees of confidence in borrowers as the natural value of commodities stands to the causes which produce the oscillations in market value. It is the supply and demand of money to be lent and borrowed which must be first considered. The quantity of money supplied against the quantity demanded—this must be broken up by analysis, referred to human motives, before it can be understood. The rate of interest is not ultimately determined by these quantities, but by the causes which determine them.

87. What then is interest, and for what is it paid? Mr. Tooke well calls it the "net profits of capital." It is analogous to wages so far as it is distinguished from profits in being fixed beforehand; profits being the uncertain residuum of total income or gross profits, when all fixed charges are paid. But it is different from wages in being paid, not for personal services, but for the services of the money. It is therefore more strictly analogous to rent, in the wide sense of the term; for rent is the sum paid for the use of goods, and interest the sum paid for the use of money. (See § 95. 41). Deducting then from gross profits, first, the fixed sum for wages, secondly, the fixed sum for rent, thirdly, the uncertain sum for labour of superintendence and insurance against losses, which uncertain sum is the residuum called net profits, the fixed sum for the use of money is what remains under the name of Interest; and, being fixed, it is of course paid before the residuum or net profit is paid, but is fixed by a previous calculation,

on the part of the industrialist, of what both gross and net profits may be expected to be.

88. Though the freedom from risk as well as from trouble of superintendence is what distinguishes the interest from the net profits of money, it is not possible to escape all risk in loans of money, however safe; but there is a great protection, in the net profits having to bear that risk in the first instance, even to their whole extent. Hence those alone are contented with pure interest for their money who wish or are compelled to incur the minimum of risk; such as trustees, for instance, and those persons, both private capitalists and bankers, who wish to have their surplus capital invested at interest, but in forms in which it may be realised at a moment's notice. Investments in shares of companies produce dividends which are partly interest and partly net profits. Only that part which is interest belongs strictly speaking to the money market; the other part, as well as the price of the whole share, belongs to the goods market, as already pointed out.

89. If a profit is to be made out of the pure interest of money, it must come from the mode in which the money lent is collected and brought into the hands of the lender. There must be in his hands to lend a greater amount of money than his own capital, if the pure interest on that money is to pay him a sum equal to net profits at the rate usual in other trades. There is such a mode of collecting money, and such a way of making profits; it is Banking; the principles of which will be described farther on. But private capitalists must either be content with pure interest, or they must purchase stock or shares which pay profits as well as interest, or they

must employ their capital in buying and selling stock and shares, not for the sake of the interest, but for the sake of the difference in their price when resold; in the second case partly, and in the third case wholly, becoming dealers in commodities in the goods market, and not in the money market, notwithstanding that the commodities dealt with are interest-bearing securities. We have then in the money market to do only with two classes of persons who lend money for pure interest, first, bankers, including those bill brokers or discounters who have bankers for their customers, as being an extension of the system of banking, and secondly, buyers of stock and shares for the sake of the interest, and not of the profits included in the dividends. There will however shortly appear a third class of dealers in the money market, whose operations are secondary to those of bankers, from dealing in the commodity which is the ultimate basis of banking operations.

90. We must now advert to a further distinction in the causes influencing the rate of interest, that between money lent for permanent investments and money lent for short periods. Those who lend money for permanent investments include not only trustees and others who are content with pure interest, but also many of those who wish for profits as well as interest. Bankers and bill discounters on the other hand are lenders for short periods. The demand for stock and shares as permanent investments of money varies very much less than the demand for them as investments for short periods; it varies with the slowly changing number and wealth of the classes who are said to live on their means. The fluctuations in their price arise chiefly from the demand for

them as investments for short periods. The habitual lenders on permanent investments are a class which varies but slowly in numbers; while the number of those who lend for short periods varies with every change in the goods market, whether in home or foreign transactions. A great effect is produced in the market for stock and shares, which are the kind of investments purchased by those who lend for long periods, by fluctuations in the demand and supply of loans for short periods, but the demand and supply of loans for short periods is comparatively uninfluenced by the price of stock and shares. No one buys stock and shares, for the sake of the interest only, and for short periods of investment, unless he has a supply of money on his hands for which he has difficulty in finding any more profitable employment, or for the sake of employing, with some return, money which he is compelled to keep where it can be realised in case of a sudden emergency.

91. Having then previously eliminated from consideration all classes of lenders but bankers and buyers of stock and shares for the sake of interest, we may now eliminate also one part of the latter class, those who lend on permanent investments, leaving only the money employed by bankers to be considered as exhibiting the variations which belong strictly to the market rate of interest. The different classes who lend for profits, or buy in order to make profit on the resale, are eliminated on the ground that these operations belong to the goods market and not to the money market; and those who lend for pure interest, but for long periods, on the ground that their operations have no effect on the fluctuations of the market rate. And the reason

for eliminating them is, that it is not here proposed to follow up, or weigh against each other in their efficacy, all the causes which may produce variations in the rate of interest, but only to analyse the mechanism of the phenomena of the money market in its strict sense.

92. The money in the hands of bankers constitutes, then, the loanable money capital of a country, the supply which, compared with the demand from time to time, governs the rate of interest. This fund however consists not only in the capital belonging to the bankers themselves and in the deposits of their customers, but in both of these multiplied, as it were, by credit, in the manner which will shortly be described. Now the very condition of this multiplication of money by credit consists in the reserve of bullion or coin, which enables the banker to meet his engagements with specie. The basis of his operations is bullion, and upon the fluctuations in the amount of bullion in the country from time to time depend the fluctuations of the credit which he enjoys and the amount which he can afford to lend. But bullion, as we have seen, is thrown upon or withdrawn from the money market in accordance with its abundance or deficiency, as it is imported or exported in payment of the balance of indebtedness arising in the goods market, upon transactions of all kinds. Here is the same phenomenon at which we arrived in par. 77, when examining the phenomena of the goods market, and here is the point of reaction upon the goods market from the money market. Bullion, which is useless in the goods market although its transmission is the final issue of the transactions in that market, and sums up as it were their results,

becomes of immense importance in the money market, not only as a commodity bearing interest, but as the basis of credit transactions to many times its own amount.

93. It is from its character as a commodity bearing interest that the secondary operations, mentioned in par. 89, arise. These consist in import and export of bullion, bought and sold by bills created for the purpose, when the rate of interest or discount differs sufficiently between any two countries to cover the cost of transmitting the bullion. Bullion is imported or exported for sale because the rate of interest is higher in one country than in another; and these so called 'bullion operations' belong to the money market, and not like the purchase and sale of bills to the goods market (par. 83), because the profit is made from the difference between the rates of interest in the two countries, and not from any difference in the value of the commodity dealt with, its scarcity or abundance, independent of what that rate may be. The supplies of bullion thus transmitted are not only governed by the existing rates of interest, but also react upon them, continuing till these rates are brought down to what we may call their specie point, when the transmission becomes unprofitable.

94. The loanable money capital, based upon these supplies of bullion, and the rate of interest resulting from the supply compared to the demand for it, are analogous to the quantities and prices of commodities in the goods market which are the condition of the speculation founded on them, as remarked in par. 69; from which speculation, together with the previous quantities and prices, the subsequent quantities and

prices of commodities result. So also it is in the money market. The present supply of money lent and the present rate of interest are the condition, at the beginning of any period, upon which speculation in the supply of money for interest is founded; and this speculation again determines the supply of money and the rate of interest at the end of the period. The speculation however is conducted by bankers, who are the dealers in the commodity money, the commodity of the money market. But the business of the money market, though thus precisely analogous to that of the goods market, is exposed to dangerous vicissitudes of a kind from which that of the goods market is exempt. It is exposed to the full weight of the changes in the quantity of bullion imported or exported, which result from operations in the goods market but directly affect the money market only, changes which cannot be prevented, and the effects of which therefore must be constantly watched and provided for. The question then is, in what way do bankers become the conductors of speculation in the money market.

95. Hitherto the value of money in the money market has been considered in connection with its quantity and value in the goods market; but, when we enter on the question of Banking, it becomes requisite to consider the relations of the different forms of currency towards each other; in doing which, however, abstraction may still be made of differences in their value, or depreciation of one with respect to another. So long as notes, or public credit currency, are de facto convertible, they are of equal value with bullion or with coin; but a specific demand for bullion, to meet payments abroad for which bullion is

the only currency, will cause notes to be returned to the bank in exchange for bullion. The difference, which is most important, is one of function and not of value. So, in transactions at home, bills which are private credit currency may be of equal value with notes or coin, but, if there is a function which notes or coin alone can perform, notes or coin will be demanded in payment of bills; and this happens, supposing notes to be perfectly convertible, whenever a contraction of the private credit currency takes place, in consequence of a contraction of credit. Again the difference is one of function, not of value, and again it produces a specific demand for one kind of currency. Res ad triarios rediit. The amount of the private credit currency fluctuates with the amount of the business which it is required to perform; it is created by that business, and destroyed when that business is concluded. But when the transactions of this business begin to lessen in amount, the amount of new creations of documents of private credit currency will be less than the amount of them already existing, which they would otherwise exchange for and replace; bills will not be renewed, but must be paid. Hence, in order to conclude the transactions, another kind of currency will be required. Notes or coin are in specific demand, as soon as speculation has begun to flag.

96. Such are the conditions of the commodity, money, in which bankers deal. What is the mode in which they deal with it? The funds in the hands of bankers arise from two sources besides their own realised money capital, first, the deposits of realised capital by customers, second, the deposits which they create in favour of customers when they discount their

bills. Mr. Macleod thus defines a banker: "A Banker is a trader who buys money, or money and debts, by creating other debts." Theory and Practice of Banking, Vol. i. p. 110, 2nd edit. The banker buys the deposits of both kinds with his credit; that is, he gives a credit in his books to the person who deposits money with him, and he does the same to the person who sells him bills, for the amount of the bills minus the discount which he charges, crediting him with the one and debiting him with the other. Both kinds of deposits may then be drawn against, or transferred, by Cheques, at the will of the depositor. All these transactions may be performed, and the latter kind must be performed, by the creation of private credit currency. It is only the deposits of money by customers, and the private capital of the banker himself, which may exist in the form of coin or notes. The deposits belonging to the customers, the cheques which are used to draw upon or transfer them, and the bills which belong to the banker, are all forms of private credit currency.

97. In what then does the profit of the banker consist? It consists in the sums which he deducts as discount on the bills. When the acceptors of these bills pay their acceptances, they pay the whole amount, against which the banker has granted a credit or deposit for the amount minus the discount. He therefore receives this difference, and also obtains the use of so much of the deposit as may remain not drawn out by the depositor, which he may use for the purpose of discounting other bills and granting new deposits. His own capital, and also the money actually deposited by customers against credits granted to them, have been used already in the same way.

There is another way also in which he may make profit; he may pay the sums drawn out by depositors in his own notes, which is meeting liabilities of one sort by liabilities of another sort, thus deferring the time and lessening the amount which would otherwise have to be met by payment of coin.

98. The banker is liable at any moment to be called upon to meet his engagements in coin. And his profits evidently depend, apart from the rate of interest, upon the amount of those transactions from which his liabilities arise. The practical question for him accordingly is, upon how small a basis of coin he can erect a given superstructure of liabilities, or how large a superstructure of liabilities he can with safety erect upon a given basis of coin. This is the temptation to that speculation, and the mode in which it is possible, which is the chief part of the speculation in the money market. The dangers to which this speculation is exposed are of two kinds; the first, which is inseparable from it, arises from the demand for credit on bills which are either unsound in themselves, or created to too large an amount, in consequence of overtrading in the goods market, and could not be avoided even if the amount of their reserves were entirely under the control of the bankers; the second, which affects the amount of the reserves themselves, arises from the varying amount of bullion in the country, owing to the fluctuations of foreign trade. By the system of banking which prevails in this country, by the country banks keeping their reserves in the hands of London bankers, and the London bankers keeping theirs in the Bank of England, the only reserve in bullion which supports the bank money of the whole country exists in the

vaults of the Bank of England. This bullion reserve accordingly has not only to meet the requirements which may arise from insecurity of credit at home, but also to bear the pressure of drains of bullion from abroad.

99. The effect of a great and continued diminution of the bullion reserve in the Bank of England, to meet a foreign drain, is to contract the advances made by bankers throughout the country, which may often cause a great destruction of wealth; and the smaller the proportion of bullion to the credit currency built upon it, the greater will be this effect upon the deposits created by granting discounts, in order to preserve the same proportion between the reserve and the deposits. This is well shown in a pamphlet by Mr. Thomas Joplin, published in 1841, entitled The Cause and Cure of our Financial Embarrassments, pp. 30-39. And this is the explanation of the fact, that the greatest pressures in the money market have always been produced by the coincidence of a drain of bullion from abroad with the close of a period of undue speculation and overtrading at home. It is of the greatest importance to avoid all such great and sudden contractions of banking credit, which are equivalent to so much destruction of real wealth; and it would seem that the only way to avoid them is by keeping an ample reserve of bullion in the Bank of England, and preventing its too great diminution by adjusting the rate of discount by the foreign exchanges, as urged by Mr. Tooke in his History of Prices, Vol. iii. pp. 185-9. And it might, I am inclined to think, materially aid in keeping up such a reserve, if the Bank of England were to adopt the plan of purchasing gold at a premium on the

present Bank price, when it was scarce, and at a discount from that price when it was abundant, according to the suggestion advocated by Mr. Seyd in his Bullion and Foreign Exchanges, Part iii. Chap. ii. Bullion and Rates of Discount.

100. But to return to the method of Banking. The deposits of money by customers, bought by credits to their account in the banker's books, are, if we put aside for simplicity's sake his own capital, the foundation of the whole business. To take Mr. Macleod's example, given at pp. 116-118 of the Theory and Practice of Banking, Vol. i., we will suppose these deposits to be £10,000, against which liabilities are created to the same amount. The first thing which the banker does is to set apart, say, £1000 of this in cash, which he keeps in his till, to meet the current demands of the depositors. He has then £9000 to trade with. He keeps the whole of this as a Reserve, either in his own coffers, or with some other Bank, or in some place where he can command it at a moment's notice, and he buys bills to the amount of, say, £40,000, by creating deposits or issuing his own notes to the amount of £39,200, deducting the difference as discount on the £40,000, supposing the rate to be 8 per cent. per annum, and the bills to be at three months. The amount which is kept to meet current payments, here supposed to be one tenth of the first kind of deposits, is determined by the experience of what sums are usually drawn out, and what sums are usually paid in, as additions to the deposits, day by day. And the amount of deposits which it is safe to create against bills, compared to the reserve, here supposed to be in the proportion of £40,000 to £9000, is determined in the

same way. The banker's accounts in the case supposed would then stand thus:

Liabilities or Deposits.		Assets.	
£10,000		Cash	£1,000
39,200		Reserve	9,000
£49,200		Bills	40,000
			£50,000

And his profit consists in the difference, £800, which being reaped four times in the year, the bills being at three months, is £3200, or eight per cent. on £40,000.

101. It makes no difference whether the banker issues his own notes or creates liabilities, in exchange for the deposits of money and bills discounted; for the liabilities may be drawn upon as soon as created, and the notes are only liabilities, so long as they remain in the hands of the public, and are not presented for payment in coin. The advantage of issuing notes is in issuing them against drafts upon deposits. It also makes no difference, so far as the nature of the transaction is concerned, whether the banker uses his own capital or deposits of the first kind, as the basis of his transactions in creating deposits of the second kind; for in both cases he keeps the whole amount as reserve, either in his own hands, or in the shape of a deposit with another bank, or in the shape of a deposit with bill brokers, or invested in public securities; in all cases having the command of the money at any moment. He then creates other liabilities, on this basis, to the extent of about four times its amount, or, in the instance given by Mr. Macleod, in the proportion of 40 to 9.

102. The general character or effect of these bank-

Book II. Ch. IV.

§ 96. Statical logic of money.

ing transactions is that of a loan of capital, part of which, and usually the larger part, is itself borrowed. The deposits of the first kind are money borrowed, the deposits of the second kind are money lent, by the banker. And the term loan is applied to all transactions where money is given in exchange for the return of an equal sum at a future time, with interest for its use. The term is too simple and too useful, as a term of denotation, to be given up; but it must be remembered that it is a denotation, or in my phrase a term of second intention only; that it requires an analysis of the transactions, and a definition of them by terms of first intention, in order to be understood. Now, as Mr. Macleod well shows, the loans in question must be analysed into the simple exchanges of which they consist; they must be conceived, not as loans, but as purchases and sales of debts; and only in this manner are they intelligible themselves, or supply an explanation of the phenomena of the money market. Exchanges, value against value, are the minima, the atoms, of the whole science of political economy; and no transactions are explained, until they are reduced by analysis into the exchanges, value against value, of which they consist. To have done this in the case of the phenomena of the money market is the great service rendered to the science by Mr. Macleod. My own obligations to his work on Banking can hardly be overstated. But I do not follow him in wishing to dispense altogether with the term loan, in describing banking transactions. It is true that the money deposited with a banker becomes his property, uncontrollable by the depositors; and it is true also that the money which he advances in discounting bills is repaid to him, not by the persons to whom he advances it, but by the acceptors of the bills. But this only shows that the transactions in question require a further analysis, that their character as exchanges of the use of money for interest, and of interest for the use of money, is distinguishable into more exchanges than one, or into exchanges between more parties than two; but it does not show that no term is needed to characterise these transactions, as cases of interest purchasing the use of money, apart from the number of exchanges and number of parties into which they may be analysed. It appears to me, that we have here another case exemplifying the nature and use of the distinction between what I have called first and second intentions. To dispense with the term Loan is like Comte's attempt to dispense with the term Cause.

103. Having thus briefly analysed the method of banking, we are in a position to return to the point departed from in par. 94, and to consider the supply and demand of money, with its resulting rate of interest, at the beginning of a period, and the speculation which operates upon it, producing a different state of demand and supply, and a different rate of interest, at the end of it. The supply of money consists of deposits or liabilities of the second kind, created by bankers in discounting bills; and it arises from two ultimate sources, first, the influx of bullion from abroad, secondly, the deposits of the first kind with bankers, together with their own capital. But the supply of bullion from abroad operates in two ways; first, it is sold by the importers to the Bank of England, where it increases the reserve of bullion, and consequently the amount of liabilities which may

with safety be created by discounting bills; and secondly, the money received for it is deposited in banks, in the shape of deposits of the first kind. The bullion is thus employed twice over, once by its owners, once by the Bank; and not only twice, for, in the use made of it by the Bank, it is not the bullion, but many times its amount, that is lent on the basis of it. Its owners sell it to the Bank of England, and then deposit the notes, which they receive in exchange, with their own bankers, where they again become a source of deposits of the second kind. "In ordinary banking" says Mr. Macleod "both parties have the complete use of the capital. The customer lends his money to the banker, and yet has the free use of it—the banker employs that money in promoting trade; upon the strength of its being deposited with him, he buys debts with his 'promises to pay,' and the person who sells the debt has the free use of the very coin which the banker has the same right to demand." Theory and Practice of Banking, Vol. i. p. 127, 2nd edit. The bullion becomes a deposit of the first kind, upon which to build deposits of the second kind, and also remains, as a bullion reserve, to secure this building, and measure the extent to which it is safe. Deposits of the first kind need no explanation; their amount depends, as the banker's own capital also does, upon the amount of money already realised in the country. Such is the nature of the supply of money in the money market.

104. The demand for it, on the other hand, consists in the demand of industrialists for advances on discount, for the creation in their favour of deposits of the second kind. And this demand depends on

the prospects of profit, or the intensity of speculation, in the goods market. It is also assisted by the demand of bankers for interest on a larger sum, compared with their reserves, which are its basis. The bankers join in the demand, for which they alone provide the supply; a circumstance which distinguishes this from every other trade. And this is what was intended by saying above, that the speculation in the money market was 'conducted by bankers,' namely, that they can create a supply to meet a demand which is partly their own, to meet their own demand for loanable capital, when it is demanded also by their customers. The degree to which they yield to this demand by creating deposits of the second kind, the amount of these deposits in comparison with the reserves their basis, which they are induced to create, is the speculation in the money market which was said, in par. 94, to operate upon the supply and demand for money, and upon the resulting rate of interest, existing at the beginning of a period, and to determine these quantities and this rate at the end of it.

105. The point, then, at which speculation reacts upon supply and demand, and upon the rate of interest, is the point where the demand is identical with the supply, where it depends on the will of one class of men to contract or extend both at once. But bankers have no control over the amount of deposits of the first kind, and no direct control over the amount of bullion in the country, which is their basis of operations; they have control only over the extent of the use which they will make of this basis. The amount of bullion in the country, depending in the first instance upon the balances of international pay-

ments of all kinds, may be decreased, if superabundant, by private speculators at home, who export it for investment abroad, or, if deficient, increased by private speculators abroad, who send it hither for investment, if that should offer them a profit. But this export and import of bullion depends upon the rate of interest at home compared with the rates in different foreign countries, rates of interest which are determined, in the first instance, by the speculation of bankers, in other countries as well as at home, by their creating or refusing to create new supplies of money. The first mover in the reaction of speculation upon quantities and rates is the banker; the second is the private speculator, who exports or imports bullion for sale to bankers.

106. Bullion accordingly has a value, sometimes expressed as its price, in a third market, the money market. It has a price proper, in other forms of currency, as shown in par. 25 et seqq.; it has a value in the commodity market, as shown in par. 59 et seqq.; and it has a value in the money market, which is interest, or the price of its use, when exported or imported for investment in securities from country to country. (See par. 53). When the price of gold is said to rise above the mint price, we must ask whether this rise is due to depreciation of the coin or paper currency in which it is paid for, or is the price paid for the use of the coin or paper given for the bullion, that is, as interest, and therefore owing to the rate of interest being higher than in other countries, interest which bullion may earn by being imported in exchange for bills. "If the rate of discount in London is 3 per cent. and that in Paris is 6 per cent., the simple meaning of that is that gold

may be bought for 3 per cent. in London, and sold at 6 per cent. in Paris. But the expense of sending it from one to the other does not exceed ½ per cent., consequently it leaves 2¼ or 2½ per cent. profit on the operation. The natural consequence immediately follows, gold flies from London to Paris, and the drain will not cease until the rates of discount are brought within a certain degree of equality. It used to be the common delusion of mercantile men that gold was only sent to pay a balance arising from the sale of goods, and that, therefore, it must cease of itself whenever these payments were made. But this is a profound delusion. When the rates of discount differ so much as is supposed above between London and Paris, persons in London fabricate bills upon their correspondents in Paris for the express purpose of selling them in London for cash, which they then remit to Paris, and which they can sell again for 6 per cent. And it is quite evident that this drain will not cease so long as the difference in the rates of discount is maintained. Moreover, merchants in Paris immediately send over their bills to be discounted in London, and, of course, have the cash remitted them." Theory and Practice of Banking, Vol. i. p. 277, 2nd edit.

107. This cause of exporting bullion is entirely independent of a previous state of indebtedness between the two countries. It is true that the same phenomenon may occur from a balance having to be paid, as soon as the exchanges reach specie point, as explained in par. 37 et seqq.; but it may occur also between two countries which have had no previous dealings with each other, or between which the exchanges would otherwise be at par, from the rate of

discount being higher in the one than in the other. Gold will then be sent solely because, being a commodity in the money market, and the only commodity in the money market which is also ultimate international currency, and purchasable by securities and interest, that is, by bills, a given quantity of it, sent to a country where the rate of interest is high, will purchase bills to a larger amount than it could purchase in a country where the rate of interest is low; for the gold which purchases the bills is their present price, and a high rate of interest or discount means that the present price of a bill is low, compared to the amount of the bill, and a low rate of interest or discount that the present price is high. And since an efflux of gold from this cause will affect banking reserves, and tend to compel a contraction of credit, it is requisite that banks should watch its operation, and include it among the data of their own speculation.

108. As the cause of efflux and influx of bullion is twofold, arising partly from indebtedness on transactions of all kinds in the goods market, and partly from the comparative rates of interest, so also is the remedy. A drain of bullion may be counteracted either by an export of commodities, or of interest-bearing securities, that is, by action on the goods market, or by raising the rate of discount. Raising the rate of discount operates directly on the price of interest-bearing securities, and only indirectly on other commodities; for interest-bearing securities belong to both markets, goods and money market, (par. 81). But bankers can only apply the latter means of counteraction directly, namely, that of raising the rate of discount; but this acts directly on

the one, indirectly on the other, of the two branches of the goods market. It acts indirectly upon prices of commodities by checking production, and causing a sale of commodities already produced. Of these two means, therefore, the only one which bankers can put in operation is to raise or lower the rate of discount, unless they go to the further and extreme measure of refusing to discount at all, which is the very evil which a prudential regulation of discounts is intended to prevent.

109. The regulation of bank speculation by the bankers themselves is the point at which, and the means by which, theory and analysis, applied to the actually existing circumstances at any time, pass into practice, the Logic of money values into the Art of dealing with them. Here therefore the logic finds its completion; and it remains, though beyond the present purpose, to apply its analysis to practice, by deduction of laws less general and more immediately applicable to existing circumstances. Banking operations, or more briefly Banking, is that which reacts upon the phenomena of money, in all its three functions; they are its condition and its object-matter, in and upon which it works. And the mode in which it operates upon them must necessarily be determined by the views and opinions held as to their nature and organisation. This is the position occupied by all state laws which attempt to regulate money matters generally or as a whole; Banking is the point at which they apply their lever. This for instance is the position occupied by the Bank Charter Act 1844, which is the dispensation under which we are still living. It would be beyond the scope of the present § to enter into any detailed discussion of that Act;

nor perhaps is it needful, so fully has it been examined by the great writers on these questions. Two points however may be briefly touched on, in order not so much to apply the foregoing analysis, as to show its applicability to the case in question; in doing which I shall found my remarks chiefly upon Sections viii. and ix. of the First Part of Mr. Gilbart's Practical Treatise on Banking, and upon Chapter xii. of Mr. Macleod's Theory and Practice of Banking, 2nd edit.

110. The first point relates to the position of the Bank itself, which is this: the greater part of its own capital is tied up in public securities which cannot be realised in gold at pleasure, and yet it is the Bank which is the ultimate depositary of the reserves of other banks, and from which all the bullion required to meet a foreign drain may be taken. It has then, properly, only its deposits, deposits of the first kind, to make into a banking reserve, to support all its issues of notes and other deposits of the second kind. It is consequently incumbent on it to consider how much of these reserves it must keep in hand, in order to support the amount of issues and other deposits of the second kind which it wishes to create, taking into account the drains of bullion, specifically, which are likely from time to time to act upon its reserve, through its deposits and issues; that is, not only ordinary banking calls upon it, but also extraordinary ones, arising from the foreign transactions of the country and the rates of interest in foreign countries.

111. To come to the second point, the Act of 1844 apparently assumes that the notes of the Bank form the only calls to be provided for, and not also

its other deposits of the second kind. It requires the Bank to keep only so much bullion as is equal to the amount of notes issued, counting besides the public securities, in which its own capital is invested, as equal to so much bullion, and as the basis of an equal amount of notes.

112. Now the distinction between notes and other deposits of the second kind is of no importance whatever, so long as bullion is plentiful and credit expanding; for advances may be made by creating deposits, and the liabilities increased beyond their just proportion to the bullion reserve, without the issue of a single note. But when credit is being contracted, and bullion is leaving the country, these deposits may be drawn upon and bullion required for the draft; and, besides this, the discounts that are required will be required in the form of notes, in order to meet engagements which can no longer be met by any form of private credit currency, as shown in par. 95. But it is precisely this form of advances which the Bank is restricted by the Act from granting. It may therefore be compelled, in order to secure itself, to contract its advances by violently raising the rate of discount, or even to refuse advances altogether, whereby all traders, sound and unsound alike, who require advances, are threatened with ruin.

113. The distinction drawn by the Act between notes and other liabilities is a distinction applicable to, and arising in, the first of the three functions of money, and is unsound when employed as a distinction belonging to the third, the money market; and the truth of the distinction, though the application is false, is that which affords to the Bank of England

a theory or principle which apparently justifies them in granting discounts and creating liabilities, without paying regard to the amount of bullion required as their basis, to meet the calls which may be made in respect of them. The Bank wants a reserve sufficient to secure its notes; the country one sufficient to secure all its liabilities, without violent alterations in the rate of discount. Without some theory of the kind, the Bank would be too much hampered in its business, by so much of its own capital being tied up in public securities, not capable of realisation at pleasure, which compels it to make the greater use of its deposits of the first kind. It is quite comprehensible that the Act should be a favourite with the authorities of the Bank; and it would no doubt be so also with the commercial public, were it not for its ruinous action in times of monetary pressure and contraction of credit. But it can be no favourite with the private bankers of the country, who, organised themselves on sound banking principles, find that Bank, upon the bullion reserve of which the security of their own reserves depends, governed, in its dealings on the basis of that reserve, by principles which endanger it when bullion is scarce, and lead to its over employment when bullion is plentiful; the Bank in both cases competing at an advantage with private bankers; for, in the first case, the rise in the Bank rate of discount compels a rise, and in the second, the lowering of the Bank rate compels a lowering, in the market rate, that is, in the rates at which private bankers grant discounts. Banking operations are thus governed, in this country, by conflicting principles, those which the Act applies to the operations of the Bank of England, and those upon which all the other banks in the country are administered. From such a conflict of principles nothing but confusion can be expected to result; and it is obvious, in such a case, which set of principles must conform to the other; for it is only by observing and not contravening the laws which govern banking under all circumstances that any voluntary modification of them, such as the Bank Charter Act 1844, can be successfully established. Natura parendo vincitur.

§ 97. 1. The examination of the phenomena of practical science is still incomplete. It has been shown in § 92 that all science, whether speculative or practical, has an aspect in which it is art, and again, what comes to the same thing, that every science has a branch or branches of art corresponding to it, which are arts of knowledge if they depend on a speculative, arts of action if they depend on a practical science. Now when we take the scientific aspect, or, what is equivalent, the sciences, whether speculative or practical, distinguished from the arts depending on them, we find that this aspect has, in every case, an historical aspect coextensive with it, and that every science has its corresponding history; a history not, of course, of the progress of the science itself, but of the object-matter which it examines. The speculative and physical sciences have each an object-matter which has followed a certain course of change or development, and this course is its history. It is not only subject to certain laws of coexistence and sequence, but it has followed a certain single course in conformity to those laws. To examine into this actual course is to treat the object-matter of the science by the historical method, as it is called, the method which is now the favourite in most subjects. The practical sciences, those of them at least which have been considered in the preceding §§, have also obviously their historical aspect and method; the object-matter of all of them has followed a certain single course, in conformity to the laws of coexistence and sequence attaching to their phenomena. There has been, for instance, a certain single course followed by the phenomena of ethic, of law, of politic; of religion, of poetry, of war, of diplomacy, of medicine, of education, of language, of wealth.

2. The difference between science and history is accordingly the following. History is the discovery of the train of sequences simple or complex, that is, of coexistences in sequence, which has actually happened; science is the discovery of the more or less general laws under which this train has happened, or of which it is a case; that is to say, it is the history stated in general terms. Science is therefore the logic of history; it is the logic, not strictly speaking of the facts or phenomena which it arranges into its hierarchy of laws, for laws are nothing but these facts or phenomena themselves, and science their arrangement in a hierarchy or logical order; but it is the logic of the facts or phenomena as they have actually happened, that is, of history; for, since the phenomena or facts are the common object-matter, and the only object-matter which exists, it is only by distinguishing the method of history from that of science that any distinction is possible between them. Method is the point distinctive between science and history, just as it is also between metaphysical and empirical science. The phenomena arranged statically, and in order of increasing com-

plexity, decreasing generality, to follow Comte's luminous distinction, are science; the same phenomena arranged dynamically, and in order of their actual occurrence and existence, are history.

3. It follows, as Comte also clearly saw, that many so-called sciences are not sciences but histories, those phenomena not having been sufficiently discovered of which their phenomena are a case; or, in other words, a sufficient number of convergent laws not having been discovered from which the phenomena in question may be deduced. Geology is an instance. Geology is the discovery of the actual changes which have taken place in the composition and recomposition of the materials of the globe. The convergent laws, or general phenomena, under which it must be exhibited as a case, in order to be raised to the rank of a science, are laws of mechanical, physical, chemical, and even vital, change; including phenomena so variable and so remote from observation, as to postpone indefinitely the hope of such a reduction. The referring the phenomena of geology, wherever possible, to general laws makes it a scientific study, but, if prediction is taken as the criterion, geology must renounce her claim to be a science. Prediction is the proof of scientific construction, because the laws, under which the phenomena in question are a case, are general, that is, equally applicable to the future as to the past, and to discoveries yet to be made as to those made already. And of course it is not intended that history is not scientific; the contrary is evident when it is called an aspect of science; the question is simply whether this or that group of phenomena can be arranged in a hierarchical order, or exhibited as

dependent upon phenomena so arranged, to such an extent as to enable a prediction of their principal changes. The question being always partly one of degree, it is clear that the decision, in the case of any history claiming to be a science, must depend upon the opinion of scientific men, applying the criterion of prediction, or, what is the same thing, deduction. History and the historical method are always the pioneers of science and the scientific method within the object-matter common to both; but scientific principles and distinctions, derived from another science, may be applied to institute and direct historical enquiry from the first, in which case they perform the function of hypotheses.

4. When we turn to the history of matters of practice, the object-matter of the practical sciences, with which alone we are here concerned, we find that history, in its large and usual sense, is the historical aspect of, or is the history corresponding to, practical sciences the arts of which are, or are contained under, ethic and politic. History, as the word is commonly used, means the history of man in society. Like the general or architectonic arts of ethic and politic, general history contains under it, or as branches constituting its whole range, the special histories of different functions and activities of man, as, for instance, the history of religions, of arts and sciences, of laws of persons and property, of production and distribution of wealth, of the origin and development of languages; which are reducible into order according as they become or show aptitude for becoming sciences. They take their classification from that of the arts of action. The list of special branches of history, within each of which other minor branches

may be ranged, is accordingly the same as the list of special practical sciences or arts.

5. When the science or philosophy of history is spoken of, the phrase can mean only this, the treatment of history in connection with its practical science, its reference to the laws of action arranged in logical instead of historical order. These laws however are laws of the comparative strength de facto, and validity de jure, of the various feelings and thoughts of man. These same laws are the guide to future practice, arts of action being founded, as already shown, upon practical sciences. Therefore it is impossible to make history a guide to practice without first taking it up into science, and thence deducing the laws of art. Only to the extent to which this is done is any practical instruction reaped from history. From this follows the explanation of the extreme delusiveness of history, in the usual sense, as a guide to action or a means of prediction; much more is expected from it than is obtainable, because its conversion into science has been as yet so imperfectly accomplished. Wherever the conversion has been accomplished, the study is no longer called a history, but either a science or an art; for instance, the art of war, the sciences of political economy and comparative philology. Even these have not reached the rank of exact sciences, partly because of the imperfect analysis attained of the group of motives on which each rests, but chiefly because of the still more imperfect knowledge of the interference of other motives or groups of motives with those constituting the group itself. No single practical science can reach the position of an exact science until all of them are near reaching it; in other words, the general sciences

of ethic and politic must approach the exact stage pari passu with the special branches which they include.

6. To treat any branch of human action as history simply, without seeking to refer the facts, as they are discovered, to the distinctions of the corresponding science, is to treat it as a matter either of personal, biographical, curiosity or of mere antiquarian research. But the moment its facts are treated scientifically, the moment it is sought to explain them, or arrange them in scientific order, that moment the history becomes scientific, and the study becomes one of forward-looking interest. In one respect the connection is closer between science and art than between history and science; science exists for the sake of art more inevitably than history for the sake of science; the interest which underlies a science and its art is one and the same, an interest in its special object-matter; while in passing from a history to its science there is a change of interest, a change from mere biographical or antiquarian curiosity to an interest in a special branch of knowledge, as part of a connected whole. But even such a curiosity, with regard to a special branch of history, will often lead those who feel it to take an interest in the subject also as a matter of science, to wish to know not only the exact detail of the facts but the reasons and causes of them, and thence the general laws of which they are instances. Mere antiquarianism, which is always purely historical, becomes thus ennobled by means of the special interest which it takes in a special subject.

7. Since however the portion of the phenomena which, in every practical science, remains historical

is much larger than that which has been reduced to science, it follows that, although the treatment of the whole of the phenomena ought to be scientific, it is an error to expect that practical guidance, that accurate prediction, from the study which it would afford if it had fully passed into the scientific stage, and had entirely converted its history into science. Political economy is held to have reached the condition of a science, and to be a science as well as an art. But even here the laws of the science are incapable of furnishing rules for guidance in detail, except hypothetically; in trade speculations, for instance, the difficulty is to know whether the case contemplated by the general rule has arisen. The science of political economy is a system of laws guiding the detailed actions of its art from a distance, by giving a general framework or logic under which to arrange the phenomena out of which trade speculations are to be made. To know the history of the case is the real difficulty to be overcome; as, for instance, the amount of cotton in the market, the amount which will come in from the next crop, the changes in the taste of the public, the competition of a new or better manufactured material.

8. So also it is, and to a far greater degree, with the architectonic arts of ethic and politic. A still greater portion of the phenomena of these arts is included in history alone than is the case with those of political economy. They supply a logic it is true, but, in regard to the complicated and obscure questions of daily life, public and private, this logic consists of hypothetical laws, the really difficult question being to know whether the case contemplated by the hypothesis, the case for the application of this

law or that, has arisen; whether, in politic, it is a time for aiming at liberty, or a time for enforcing justice, by repealing or enacting this or that special law; whether, in ethic, it is a time for throwing off old observances, or a time for adopting more stringent ones, as a means of self-education. It is clear that in politic the distance is enormous from which its logic sends guidance and help to the decision of details. And in ethic it is equally unreasonable to expect the logician to furnish rules for the guidance of individual conduct, which must vary according to the character and circumstances of every individual. The logician who attempted such a task would beat the air, either with meaningless platitudes, or with subtil but random distinctions and refinements. Exhortation, the weapon of the preacher, is not his province; and beyond this, wherever particular counsel for particular cases can be given, it must come from that practical wisdom which is the fruit of experience, that is, from observations which have not yet been reduced to science. Even with a logic of ethic and of politic, and even with one or two undoubted special sciences of practice, the phenomena of history still unreclaimed bear an overwhelming proportion to those of its science, the phenomena which cannot to those which can be predicted, the phenomena in daily life of which we are ignorant to those of which we are cognisant. In proportion as this line of separation is pushed forwards, more questions are brought under the decision of logic; and the dominion of ethic and politic is extended by every stroke which extends that of science; for these are but the main branches of that practical science into which history is converted by increasing knowledge.

9. There is then no other science of history but the practical science, still in process of formation, of which ethic, politic, and their subordinates, are the members already constituted as sciences. But the question may be asked, How the rank of science can be claimed for these portions, while it is denied to the whole which they constitute, and which remains still in the condition of history. The answer to this is the following.—History has two great branches, its phenomena are of two kinds, physical phenomena which require investigation by the physical and speculative sciences, and phenomena of consciousness which require treating metaphysically. We have come round to the point touched upon in § 4, where it was said that physical history, physiology, and analysis of conscious states, were three great branches of one science of man, which could only be complete by their combination. This entire group of studies is what we have now called History. That branch of it which consists in the analysis of conscious states has been so far pursued in Book I. as to warrant us in founding a logic of practice upon it in Book II. And the logics of ethic and politic venture only so far as the phenomena of conscious action are known or thought to be known. The filling up of their outlines, the carrying their laws out into detailed provisions, was expressly left in § 86. 1-2 for future knowledge; and the greatest lack of this knowledge is in the physical and physiological, not in the metaphysical branch. It is clear then that we have neither a Science of History, nor an Art of Life, in all its details; but we have a logic of ethic and of politic so far as we have a scientific analysis of conscious voluntary action. And the detailed art of life, when

and as it grows up, will be the continuation and amplification of ethic and politic, considered as arts, just as the science of history, which will be its foundation, will be the amplification of them considered as sciences; for physical and physiological phenomena come into history only so far as they stand connected with human action and feeling; the scope of history, and the circumscription of the physical phenomena to be included in it, are marked out from a subjective centre; and its science is the completion of the series of the subjective and practical, as physiology is of the physical and purely speculative sciences.

§ 98. 1. While disclaiming therefore the ambitious name of the Science of History, as having to express an aim and a wish rather than anything already realised, we cannot give up the endeavour to make history scientific, and thus raise it to the desired rank. The conception which we have been led to form of it may perhaps be expressed by the name Historical Science, or history treated scientifically. So treated, the subject has, it has been shown, two great branches; the first including all physical phenomena which have influence on man, phenomena which must first be investigated separately, from the point of view of physical speculative science; and the second including the phenomena of consciousness, as well those of the individual alone as those which result from his action on and intercourse with other individuals, a study also to be pursued separately at first, and then completed, along with the former branch, by studying the two series of phenomena in combination, the state in which they are actually presented in experience. Physical phenomena may again be distinguished into two orders, those which operate upon man's motives of action directly, as, for instance, a fertile valley which attracts his settlements, a mountain chain which bars his progress, and those which compose his physiological nature, in structure and function, or which act upon him by modifying this nature, as climate, food, physiological peculiarities of race, of mixed races, of alternation in generations, and physiological causes of the birth of exceptionally powerful minds.

2. The distinction of the two main branches of historical science is parallel to that which was drawn in § 60 between the character of the individual and influences operative on the character. The method to which this distinction led, in the analysis of the individual, is equally commanded by the parallel distinction in the case of mankind at large. Distinguishing the physical and physiological influences, operative on the individuals and the nations composing mankind, from the systems of thought and feeling which they mould, and which react upon them in turn, it is the latter group of phenomena which we must lay at the basis of the enquiry, the changes of which must be the thread or clue to which we refer the modifying influences. It is these which constitute the end or purpose of historical, being practical, science; it is these therefore which we must keep always in view, whatever are the physical phenomena modifying them. Accordingly, the first question to be asked relates to the normal course of development of systems of thought and feeling among mankind, whether there is such an one discoverable, and in what it consists. This is the position occupied by Comte's famous law of the three states. It is by no means, in my opinion, a law of history as a whole; it is a law

of the normal course of development of the character of mankind generally.

3. To pursue historical science on either of its two great branches alone, exclusively of the other, is to mistake its character as well as to narrow its scope. But since it is practical science, deriving its interest from man, the danger of paying exclusive attention to the branch of character is greater than the opposite. The danger on this latter side is rather one of attributing too great potency to physical and physiological phenomena, too great modifiability to character, than of denying the influence of character altogether; while on the other side there is the danger of treating the character and its normal course of development as an absolute, its end decreed from the beginning, and thus essentially independent of physical circumstances, or dominating them without reaction. Neither branch alone, how far soever its investigations may be successful, can be the whole of historical science, unless we are prepared to admit, either that man has no reactive power on nature, or nature none on man. The power which nature exerts over man, the extreme variety and remoteness from observation of the forces which have acted or may act upon him, seem to remove all hope of his history, as a whole, ever reaching the position of a science of prediction. For we have seen that geology is not a science in this sense, § 97. 2; and all the phenomena of geological science are phenomena also of historical, being phenomena which condition the possibility of man's existence. The physical branch of history is the one which opposes the greatest obstacle to its ever ranking as a science of prediction. If we discovered the course of development of character down

to the most minute changes, if we discovered the law which governed these changes so far as they depended on human feeling and thought, we should still have a science of history conditionally only, on the condition of physical phenomena continuing to follow a normal course, of which we should have no guarantee.

4. But even apart from such physical conditions as may be called conditions of major order, and assuming that the earth will continue to exist in much the same habitable condition as at present, historical science would still remain conditional with regard to physical and physiological conditions of a minor order. Earthquake, famine, epidemic disease, blight, storm, all the category of so-called physical accidents, are to a very small extent capable of being predicted, still less of being averted or neutralised. Conceivably, however, any of these may change, indeed for aught we know may have already changed from what it would otherwise have been, the history of mankind, may have barred its progress or diverted it. And although we might be able, from a knowledge of human character, to say what would be the effect in history of any of the occurrences now mentioned, we should still be uncertain when or whether they might happen, or whether others, new in kind but equal in potency, might not suddenly spring forth from nature's arsenal. We may indeed be guaranteed against a new irruption of barbaric nations, but can we be so against new combinations of physical and vital forces? Accordingly, we must conceive the problem of historical science as twofold; first to discover the effect of physical and physiological circumstances upon the normal course of mental

development, and at different periods of it; secondly to discover when and in what measure these circumstances have been or will be brought into operation on it, a question which depends upon physical and speculative science.

5. At every step in the enquiry the question which arises is distinguishable into these same two branches; and each branch, followed up by a further question, again divides in the same way, and so on perpetually. This may be seen in that method of treating history which is certainly not without advantages, inasmuch as it is one which keeps real facts in view, and seeks solutions where there is a possibility of finding real antecedents, namely, the method of imagining some circumstances different in actual events and states of history, and then endeavouring to follow this change downwards to the changes it would involve in the subsequent history, and then again following backwards or upwards the causes which it would be necessary to imagine as antecedents of the imagined change. Thus for instance Dr. Mommsen says, in his History of Rome, Book iv. Ch. v. (Dr. Dickson's Transl. Vol. iii. p. 194, ed. 1868), "It is impossible to tell what might have happened, had the Cimbrians immediately after their double victory" at Arausio, B.C. 105, "advanced through the gates of the Alps into Italy. But they first overran the territory of the Arverni, who laboured to defend themselves in their fortresses against the enemy; and soon, weary of sieges, set out from thence, not to Italy, but westward to the Pyrenees." This delay on the part of the Cimbrians, he implies, may possibly have saved the Roman power from dissolution. Following the consequences of their supposed move-

ment into Italy, we cannot indeed see what they would specifically have been, but we may see that they would have consisted, at each step, of the mental energy of the Romans under the influence of alarm and confusion, balanced against that of the Cimbrians, under physical circumstances, such as the determination of the battle ground, partly influenced by that alarm. Following the causes which might have produced the supposed movement into Italy, we may see that they are resolvable into the same categories, want of attraction elsewhere, insufficient quarters, personal influence of adventurous chiefs, and so on. The personal influence of an adventurous chief, however, may depend partly on physiological causes, partly on physical circumstances which have enabled him to display his character, as well as on the attraction of that character on his tribesmen. Now the reversal or omission of even the minutest circumstance of actual history is an impossible supposition, since natural laws are invariable and inevitable in their operation; but the use of taking an illustration from actual history is to give definiteness and reality to the circumstances imagined as cases of general laws. To imagine a law as general and to imagine specifically different modifications of it are one and the same thing. To take an instance of a general law from actual history is to abstract, for the time, from the fact that it is an actual, that is, an inevitably determined fact, determined by antecedents and contributing to consequences which appear accidental and variable only because the antecedents are unknown. The changes imagined in actual history are the modifications of a general law, the actual circumstance, changed from in imagination, being another modification of it; if illustrations are sought in actual history, imagined changes of actual, unchangeable, events are the only means of generalising, for all scientific or generalised arrangement is imaginary.

6. Historical phenomena may accordingly be approached in two ways; first, from the side of history, beginning with them as a series of actual events, which is Mr. Mill's Inverse Deductive or Historical method; secondly, from the side of science, beginning with the laws of human nature, which is Mr. Mill's Direct or Concrete Deductive method. (System of Logic, Book vi. Chapters ix. x. 6th edition). In the former case, we take the facts known to have existed, and then seek their explanation by referring them to general laws of human nature; in the second we attempt to construct or prove the existence of facts, whether past or future, whether as discovered or predicted, from a previous knowledge of the general laws which must operate or have operated at the time and under the circumstances in question. Almost every considerable piece of historical reasoning, however, includes the alternate use of both methods, so that, as a whole, it can only be said to belong to one or the other method, as the use of either predominates in it.

7. A brilliant instance in which the direct deductive method predominates is found in Mr. MacLennan's construction of the early stages of some departments of human development, in his Primitive Marriage, Chap. viii., to which reference has once before been made. He traces the development of the earliest groups of men, which, he shows, were or were assumed to be homogeneous, through a stage in which kinship through females only was recog-

nised; through two stages of polyandry, a lower and
a higher; through a stage of recognition of kinship
through males as well as females; to a final stage
of kinship through males only, the stage to which
belong the agnatic bond of relationship and the patria
potestas of the early Roman law. Every preceding
stage contains the germ of the succeeding, every succeeding stage abolishes some features of the preceding; and the means of progression are found in the
ordinary feelings and motives of men, acting in the
ordinary way upon the circumstances offered by each
stage. A bridge is thus thrown over an early portion of history, of which no written record has probably ever existed.

8. By whichever of the two methods the phenomena of history are approached, their scientific treatment consists in generalisation, in the exhibition of
the phenomena as a case or cases under general laws.
The generalisation here intended is generalisation
by analysis; it does not consist simply in making a
general statement which will cover several particular
cases, actual or imagined. It is true that the history
of one nation is often analogous to the history of
another, the history of one group of nations to that
of another group, and that history thus, as it were,
repeats itself with variations; and farther, that these
variations of analogous cases supply our best means
of discovering the general laws applicable to all. But
this generalisation is not the scientific generalisation
here intended; if this were all, history would not
be scientific, it would consist merely in grouping and
classifying phenomena, not in classifying them logically, that is, in discovering principles or laws under
which they become capable of classification. History

would be in the position of botany apart from vegetable physiology. Just as physiology which is founded on the analysis of the structure and function of plants is the reason and explanation of the classifications of botany, so the generalisation which explains the phenomena of history is given by a further analysis of those phenomena themselves. There is no series of historical phenomena but one, and the generalisation which is to explain this series must be founded on an analysis of the phenomena more searching and minute than that which arranges them into similar or analogous groups. It is an analysis of the very same phenomena as those which are to be explained. The breaking up the whole series into parts, into histories of different nations, running their course simultaneously or successively, and the observation of analogies between these histories, are the mere preliminaries of the enquiry. The history of each nation or state is not to be explained by pointing out similar histories elsewhere, but by a more complete and minute analysis of its own phenomena. This more minute analysis of the very facts to be explained, an analysis into motives and their laws, furnishes the means of generalising them in the sense here intended.

9. All historical states and events are composed of human actions spontaneous or voluntary, and the only causes of human actions are feelings in dependence on physical or physiological circumstances. In other words, the analysis of the states and events of history is into spontaneous and voluntary actions, and the analysis of these actions is into feelings as causes and effects of each other. The feelings of men are capable of distinction and arrangement in classes;

there is a certain number of kinds of feeling, similar in every individual; and the varied play and succession of these feelings is that which produces the action of individuals and masses of individuals. The same feeling recurs at a countless number of times, with variations according to circumstances, but always subject to certain fixed laws of change. This enables us to generalise the laws of feeling and of action; and this generalisation is a second classification of the phenomena, by the side of the first; it is a classification of the constituent elements of the phenomena in addition to the classification of the phenomena as wholes; and it is, besides, a classification of those elements which are causes of the phenomena taken as wholes, or in which the motive or the guiding power of the whole phenomena resides. All science is ultimately, or in the last resort, analysis; but a more minute analysis is the explanation of one less minute.

10. Wherever phenomena can be thus analysed twice, or at two stages, there the explanation is not complete until the second analysis has been given. The phenomena of history are of this kind; they are a congeries of phenomena which separately belong to other sciences than history, namely, to the physical sciences, to physiology, and to metaphysic or subjective analysis of states of consciousness. The explanation of them, therefore, cannot lie within history itself, in the mere description and classification of the phenomena as repeated at different times and places in history. The explanation of such heterogeneous phenomena includes the assignment of the causes of their coming together from their triple source, and assuming the shape of historical phenomena; and

these causes can only be assigned when the phenomena have been analysed, each in its own science; but the phenomena of ultimate sciences are susceptible of no causal, but only of an analytical, explanation. Hence the phenomena of history are explained when exhibited as cases, not of mere historical but of ethical generalisation, not of a pretended predestined course of human affairs but as results of the feelings and motives of individuals, acting together in masses or mutually influencing each other. For instance, the explanation of republicanism in America is not found in the existence of republicanism in Switzerland and in Greece, or in enumerating and describing the differences characteristic of it in the several cases, but in the feelings and motives operative in individual Americans. That similar feelings and motives have operated in similar ways, at other times and places, is a proof of the constancy and force of the motives, not an explanation of the result without them; without these motives the additional instances of the phenomenon of republicanism would be but a multiplication of the phenomena to be explained.

11. We have now come back to the point touched on in § 7, the relation between history, physiology, and ethic; and it is clear in what sense ethic is one source of history, in what sense its phenomena and their analysis supply the explanation of history, and help to make the entire study a science. For it is history in the ordinary acceptation of the term, namely, a connected narrative of human actions, that is the third member, with ethic and physiology, in the group of sciences which, in § 7, were said to require scientific treatment as a whole, before practi-

cal conclusions could be drawn to guide detailed or doubtful cases of moral and political conduct. This group as a whole is history in the true and wide sense of the term, the scientific treatment of which depends upon the previous and separate analysis of the phenomena belonging to each of its three members. Of these three, however, ethical analysis of the phenomena of consciousness is that which is the groundwork of the whole, that without which the other analyses would have no reason for being entered on, and if entered on no bond of connection with each other. It is ethical analysis of the phenomena of consciousness which supplies the knowledge of that organism which is the object of historical science, physical and physiological analysis which supplies that of its environment. An analysis of the phenomena of consciousness must therefore be the corner stone, or rather let us say the entire substructure, of the whole building of historical science.

§ 99. 1. When from the point which is now reached we cast a glance of retrospect over the whole previous course, the reflection occurs, that there is no science, no phenomenon in any science, which is not included in the purview and treatment of the metaphysical and subjective method. The whole field of fact and of knowledge may be organised from a subjective point of view, in its relations to the nature and desires of man. This is clearly the case with the analysis of the phenomena of consciousness as such, and no less clearly with those constructive and practical sciences which are built upon that analysis; for the phenomena of these sciences are nothing more than the same specific and general feelings which were analysed in Chap. ii. Book i., differently massed and connected. From the simplest distinctions of form and matter in sensations, of different special sensations from one another, to the minutest rules of conduct which may be given by ethic or by any of the branches of practical art in subordination to it, the course is uninterrupted and homogeneous, the series of sciences continuous and organic. All the practical sciences, then, depend ultimately on subjective and metaphysical distinctions. But there is another class of sciences and phenomena which are more purely speculative, the series of physical sciences; are these also included in the purview of metaphysic, capable of subjective treatment, capable of being brought into the same series, homogeneous and continuous with the practical series, capable of organisation from the same centre with them? The answer must be, that they are so in point of method.

2. All the physical sciences, from mathematic to physiology, in their construction and organisation as sciences, in the discovery of their phenomena and laws, and in the arrangement of these phenomena and laws into a hierarchical system, are obedient to the laws of logic, obedient to the purposes proposed by that volition which is reasoning; laws and purposes which can only be known and comprehended by subjective and metaphysical analysis, only modified by a further reasoning which is reflection. The very principle upon which Comte established the hierarchy of these sciences, increasing complexity and decreasing generality in the phenomena and laws arranged by them, is a logical principle, that which is seen in its simplest shape as the increasing intension and decreasing extension of logical terms, that

which gave rise to the logical categories of summum genus and infimæ species contained under it. (See "Time and Space," § 52). This logical principle, which is applicable to all phenomena indifferently, is directly founded on the logical law of Parcimony, a law for the conative element in reasoning; and fulfils its commands by holding together in one view the greatest diversity and multiplicity of particulars with the greatest simplicity of general conceptions under which they can be brought. These logical laws are universal and necessary, asserting their own validity under all circumstances, ruling the conceptions of the Positivist no less than of the Scholastic; the error of the latter having consisted, not in holding fast the logical framework, but in attempting to discover, by examining and refining on it, the phenomena of nature which, when discovered by observation, experiment, and reasoning, would of themselves have grouped themselves under it, and supplied the refinements exemplifying its distinctions. So far therefore as the physical sciences are methods or processes of reasoning, so far as they are practical sciences or arts (according to the distinction in § 92. 1), they are members of the same series with those of consciousness and of practice, which must be treated subjectively. Not only are the phenomena which the speculative and physical sciences discover and arrange, or which are their object-matter, objects also of the sciences of practice, owing to the use which may be made of them for human purposes, but these sciences are themselves practical in their own use of the phenomena which are their object-matter, in respect of their being methods and processes of reasoning, which is a process of volition.

3. We thus apply the distinction between art and science, laid down in § 92, and distinguish by its application the whole field of knowledge and of fact into two aspects, that in which it is a process, and that in which it is a result; aspects inseparable from each other, and affording reciprocal support. Every science is a practical method, and in this respect is a portion of a subjective series; every science is a complex of actually existing phenomena, and in this respect is a portion of an objective series. From this point of view it is indifferent what kind of phenomena are the objects of any science, whether they are physical, or whether they are mental; as phenomena they are objective, as method they are subjective. States of consciousness, the object-matter of metaphysic and of the practical sciences, are objective phenomena, as much as the atoms, molecules, and masses, which are the object-matter of the physical sciences; and they need only the completion and recognition of their analysis, and its fixation by terms of definite and accepted meaning, in order to be recognised and treated as such objective phenomena. The fact that they are treated by reasoning, that they compose trains of reasoning, that they are a method of scientific sequence as well as separate phenomena, is that which makes them members of a single subjective series in the sense now intended.

4. But it must be admitted, that this distinction of aspect only partially answers the question with which we began. When we turn to the differences between the phenomena which are respectively the object-matter of the physical and practical sciences, we find them so striking as to warrant the distinction of two groups of sciences, of which the physical may

in one sense be called objective, the practical subjective sciences. We have in this an empirical not a metaphysical distinction; two complete groups of sciences, not two aspects of all and every science. So distinguishing, the subjective method which dominates the practical sciences has a less dominant function in the physical. Although the phenomena of each series have both an objective and a subjective aspect, and although the method of dealing with each is logical and therefore subjective, yet the phenomena of the physical series are best studied in their objective, those of the practical in their subjective aspect. It is as if we were examining the tapestries along the wall of a long corridor, and up to a certain point were to examine them in front, beyond that point were to change the side and examine the remainder from behind. This difference arises from the phenomena of the physical series, atoms, molecules, and masses, in their interweaving with, their action and reaction upon, each other, having been formed into complete or empirical objects by a process of perception of remote objects (see § 13. 2, 4, and the reff. there given) long continued indeed but long ago forgotten, the results of which, the remote objects themselves, the bodies in three dimensions of space, the atoms, molecules, and masses, remain alone, as a recognised starting point for thought, as a kind of existences, named "matter," which may be thenceforward examined by themselves without reference to the subjective history of their original formation from sensations of sight and touch in two dimensions of space or superficial extension (see § 10. 4, 5). But it is the same subjective process of formation which is continued in the combination of the emotions and the growth of the practical sciences, and which must be examined for itself in the analysis of their phenomena, since it has not yet resulted in the formation of complete empirical objects out of emotions and images corresponding to those formed out of sensations, which are the objects of the physical sciences. The phenomena of the practical series can therefore only be treated from their subjective, those of the physical only profitably treated from their objective side, notwithstanding that the method is subjective in both, and notwithstanding that both classes of phenomena have equally a subjective equally an objective aspect.

5. When therefore the sciences are distinguished empirically from one another, in order to be grouped in a certain order or hierarchy, it is impracticable to arrange them in a single series from a single point of view. The series is broken at the point where nerve movement causes consciousness; see § 49 and the diagram there given. Below this point the series embraces the physical, objectively treated, sciences; above it comes the series of practical, subjectively treated, sciences. Beyond this point, advancing from the physical end, the objective treatment of the practical series, that is, of the several branches included in historical science in the large sense, is an endeavour to be more fully realised; beyond the same point, advancing in the opposite direction, the subjective examination of the physical phenomena is also something to be more perfectly attained, but the means for which are already secured, partly by metaphysical enquiries such as those of Berkeley, partly by the logical organisation given by Comte. But the perfect fusion of both series into one, having

in all its phenomena and in all its sciences an objective and a subjective aspect, is not to be expected until the phenomena which are the object-matter of the practical sciences have become capable of objective treatment, until history in its large sense has become a science of prediction, at least of prediction conditioned only by circumstances which were called, in § 98. 4, conditions of major order. The mode of the conditioning of consciousness, sensation, emotion, thought, by nerve action, of the conditioning of nerve action by physical influences, and the order or law of these processes, for man collectively as well as individually, are discoveries which must be made before either the phenomena of consciousness can be treated objectively, or history become a science of prediction. The order of occurrence, the place occupied by one state of consciousness, defined by its analysis, in relation to other states, in order of coexistence and sequence, the knowledge of which depends on a knowledge of its physiological condition, is equally necessary with the subjective analysis of the state itself, in order that the treatment of it, and of the series to which it belongs, should become objective. Each phenomenon of practical science must be known in its cause and its consequent as well as in itself, in its history as well as in its nature, before it can be considered as an object for its science in the same sense as bodies visible and tangible are objects for mechanic or chemistry. The subjective metaphysical analysis of states of consciousness is therefore but the first step towards the completely objective treatment of them. Whether this consummation is destined ever to be realised may be doubtful, but it is not doubtful that some steps towards it may be made.

6. If in the present state of scientific knowledge it is impossible to organise all the sciences into a single series from a single point of view, it is equally impossible to deny the existence of either series. The unity which would be thus effected would be an unity of a part of the whole field of knowledge and of existence, not of the whole. There are two groups of sciences which, as yet, are only homogeneous in respect of the common feature of having a subjective and an objective aspect, and in respect of their logical method as products of reasoning. The attempt to coordinate them into a single series, from a point of view supplied by their phenomena, must at present fail, from the circumstance that some of these phenomena must be treated subjectively and others objectively. History, for instance, ethic, politic, and their subordinate sciences, cannot be added to the physical series as dependents on or deductions from physiology; nor can mechanic, physic, chemistry, physiology, be constructed a priori out of sensations of sight and touch in time and space relations, such as number, weight, duration, magnitude, velocity, and so on, notwithstanding that the object-matter of pure mathematic, the pure relations of space, time, and number, have precisely the same character whether objectively or subjectively taken, or, in other words, notwithstanding that their objective and subjective aspects are indistinguishable from each other; which character they owe to this, that time and space, the formal element, is the one, unchanging, common, element in feelings, whether these are regarded as portions of consciousness or as portions of the world

of objects. We must therefore be content to regard the great building of science as unfinished, as possibly destined to be unfinished for ever. The greatness of the work is its interest, and this is perhaps the greater for each removal of its goal, for each renewed perception of its incompleteness.

7. Two attempts have been made in the present century to organise the sciences into a single series, one from the metaphysical, the other from the physical point of view; the former by deducing all phenomena and laws of phenomena from the nature and law of thought, and thus gathering up all into a single absolute or ontological system,—which was the attempt of Hegel; the latter by excluding metaphysical enquiries altogether, as a worn-out method, from the hierarchy of positive sciences,—which was the attempt of Comte. I have given in "Time and Space," § 45, my reasons for rejecting the Hegelian metaphysical Ontology; but this is not the only alternative of the physical ontology of Positivism. There is a metaphysical positivism; a metaphysic which is not ontology, a positivism which is not exclusively physical, of the existence of which the physical positivists have not been aware. They have been unaware, apparently, how much was contained in their own admission of the relativity of human knowledge; they have passed over the conceptions of Berkeley and of Kant, confounding both in their condemnation of the a priori method of deducing physical phenomena from the laws of thought; they have supposed themselves to have a beginning of speculation in the conception of body, or as it is usually called "matter," a beginning which is in truth as much an Absolute as Hegel's pure thought itself.

The reaction against metaphysical ontology has carried them too far, and forced them into an opposite extreme, into an ontology of a different kind; their analysis has not been sufficiently searching, their purview of phenomena not sufficiently comprehensive. They have denied too sweepingly the metaphysical truths contained in the ontology which they rejected, affirmed too sweepingly the all-sufficience of the physical truths contained in the ontology which they asserted. For, if they should reply that they maintain no doctrine about the nature of "matter," but are content to leave it as beyond our faculties, and therefore are not ontologists, they place themselves in this dilemma: either they maintain such a doctrine, and then they are ontologists, or they abstain from maintaining any doctrine on the point, and then their system is incomplete, a scientific not a philosophical one. The only philosophical doctrine about "matter" which is not ontological is necessarily metaphysical.

8. It remains then to bring the sciences of the practical series into harmony with those of the physical, by means of metaphysical conceptions, the only conceptions which are common to both, or can be applied to harmonise them without doing violence to those of the sciences themselves. And as a first step towards this harmony, the order of the practical sciences, and their relation to metaphysic, must here be given. For this purpose two things are requisite, the method must be subjective, and the distinctions must be metaphysical not empirical. We have seen that the whole series of the sciences, divided though it be into two portions, one the physical, one the practical or conscious portion, is never-

theless a single series with a double aspect, subjective and objective. The physical portion is eminently objective, the conscious eminently subjective; but the whole series may be approached in either manner, and from either portion. The relativity of all phenomena is thus the fundamental fact which determines the double series of sciences, each traversing the same ground in opposite directions; or, in other words, the fact that every phenomenon has a double aspect, subjective and objective, is the cause of there being two ways of treating it, that is, in all the phenomena taken together, two series of sciences. Now what mathematic is to the objective series that metaphysic is to the subjective, besides and apart from its position at the head of the subjective treatment of both; it is the analysis of consciousness in two great branches, analysis of its Formal and of its Material element; and upon these depends the rest of the series, consisting of sciences which are all less general than metaphysic, and derive from it their logic. First comes pure logic, then the logic of ethic, then of politic and history, then of the different branches of politic and history, then of the sciences which treat man as an individual, such as medicine, then of the different material arts, which consist almost entirely of results obtained from the sciences of the objective series. These sciences themselves, the logic of which is thus derived from metaphysic, still await, in many cases, even their formation, but in all their combination into a hierarchy such as Comte has supplied for those of the objective series. Such is the order, as yet only partially realised, of the sciences which belong to the practical or conscious series.

9. The grouping of the sciences of both series is then the following. Metaphysic itself, as a separate body of distinctions and doctrines, or as a particular positive science, the centre or central moment of which is the act or moment of self-consciousness, the Ich denke, distinguishing the Object from the Subject, stands at the head of both the objectively and the subjectively treated series; the sciences of both alike ultimately hold of Metaphysic. Mathematic, which is the first or highest science in the objective series, having pure space and time relations for its object-matter, an object given only by a metaphysical distinction, is as much subjective as objective in its method; its verification is subjective and objective at once. But the remaining sciences of the objective series are only to be profitably treated objectively, their object-matter consisting of concrete, empirical, remote, objects, each of which is known and distinguished as such by its name, and the laws of which must be learnt by objective observation and experiment. The sciences in the subjective series, on the other hand, can be treated only by the same subjective method as metaphysic itself, that is, by subjective observation and analysis, verified by external, empirical, and in this sense objective facts, which again must be subjectively interpreted. Here it is not, as in the objective series, the nature and sequence of external facts, but the nature and sequence of internal feelings, which are the object-matter of the sciences. Their connection with metaphysic is uninterrupted, not merely in respect of their method being logical and logic having its laws discovered by metaphysic, but also in respect of their distinctions being metaphysical, and their object-matter consist-

ing of states of consciousness, treated as such, and not as empirically separate objects.

10. Next as to the first of the two requisites of the method of ordering the sciences of the conscious series, namely, that it must be subjective. The development of the conscious sciences, with their subjective method of treatment, is a fact which becomes more and more prominent in the history of science and philosophy. It will be sufficient to take the cardinal instance of the relation between ethic and politic. The term 'state' no longer means a social and political structure independent of the individuals who compose it, and to the supposed advantage of which the advantage of the individuals must be made to conform; it is a collective term for the individuals themselves in certain relations to each other, and its structure is confessedly to be adapted to their advantage. Nor is Comte's view any exception to this universally admitted doctrine. Now the adoption of the subjective point of view is the only logical basis for this reversal of the ancient relation between politic and ethic. (See § 3). The logical treatment of the two sciences in connection compels their subjective treatment, and in this way; man in society is, logically, a part of the whole subject of man generally, his social nature a logical subdivision of his nature as a whole; but the treatment of man's nature as a whole is Ethic, that of his social nature Politic. Ethic however was, and indeed still is, a science requiring subjective treatment, while politic had been long objectively treated, as having for its object a social structure independent of the individuals composing it. To subordinate politic to ethic was therefore to treat politic in the only way also applicable

to ethic, that is, subjectively. The old objective method was now recognised as illogical; for to take man as a part of society, and the community as the whole of which the individuals were parts, was to take both empirically; the individual as an empirical part of an empirical aggregate, as a body among bodies, although at the same time (as it happened) a body endowed with powers of locomotion, sensation, emotion, and thought. The logical point of view on the other hand coincided with the subjective, and together they supplied the possibility of organising the practical sciences of ethic and politic in a scientific as opposed to a merely historical manner. To subordinate politic to ethic is therefore not only required by logic, but also itself requires in turn the adoption of the subjective method.

11. As to the second of the two requisites, the employment of metaphysical and not empirical distinctions is involved in the use of the subjective method; for the moment any phenomenon is taken subjectively, from the simplest state of consciousness to the most complex, two elements at the least are found inseparably involved in it, form and matter; and this inseparable union of elements, in every phenomenon, determines the necessity of metaphysical and not empirical distinctions being employed in all subjective science, just as the universal relativity of all phenomena determines the necessity of a series of subjective sciences. Accordingly, the chief objection which I have to urge against Comte is, that while his method has become subjective, his distinctions remain too completely empirical. The instance I shall take in proof of this is a capital one, since it lies at the basis of his conception of the future order of humanity;

the foundation for his practical construction of which may be seen laid in his Tableau Systématique de l'Âme, in the first volume of the Politique Positive. He there distinguishes eighteen cerebral organs, ten of which are emotional, five intellectual, and three practical, corresponding respectively to principle or motive of conduct, means, and result; or, as he also expresses it, to impulse, counsel, and execution; or, as he again varies the expression, to the heart, the mind, and the character. That is to say, he first separates the functions, and then brings them into reciprocal action on one another; the fact being, that not one of these functions but includes in itself one or both of the others, thus forbidding its separation from the others, though only as a preliminary to its future recombination with them by means of reciprocal action.. In short we find here the familiar psychologist's distinction of feeling, cognition, and volition; and that too fixed in separate cerebral organs appropriated to each. Comte then has not, in my opinion, carried metaphysical distinction far enough, but has given us general characterising terms instead of ultimate analytical distinctions, and thus added a new complication to the problem which he proposed to solve.

12. Let us finally fix our attention once more upon the sciences of both the series taken collectively, and endeavour to discover the law of their alternately subjective and objective treatment. There are three stages, or methods, through which every science, or, what is the same thing, every group of phenomena, passes; stages not destructive of each other, but superposed, each subsequent one recognising and involving, or, in Hegelian language, aufhebend, its

Book II.
Ch. IV.

§ 99.
Arrangement
of the
Sciences.

antecedent.—The first stage is purely objective; when phenomena are observed without reflection; when their subjective side is not perceived as such, its existence not suspected, but phenomena appear as immediately present to the observer, no question asked as to how or why there should be phenomena at all. This stage is seen in children and in the early history of mankind.—The second is when reflection has arisen, when both sides, subjective and objective, are perceived, the knowledge of phenomena distinguished from the reality, as it is called, the subjective knowledge from the objective truth. While sciences are in this stage, either side of the phenomena may be taken, followed up, and reduced to scientific organisation, according to the exigences of the object-matter; "matter" requiring objective, "mind" subjective treatment (par. 4); but neither side being separable from the other, except by abstraction for the purposes of examination.—The third is when both sides are equated, and brought to be perfectly expressible either in subjective or in objective terms; when the phenomena which have been treated objectively, those of the physical sciences, are seen to be resolvable into sensations of sight and touch in three dimensions of space, and the phenomena which have been treated subjectively are seen to be capable, not only of subjective analysis, but also of dynamical, empirical, historical arrangement, in dependence upon phenomena of the physical sciences. With regard to these subjective phenomena, the attainment of this third stage is the attainment of a second or double objectivity, one which changes yet preserves the objectivity of the first stage. With regard to the phenomena of the physical sciences, this third stage is the attainment of a second subjectivity, the first having been involved, but unsuspected, in the objectivity of the first stage. But throughout the whole process, the two aspects are permanent and inseparable; so that the attainment of the second objectivity is not a return to the blind objectivity of the first stage, not a laying down but an incorporation of subjectivity, henceforth never to be laid aside. To suppose that it can be laid aside, to imagine an objective without a subjective aspect of phenomena, in other words, an Absolute, is either to hold a contradiction in terms, or it is an actual falling back into the first and rudest stage of intelligence. Bare existence itself, the Seyn-Nichts of Hegel, is a bare notion of existence, that is, subjective as well as objective.

§ 100. 1. The importance of the establishment of the complete and exhaustive relativity between consciousness and objective existence cannot be overrated. It is the corner stone not only of metaphysic but of all science, of all branches of human thought, feeling, and action. Now it is only the metaphysical conception of this relativity that is complete and exhaustive, and consequently fitted to be such a corner stone of science. When Auguste Comte, blaming Kant's metaphysical conception of it as inexhaustive, which in a certain respect it was, proceeds to give his own view of relativity, we find that he conceives it as a relation between the human living organism and its environment; and the complete establishment of this relativity he conceives to consist in showing, first, the dependence of the organism on the environment, secondly, the mutability and gradual development of intelligence within the limits of the organism, assuming the organism to remain unchanged in its general constitution. (Philosophie Positive, Leçon 58, Vol. vi. pages 618-623, ed. 1864, a passage beginning A cette appréciation logique, and ending et dès lors une consécration dogmatique.)

2. Now in the first place, the metaphysical relativity between subject and object, as I conceive it, (§ 13), has nothing to do with either the mutability or the immutability of intelligence; whether there was a fixity in certain perceptions or conceptions, or in their elements, or whether there was no such fixity, in either case the merely general, characterising, truth of the relativity between consciousness and its objects would remain untouched. In the second place, the conception of the relativity between organism and environment is no escape from the conception of an Absolute; unless the relativity is between consciousness and objects of consciousness, between knowledge and things known, the absolute is not eliminated; because the two things between which the relativity is established are both of them objects of consciousness, both of them things known; and therefore to establish a relativity between them, however thorough-going, is merely to distinguish the absolute into two parts, in the present instance organism and environment, in other cases mind and matter, or to make two absolutes instead of one. We may call this an empirical relativity.

3. The shortcoming of the empirical relativity consists in this, that it does not eliminate the Unknowable from science; it leaves in the unknown parts of the uneliminated absolute, (for of course the merely unknown is to everyone infinite), a possible existence which is unknowable, unknowable and yet possibly existing. It says: Our knowledge is limited by our

organisation and circumstances; beyond these limits we cannot know anything; but what existence there may be beyond them, into this we have not the power to enquire, nor is it worth while to do so. Thus is admitted the possibility of an existence in relation to which there is impossibility of knowledge. Now it is true that, even on this view, it may be a counsel of true prudence and wisdom to abstain from attempting the enquiry into such a possible existence, and to limit thought to positive methods, and to actual existences whether known or as yet unknown. This in fact is the continual exhortation of the positivist school. But suppose any one to be unwilling to attend to this exhortation, to be bent on changing the limits between what is now supposed possible and what is now supposed impossible to knowledge, to come forward with a Revelation from that admitted possible, though unknowable, Existence,—where is the defence, what is the reply, of positivists, holding merely an empirical relativity, to such speculative incursions? I confess that I see none. They have left behind them an inexhaustible officina miraculorum. And, the possible existence of an unknowable once granted to those who may be interested in the Revelation of it, all the arguments would at once be brought into play which show, and show irresistibly, that to conceive an existence possible is eo ipso to have some knowledge of that existence, whereby the previous admission of its being unknowable would be sophistically reversed. But such sophistry is rendered once for all impossible by the equation of possible knowledge and possible existence, that is, by the metaphysical relativity between consciousness and its objects.

4. The tendency to believe in an Absolute is perhaps more deeply rooted in human minds than anything which is not itself part and parcel of the nature of mind. Belief in it is the strongest of merely habitual and hereditary beliefs. Belief in an absolute, or in objects as absolute, is the name given by metaphysicians to the first unreflecting attitude of the mind in presence of objects or states of consciousness. (§ 99. 11). Its characteristic is, that it uses the word "is" or "am," or the term "existence," as if their meaning required no further explanation. Depth or intensity of impression in the speaker is what they really signify, not his analytical knowledge of the thing which, he says, exists or is; "It is, aye *that* it is!" which is Plato's τὸ ὄν, τὸ ὄντως ὄν. Now to show that every case of existence is also a case of consciousness, which is the metaphysical refutation of belief in an absolute, or the metaphysical relativity, leaves entirely untouched this depth or intensity of impression. The world is just as real and as true after perception of the distinction as before. It is the old attitude of the mind in presence of objects and states of consciousness, an attitude as if they had a separate existence, or were "things-in-themselves" not modes of consciousness, that is now exchanged for an attitude which brings them into homogeneity with the mind; without any diminution of their reality or intensity of meaning, notwithstanding that the old expressions "it is, aye *that* it is," τὸ ὄντως ὄν, and so forth, contained undistinguished both significations. The world is the same world as before, except that a veil of Maya has been lifted, a menti gratissimus error removed.—It may be remarked here, that the question as to the real exist-

ence of "matter," so much debated since Berkeley's time, has two distinct heads, 1st, as to the real existence of "matter as we perceive it," independent of the perceiving mind, 2nd, as to the real existence of "matter per se," or the unknown substratum of matter as we perceive it. If "matter as we perceive it" is not a mere orderly phantasmagoria in the perceiving mind, it has behind it (so it was thought) an unknown substratum, "matter per se," as one limb of the cause of perception, or of "matter as we perceive it." For that the mind contributes *something* to that perception was admitted on all hands; and, if it did not contribute *all*, the other part must come from "matter per se," or matter not known to be as we perceive it. To save the real existence of "matter as we perceive it," recourse was had to the conception of "matter per se," which had to be conceived as more real than "matter as we perceive it," and as one cause of its existence as we perceive it. Hence the question as to the real existence of "matter," the ὄντως οὐσία of it, is the same question as that of the real existence of "matter per se," or an unknown substratum of matter. But in truth this substratum can never be more real than "matter as we perceive it," because it is but an inference from that perception. The thing of which we are immediately certain is "matter as we perceive it," apart from all question, —and this is the important point,—as to its dependence or independence on the perceiving mind. Of this no one doubts; and this, and this alone, is the firm and ultimate basis of all philosophy, so far as it relates to the material world.

5. There are two chief sources of belief in an absolute, or rather the objects which are believed in

as absolutes are grouped naturally under two heads. The first comprises all visible and tangible matter, or remote objects of perception formed out of these sensations, that is, "matter" in its popular sense, and motion in that matter. The effect upon sensation of such visible and tangible objects is so powerful and so inevitable, that we cannot shake off the belief in their separable existence, that it overshadows the perception of their being, in the analysis of their nature, modes of consciousness. And this belief is farther strengthened by the proof, given in the special physical sciences, that all phenomena are due, in the last stage of physical analysis, to combinations of such "matter," atoms and molecules, in various modes of motion. The second group is founded on the perception of pleasure and pain, in all the various modes of consciousness in which they come forward. Nothing can be indifferent to us in this respect. Pleasure and pain we cannot but feel, often most intensely, and cannot attain to a state of not caring whether we feel them or not. The ideal state of some schools of Hindu moralists consists, as is well known, in such a state of not caring for pleasure or pain. We are led therefore, just as in the case of visible and tangible matter, to believe in the separable existence of something causing pleasure and pain, to believe in pleasure and pain as absolutely inherent in the nature of things, in consequence of their inevitableness and their importance to us. And from this comes the belief in the special absoluteness, so to speak, of certain kinds of pleasure, according as they are judged to be of special moral worth and dignity; as, for instance, the special absoluteness of the pleasure of morality, or of the pleasure of religion, together with the objects of these pleasures, duty and God. Such are the two forms which the popular belief in an absolute has taken in Europe; as to a possible absolute founded neither on "matter" nor on pleasure and pain, such as, for instance, the philosophical absolute of the Hindu systems mentioned above, or the Substance of Spinoza, it does not concern us here; all such cases will be found to elevate some abstract mode or object of thought, conceived as underlying other more obvious modes or objects, into an absolute, separable, or independent, Existence, without thinking it necessary to explain what may be the meaning of the term 'existence' itself.

6. All such beliefs in an absolute are precluded by the conception of the complete relativity and coextensiveness of consciousness and its objects, of the subjective and objective aspects of phenomena. The two characteristics of that conception, to which it owes its precluding power, may be mentioned here. The first is, that the two kinds of elements in all phenomena, the material and the formal, are conceived as equally and alike objective, equally and alike subjective; instead of being referred, as they have usually been hitherto, one to the mind, as the subjective, the other to things external to the mind, as the objective element, in consciousness or in the world. (See "Time and Space" § 11). The second characteristic is the infinity of the world or of consciousness, freed from the apparent contradiction of their finiteness when fixed on by volition, as a definite object, or concept, for the purpose of reasoning. ("Time and Space" § 17). These two points or traits in my method of conceiving the relativity of consciousness and its objects will be found, I think,

a sufficient guarantee for the exhaustiveness of that relativity. But I would add that, whenever relativity of the subjective and objective aspects of phenomena comes under review, the true meaning of that doctrine cannot be understood without connecting it with the distinction between nature and history, or, what in this case is the same, between the statical and metaphysical view of phenomena, on the one hand, and the dynamical and empirical view of them on the other, which has been given, at some length, in § 13. 6-9, of the present work.

7. If truth is important in important matters, I cannot but think that it is important to weigh thoroughly the validity of the old conception of an absolute with that of the new conception of an exhaustive relativity between consciousness and its objects, or, in other words, between consciousness and existence in any and every shape. Knowledge is not narrowed, a domain once possessed is not cut off, by this conception; rather what was once the absolute is included in a relation, and the bounds of knowledge and of existence at once extended. Everything that could be thought of before as belonging to absolute existence can be thought of still, and with more definiteness and security of aim. Analysis is substituted for a search into Causes; the last word of science is Analysis. Enough, I think, has been brought forward, in the course of the foregoing enquiry, to show that morality and religion at least have nothing to fear from analysis, though it should be a more searching one than the present. I cannot myself conceive it possible that they should. Were it possible, they would not possess that eternity of promise which is one of their essential characteristics.

6. Vain are the fears of the danger to arise from overturning doctrines which have hitherto been believed. Turn to the various religious systems of the world; what do we see? The same human nature working everywhere to similar results, with similar conceptions, similar emotions, and through similar stages of development. It is not the doctrines held from time to time, though they may be felt at the time as an indispensable embodiment of the morality and the religion, which are the guarantee of its permanence and of its progress. It is the human nature, their parent, which is the guarantee. Those who complain of new theories as dangerous to religion or morality do too much honour alike to the new theories and to their own. To the new as having power to alter the course of nature, to their own as essential to its maintenance. If the course of nature establishes religion and morality, they are established beyond the power of any theory to overturn; if it does not, no theory has power to establish them. In a better sense, and as the ground of hope, we may apply Gloucester's words in King Lear, "Though the wisdom of nature can reason it thus and thus, yet nature finds itself scourged by the sequent effects." The same nature, the same mental constitution and laws of its working, which lead us to make virtue and truth, morality and religion, important matters, will also secure their development. It is upon this constitution as it really is that the development depends, not upon the philosophical theories which may be formed of it. Their function is performed if they strive to attain a true conception of what that constitution really is; their end is reached so far as they attain it; and from their truth to fact all their efficacy is

derived. But in a logical sense, and not only so but in a practical sense also, those theories are the most valuable which, while giving back a true conception of the facts, give it back also in the simplest form, a form into which it is impossible to introduce distinctions more subtil than its own, like faultless armour invulnerable by the sharpest edge of doubt. Such a theory, if it could arise, would be not only true but known and felt to be so; being the result of all the past, it would have the promise of all the future; repose and confidence would be in its keeping, hope would bloom under its shelter.

9. The great aim of all philosophy, an aim which is its ethical justification as the pursuit of a life, is to give unity of conception to all branches of knowledge, as the basis of unity of action. The unity must extend to all conceptions in the individual mind, as the condition of uniting individuals, and finally nations, in the same philosophical system and the same general plan of action. It must be an unity which contains and allows for all possible differences, whether of character or of creed, assigning them their place in the history of belief, and their function in the direction of practice. No partial philosophy can fulfil these conditions. The philosophical task of the present century has been one of construction; but this is not a task which can be completed at a blow. The foundation had been laid by Vico. But there was still needed much critical and destructive work, which the last century supplied. The two great constructive minds of this century have been Hegel and Comte; both aimed, but by different methods, at an all-embracing system of philosophy; and Comte may be regarded as the Andersseyn, the Nega-

tion of Hegel. Neither the one nor the other system is complete in itself; each finds its completion only in ideas peculiar to the other. The task of the future is to combine the two contradictories in a system which shall be the Truth of both, a system at once metaphysical in its method, positive and experimental in its content. Such at least is the problem immediately to be solved, whatever be the next step which may be revealed and proposed by its solution. To contribute in some measure to this solution has been the endeavour of the present work.

THE END.

www.ingramcontent.com/pod-product-compliance
Lightning Source LLC
Chambersburg PA
CBHW051200300426
44116CB00006B/378